SCEPTRED ISLE

Also by Helen Carr

The Red Prince

What Is History, Now?

HELEN CARR

SCEPTRED ISLE

A NEW HISTORY OF THE FOURTEENTH CENTURY

HUTCHINSON
HEINEMANN

HUTCHINSON HEINEMANN

UK | USA | Canada | Ireland | Australia
India | New Zealand | South Africa

Hutchinson Heinemann is part of the Penguin Random House group of companies
whose addresses can be found at global.penguinrandomhouse.com

Penguin Random House UK,
One Embassy Gardens, 8 Viaduct Gardens, London SW11 7BW

penguin.co.uk
global.penguinrandomhouse.com

First published 2025
004

Maps © Darren Bennett at DKB Creative Ltd (www.dkbcreative.com)

Typeset in 12/14.75pt Bembo Book MT Pro by Jouve (UK), Milton Keynes
Printed and bound in Great Britain by Clays Ltd, Elcograf S.p.A.

The authorised representative in the EEA is Penguin Random House Ireland,
Morrison Chambers, 32 Nassau Street, Dublin D02 YH68

A CIP catalogue record for this book is available from the British Library

ISBN: 978–1–52915–165–7 (hardback)

For Henry – an actual hero

'*Sometime he angers me.*
With telling me of the moldwarp and the ant,
Of the dreamer Merlin and his prophecies,
And of a dragon and a finless fish,
A clip-wing'd griffin and a moulten raven,
A couching lion and a ramping cat,
And such a deal of skimble-skamble stuff
As puts me from my faith.'

William Shakespeare, *Henry IV*, *Part 1*, 3.1, 144–51

'*A great historian, as he insisted on calling himself . . . glories in his*
copious remarks and digressions . . . We belated historians must not linger
after his example; and if we did so, it is probable that our chat would be
thin and eager . . . I at least have so much to do in unravelling certain human lots,
and seeing how they are woven and interwoven, that all the light I can command
must be concentrated on this particular web, and not dispersed over
that tempting range of relevancies called the universe.'

George Eliot, *Middlemarch* (Chapter 15)

Contents

PART THREE

Arthur and Saint George

PART FOUR

The Age of Apocalypse

PART FIVE

The Age of Revolution

Author's Note

There are many characters within this book, and though many of their titles changed over the course of their lives I have tried to keep names consistent – prioritising fluency and readability where I felt appropriate. Some major characters, namely Edward III's sons, are named after the places they were born, for example Lionel of Antwerp, John of Gaunt, or Gaunt's son Henry Bolingbroke. For the nobility, I have either referred to them by their title, for example earl of Lancaster, or by their family name – Despenser or de Clare. On occasion, I refer to a character on a first-name basis, i.e. Henry or Thomas. In regard to French or Spanish kings and characters, I have used the contemporary spellings of their name, for example King Jean II of France, or Pedro of Castile, to demonstrate the multilingual nature of medieval Europe. I hope the Cast of Characters that I have provided will help readers navigate the many players who feature within the book and see for themselves how they are interwoven into various European medieval dynasties.

For place names I have tried to retain consistency throughout, though there can be some confusion in reference to Aquitaine. I have largely used 'Aquitaine' to describe the large, (mostly) English-held territory in France, but in some instances I refer to Gascony rather than Aquitaine. Though both names can refer to the same area, Gascony is a slightly smaller duchy contained within the larger territory of Aquitaine. I have used the term 'Gascony' when it is referred to as such in the record. For distances between places I have rounded the number to the nearest whole figure, for readability.

Throughout the book I have kept currency at contemporary sums. Most figures are to the pound but in regard to the 1381 rebellion I use 'd' meaning 'pence' and the unfamiliar term 'groat'. In the fourteenth century there was roughly twelve pence to the shilling and twenty shillings to the pound. A groat was worth four pence.

In order to understand the value of fourteenth-century currency by today's standards I have used the currency converter available on the National Archives website, and where appropriate noted the converted sum in my endnotes.

All quoted primary sources from the archive are quoted as written and have been transcribed and translated by me, or left in the contemporary French with a translation alongside. Where I have quoted from printed primary sources, I have quoted them as read.

Cast of Characters

Edward I (1239–1307), king of England (from 1272), also known as 'Edward Longshanks' and 'Hammer of the Scots'

husband of:

    Eleanor of Castile (1241–90), wife of Edward I (from 1254)

    Margaret of France (*c.*1279–1318), wife of Edward I (from 1299); sister of Philip IV of France

father of:

    Joan of Acre (1272–1307), daughter of Eleanor of Castile

    Mary of Woodstock (1278–1332), daughter of Eleanor of Castile

    Elizabeth (1282–1316), daughter of Eleanor of Castile

    Edward II (1284–1327), son of Eleanor of Castile; king of England (from 1307)

    Edmund (1301–30), son of Margaret of France; earl of Kent; father of Joan of Kent

★

Isabella of France (*c.*1295–1358), wife of Edward II (1308–27), 'She-wolf of France', daughter of the French King Philip IV and Queen Joan I of Navarre

Children of Edward II and Isabella of France:

    Edward III (1312–1377), king of England (from 1327)

    John of Eltham (1316–36)

    Eleanor (1318–1355)

Joan (1321–62), queen of Scotland (from 1329) as the first wife of David II of Scotland

★

Philippa of Hainault (1314–69), wife of Edward III (from 1328)

Children of Edward III and Philippa of Hainault:

Edward the Black Prince (1330–76), earl of Chester (from 1335), duke of Cornwall (from 1337), prince of Wales (from 1343) and Aquitaine (from 1362); husband of Joan of Kent (from 1361)

Isabella (1332–*c*.1382)

Joan (1333/4–1348)

Lionel of Antwerp (1338–68), earl of Ulster (by 1347), duke of Clarence (from 1362); husband of Elizabeth de Burgh (1352–63) and Violante Visconti (1368)

John of Gaunt (1340–99), earl of Richmond (1342–72), earl of Derby, Lincoln and Leicester and duke of Lancaster (from 1362), duke of Aquitaine (from 1390), king of Castile and Léon (title claimed 1371–88); husband of Blanche of Lancaster (1359–68), Constance of Castile (1371–94), daughter of Pedro I, and Katherine Swynford (1396–99)

Edmund of Langley (1341–1402), earl of Cambridge (from 1362), duke of York (from 1385)

Mary (1344–61)

Margaret (1346–61)

Thomas of Woodstock (1355–97), earl of Buckingham (from 1377), duke of Gloucester (from 1385)

★

Richard II (1367–1400), son of Edward the Black Prince and Joan of Kent; king of England (1377–99), known as 'the White Hart'; earl of Chester, duke of Cornwall and prince of Wales (1376–99); husband of Anne of Bohemia (1382–94) and Isabella of Valois (from 1396)

Joan of Kent (*c.*1328–85), wife of Edward the Black Prince (from 1361) and mother of Richard II; countess of Salisbury (1344–9), countess of Kent (from 1352), princess of Wales (from 1361) and Aquitaine (from 1362)

Anne of Bohemia (1366–94), daughter of the Holy Roman Emperor Charles IV; wife of Richard II (1382–94)

Isabella of Valois (1389–1409), duchess d'Orléans (from 1407); second wife of Richard II (from 1396)

John Holland (1352–1400), earl of Huntingdon (from 1388), duke of Exeter (1397–9) and half-brother of Richard II

Henry IV (*c.*1367–1413), son of Blanche Lancaster and John of Gaunt; king of England (from 1399); also known as Henry Bolingbroke and Henry Lancaster

Other noteworthy players from noble families of England

Piers Gaveston (*c.*1284–1312), close companion of Edward II; the earl of Cornwall (from 1307); husband of Margaret de Clare (from 1307)

Thomas of Lancaster (*c.*1278–1322), second earl of Lancaster, Leicester and Derby (from 1296) and the earl of Lincoln and Salisbury *juxe uxoris* (from 1311); grandson of Henry III and cousin of Edward II; husband of Alice de Lacy (from 1294)

Alice de Lacy (1281–1348), countess of Lincoln; daughter of Henry Lacy, the earl of Lincoln; wife of Thomas of Lancaster (from 1294)

Henry of Lancaster (1281–1345), third earl of Lancaster; younger brother of Thomas Lancaster and grandfather of Blanche of Lancaster

Blanche of Lancaster (1342–68), wife of John of Gaunt (from 1359); mother of King Henry IV and grandmother of Henry V

Hugh Despenser the Elder (1261–1326), earl of Winchester (from 1322); husband of Isabella de Beauchamp (from 1286)

Hugh Despenser the Younger (*c.*1287–1326), son of Hugh Despenser the Elder; lordship of Glamorgan (from 1317); husband of Eleanor de Clare (from 1306)

Eleanor de Clare (1292–1377), wife of Hugh Despenser the Younger (from 1306) and William la Zouche (from 1329); granddaughter of Edward I; daughter of Gilbert de Clare, seventh earl of Gloucester, and Joan of Acre, daughter of Edward I

sister of:

> **Gilbert de Clare** (1291–1314), eighth earl of Gloucester; husband of Maud de Burgh (from 1308)

> **Margaret de Clare** (1293–1342), wife of Piers Gaveston (1307–12) and Hugh de Audley (from 1317); daughter of the seventh earl of Gloucester

> **Elizabeth de Clare** (1295–1360), wife of John de Burgh (1308–13), Theobald de Verdun (1316) and Roger Damory (from 1317)

★

Roger Damory (d. 1322), Lord Damory, baron d'Amory in Ireland, constable of Corfe Castle; favourite of Edward II along with Hugh de Audley and William Montagu

Elizabeth de Burgh (1332–63), duchess of Clarence; wife of Lionel of Antwerp (from 1352)

Roger Mortimer of Chirk (1256–1326), uncle of Roger Mortimer of Wigmore

Roger Mortimer of Wigmore (1287–1330), earl of March (from 1328); nephew of Roger Mortimer of Chirk; husband of Joan de Geneville, baroness of Geneville (from 1301); lover of Queen Isabella, mother of Edward III

Alice Perrers (1348–1400), mistress of Edward III

Thomas Beauchamp (1338–1401), earl of Warwick; one of the chief opponents of Richard II

Richard FitzAlan (1346–97), earl of Arundel; one of the chief opponents of Richard II

Robert de Vere (1362–92), earl of Oxford and Marquess of Ireland; favourite of Richard II

Thomas Mowbray (1366–99), duke of Norfolk

Main players in royal and noble families of Scotland, France and Castile and León

Scotland

John Balliol (1248–1314), king of the Scots (1292–6)

Edward Balliol (1283–1364), ruler of parts of Scotland (1332–56)

Robert Bruce (1274–1329), king of the Scots (from 1306); husband of Elizabeth de Burgh (from 1302)

Edward Bruce (*c*.1280–1318), earl of Carrick, high king of Ireland (from 1315); brother of Robert Bruce

Isabella Macduff (d. 1358), countess of Buchan

Elizabeth de Burgh (1289–1327), wife of Robert Bruce (from 1302)

David II (1324–71), son of Robert Bruce and Elizabeth de Burgh; king of the Scots (from 1329); husband of Joan of England (1328–62); daughter of Edward II and Margaret Drummond (from 1364)

James Douglas (*c*.1286–1330), also known as 'Black Douglas'

France

Philip IV (1268–1314), king of France (from 1285); husband of Joan I of Navarre (from 1284); King Philip I of Navarre (1284–1304), count of Champagne

Philip V (1292–1322), king of France (from 1317)

Charles IV of France (1294–1328), third son of Philip IV; king of France (from 1322), the last Capetian king of France

Philip VI (1293–1350), king of France (from 1328), the first Valois king

Jean II of France (1319–64), king of France (from 1350)

Charles V (1338–80), king of France (from 1364)

Charles VI (1368–1422), king of France (from 1380)

Castile and León

Alfonso XI (1311–50), king of Castile and León (from 1312 as a baby; reigned from 1325); husband of Queen Maria of Portugal (from 1328)

Pedro I (1334–69), son of Alfonso XI and Queen Maria of Portugal; betrothed to Joan, daughter of Edward III, but she died before they were wed; king of Castile and León (from 1350)

Constance (1354–94) and **Isabella** (1355–92), daughters of Pedro I; both later wives of the Black Prince's brothers John of Gaunt and Edmund of Langley, respectively

Maps

THE
BRITISH
ISLES

*North
Sea*

*Atlantic
Ocean*

Ness

S C O T L A N D

• Inverness
• Aberdeen
• Dundee
Perth •
■ EDINBURGH

Tay

Tweed

• Berwick-upon-Tweed
• Alnwick
• Newcastle
Carlisle • • Durham

Tyne *Tees*

• Derry

Bann

Annalee

I S L A N D   O F   I R E L A N D

Roscommon •
• Tuam
Drogheda •
DUBLIN ■

Barrow

• Cashel
• Wexford

Blackwater

Waterford •

ISLE
OF MAN

Irish Sea

E N G L A N D

Ouse

York •

• Lincoln

Nottingham •

W A L E S

MARCHIA WALLIE

Severn *Trent*

• Norwich
Cambridge •

• Worcester
• Hereford
Oxford •

LONDON ■

Thames

CARDIFF ■

Windsor •
Canterbury •

Salisbury •

Exeter •
Plymouth •

English Channel

| 0 | 40 | 80 | 120 mi |

| 0 | 40 | 80 | 120 | 160 km |

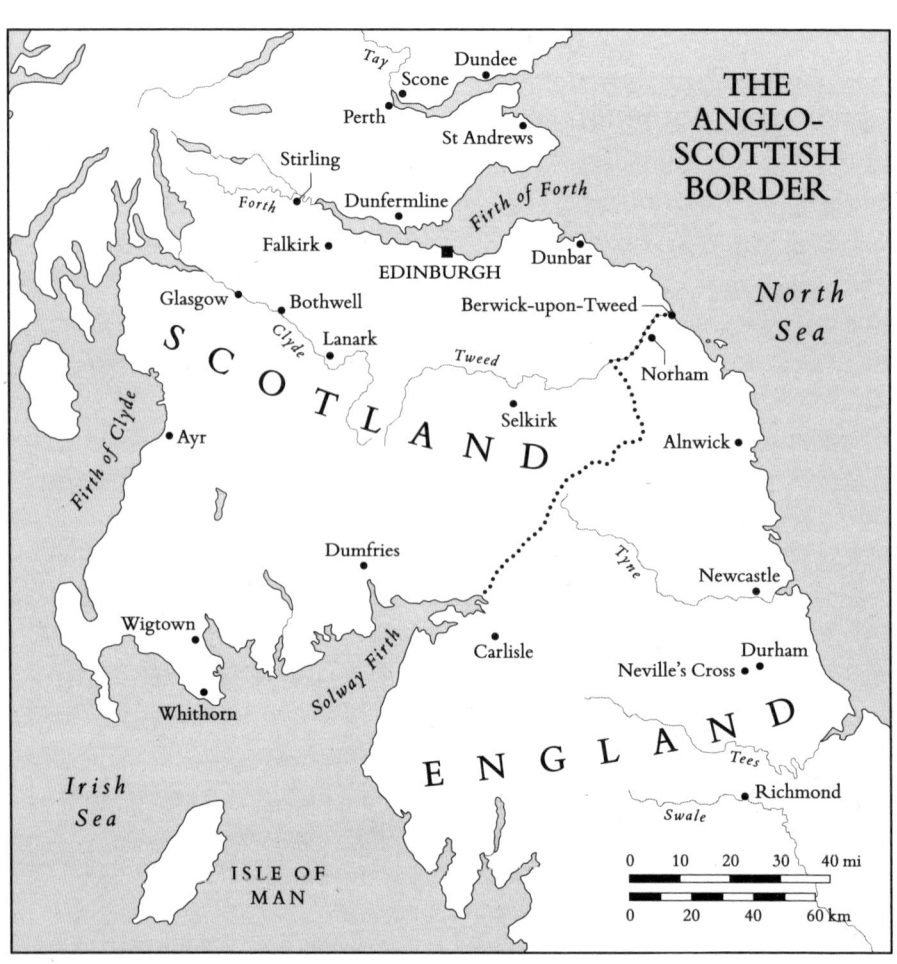

THE
ANGLO-
SCOTTISH
BORDER

Tay
Dundee
Scone
Perth
St Andrews
Stirling
Forth
Dunfermline
Firth of Forth
Falkirk
EDINBURGH
Dunbar
Glasgow
Bothwell
Berwick-upon-Tweed
North
Sea
Clyde
Lanark
Norham
Tweed
S C O T L A N D
Selkirk
Alnwick
Firth of Clyde
Ayr
Dumfries
Tyne
Newcastle
Wigtown
Carlisle
Durham
Solway Firth
Neville's Cross
Whithorn
E N G L A N D
Tees
Irish
Sea
Richmond
Swale

ISLE OF
MAN

| 0 | 10 | 20 | 30 | 40 mi |

| 0 | 20 | 40 | 60 km |

THE IBERIAN PENINSULA

Santiago de
Compostela

Oviedo •

ASTURIAS · BISCAY

Pamplona

Minho

• Leon

Ebro

GALICIA

Nájera •

NAVARRE

Tudela

Girona •

Burgos

LEON

Lleida

Barcelona •

Douro

CASTILE

OLD CASTILE

ARAGON

CATALONIA

Coimbra •

PORTUGAL

MADRID ■

Toledo •

&

LEON

MINORCA

MAJORCA

Tagus

NEW CASTILE

VALENCIA

LISBON ■

Valencia •

IBIZA

Guadiana

Elena •

CORDOVA · JAEN

MURCIA

Cordova •

Murcia •

*Mediterranean
Sea*

Seville •

Jaen •

GRANADA

Cartagena •

SEVILLE

Guadalquivir

Granada •

Almeria •

Cadiz •

Malaga •

Algeciras • — Gibraltar

Ceuta •

0   50   100   150   200 mi

Tangier

0   100   200   300 km

LONDON

ENGLAND

English Channel

Calais

Bruges

FLANDERS

Scheldt

Crecy
Abbeville

Rouen

Oise

Reims

Meuse

Moselle

Rhine

English Territory
after the Treaty
of Bretigny 1360

Caen

N O R M A N D Y

PARIS

Evreux

Seine

Marne

Troyes

Yonne

Brest

B R I T T A N Y

Rennes

Bretigny

Le Mans

F R A N C E

Orléans

Cher

Allier

D U C H Y   O F
B U R G U N D Y

Saône

Dijon

Nantes

Angers

Tours

Loire

Bourges

Poitiers

Vienne

P R I N C I P A L I T Y
O F   A Q U I T A I N E

S A V O Y

Lake
Geneva

La Rochelle

Limoges

Dordogne

Loire

Lyon

FRANCE
IN THE
FOURTEENTH
CENTURY

Bordeaux

Rhône

Isère

Grenoble

DAUPHINY

Garonne

Lot

Rodez

Tarn

Avignon

Durance

Bayonne

Adour

Alby

Nimes

Arles

PROVENCE

Toulouse

Narbonne

Carcasonne

0	40	80	120 mi

0	80	160	240 km

*Mediterranean
Sea*

Introduction

The fourteenth century in England has been dubbed 'the calamitous fourteenth century', known to posterity for everything that went wrong: a crisis period of famine, plague and war.[1] It can, from a distance, look like everything went terribly awry from 1300 onwards – a prosperous realm tumbling into destitution. This dramatic change in personal and political circumstances is written about and visualised in medieval philosophy, literature and manuscript culture through the motif of the Wheel of Fortune. Spun at random by the goddess Fortuna, the Wheel is a recurrent and potent textual and artistic symbol that appears across manuscript illumination and storytelling, evidencing a sense of circularity in life and the changeable nature of fate.

Medieval society was fatalistic and also, at the start of the fourteenth century, intensely hierarchical. Society was divided into around seven categories: serfs, peasants, merchants, knights, lords and nobility, the Church and the Crown. People rarely moved outside of their social spheres, bound by feudal law – an important legal aspect of medieval society – where all land was held from the king in return for homage and service in times of war. Even ecclesiastical tenants were expected to provide spiritual services as remuneration. Time itself was similarly dictated by the major powers of the medieval world: the Church and the king. Dates were recorded with reference to the feasts and saints' days of the liturgical year, as well as the number of years the current monarch had been on the throne: 29 September was known as Michaelmas, and after Edward II succeeded the throne, 1307 became known as the 'first year of Edward II's reign'.

In 1307, the new monarch Edward II inherited a prosperous but troubled kingdom. His father, Edward I, had ruled for over thirty years. Edward I was a fierce warrior and charismatic leader who was both revered and feared, making his presence felt across medieval Christendom. By 1300 he had conquered Wales, controlled Ireland

and had successfully invaded Scotland, with the intention of conquering the country entirely, thereby practically if not legally making himself supreme king of the British Isles. With Edward I at England's helm, the start of the fourteenth century saw a realm thriving. Its population was growing, it had a flourishing European trade network and an expanding economy. But as soon as Edward II ascended the throne, the political atmosphere changed.

This book begins with the start of Edward II's tumultuous reign and ends with the deposition of Richard II in 1399. Enclosed between these complex and intriguing reigns was a war with Scotland which lasted – on and off – into the sixteenth century, as well as the beginning of the Hundred Years War, which began in 1337 and ended in 1453. Northern Europe also saw catastrophic famine, followed only twenty years later by the largest human catastrophe in known history, the Black Death. Taking place halfway into the fourteenth century the Black Death reshaped the western world; its governance, social structures and the way people considered life and death. Half the population died, and into the seventeenth century people continued to live with the near-constant spectre of plague. Major movements and cultural changes emerged in England after the 1348 wave of the plague, mostly notably the 1381 rising known as the Peasants' Revolt. These ran in tandem with the growth of a merchant class, wider access to education, religious reform and a period of self-betterment. The vernacular also changed, with the language of the court shifting from French to English, producing some of the greatest works of the English literary canon. By the end of the century England had become more Anglocentric. A pause in the war against France (which would resume under Henry V the following century) meant that the focus of power was domestic, rather than concentrated across the Channel.

Covering almost one hundred years of history, the book is broken into five sections, each looking at the political or social changes during the century. Part One looks at the early reign of Edward II, showing how the accepted power structures and social stability of medieval England were thrown into tumult by weak leadership and favouritism. Part Two narrates the collapse of opposing powers through the contemporary symbol of the Wheel of Fortune, and

Part Three examines a new age of hope, European interest and national spirit. Part Four presents the century's nadir, when it was ravaged by the inhumanity of war and the outbreak of plague and the plague's consequences. Part Five looks at England as it found itself in a fragile and vulnerable position, ruled by a child who became a tyrant, and explores how the latter part of the fourteenth century became a space of great radical change.

The leading characters are the last of the Plantagenets, a royal dynasty that ruled from the twelfth century to the end of the fourteenth. Henry IV, who ruled from 1399, had Plantagenet ancestry, but he was the first king in two centuries who did not directly inherit the crown. I have therefore chosen to end the age of the Plantagenets with the deposition of Richard II.

In *Middlemarch* George Eliot explores human experience, morality and ego. On pondering the role of a historian, or even an observer of people, she writes, 'I at least have so much to do in unravelling certain human lots, and seeing how they are woven and interwoven . . .' This is a book about unravelling certain human lots and has two themes to its narrative – power and humanity. There is so much we do not know about the people who lived during the fourteenth century, but what we do know is that they were human beings whose lives were dictated by power: the power of God and the power of kings. Three very different monarchs ruled during the fourteenth century, each with different ideas of what it meant to wield power; in doing so, they revealed their own humanity. One was corrupted by power, another overexerted his, and another demonstrated that power wielded through violence and fear is only ever temporary.

This book is told through the lens of the last Plantagenets but includes a wider focus on the people who coexisted with them. I am interested in a storytelling culture, in people who believed that their fate was intertwined with divine favour and that miracles could happen, who saw their lives as ruled by portentous signs and symbols. Although kings, queens and the nobility carry the narrative forward I have included – where possible – the experiences of common folk, women, and those living outside the royal sphere. I have also included, where appropriate, examples of the art and literature of the age in order to offer a sense of what people imbibed from their environment. Culture is a fundamental part of human experience and although medieval people only saw as many images in their entire lifetime as we experience in one day, the cultural fabric of their world was immensely rich.

Over the last five years, and the course of writing the book, mankind has experienced a pandemic, the impact of climate change, two appalling wars and the unsettling rise of major Eastern and Western political powers. Now, perhaps more than ever, we can gain empathy for, and perhaps a fragment of insight into, how people of the fourteenth century felt about the world they lived in, when they endured famine, plague and brutal conflict at home and abroad.

By looking closely at the information available to us, asking questions of sources and 'reading against the grain', it is possible to access the emotions and humanity of people living in the fourteenth century.[2] It is possible to study the psychology of kings – who above all were just people – and to reconsider canonical moments in history (which always favours the victors) with humanity and empathy. It is essential to consider history as human experience. If my readers come away from this book feeling they have come to know the characters as human beings and can reflect with empathy as well as intrigue upon the world they lived in, I will consider my job well done.

Helen Carr
Cambridge, November 2024

Prologue

Avalon

Torches flickered in the biting spring breeze as twilight sent Glastonbury Abbey into darkness. To the sound of crows and the evening chorus of birdsong, an eerie and private ceremony began. In April 1278 the monks of Glastonbury had briefly paused traditional Easter liturgy, for Edward I, the king of England, had arrived in person with his queen, Eleanor of Castile, for another holy ceremony – the exhumation and reburial of a legendary king. From underneath a decrepit slab reading, 'Here lies buried the renown King Arthur in the Isle of Avalon', two wooden coffins, chipped and crumbling with age, were carefully lifted from the damp ground and cracked open under a wash of candlelight. Each revealed one skeleton, the first, the saviour of the Britons – 'Rex Arturius' – and the second, his queen, 'Guinevere'. The skulls were carefully removed for 'the veneration of the people', the remaining bones delicately wrapped in silks and interred inside a black marble tomb flanked by two lions, with an effigy of Arthur himself. The tomb was then fitted into place at the abbey's high altar. It remained a talisman of medieval kingship for the next three hundred years in Glastonbury, or as mythology told it, 'Avalon' – the mythical meeting place of the dead.

Almost five centuries later in London, like 'Arthur', Edward I was also exhumed. Dr John Thomas, the dean of Westminster, sanctioned a request to exhume the illustrious king. The lid of his vast tomb was removed and its contents inspected, revealing a corpse 'adorned with ensigns of royalty': wrapped in a wax cloth, wearing a crimson mantle and gold and red royal robes, a crown planted upon its decaying head. Edward's body was 'almost intire, not withstanding the length of time it had been entombed . . . after the spectators had taken a sufficient view, the top of the coffin and the covering stone of the tomb, were restored to their proper places, and fastened down by a strong cement of terrice before the dean retired from the chapel'.[1]

Like Arthur, Edward I had become a posthumous icon – important enough to be exhumed. But the carefully inspected bones were a reminder of Edward's mortality. The long-limbed, short-fused 'Longshanks'. The astute and severe Plantagenet king who lived and ruled, played his role in shaping England as a realm. But Edward I lacked the longevity and omnipotence of legend. When in 1278 Edward exhumed 'Arthur' (or the corpse he believed to be Arthur) from the damp earth, he did so intending to reshape the institution of Plantagenet kingship. He exhumed a model of governance, one that the kings who followed him would either be burdened by, or would embrace and build upon. The marble lid of Arthur's new tomb was sealed from all worldly light, but his ghost rattled into the fourteenth century. It carried a haunting prophecy of goats and boars, of war, famine and conquest. It carried whispers of what was to come for the last of the Plantagenet kings and this sceptred isle they governed.

PART ONE

Unto Destruction

'But now concerning the demeanour of this new king, whose disordered maners brought himselfe and manie others vnto destruction; we find that in the beginning of his gouernement, though he was of nature giuen to lightnesse, yet being restreined with the prudent aduertisements of certeine of his councellors, to the end he might shew some likelihood of good proofe, be counterfeited a kind of grauitie, vertue and modestie.'[1]

Raphael Holinshed, *Chronicles of England*

Never has our future   we depended
so much on political forces that cannot be trusted to follow the rules of
common sense and self-interest – forces that look like sheer insanity, if
judged by the standards of other centuries.

Hannah Arendt, *The Origins of Totalitarianism*

1. The King Is Dead

The beginning of the fourteenth century was marred by a bitter conflict between neighbouring realms. The border that divided them was a frontier blackened by fire. England and Scotland had been at war since 1296, when King Edward I invaded Scotland, asserting English royal authority over the country. The relationship between England and Scotland had historically been a peaceful one, a coexistence of two kingdoms with a permeable border and shared interests. But in the late thirteenth century Scotland faced a power vacuum.

The trouble started on a bleak stormy night in 1286, when the king of Scotland – and friend of the English – Alexander III left Edinburgh Castle on horseback. Riding through a tempest, the Scottish king tumbled down a deep ravine and broke his neck. Scotland became a country without a king. Edward I of England was invited to arbitrate what was originally a civil argument of succession. As feudal superior, Edward was effectively asked to oversee who the next monarch of Scotland should be. Edward played his part and John Balliol was installed on the throne, a weak king who allowed Edward to pull the strings of power in Scotland. Soon tired of serving as Edward's vassal, Balliol tried to reclaim his authority and in 1295 entered into an alliance with the French. As France was an age-old enemy of English kings, this was the ultimate rebuff to Edward's authority. Edward, famed for his fierce nature, was infuriated but also saw this as an opportunity to exert further power over Balliol. In 1296 he invaded Scotland and in one fell swoop claimed overlordship of the country and its people by force. Edward I had already been a successful conqueror. In Wales he had quelled the rebellions of princes and fortified the country with a ring of formidable garrisons. After his conquest of Wales, a country that had been once ruled by princes of Wales as vassals to the king was now ruled entirely by Edward. He was now able to name his own son, Edward, as prince of Wales. Much of Ireland had been colonised over the previous century, with Edward having been granted the lordship as his apanage before coming to the throne. To control Scotland as he did Wales – possibly even marrying his son into the Scottish line of succession – would mean that Edward would be crowned and sceptred in Westminster, with his power stretching across the Isles as their ultimate overlord. But Scotland would not surrender, even as Edward took the country by village and town, beginning with Berwick-upon-Tweed.

The steep crenellated walls of Berwick Castle loomed over the River Tweed. Berwick was a bastion of defence, sitting so close to the edge of the yawning river that the water licked at its foundations. Garrison and port, town and royal castle, it straddled the border between England and Scotland, and was visible for miles. Dubbed another Jerusalem, it was besieged almost as often as the city in the Holy Land, as both England and Scotland demanded control of the north's most powerful stronghold. Berwick was taken by Edward I in a brutal siege in 1296, during the first months of the first Scottish War of Independence – a siege that cost the lives of all the men who had tirelessly defended it. It was, by the start of the fourteenth century, the place Edward kept his most important Scottish prisoners, including women.

Strung up from the highest towers, exposed to the punishing elements, was a cage, 'well inforced [sic] . . . of strong wooden lattice and planking secured with iron'. Inside was a woman. Isabella, countess of Carrick and Buchan, who was being punished as a traitor. Edward had ordered that, 'Because she did not strike with the sword, she will not perish by the sword . . . however, on account of the illicit coronation which she carried out', she would be imprisoned, 'in a little enclosure made of iron and stone in the form of a crown, solidly constructed, let her be suspended at Berwick under the open heavens, so as to provide, in life and after death, a spectacle for passers-by and eternal shame.'[1]

The countess's crime was that in 1306 she had placed a crown on the head of Robert Bruce, a Scottish noble born into one of the most powerful families in Scotland and England, holding land on both sides of the border. Bruce was once loyal to Edward I but after John

Balliol was forced to abdicate, imprisoned by Edward I in the Tower of London, Scotland needed a new king to lead the country against the invading English. Bruce's claim to the Scottish crown was in his blood; it was a role once coveted by his grandfather during the original arbitration a decade earlier, which went in favour of Balliol. At Scone in Perth – the site of all Scottish coronations – Robert Bruce had his chance and, per tradition, was crowned by a member of Clan Macduff: Isabella of Buchan. A clan member by birthright, she was considered the appropriate Scottish noblewoman to do the deed. Firmly placing the crown on Bruce's head, Isabella made Bruce king of Scotland and herself a traitor in the eyes of Edward I. In response, Edward I would stop at nothing to exact punishment and revenge.

Robert Bruce inherited a country oppressed by English force, with Edward packing garrisons across Scotland with English soldiers, and his opposition against the formidable English king was initially futile. Bruce went into hiding while he was hunted by English spies and soldiers. When he could not be found, Edward's men turned on his people and his family.

In a bloody rout in 1306 at Kildrummy Castle in Aberdeenshire, Bruce's family were captured. Robert's sisters, Mary Bruce and Christina Bruce, with his daughter Marjorie, were taken to Berwick alongside Isabella and his queen, Elizabeth de Burgh, as prisoners. The castle went up in flames and Bruce's brother Neil was murdered along with the rest of the castle's residents.

Isabella and Mary (who was moved on to Roxburgh Castle and whose own 'kage' was built into its walls for all to see) were meant to be a spectacle and a warning. Where the men were butchered and their remains picked on by birds, these women were caged and tormented. Thomas Bruce – Robert's brother – was captured and 'drawn at the tails of horses in Carlisle' before being 'hanged and afterwards beheaded'.[2] After one particularly chilling day, six rebel heads decorated the three gates of Carlisle, England's principal northern fortress. By the beginning of the fourteenth century, England's warrior king was seen by Peter Langtoft – a chronicler from Yorkshire – to have inflicted on Scotland 'such slaughter I never saw before'.[3] This was what happened if you moved against Edward I.

In the late summer of 1306, as Isabella dangled over Berwick-upon-Tweed, encased in iron, 'so well and securely guarded in the same cage that she may not leave it in any way', Edward was marching north.[4] The king planned to join his men and his eldest son, Edward, prince of Wales, in Scotland, where, having captured Bruce's family, they had been hunting the so-called traitors. In his pursuit and to incite terror, Prince Edward perhaps raised the dragon banner, 'the royal standard, which they call the dragon, brothers – presenting themselves for the deadly judgement of combat'.[5] The Scottish force was led by noblemen with land and title on both sides of the border, but Edward ordered his men to 'put to death all enemies and rebels'.[6] Their status bought them no clemency.

While Edward's dragon banner was a harbinger of terror and doom in Scotland, the 67-year-old Edward himself did not intimidate as he once had. Nicknamed 'Longshanks', the formerly tall, muscular and imposing figure was now ageing, sick and increasingly troubled by pain in his joints. Dosed up with pomegranate wine, rose water and a concoction of herbs, he was occasionally carried on a litter, his legs – bound in tight leather leggings – rendering him incapable of walking.[7] Edward's ailments meant that the march north was cumbersome and deathly slow. Eventually, the king and his company were forced to wait at Lanercost Priory, an Augustinian house built largely from the stones of Hadrian's Wall. Edward was in so much pain he physically could not carry on and had to stay there for months. Glass windows were specially fitted to keep the icy wind from the old king's bones.[8]

By the end of 1306, with Robert Bruce on the run, the rebellion had been quelled. Scottish nobles were slaughtered and dragged through the streets of Newcastle, even clergy and women – normally immune from punishment due to their religious status and chivalric law – were stripped of everything they had and imprisoned in order to assert Edward's aggressive policy for pacifying Scotland. But Edward maintained his resolve, determined to hunt down Bruce and the remaining rebels before his days were done. Dragging himself from Lanercost Priory, the king held parliament at Carlisle before moving forward to Scotland in early July 1307. His baggage train wove through the undulating, craggy hills of Cumberland, the sound of steel rattling across the valleys. Despite a Herculean effort, Edward never reached Scotland. As Robert Bruce crept out of hiding, raising men on the white beaches of the Scottish Isles, Edward turned off the north road and moved west. He was destined for the old Hadrianic fortress town of Burgh by Sands. The move to march an army off the road that led directly north made no sense, unless Edward was going there to die.

Burgh by Sands was steeped in folklore. Aballava was the name of the Roman fortress at Burgh, otherwise called Avalon, and it was suggested by the twelfth-century French writer Marie de France, in her poem *Lanval*, that Avalon was found in Cumbria.[9] To fourteenth-century minds, this could mean that Burgh by Sands was Avalon, the place Arthur – according to legend – drew his last. Not Glastonbury, where Edward had recovered and re-interred his said-to-be corporeal remains. It is possible that Edward, who had cast himself in the role of Arthur, hedged his bets in his dying days. That he wished to die in 'Avalon'. The elements hammered at the sides of Edward's tent as he was nursed in his bed, withered by dysentery and age. Finally, when it was seen fit to move the gasping king, he was carefully lifted from his sheets in order to allow him to sit and eat something. Instead, that morning, on 6 July, Edward I, the formidable 'Hammer of the Scots', died in the arms of his servant.

Marking Edward I's obsession with conquering Scotland, the chronicler Jean Froissart later relayed that his son the prince of Wales was made to swear to his father that 'he would have his body boiled in a large cauldron until the flesh should be separated from the bones; that he would have the flesh buried, and the bones preserved, and that every time the Scots should rebel against him he would summon his people, and carry with him the bones of his father'.[10] Froissart's account builds on the image of Edward I as a king that was feared. But Edward's bones were not boiled. This later description of Edward's wishes was simply a eulogy to his fearsome reputation. Like Plantagenet kings before him, Edward I was interred at Westminster Abbey, a mausoleum for his ancestors, presided over by the patron saint Edward the Confessor. A glimmer of Edward's legacy is etched in the Purbeck marble of his tomb in a laconic inscription: 'Edward the First, Hammer of the Scots. Keep Troth'.[11]

The succession was set: the crown and responsibility of the realm would go to his only surviving son, Edward Caernarfon, prince of Wales – named after his father, but, his contemporaries believed, entirely unlike him. Where Edward I cast himself in the image of the legendary King Arthur, who united the Britons, Edward II was destined to do the opposite.

Affable and charismatic, Edward II was as likeable as his father was menacing. To many, the transition from father to son may have come with a sigh of relief. Edward II, according to a contemporary, was 'a handsome man, strong in body and limb'.[12] He cut the figure of a king but lacked the important features necessary to retain control over an entire kingdom: nous, political strength and popularity. Edward's interests were more basic and his friends more rustic. He preferred sport, rowing or labouring to governing. He was known to bring ale to the thirsty on hot days, befriend workmen and take an interest in building and construction.[13] On one occasion, Edward is said to have almost drowned rowing, 'with a great company of simple people', on the Cambridgeshire Fens, when his boat overturned.[14] The oldest son of Edward I and Eleanor of Castile, Edward's only full surviving siblings were his older sisters, Joan, Margaret, Eleanor, Mary and Elizabeth. After the tragic death of Queen Eleanor of Castile in 1290, his father had married the French princess Margaret, forty years his junior, and had two sons, Thomas and Edmund. However, these boys were much younger than Edward. What he lacked and longed for was fraternal company. In the latter years of Edward I's reign, the prince began to form attachments to other courtiers, most notably a young squire called Piers Gaveston, placed in Edward's household when the prince was a boy. 'Handsome, nimble, quick witted, of an inquisitive disposition and fairly well practiced in the arts of war' is how one chronicler described Piers Gaveston. It is possible that Gaveston – probably slightly Edward's senior – was meant to befriend Edward, or even inspire him to take interest in warfare, tournaments and the chivalric celebrations enjoyed by his father, but not Edward himself.[15] The friendship blossomed and Piers Gaveston became Prince Edward's favourite friend. It was not long, however, before Gaveston began to push the boundaries of noble hierarchy.

Around the time of Edward I's final campaign to Scotland in 1307, the prince approached the king's treasurer requesting the county of Ponthieu in northern France be given to his friend. The prince could be easily manipulated by the charming and persuasive Gaveston, but not his battle-hardened and intimidating father. Edward's relationship with his father had always been volatile but this bold request was incendiary. One account describes the old king boiling himself into such a rage with the prince of Wales over requesting that land should be given as a gift to Gaveston that he grabbed him and tore out a fistful of his hair, spitting: 'You bastard son of a bitch! Now you want to give lands away, you who never gained any!'[16] Gaveston was given two months before he was sent into an exile which was perhaps as much of a punishment for Prince Edward as it was for Gaveston. Edward I clearly saw the relationship as a serious threat and it was allegedly stated by the dying king that under no condition should Gaveston be allowed to return to the realm and the company of the prince.[17] It is more likely, however, that this deathbed scene is a flourish, adding fuel to the later argument that Piers Gaveston and Edward II had developed a homosexual relationship, that 'he had bound himself with him before all other mortals'.[18]

Accounts of supposed homosexual relationships in the Middle Ages rarely offer clear evidence of those involved identifying as such, and the term itself was not yet in existence.[19] People around Edward related how he treated Gaveston with 'love' and 'tenderness' and after around three years in the prince's household, Gaveston was described as his 'socius' or 'companion', which was not uncommon for young men, particularly soldiers.[20] Their relationship was later portrayed as homosexual based on these contemporary accounts, yet there is no direct evidence to prove this. The nature of the relationship between Piers Gaveston and Edward II is tantalisingly obscure, but it appears to have been deeply loving and romantic – to contemporaries, this could have appeared 'queer', in that their physical closeness did not look to be within the paradigms of conventional sexuality. Another reading of Edward and Piers Gaveston's love is that they entered into a ritual brotherhood.[21]

Ritual brotherhood was rooted in military and chivalric practice. An established formal binding of two men, perhaps before God. It rendered two soldiers, not related by blood, as 'brothers'. It was an affirmation of masculine power but also a human demonstration of loving feeling. This looked more like homosocial desire than homosexual desire, where intimacy replaced sex.

The clearest parallel is the relationship between David and Jonathan in the Old Testament, which depicts David as a formidable soldier. Jonathan gave David weapons and armour as symbolic gifts of masculine affection and love. In manuscript illuminations circulated in the fourteenth century, images of David and Jonathan even demonstrate kissing and physical closeness.[22] These images were perhaps more than anything meant to mirror the practice of ritual brotherhood in the Middle Ages, for then, like now, people enjoyed seeing themselves represented in imagery and storytelling.

Male love was not exclusive to scripture. It also featured within romances of the time, tales from antiquity such as Achilles and Patroclus, or Roland and Oliver in the French epic *The Song of Roland*. But it was perhaps the story of Lancelot and Galehaut in Arthurian legend that was best known. Edward would have been educated in tales of Arthur and his knights – after all, he was expected, like Edward I, to rule in the mythical king's image. The story of Lancelot and Galehaut echoes ritual brotherhood in its military nature, but it is also infused with humanity and unconditional love. Lancelot accepts Galehaut's companionship, but it is Galehaut who sacrifices his power and agency and eventually his life for Lancelot. The epitaph on his tomb reads, 'Here lies Galehaut, the son of a giantess who died for the love of Lancelot.'[23] On Lancelot's death, the Lady of the Lake has the two men buried together in eternal fidelity. This type of brotherly burial became a minor trend between soldiers in this period, as a means of demonstrating a deeply affectionate relationship that was not necessarily sexual.

Stories of brotherly bonds both biblical and literary would have been a part of both Edward's and Gaveston's cultural upbringing and perhaps made space for an unconventional relationship. Both Edward and Gaveston had a military background, having campaigned together in Scotland. Edward, in his youth, was known to idolise Gaveston. For Edward, the relationship was likely rooted in a sense of amity and brotherhood – in the written record such as Edward's personal accounts and even more publicly in parliament, he frequently referred to Gaveston as his 'brother'. This was also the case for Gaveston, though he was also clearly conscious of the glittering prospect of all he could grasp under Edward's loving gaze.

Ritual brotherhood was both praised and condemned and there were anxieties around what such male love entailed. But this only became problematic when it became political, such as when Piers Gaveston became more powerful as a result of the relationship. It was only then that their behaviour was described as 'immoderate'. At the very end of Edward's reign, he was accused of sodomy in a hectoring attack by the bishop of Hereford. Yet again this served as political slander against Edward's problem of political and personal favouritism. However, the single most influential reason for the rumours of homosexuality between Edward and Gaveston is the depiction, appearing centuries after the fact, of the relationship in Christopher Marlowe's play *Edward II*, which encourages its audience to believe the men were lovers. In reality, it is perhaps more appropriate, then, to consider Edward II and Piers Gaveston's relationship as a ritual brotherhood that *possibly* became sexual, and embrace it, with all its complexity.

Gaveston's importance to Edward on his accession to the throne was immediately clear. The corpse of Edward I was barely cold before Edward II revoked Gaveston's banishment. While in the north of England, dealing with the transition from one king to the next as his father's body was embalmed and prepared for internment, Edward II endowed Piers Gaveston with a new title and new land.[24] He was granted the earldom of Cornwall before a collection of lords, including a roster of his future adversaries. Edward was so fresh to the role of king he even had to use his father's seal.[25] Through this act, Gaveston was elevated into the highest echelons of the nobility. His new status was bolstered further in October when he was married to

Margaret de Clare, the king's niece – daughter of the wealthy earl of Gloucester and Joan of Acre, Edward's sister. Before Edward was even officially crowned, Piers Gaveston's position was raised to the same level as members of the royal family – most notably the king's cousin Thomas of Lancaster. In the charter granting Gaveston his new title the parchment is delicately decorated with Cornish choughs, little black birds with orange beaks, but most starkly the royal coat of arms at the top of the charter is set in-between Gaveston's arms and those of his wife, Margaret de Clare. The royal arms are at the heart of an eagle with its wings outstretched, wrapping tenderly around the arms of Gaveston and Margaret on either side. The message here is clear: this is the king's beloved family. Gaveston's unprecedented rise in power prompted the annalist writing out of Saint Paul's Cathedral to comment that there were 'two kings reigning in one kingdom, one in name, the other in deed'.[26] It was said by the contemporaneous author of the *Vita Edwardi Secundi* (the Life of Edward II) that Gaveston appeared as if a 'second king'.[27]

Despite his close relationship with Gaveston, Edward needed a queen; he was, after all, one of the most eligible bachelors in Europe. While Edward II began to unpick his father's orders over Gaveston, he honoured the marriage agreement Edward I had been painstakingly brokering across the Channel. Over the course of months of back and forth, Edward I had been working to secure an excellent match for his son. Isabella of France was the eldest daughter of the king of France, Philip IV, and Queen Joan of Navarre. This marriage was important. It would unite the two countries politically and dynastically and formalise a peace that was sorely needed after years on the precipice of war, the result of a power struggle over the once English-held territory of Aquitaine. Aquitaine was a large and wealthy region in south-west France, formerly owned by Eleanor of Aquitaine and, by proxy, her husband Henry II of England. Aquitaine had been held as a vassal state to the French king while the rest of English land in France – steadily acquired by Henry II – was lost to the French due to the grievous errors of King John. An obsession with recovering it was handed down by successive Plantagenet monarchs, carrying a weight of expectation as heavy as the crown itself.

In one final push to reach a marriage settlement as Isabella turned twelve (a normal age to marry), the belligerent Philip IV offered to return Gascony to Edward II, with the proviso that he would have to regularly travel to Paris to pay homage to Philip for his lands. This was a formal and public declaration of fealty to the French king that some would consider to be an ignominious display of subjugation. Philip IV considered this offer generous and believed the king of England would do well to accept it. With little room to manoeuvre, Edward prepared to travel to France, where the marriage would take place in Boulogne in late January 1308. Almost exactly a month later, having returned to Dover, the couple would be crowned king and queen of England.

Before Edward set sail to meet and marry Isabella of France, he spent an intimate Christmas with Gaveston at Wye in Kent, where he appointed him *custos regni*, 'keeper of England during the king's absence beyond seas'.[28] This made Gaveston, in Edward's absence, effectively regent of England. An 'astonishing thing', wrote the author of the *Vita*, 'he who was lately an exile and outcast from England has now been made governor and keeper of the same land!'[29] When Edward and Isabella landed back at Dover in early February the atmosphere was tense.

The pervading problem for almost every Plantagenet monarch was the nobles, the lords of the realm – some quasi-royal – who for centuries had owned land across predominantly England but also Ireland, Wales and even Scotland and northern France. Their feudal vassals – those who lived on their land and paid rent – provided the manpower for war or worked the land to keep the economy moving and supply the lord's table. The nobility were important and they had to remain loyal, or at least fearful of their king, for government to run smoothly. A sure way to enrage and ostracise these powerful men was for the king to direct his gaze, his affections and especially his grace and generosity towards one individual – particularly one of comparatively low birth – thereby threatening the established hierarchy of power in the realm. The whiplash elevation of Gaveston was enough to have many nobles twitching. When Edward was reunited with Piers Gaveston before a collection of red-faced lords, he allegedly embraced his friend with kisses and obvious affection. The deepest affront was not to the lords, but to the shocked new queen.

As the coronation ceremony crept closer there were rumblings of discontent over the king and his favourite. A dark and foreboding cloud circled Westminster, carrying with it the promise of a thunderous start to the reign of Edward II.

2. Two Kings

Coronation was the most sacred rite of passage for any English monarch. A deeply religious ceremony, steeped in symbolism and holy ritual, it was also a major political opportunity: a chance to show the realm who the new king was and how he meant to rule. Citizens from London and the neighbouring shires, lords and ladies of the realm, elite merchants, earls, barons, bishops and archbishops – were all present.

The lead-up to the coronation ceremony at Westminster had been fraught with problems. Having invested much of the Crown's wealth into war with Scotland, Edward I passed on to his son a palace that was falling apart. Purpose-built only a stone's throw from Westminster Abbey, the palace consisted of a large complex of towers, outbuildings and courtyards encased by a wall and the river. As the location of state ceremonies, parliament, and serving as the main royal residence in London since the eleventh century, the palace rivalled the abbey in size and grandeur. But in 1298 a fire had destroyed parts of Westminster, leaving only the Great Hall and the king's chambers unscathed.

With much of his focus on the war in Scotland, Edward I abandoned the palace to the elements when he marched north. Wind battered the exposed walls, windows were cracked and broken, and rot set in, leaving a pervading stench through the maze of hallways and chambers.[1] The palace was not fit for a king, let alone his new queen, on their coronation day. Within a month of his father's death, Edward II demonstrated his particular interest in the renovation of Westminster by giving his own orders to the workmen. Richard of Wytham was given the important job of master craftsman, tasked with overseeing the restoration process and managing a team of workmen, cutting and dressing stone and marble as well as shaping timber, forging ironwork, painting walls and glazing windows. Seven thousand tiles were sourced from east Smithfield and seven boatloads of sand were dragged up from the Thames in order to make cement.[2] So many men were employed as skilled labourers that a horn had to be blown to summon them in the morning and dismiss them in the evening.[3]

As the February coronation approached, fears grew that the deadline for the completion of the glittering new renovation of Westminster might not be met. In order to extend the working day, hundreds of candles were carted into Westminster so the workmen could continue their work by flickering light. Nonetheless, it became evident that the palace would still not be ready come February. A makeshift space would have to be cobbled together. Oaks were chopped down and the timber shipped to London in order to build a temporary hall.[4] It was vast, and strengthened to accommodate the mass of spectators, spanning the entire length of the river wall of the palace – around five hundred feet. Tables were erected in every possible free space inside the palace to aid the banquet in Westminster Hall. Forty ovens were installed and lead piping fitted to service a fountain that would flow 'day and night with red and white wine'. Inside Westminster Abbey itself, a stage was erected so high that 'men at arms could ride on horseback beneath it without stooping', upon which stood two thrones, one for the king and the other for his new queen, Isabella of France.[5]

Image was everything. This was something Edward I knew well. Though the former king would never witness his son's coronation, he wanted to ensure that his legacy would be etched into the symbolism of the ceremony.

When Edward invaded Scotland for the first time, he had removed the very emblem of Scottish kingship, the Stone of Scone. Otherwise known as the Stone of Destiny, this was the stone that every Scottish king sat upon as he was crowned. Legend had it that the Stone had belonged to the biblical figure Jacob, who had used it as a pillow. At some point the Stone had fallen into the hands of the Scots and it became interwoven with Scottish monarchal identity, mythology and folklore. In 1296, leaving Scotland burning, Edward I had the Stone of Destiny carted back to Westminster. There he commissioned a new throne wide enough to encase the Stone of Destiny beneath it. Made of oak, the 'gilded' chair was decorated with painted birds and foliage, with the figure of a king on the back, his feet resting on a lion. Each arm was to be a gilded leopard. Meant to be placed 'in the Abbey of Westminster, next to the shrine of Saint Edward', the chair and the Stone were ensconced within the symbolic confines of English kingship.[6] In 1307, shortly before his death, an inventory was compiled for Edward I. The chair appears, 'which the king had ordered in order that the kings of England and Scotland might sit on it on the day of their coronation in perpetual memory'.[7] The point of the chair was that Edward II would be the first king to be crowned in England while also seated on the Scottish coronation stone. It was a symbolic crowning of the first king of England *and* Scotland.

The panic to ready Westminster for the coronation led to shortcuts and compromises in the construction work. Scaffolding still decorated the palace, which, by the day of the coronation was bulging with people, so much so that Edward and Isabella had to leave via a back door, unable to squeeze past the masses. A short distance from the abbey, Edward and Isabella walked along a woollen carpet, strewn with fresh flowers, and beneath an embroidered canopy, carried by the lords who controlled the Cinque Ports – Sandwich, Dover, Hythe, New Romney and Hastings, franchised ports along the south coast of England. The most notable and important lords of the realm had a major part to play in Edward's coronation – ceremonially carrying the coronation regalia. This act was meant to serve as both a demonstration of their own prestigious lineage and the nature of noble hierarchy, with the king at the pinnacle of power. The thirty-year-old Humphrey de Bohun, the earl of Hereford, a scion of one of the most revered families on the Welsh Marches – the borderlands between England and Wales – and a veteran of the war in Scotland, carried the royal sceptre. *Curtana*, otherwise known as the Sword of Mercy, was carried by the king's cousin, Thomas, earl of Lancaster. The vestments were carried by Hugh Despenser the Younger (the son of Hugh Despenser the Elder, a loyal diplomat in Edward I's service), and Roger Mortimer of Wigmore, another Marcher lord with influence across the border between England and Wales. These roles were important to the ceremony, but were

considered paltry in comparison to the star of Edward II's coronation, Piers Gaveston. He was allocated significant responsibilities:
carrying the sacred crown of Saint Edward – the very crown that
would be placed upon the king's head, said to have once belonged to
Edward the Confessor. The Saint Paul's chronicler sniped that Gaveston had dressed as if he were 'the God Mars', wearing purple and
dripping in pearls.[8] More worrying, though, were the tapestries that
hung above the royal couple's thrones. Edward II's arms were emblazoned in vivid detail. Beside them, however, were not those of his
new queen, but, awkwardly, the heraldry of Piers Gaveston.

To any unknowing onlooker, this would have appeared more like
the coronation of Edward II and Gaveston. The decision to show-
case Gaveston's importance to Edward, in circumstances as sacred as
the coronation, was reckless, but Edward clearly sanctioned the idea.
Gaveston had become untouchable, protected by the king and by the
status he had been gifted. This behaviour inspired 'general resentment and a wicked hatred of his personality, in that he challenged
prerogatives which pre-eminently belonged to the nobility alone'.[9]
One of Queen Isabella's relatives who was attending the coronation –
possibly her brother – was allegedly so offended by the tapestries that
he threatened to kill Gaveston there and then.[10]

Despite the thrumming resentment and confusion over Gaveston's involvement in the ceremony, this coronation marked a new
era, with major changes to the established order. Edward II swore
his coronation oath in French, to be more understandable for those
present, when it was traditionally recited in Latin, and there was even
a change to the oath itself: Edward II added that he would uphold
the 'laws and rightful customs which the community of the realm
shall have chosen'.[11] This change in wording carefully acknowledged
Magna Carta – literally meaning 'great charter' – sealed by King
John in 1215. The core principle of the charter was that the authority
of the monarch was not absolute. Kings and queens would from that
point onwards also be bound by law. Magna Carta had been reis-
sued several times during the thirteenth century, and most recently
in 1300. The point Edward was trying to make was that he wished to
be a king for his people and to be inclusive in his kingship, changing

elitist coronation traditions and raising the importance of Magna Carta, a precedent for fair rule, avoiding tyranny and despotism. Edward's oath aligned with this same principle and promised political amity. A kingship that would develop *with* the realm rather than against it. As part of his coronation Edward promised political harmony, but politics was already fragmented. It would become clear that the decisions he made for his coronation were not reflective of his duty to the Crown or to the realm, but served his relationship with Piers Gaveston.

Soon the kingdom began to fracture under the weight of Edward's poor choices. Weeks after the coronation, dispute among the powerful nobility threatened the stability of the realm. These were the men who upheld Edward's kingship, who managed land and people. Instability among the nobles threatened to dismantle historic loyalties, divide families and threaten the security of the borders and the beaches. At the heart of it all was Gaveston. It was observed that 'almost all the earls and barons of England rose against Piers Gaveston and they were bound by a mutual oath never to cease what they had begun until Piers had left the land of England and given up the earldom of Cornwall.'[12] Gaveston's constant access to the king was the main problem for the nobles. The medieval hierarchy of power was clear: the king reigned at the top, followed by the nobility in order of rank. Those who disrupted the order of things were considered a threat: was it the king making decisions or was it Piers Gaveston? However much pressure the barons placed on Edward to restore the normal structure of power within his inner circle, this was never going to happen without a fight and by March 1308 Edward began to ready himself for war. Time and money were dedicated to the reinforcement of royal castles across the country and Gaveston was appointed as a custodian of some of the major fortifications in England alongside one of the only remaining loyal lords, Hugh Despenser the Elder. Though steadfast during Edward II's rocky accession, Despenser's motives were questionable. It was said that the old earl was only ever out to line his own pocket.[13]

Despite his efforts to bolster the defences of the Tower of London, the king decided to take refuge at Windsor Castle. Gaveston joined him in April after mustering his own forces. Edward had prioritised strengthening the 'houses, tower, walls and bridges of the castle' as well as its fences and walls in preparation for a siege launched by the earls.[14] Elsewhere in the country, towns and villages waited anxiously for the imminent breakout of rebellion. In a gathering at Pontefract, furious members of the nobility laid down their grievances against Piers Gaveston. It was decided that an official document should be drawn up and presented to the king at the parliament due to be held at the end of the month. Magna Carta set a precedent against kings doing as they liked, when they liked, and this document, they hoped, would offer a legal solution to the issue of favouritism.

In April, ten earls, forty-seven barons and thirty-six royal judges and clerks arrived at Westminster Abbey for the spring parliament concerning 'various affairs touching the state of the king and of his kingdom'.[15] They were joined by the archbishop of York, fifteen bishops, twelve abbots and two priors. The gathering was hostile. As the earls clattered into Westminster, with their fully armed retinues, they came up against one another with the prospect of battle hanging by a thread. The ten earls present included Lancaster, Gloucester, Lincoln, Warwick, Surrey, Hereford, Arundel, Pembroke and Oxford. Though the sight of each of the most powerful lords in England armed for combat was an intimidating spectacle, they saw their preparations as a case of self-defence rather than an offensive exercise, should Edward decide to have them arrested. No swords were drawn that day. Nonetheless, Edward decided to keep away from parliament. Instead, he paced the halls of Westminster Palace awaiting updates.[16]

As proceedings began, the document drawn up at Pontefract was presented. Three articles within it argued that the earls were justified both legally and constitutionally to reprimand Piers Gaveston. He had exercised authority beyond his remit and encroached on the auspices of the Crown, causing 'discord' between the king and his people. They argued in defence of the Crown, stipulating that it was within their right to demand the removal of 'a robber of the people and a traitor to his liege lord and his realm'. They continued by saying that 'the people rate him as a man attained and judged, and pray the king that, since he is bound by his coronation oath to keep the laws that the people shall choose, he will accept and execute the award of his people'.[17] The threat against Gaveston from Robert Winchelsey, archbishop of Canterbury, was that he would be excommunicated should he continue advising the king, and to Edward the demand was clear: Piers Gaveston must be exiled or the king would be considered in breach of the oath that he made on his coronation. As expected, when the document was presented to Edward inside the walls of the palace, he did not accept the articles or the demand of the earls who composed it. Edward flatly refused to exile a person who was not only beloved to him but who he considered to be an 'adoptive brother'.[18] But as the weeks went on, the pressure to oust Gaveston came not only from the barons but also from across the Channel.

Philip IV, Edward's father-in-law, had been unimpressed by Gaveston's performance at the coronation ceremony and informed his son-in-law that unless Gaveston was forced to 'leave the country' he would consider all those in favour of the troublesome earl his 'mortal enemies'.[19] Though described as 'fair' in looks, Philip IV was not forgiving: in 1314 he had two knights from the French court flayed alive for having had a series of affairs with his daughters-in-law. Piers Gaveston, having humiliated Isabella at the coronation ceremony, would have received a similar punishment had Philip IV been given the opportunity.

Backed into a corner, Edward II had little choice other than to capitulate and exile his 'brother'. In June 1308 Gaveston prepared to travel to Ireland by ship, accompanied by a large household who would provide the comforts he had become familiar with.[20] Though living in a state of regal luxury, he remained trapped in Ireland until Edward attempted to liberate him in 1309.

The Channel was bitterly cold in March 1309 as wind filled the sails of an English ship carrying envoys across the water. The party of carefully selected emissaries had been dispatched by the king of England with an important mission. They were tasked with riding to the Holy See of Avignon, home to the Catholic Church since 1309 when the new Pope Clement V refused to move to Rome, bringing the papal court to the enclave in Provence. There, on behalf of Edward II, they would ask Pope Clement V to revoke the exile of Piers Gaveston. Edward had gone to the highest power in Europe to return his friend. But it was clear he would also need to convince his father-in-law. En route to Avignon the envoys were expected to visit the French king and win his support. Since Gaveston's exile, Edward had tried to repair relations with his magnates. Generous by nature, he showered them with gifts and honours and considered requests to reform the realm.[21] Yet, suspicion was rife. The lords who had pushed for Gaveston's exile knew it was only a matter of time before Edward brought him back again.

These lords had gathered in early April 1309 for a tournament that took place in Dunstable. The topic of discussion was the forthcoming parliament at the end of the month and whether Edward would request Gaveston's return. Under no circumstances would the major magnates of England accept the return of his favourite, even if Edward agreed to some of their requests.

Around this time there was some hope for Edward, for he received word from Avignon. Pope Clement V had sympathy for his plight and issued a papal bull annulling the prospect of excommunication against Gaveston on the grounds that internal Church laws and regulations had not been observed by the archbishop of Canterbury when making threats against the troublesome earl. The pope wielded the same level of authority – if not more – than the king and with Clement V on his side, the balance of power in England tipped drastically in Edward's favour. The elite members of the English Church gathered to hear the bull read aloud on a summer's day. Though disgruntled, they had no choice but to accept the pope's decree. A relieved and jubilant Edward quickly set off to Chester where he greeted Gaveston, who had sailed from Ireland, 'joyfully . . . with honour as his brother'.

Enjoying a brief period of calm, Gaveston travelled with the king, 'talking daily and fully making up for the former absence by their long desired closeness'.[22] However, the arrogance and conceit that had invited so many to stand against Gaveston had not diminished during his period in Ireland. The *Vita* chronicle details Gaveston making up snide and offensive nicknames for the nobility. Among the names he afforded his contemporaries were 'whoreson' for Gloucester, 'the black dog of Arden' for the earl of Warwick, 'burst belly' for the sixty-year-old earl of Lincoln and 'churl' for Lancaster – effectively calling him a peasant. The nobility were not the only recipients of Gaveston's sneering. His valet was named in Gaveston's accounts as Richard 'Whiteflesh' – possibly a remark on his pasty complexion.[23] All of this added to what was already a roster of complaints against Gaveston, which led to the earls of Lancaster, Warwick, Arundel, Lincoln and Oxford refusing a request from the king to meet in York. They could no longer stand to be in the same room as Edward's favourite. Despite Gaveston's brief exile and all that had happened since, the king, Gaveston and the barons of England found themselves in the same uncomfortable, simmering dynamic as they had the day of Edward's coronation. This led to a bloody showdown that would cast a bleak and vengeful shadow across the rest of Edward II's reign.

3. Blacklow Hill

It was said that the 'chief enemy' was 'lurking in the king's bedchamber'.[1] The leading earls of England had made a stand against the king. Parliament was due to begin at Westminster in April 1310 and the earls made it plain that Piers Gaveston must not be present during proceedings. If he was, they would attend armed. For almost three weeks, both sides held to their positions, until the king capitulated and arranged for Gaveston to stay away from Westminster for the duration of parliament, perhaps more for the safety of his friend than out of amity to his earls.

When parliament finally and awkwardly began, the earls wasted no time in making their grievances against the king's judgement known. The earl of Lancaster – Edward's cousin – was probably the one to deliver the first blow by presenting Edward with a petition on behalf of the leading magnates of the realm. He was accused of 'shaming the land by unsuitable and evil counsel', a reference to Piers Gaveston, of crippling the realm financially so that 'he could neither defend' from the Scots who had set about attacking the borderlands, and of failing to 'maintain his household'. To emphasise the damage the king had done, the petition said he was in breach of Magna Carta. Instead, they had their own proposal: they had produced a document outlining eleven articles designed to reform a realm they did not believe was being governed in accordance with Magna Carta. At the end of the month, the earls and barons appeared at parliament in Westminster, where they presented the king with their demands. Pushed into a corner, Edward was careful to remain neutral.

The anger levelled at Edward for his mismanagement was justified. Following Edward's accession to the throne, his father's greatest enemy, Robert Bruce, led raids into the north of England and attacks on English-held garrisons across Scotland with unbridled vengeance. As a result, the English were in peril of losing strength in Scotland, a

power that Edward I had dedicated the latter part of his reign to establishing. The earls were incensed. However, the major issue was not
lack of initiative, but the miserable financial state of the realm – the
earls blamed the king for squandering Crown funds on his generosity
to his family and friends and blatant favouritism. They pointed the
finger at Piers Gaveston and demanded reform.

The heat of parliament threatened to blaze into the fire of rebellion, one Edward knew he would not necessarily control. Forced to
hear the demands of the earls and barons, he agreed on reform. It was
decided to elect twenty-one officials from among the 'powerful and
discreet men of the kingdom' as 'Ordainers' – men who would oversee the king and control major aspects of his government. Edward had
avoided accepting them then, but now he had little choice. By February 1311, Thomas of Lancaster was among the leading earls involved
'in the process of deciding certain matters': adapting and perfecting
a series of documents in order to put a new and more formal set of
rules to the king at the end of May.[2] These became forty-one clauses
designed to reform a realm they did not believe was being governed
in accordance with Magna Carta. They named these the Ordinances.
Issued alongside the original provision of Magna Carta and signed by
ten bishops, eight earls and thirteen barons, they covered a variety of
regulations including the king's right to issue pardons and to give his
lands away without baronial consent.[3] They also ensured parliament
met twice annually and stipulated that the king must cease to issue
writs under his privy seal that went against common law – essentially stopping the king from taking the law into his own hands. The
major point to the Ordinances was the removal of Gaveston from his
position of incomparable power. It was stated that he was the 'evident enemy of the king and of his people', that he had 'badly advised
our lord the king . . . especially in estranging the heart of the king
from his lieges'. It was determined that he should be 'ejected and dis-
missed altogether'.[4] Initially, Edward stood his ground, stating that
the other Ordinances 'shall be established at your request and remain
in force forever. But you shall stop persecuting my brother Piers, and
allow him to have the earldom of Cornwall'. In a bitter exchange
the Ordainers determined that with or without the king's consent,

Piers Gaveston would be exiled 'or each man would consider how to defend his own life'.[5]

The Ordinances, however much they tethered Edward to rule by the book, served as the opportunity to exercise better judgement and act accordingly. Yet Edward was not motivated by his own need for power, he was drawn to others. It was his emotional inability to rule alone, without close guidance, that marked Edward's problematic reign from the outset. The king could not see beyond his own obsession with Gaveston and his fear of losing him. The situation could not be unpicked and put back together again, for the pieces of the puzzle could never fit. The nobility wanted a leader, and Edward wanted to be led. However much Lancaster buried himself in his papers and carefully constructed means to bring the king to heel, Edward could never effectively rule alone.

In late 1311 Gaveston was exiled for the third time, but only for a matter of weeks. By early January 1312 Edward changed his mind and not only rejected the Ordinances but recalled Piers Gaveston. This sudden change of heart is curious, as though Edward had counselled himself – or someone else had – not to be bullied. Whatever the cause of Edward's shift in mindset it was a reckless one, for as a result an irreparable wedge had been driven between Edward and his nobles, none more so than his cousin Thomas, earl of Lancaster.

Of the four earls trying to force the Ordinances upon the king, Thomas of Lancaster had appeared most dedicated to the cause. As a result, from 1311, a great gulf began to crack open between Edward and his cousin. Where Edward was generous and affable, Lancaster was haughty, hostile, inflexible and dogmatic. He found it difficult to inspire loyalty from others and he preferred his northern castles to the king's court at Westminster. However, as a direct descendant from both the Plantagenet line and the French Capetian royal house, he was still a major power among the nobility.

And if his lineage did not already make him a threat to Edward, by 1311 his growing power and wealth rendered him even more dangerous. That summer his father-in-law, Henry de Lacy, earl of Lincoln, had passed away, leaving two earldoms to his daughter

Alice, which meant that Lancaster had amassed more wealth than any other nobleman in the realm as well as holding five earldoms, including Lancaster, Derby and Leicester. It was foolish to alienate him, and yet this was exactly what Edward's actions seemed designed to do.

Rumours about Piers Gaveston and his whereabouts proliferated. What is clear is that somehow, after Christmas, Gaveston had found his way north. Accompanied by one of Edward's household knights, Gaveston arrived outside York in early January 1312. Gaveston took refuge in the home of the treasurer of York Minster before quickly moving on to Knaresborough Castle, where he was reunited with the king – his 'brother'. Together they tried to forge a plan that would both protect Gaveston from the malice of his enemies and allow Edward to keep his crown. This was entirely futile.

As soon as the winter frost melted, the barons of England initiated a manhunt. Cautious not to panic the realm, a series of tournaments were held across the country: a ruse to allow them to gather arms without drawing undue suspicion. On hearing that Gaveston and the king had gone against the Ordinances, the earls of Warwick, Lancaster, Pembroke, Arundel and Hereford met with Robert Winchelsey, the archbishop of Canterbury who had previously threatened excommunication against Gaveston for not adhering to his exile. The author of the *Vita* notes that 'what had been done there later became clear' and goes on to give this detailed version of events.[6]

A plan started to take shape and it was crucial that the men moved cautiously and kept peace in order not to alarm either Edward or the population at large. Thomas of Lancaster agreed to go north to track down Gaveston; at Newcastle he discovered evidence of the king and his favourite gathering their own arms.

The earls had only one chance to capture Gaveston, who had fled to Scarborough Castle for his safety and, probably, for its location on the coast, crucial to receive supplies or escape by sea.[7] While Gaveston lodged at Scarborough the threat of excommunication that had been held over him for years was formally declared by the archbishop. Gaveston was not only on the run but he was without papal support.

On 14 May 1312 Edward travelled back to Knaresborough Castle, with the pregnant Isabella, who had been dragged across North Yorkshire on her husband's quest to save Gaveston. As Edward left Scarborough, he left his friend for the final time.

Circling the area, Aymer de Valence, the earl of Pembroke, together with Guy de Beauchamp, the earl of Warwick, were charged with the arrest of the king's favourite; they quickly moved in and took the castle by surprise. With little choice and insufficient defence, Gaveston was forced to surrender to Pembroke, but on the condition he would be heard before parliament. Accepting Gaveston's surrender and condition as the laws of chivalry dictated, Pembroke took his prisoner south with the expectation that he would enter into formal negotiations with Edward for his release.

The earl of Pembroke arrived with his captive at the sleepy village of Deddington in Oxfordshire, 'a pleasant place with ample lodgings', on the evening of 9 June 1312.[8] Pembroke had chosen Deddington because his wife was based at nearby Bampton Manor; he left Gaveston lightly guarded at his Deddington lodging so that he could spend the night at Bampton. Whether Pembroke knew what would happen next is uncertain, but if he had expected to return Gaveston to the king alive, following negotiations, his decision was foolish.

As Pembroke left Gaveston to join his wife, the earl of Warwick, 'whom Piers called Warwick the Dog', moved in, clattering into the courtyard of Castle House, the manor where Piers was staying with a small armed guard.[9] He yelled up to Gaveston's bedroom: 'Arise traitor, thou art taken.' Jolted awake, Gaveston dressed, leaving aside his 'belt of knighthood', was arrested, and left his lodgings in chains. On the road to Warwick 'blaring trumpets, yelling people and savage shouting followed Piers', as though he were a 'thief and a traitor', and he was taken to Warwick Castle to await his fate at the hands of the earls.[10] Within days the rest of them had arrived, including the earl of Lancaster. The earl of Pembroke was allegedly horrified that Gaveston had been snatched from under his nose and ardently protested to the earl of Gloucester, 'beseeching him with tears to vindicate the wrong that had been done to him'.[11] Pembroke's weeping changed nothing. It was soon decided that Gaveston must be put to death after a show trial; he was accused of treason, having led the king into wrongdoing by breaching the Ordinances. It was, however, to be done honourably – he would be beheaded as 'a nobleman and a Roman citizen would'.[12]

As a small act of courtesy, Gaveston was given time to 'look to his soul' and prepare himself for death. On 19 June, he was taken from his cell and brought before Thomas of Lancaster; in a desperate plea he threw himself on the ground and cried, 'Noble earl, have mercy on me!' Unmoved, Lancaster spat, 'In God's name let him be taken away.'[13] Gaveston was taken to Blacklow Hill – Lancaster's land – where two Welsh executioners were paid generously to end his life. At the top of the hill, one of the men savagely ran him through with a sword before the other struck a mighty blow and took off Gaveston's head.

His remains were not left to fester on Blacklow Hill. Dominican friars attended to his corpse, gathering him up and carefully stitching his head back onto his body before they carried him to Oxford. Unsure what to do with the body of the excommunicated earl, they left him in the care of the Dominicans in Oxford so that Edward could decide how to honour his beloved friend and 'brother'. Unable to be laid to rest until his excommunication was revoked, Piers Gaveston's corporeal remains were in limbo for two years. His fetid body was embalmed and cloth of gold – ordered by Edward and Margaret de Clare, Gaveston's wife – was carefully draped over his corpse.[14] This grief was interwoven with bitter anger. Piers Gaveston had been murdered – an unjust, cruel and reckless act. At some point Edward made it plain that he 'had already decided to destroy those who killed Piers'.[15]

Those involved in Gaveston's capture and execution certainly feared the consequences. Soon after, Henry Percy, a northern lord and warden of the Scottish Marches, wrote to Humphrey de Bohun, the earl of Hereford, reminding him that they must remain united, even in fear. Discussing Thomas of Lancaster, who ultimately had Gaveston's blood on his hands, he said: 'We are bound to defend, save, maintain any damages that might occur to him, live and die in aid and in defence of him in the aforesaid quarrel.'[16] The lords sought to ensure that no man could be singled out for punishment by the king and that Gaveston's death would remain a triumph for the nobility in the face of tyranny.

The grieving Edward soon found some joy. On 13 November 1312, sixteen-year-old Queen Isabella gave birth to a healthy son, who was also named Edward. The king had an heir. The precious baby was baptised in the chapel of Saint Edward at Windsor Castle amid immense celebrations: an elaborate pageant was held by the London guild of fishmongers to celebrate Isabella and the safe arrival of the prince. Yet as winter melted into spring, no significant progress had been made between the king and his earls. Edward was unwilling to accept that Gaveston's death was anything other than murder.

Without resolution, Edward turned his attention to duty and an event across the Channel in France: Edward and Isabella were invited to attend the knighting of Philip IV's sons at Amiens. This was no empty ceremony. The *grand' feste* held in honour of the event was unprecedented in scale and ceremony, and began when Edward and Isabella entered Paris on the eve of Pentecost, when 'the whole city rose up and went forth to meet them'.[17]

The trip was a marital success. Having escaped Edward's stalemate with his earls, and without Gaveston coming between them, Edward and Isabella's relationship improved. The couple appeared to be so distracted by one another that they were oblivious to royal commitments. It was said that Edward was late for a meeting with the king of France because he stayed too long in bed with Isabella. Yet the trip ended badly. One night in July a fire broke out in Edward's rooms and the flames quickly spread to the soft furnishings. With many of their belongings destroyed, the couple were forced to flee semi-clothed into the courtyard. Edward was said to have helped Isabella from the fire, but the flames were so intense that she was badly injured. The burns to her hands took months to heal. Odo, the queen's apothecary, sold her violet flowers, cardamom, grains of paradise, tamarind and papillon as well as rose water to help the healing process.[18]

On the couple's return it was time to settle the matter of Gaveston's death. After months of animosity, the king and earls finally made peace on 15 October. A pardon was agreed in parliament and announced the next day, absolving Lancaster 'and his adherents, followers, and confederates' for their crimes against the king, which Edward considered to not only include Gaveston's murder but 'forcible entries into . . . towns or castles, or any sieges of the same; or on account of having borne arms'.[19] There is no reference to Gaveston being named a traitor; peace had been made on the king's terms. 'The earls approached the lord king and greeted him, as was proper, on bended knee. Receiving them graciously he at once raised them and kissed them one by one, wholly absolved them of every crime of which they were accused.'[20] The matter was dealt with and the bubbling resentment Edward held, particularly for his cousin Lancaster, was brushed aside in order to finally deal with the most urgent threat to the realm: the Scots.

4. The Road to Bannockburn

In summer 1313 an army of Scots laid siege to Stirling Castle, one of the last English strongholds in the Forth Valley. A great edifice built upon a steep crag overlooking the River Forth, Stirling was crucial for Robert Bruce if he was to recover authority in Scotland and rule as king.

Since assuming the crown, Edward had been too consumed by internal politics to take up his father's mantle of 'Hammer of the Scots'. Instead, it was left to weary commanders garrisoned in both Scotland and on the English side of the border to put up their best defences against a growing threat of Scottish resistance.

Edward's distractions allowed Robert Bruce to gather his strength and launch a series of attacks on border towns. In parallel, he attempted to negotiate with Edward II, imploring the English king to allow Scottish people to live in peace with Bruce as their king. In October 1310 the king of Scotland wrote to the king of England, asking 'to beseech your highness more devoutly so that, having God and public decency in sight, you would take pains to cease from our persecution and the disturbance of the people of our kingdom in order that devastation and the spilling of a neighbour's blood may henceforth stop'.[1] But this plea was also a warning.

Robert Bruce was a risk-taker and a brilliant military strategist but above all he was an opportunist. With Edward's back turned in the summer of 1311, Bruce and his men invaded England by crossing the border, raiding towns and starting fires across Cumbria – one of many examples of Bruce dipping his toe into England to test how much resistance he faced, bringing fire and sword to English communities and plundering their resources. Finding little, he returned again, attacking Corbridge, Durham, Northumberland and Dunbar as well as the battle-hardened edifice of Norham Castle, which overlooked the River Tweed. In 1312, the people of Durham despaired over the crippling wave of Scottish attacks and negotiated directly with Robert Bruce, offering him 'two thousand pounds to obtain truce' for the next year, which resulted in the Scots negotiating 'free access and retreat through the land of the bishopric whensoever they wished to make a raid on England'.[2] These sorts of agreements, verging on treason, were not made lightly, but the population were increasingly scared and forlorn. Entire towns and individuals tried to appeal to King Edward for aid.

Cries for help were sent to Edward in the form of various petitions. As lords yawned and shuffled their feet along the stone slabs of Westminster Hall, the voices of the desperate rang out through the oration of their petitions in government, read out loud, possibly by the chancellor. In 1310, after a particularly punitive Scottish raid on Bolton Abbey in the valley of the River Wharfe in Yorkshire, the prior of Bolton petitioned Edward to restore abbey 'goods and chattels', including the 'king's charter', which was also lifted by the Scottish raiding party.[3] Some wished to take matters into their own hands. Bernard le Poleter, a merchant from Carlisle, grew tired of defending the town and requested permission from the king to take four men into Scotland and retrieve 'cattle and other merchandises taken by the Scots'.[4] Others agonised over how the warring had irreparably destroyed their property, such as that belonging to Margaret de Gironde, a widow whose 'land [was] ruined . . . castles destroyed and . . . goods lost as a result'.[5] Perhaps from the comfort of Westminster it was hard for the king and his nobility to empathise with the plight of wretched people in the north. But what was plain to them was that Robert Bruce was testing English power by pushing further across the border than any Scottish rebel before him.

Aside from harrying the borderlands and extorting the English, a major objective for Robert Bruce was to remove any English presence in Scotland and reclaim the country as a nation independent of English sovereignty. The English had occupied Scotland in various garrisons since Edward I's conquest and in doing so they dominated the surrounding countryside. These castles also served as a base for invading armies marching north from England. The only way to remove them was to burn them out. From 1309 to 1313 Bruce began laying siege to, and then razing, English castles. The fleeing English were left to the mercy of the unfamiliar and unforgiving Scottish landscape. Robert Bruce had initially torn through the Lothian – the Scottish lowlands south of Edinburgh – at such a rate that by March 1313 he had created the space and means to take the strategically important castle of Perth, as well as Roxburgh, Dumfries, Banff, Dundee, Ayr, Loch Doon, Dalswinton, Buittle and Caerlaverock. Only two important castles remained under English control: Bothwell and Stirling, the latter being the gateway to the north of Scotland. Stirling had to be taken and Bruce allocated this momentous task to his brother, Edward Bruce, an experienced warrior. Camped outside the castle, Edward Bruce was forced to commit to the drudgery of a siege and simply wait for the inhabitants of Stirling to run out of supplies.

With Stirling under siege, an English campaign into Scotland was necessary. Robert Bruce had built too much power to be ignored and the pressure he put on the border was no longer sustainable for those who fought hard to protect it. A mighty expedition into Scotland could also harness support Edward had lost after Gaveston's execution, echoing his father's ability to rally men behind his sword. The problem was that it was too late. Bruce had begun to unravel the web of English power that had been in place in Scotland, imposed by both pen and sword. In October 1313, Bruce swore that any person in opposition to his rule would lose their lands. For centuries, noble families, both English and Scottish, had held lands either side of the border. Family trees ran through both royal lines and a cross-border community of people had coexisted for generations. Bruce's threat sought to disrupt ancient social structures, dismantle communities and disinherit vast numbers of nobility from their land. Under the new law, these families were forced to pick a side, which, for some, would force brother and cousin to turn on one another. A binary border meant the loss of the human structures and societies that had previously defined it.

In a bid to prevent this border divide, which would oust all English loyalists from Scotland, Edward had to liberate Stirling. He mustered the best men available to him, ordering them to gather at Berwick-upon-Tweed by 19 May 1314. A fifteen-thousand-strong fighting force, mostly infantry, was summoned from English counties and another contingent called up from Wales.[6] Some of these men had experienced victory against rebel Scots led by William Wallace at Falkirk in 1298 and as a result were considered the most proficient warriors in the realm. Edward went to exceptional lengths to secure the best soldiers he could. Sir Giles d'Argentein, an esteemed Norman knight who had been captured by the emperor of Byzantium while crusading with the Knights of Rhodes, was ransomed by Edward so that he could make it back to England in time to join the army in Scotland. He was asked to ride beside the king as his personal bodyguard.

By June 1314 the massive English army was finally ready to march. Under the midsummer sun, a twenty-mile-long procession snaked north from Berwick-upon-Tweed with Edward II at the helm; 'in that company' there were 'quite sufficient to penetrate the whole of Scotland . . . indeed all who were present agreed that never in our time has such an army marched out from England.'[7] Convinced of victory, Edward led his army as if he were on a pilgrimage.

A Northumbrian knight named Thomas Gray, who rode in the company of the nobleman and military leader Henry de Beaumont, would later provide one of the only eyewitness accounts of the battle. Years later, his son penned his father's account on parchment.[8] Alongside archival records and other chronicle accounts from both sides of this battle, the events that took place after Edward II finally brought his army within sight of Stirling Castle provide the following account.

A few miles from the castle on the afternoon of 23 June the army paused as the vanguard went ahead to assess the terrain. Among them was the nobleman Henry de Bohun. Hoping to achieve a wide view of the field ahead, he spied the shadows of men in the distance, half concealed in the New Park, thick woodland that stretched across the valley below. Addressing them was a man on a small grey palfrey, wearing a helmet with a gold circlet – the symbol of a king. Bruce was an open target. Henry de Bohun had moments to grab glory. He lowered his lance and charged. The sound of clinking armour and thundering hooves caused Bruce to turn towards the knight and charge. In the moment of contact, he spun to one side, stood high in his stirrups and hurled his axe down on Henry de Bohun's head, crushing his helmet and skull in one brutal blow. The esteemed English knight toppled from his horse and was dragged through the grass a dead man.

While the Scots were ignited by this small but significant victory, the atmosphere in the exhausted English camp soured at the news. As dawn broke on Midsummer's Day, Edward's army found itself far from ready for battle. Edward was already at loggerheads with his men. The king's nephew, the earl of Gloucester, pushed his uncle for patience, urging the need for rest. But, furious under the pressure of imminent battle, Edward was eager to fight and saw Gloucester as patronising and meddling. He 'scorned the earl's advice, and grew very heated with him'. When he challenged Gloucester's loyalty, his nephew stormed off and prepared himself for battle against his better judgement. He is said to have exclaimed, 'Today . . . it will be clear that I am neither a traitor nor a liar.'[9]

The king would have done well to accept Gloucester's counsel. The exhaustion of a fast march towards Stirling and dilapidated morale after the death of one of their vanguard meant that the glum atmosphere in the camp was palpable; with little time to grapple with the terrain, the English army, whatever its size, was in a bad position. They were enclosed by low-lying marshland at their backs and the Bannock Burn – a small river – and the Pelstream Burn on either flank. Dawn broke on 24 June and the morning fog slowly dissipated. The English army had already crossed the burn from the west under the cover of darkness and by sunrise were lined up to do battle. Overnight, Robert Bruce marched his men entirely on foot from the New Park Wood so that they would wait for the English to find their ground. Before sunrise, the Scots marched downhill so that they had an area of dense woodland at their backs. There they arranged themselves into three schiltrons – their shields locked together in front and overhead. This 'thick-set hedge' was a powerful defence 'which a sword would not easily penetrate' – a hedgehog formation of razor-sharp steel.[10]

The English cavalry was led by Gilbert de Clare, earl of Gloucester, the king's furious nephew. Each horse carried a fully armoured knight holding a twelve-foot lance, along with an axe, mace or sword. The Scots had no visible cavalry. It might have seemed like easy pickings for the English, and Edward likely thought as much as he scanned the line of Scots. Seeing they were kneeling, he initially assumed this was in submission. But he was soon put right. 'No, my lord. They kneel before God,' said Sir Ingram de Umfraville.[11]

Drums started and archers stepped forward to begin the battle. These archers were the best weapon Edward had and they would do the most damage to the Scottish army throughout the battle. Then it was time for the vanguard to attack. Gloucester, still reeling from his argument with Edward, had forgotten to wear his surcoat. The cavalry prepared to advance, hurling the full weight of galloping horses against the Scottish spears, but their position rendered the cavalry ineffective. The confluence of the two burns trapped the cavalry by pushing the horses together, their flanks haplessly bumping into one another as they tried to launch into the charge. Instead, they were pushed back, squashed tighter together by the incoming offensive juggernaut of the Scottish schiltrons. Those that did manage to advance hurtled into a death trap. On impact, knights were flung from their horses to the ground, where they were met by Scottish axes. A massacre ensued. The earl of Gloucester had tried to break up the schiltrons, to give the cavalry space, but was not recognised by his arms. He would have been a lucrative ransom, but in the heat of battle, he was butchered on the spears of the Scots.

Penned in, the English cavalry became a bloodied blockade for the English infantry. In moving forward, the foot soldiers only added to the confused melee. With thousands of arrows to use, the skilled English archers hurried to the north side of the battle where they could rain arrows onto the Scottish flank. But this was futile – Bruce ordered his light cavalry forward and horsemen swept through the archers, cutting them down with ease. Bannockburn was lost.

Edward was dragged from the battle and across the Pelstream to safety before its waters ran with blood from the bodies of English soldiers. 'Bannockburn was spoken about for many years in English throats,' wrote the Lanercost chronicler. As English men and mercenaries were bloodied, Edward and his closest allies, 'like miserable wretches', fled for Dunbar Castle, 'leaving all the others to their fate', for 'the inhabitants of the countryside, who had previously feigned peace, now butchered our men everywhere.' The English deserted with such speed and terror they left behind their entire baggage train.[12] The king, having barely stopped for breath when he reached Dunbar, took the soonest boat to Berwick.

Chroniclers were left aghast at the outcome of Bannockburn. Some called it a moral reckoning, a punishment on Edward II for pillaging monasteries on his way to Stirling. Some blamed revelling soldiers the night before battle, so confident in their impending victory they drank heavily and did not prepare themselves. Others blamed the absence of major English noblemen, such as Thomas of Lancaster, who had refused to participate in the battle because he thought it went against the Ordinances. One thing that was agreed, however, is that Bannockburn was the greatest military disaster the English army had suffered. It would not recover during Edward's reign.

The victorious king of Scots had his own agenda: forcing every elite member of the realm to attest their allegiance or be stripped of their land, wealth and titles. This would shape the relationship between England and Scotland for ever. The effects of the Battle of Bannockburn – political dilemmas, rebellion and civil war – were felt through the rest of the fourteenth century. The victory gave Bruce and his men a boost in morale and the confidence to extend his power elsewhere in the British Isles, taking a keen interest in Ireland and the north of England. Yet the battle itself achieved nothing. Bruce wanted independence and Edward would not agree to his terms. In this stalemate between royal powers it was the people who suffered.

Where Bannockburn achieved little in regard to Scottish independence, Ireland, which had been colonised by English forces since the twelfth century, was reinvigorated by the Scottish victory. Domhnall O'Neill, king of Tyrone, was so impressed by Bruce's efforts, he offered the high kingship of Ireland to Edward Bruce. The hope was to oust the English from Ireland with Scottish help and achieve national independence in the same manner as Bruce had intended. As a result, there was a reshuffle of power dynamics across the Isles. For Edward II the loss was personal; an unpleasant lesson in martial failure. He had lost because he had thoughtlessly chosen poor terrain and ignored the advice of his commanders. Edward was more vulnerable than ever and England faced a crisis of security. The border was unstable, English power was entirely lost in Scotland and Edward had lost the bulwark of his northern nobility, men whose strength and armies he relied upon. The balance of power was dramatically tipped in Thomas of Lancaster's favour. Edward's failure to achieve the military success of his father exposed and reopened the rift between Edward and his cousin, with Edward forced into political submission as the reins of government were handed to the more capable Lancaster. Alongside this, the death of the wealthy noble Gilbert de Clare created a power vacuum in his ungoverned ancestral lands across the England–Wales border. This conglomeration of misfortune, poor decision-making and the clash of egos and ideals shaped the future of England for the first half of the fourteenth century.

5.   The Third Apocalypse

The Book of Revelation speaks of a scroll bound by seven seals that was held in the right hand of God. When four of the seven seals are cracked open, four horsemen leap into the mortal world, descending from the heavens in a furious gallop. The black horse is Famine, the white horse is Conquest, the red horse is War and the pale horse is Death. Famine, Conquest, War and Death: these are the bringers of the Apocalypse. It is written that the world into which they thunder will descend into doom.

After the loss at Bannockburn, England fell into a state of desperation and destruction. The black horse, Famine, visited towns and villages across the country. Emptying grain stores and felling livestock, it left rural communities destitute. The white horse with its crowned rider clutching a bow, Conquest, came in the guise of the Scots who ravaged northern communities. The red horse came as the red rose, the emblem of the House of Lancaster, as Edward II and his cousin continued their descent into civil war. All carried the promise of Death.

At the turn of the fourteenth century England had prospered. There was enough food and the population thrived, enjoying a series of successful harvests. After Bannockburn it was as though the heavens wept for all those bloodied and lost. The skies opened and a torrent of rain fell almost relentlessly for the next three years, plaguing northern Europe with scenes reminiscent of the biblical Flood. Freshly sown seeds were washed away and livestock drowned as rivers burst and bridges collapsed. Barley, oats, peas and beans all increased in price while grain and salt rose up to eight times their usual value. The poor starved but the wealthy paid the swelling asking price for daily bread. Food production, trade and commerce ground to a halt and this relentless hunger became known as the Great Famine.

The lack of ample sustenance and the presence of near-constant rain – sodden earth being the ideal breeding ground for deadly bacteria – meant that infection spread fast among livestock. As the famine held a tight grip on England, a 'murrain', or infection, began to kill off cattle, young bulls and oxen. Religious ceremonies and rites were performed during their feeding in the hope of salvation from the cruelty of the climate. Pastures became swampland, with farmers desperately trying to drag their wagons through boggy earth. A misery 'such as our age has never seen' resulted in soldiers garrisoned in Berwick picking the bones of their dead horses, people boiling and eating tree bark, dogs, cats and other 'unclean things' – possibly vermin – and according to some more graphic accounts, resorting to cannibalism.[1] Many suspected that an impending apocalypse was the source of this suffering. Was it an expression of the wrath of the Almighty, angered by their sinful lives? The archbishop of Canterbury ordered every parish church in the realm to partake in a series of processions, to purge communities of the 'wickedness of the inhabitants'. Clergymen trudged barefoot through the mudcaked streets of England, rain trickling down their faces. Prayer, fasting and giving of alms (donations of money or goods to charitable foundations) were believed to be the way to appeal to the mercy of the Lord. But the rain kept coming.

In February 1315 'the earls and all the barons met in London, to discuss the state of the king and the realm'. The king could not make the rain stop and the crops grow but something had to be done. The remedy proffered at this parliament was to fix the prices of food: 'oxen, pigs and sheep, for fowls, chickens and pigeons, and for other common foods'. Corn and other foodstuffs were sourced from overseas with merchants being granted safe conduct to travel, seeking goods to feed the starving realm. However, this had little positive impact. The Great Famine, coupled with the 'murrain' among livestock, meant that farmers were forced to plough with horses rather than cattle. Even royalty was affected: the king lost half of his flock of sheep at his farm at Clipstone in Sherwood Forest.[2]

Against this backdrop, the earls and barons had another pressing concern: Scottish raids had become worse after Bannockburn.

Northumberland, Cumberland, Durham, Teesside and even parts of Yorkshire were under threat and Edward could not help them. Incapable of finding a solution, the government in Westminster effectively cut off the north from the rest of England by offering little to no protection. It was a problem that, for now, was better ignored. The north had become frontier land: lawless, barren and highly dangerous. Scottish raiders, led by Edward Bruce and James Douglas (known by his moniker 'Black Douglas'), descended into the valleys and launched their attacks. One account describes how in November 1314 the Scots 'devastated almost all Northumberland with fire, except the castles'.[3] Some people were able to buy themselves safety, paying custodians of northern garrisons for the privilege of protection, but most could not afford to do so. After the Scots ravaged Northumberland they raided Richmond in Yorkshire, stealing cattle and taking slaves 'without resistance'. Many 'fled south or hid themselves in the woods except those who took refuge in the castles'.[4] After a week of raiding, the Scots reached Westmorland, where they interrupted court proceedings by bursting into the castle of Appleby, to the screams of its inhabitants.

Increasingly, the only way to obtain safety was to buy it; 'ransoming' safety became normal practice for survival. Robert Bruce knew that wealthy cathedral cities like Durham could and would pay for immunity against Scottish attacks and as a result raiding – or receiving tribute payments to prevent Scottish attack – became a means of generating vast sums of money for Bruce in order to fund his war effort. Unlike the raids that took place in the late thirteenth century under the rebel William Wallace, which lasted a number of weeks, Robert Bruce ordered his men to move fast, darting in and out of the northern counties, frequently returning to Scotland. This way they would not be hindered by supplies, the need to garrison men or by dragging around booty for months on end. Durham continually extended their agreement with the Scots, buying immunity from the punitive raids. Garrisons at Alnwick and Bamburgh followed, purchasing safety, at a crippling cost, from the Scottish king. Multiple deals with northern towns and communities saw well over twenty thousand pounds of tribute money paid directly into Bruce's purse.

With no resistance from Westminster, he had effectively become a king in the north.

English accounts of the Scottish raiding parties paint a picture of godless, lawless barbarians with murderous intentions that spared nobody. The reality was that these accounts were entirely partisan. Not all were written from first-hand experience; they leaned largely towards the gruesomely sensationalist. Reflecting on a Scottish raid conducted by William Wallace back in 1297, a monk from Saint Albans Abbey – nowhere near the border – claimed that: 'driving together English men and women, the vile Scots tied them together and whipped them until they dropped. They even snatched up babes from the cradle or from their mothers' breasts and cut them open, and they burned alive many children in churches and schools.'[5] Though atrocities certainly occurred, often the point of these horror stories was to invoke hatred and to shock people into fearing the Scots to prevent them from siding with Bruce.

Surviving records show that money was not the only motive for the Scots' exploits. The famine affected both sides of the border, with stocks of foodstuffs reaching an all-time low.[6] Grain was stolen and sheep and cattle were driven off farmland and pushed back towards Scotland, trampling crops as they moved. Household items were snatched: plate, bedclothes, utensils, clothing and, where it was available, iron. When the Scots raided Furness in Lancashire they were 'delighted with the abundance of iron they found'. Iron was sought after because it was needed to manufacture valuable weaponry and armour.

Since Bannockburn, Bruce's power, and thus his ability to negotiate, had increased drastically. He had the north of England in the palm of his hand and a collection of English noblemen as his prisoners, including the important earl of Hereford. But relationships and people were also important to Robert Bruce, particularly those he loved, and Edward still held the most precious prize of all: Bruce's family.

His sister, wife and daughter had been held in captivity for eight years by the time, on Michaelmas Day 1314, two months after Bannockburn, their freedom was exchanged for that of the Earl of

Hereford.[7] The record is silent about this reunion; we know only that Bruce had them restored either at Saint Andrews or Arbroath, where he remained to oversee administrative problems – removing English loyalists from their castles in Scotland. The coming together of a family, torn apart by war, must have been a great relief. Perhaps Bruce spent time at Arbroath to be close to the women he had been separated from for so long.

This prisoner exchange was both political and in the interest of those who had been held captive. Edward had owed a duty to the earl of Hereford, to whom he was bound in honour, to not leave his man in the hands of the enemy. Bruce simply wanted to be reunited with his family. The handover did nothing to restore security to people in the borderlands. Complaints poured into Westminster via another catalogue of petitions. Grievances were read out, from 'the men of South Tynedale' complaining how men from other counties had sided with the Scots.[8] 'Furthermore, sire,' the speaker addressed the king, 'they pray for a remedy against the people of the said counties of Cumberland and Westmorland, who have come by night, and have taken their wives, chattels and other goods and carried them off into the said counties'. The petitioners pleaded that 'these wrongs might no more be perpetrated, but that the trespasses committed before might be put right, if it please our said lord the king.'[9] Tenants from Kirkby Lonsdale complained that they were 'so impoverished by the coming of the enemy' they were unable to repair damages caused by the Scottish incursions.[10] The prioress of Gyseburn in Yorkshire relayed that her church had been 'burnt, robbed and destroyed' and the people of Newcastle-upon-Tyne requested financial aid in defending the city, for 'the surrounding countryside is devastated by the war, neither the merchants or craftsmen have anything to live on'.[11]

The vulnerability of people on the borders is most clearly demonstrated through the testimonies of the women widowed after Bannockburn. Christina de Woderington pleaded for help after her lands were 'burnt and destroyed by the Scots, and her chattels stolen, leaving her with three young children and no support'.[12] Despite the prevalence of these issues, they were not Edward's top priority in parliament – a major political power struggle was brewing and this took up much of Edward's attention. Had Edward won Bannock-burn he would have been able to shake free from the Ordinances that bound him. But with his appalling defeat, authority was thrust into the arms of Thomas of Lancaster. Edward's loss in battle was his greatest rival's gain.

The campaign north had not been sanctioned by parliament, it was a war entirely on Edward's terms. Lancaster had refused to fight, claiming that moving an army into Scotland without the support of parliament was going against his Ordinances. As Edward returned, demoralised by defeat, the self-righteous Lancaster could relish seeing his point proven: Edward had acted rashly and without con-sent from the lords, and as a result lost the best of the English army. Initially, the two cousins tried to coexist in the face of adversity but they were almost constantly at loggerheads, eventually agreeing to disagree and avoiding each other. Lancaster spent most of his time in the north, preferring the chill of the northern wind at Pontefract to Edward's brisk company in Westminster.

Morale was low, the country was on the brink of starvation and the north of England had been lost to Bruce's raiders. As parliament in Westminster was prorogued for Easter in March 1315, exhausted lords went back to their castles, grumbling about the state of the realm and the king's persistent bickering with his cousin. But as early signs of spring appeared in the trees and the chill of the Scottish winter eased, the self-proclaimed king of Scotland had formed his own agenda: to take the formidable English fortress at Carlisle.

Carlisle was 'indeed always hateful to the Scots; it was always feared by them, for it frequently intercepted their raids and many times hindered their flight.'[13] Lying on the western border between England and Scotland, the castle was, like Berwick, important to both sides. Over the course of the Scottish Wars of Independence these two major garrisons were crucibles of power: whoever held them held the borders.

Carlisle Castle had been built into the circular twelfth-century wall that wrapped around the town, creating a formidable defensive fortress. As with most walled towns and cities of the time, access was possible only through a series of gates with imposing portcullises.

Carlisle had three such gates and the Scots unleashed their full force on each of them. By July 1315, smoke circled the walls of the town as wooden homesteads were consumed by the white heat of the inferno unleashed by Robert Bruce.

Andrew Harclay, a battle-hardened veteran familiar with fighting Scots across the border, was tasked with the defence of Carlisle. Robert Bruce, anticipating strong resistance, employed a trebuchet to launch rocks into the walls, killing one English soldier in the process. Yet this single trebuchet was no match for the weaponry the English had to hand. English siege engines were rolled up to the inner walls, hurling back eight times as many stones and debris as the Scots were able to. Bruce was undeterred, bringing forward 'a moveable towerlike structure for sieges . . . considerably higher than the city walls'. Though this might have been enough to change the course of the siege in other conditions, Carlisle had been hammered by rainfall and the ground was sodden. As the Scots wheeled their towering beast of a siege engine up to the wall, it was claimed by mud and Robert Bruce was forced to abandon it.

In a final attempt to get men inside, the bold – but mostly reckless – James Douglas launched an ambitious attack at the more lightly defended higher part of the wall. It was said that 'there they set up long ladders which they climbed, and the bowmen, whereof they had a great number, shot their arrows thickly to prevent anyone showing his head above the wall'. Even Douglas could not conquer Carlisle: he was 'met with such resistance there as threw them to the ground with their ladders'. After ten days of attack, Robert Bruce marched his army back to Scotland, 'leaving behind them all their engines of war' in the soaked ground.[14]

For Edward it was a small victory. It brought some hope to what had felt like a doomed cause in a doomed year; and crucially it allowed a momentary respite in raiding. Robert Bruce, bloodied in defeat, shifted his focus to Ireland, where his brother Edward had landed an army on the north-east coast. As spring arrived, Bruce prepared to form an alliance with Irish neighbours in the attempt to put pressure on Edward II through a Gaelic union.

If Edward was to rescue all that his father and the Plantagenet kings before him had worked towards, he would be forced to reconcile his differences with Lancaster – going to war *with* his cousin rather than against him. The problem was that Edward II had locked horns with the lords that surrounded him at Westminster since the start of his reign. This had created a chasm at the heart of government that compromised the structures of power elsewhere in the realm. Borders were unsafe, people starved through lack of initiative to combat famine, and Robert Bruce was sourcing allies in Ireland. A decade into his reign, Edward II was learning the hard truth that a sovereign had to be united with the nobility in order to keep the wheels of government turning smoothly. The survival of the realm depended on it. Yet the situation was at an impasse. Lancaster's uncompromising nature and Edward's insecurity and reliance on close friendships rendered the recovery of the realm impossible. As Lancaster suffocated Edward with his insistence on his Ordinances, Edward once again edged closer towards a cabal of men who he needed to advise and encourage him, but who the rest of government – indeed the realm – could not trust. New favourites emerged at court, most notably Hugh Despenser the Elder and Hugh Despenser the Younger. These men would stop at nothing to advance their positions and claim the ear and heart of the king.

6.   A Song of Steel

A vast cavern of Purbeck marble, stone, slate and wood, Westminster Hall was built by the son of William the Conqueror, William II. On its completion in 1097, William stood and admired his Great Hall, a space that he would preside over with majesty. Allegedly, when a member of his household criticised the hall for being 'too big' William scoffed that it was 'not half large enough . . . a mere bed-chamber when compared to what he had in mind'. The hall had a self-supporting roof and stone walls two metres thick, as well as a wall passage on four sides that could serve as a gallery. Draped with royal tabards and tapestries, it was the cathedral of kings.

In May 1317 Edward II hosted a great feast in the hall to celebrate the Pentecost. A moveable feast in the Christian calendar, Pentecost marks the moment the Holy Spirit descended from the heavens to visit the Apostles. For a medieval king, it was a time when food, drink and dancing could be enjoyed in abundance. Peacocks and sugar sculptures adorned the tables and minstrels played to guests as they ate. The king was surrounded by his new collection of favourite men, including the Despensers – Hugh the Elder and Hugh the Younger. Along with Hugh Despenser the Younger sat two more handsome and ambitious knights, Hugh Audley and Roger Damory. But the warm mood turned cold when an unexpected guest was permitted entry. The heavy doors swung open to reveal a woman, masked, on horseback and dressed in costume. The king, perhaps suspecting this was part of the celebrations, was untouched by fear as she trotted towards his table. She reached down from her horse and handed him a letter before circling her mount and exiting. The king ordered that the letter be read aloud. Much to his surprise, the letter was highly critical, shaming him for neglecting important men of the realm. He was also accused of favouritism by promoting others 'who had not

borne the heat of the day' – a blatant nod to the dashing young courtiers surrounding him.[1]

Seized before she could get away, the mysterious woman confessed
that she had been paid by one of Edward's knights to deliver the
accusation. The knight in question confessed in a panic, stating that
he had not expected the letter to be read aloud. Intended, perhaps, to
serve as a warning to the king rather than a threat, this letter and the
manner in which it was delivered cast an ominous shadow over the
king of England's authority and drew attention to the corruption
and conflict that existed within inner court circles. The precarious
state of Edward II's domestic affairs continued to prove an unfortunate distraction from a much greater problem, namely Robert Bruce
and his intentions in Ireland.

At the start of the fourteenth century, the English held power over
most of the south and east of Ireland, with English lords controlling land and castles across the region in the name of King Edward.
These English-Irish lords were descended from noble families who
attempted to colonise Ireland in the twelfth and thirteenth centuries
but they were yet to take parts of the north and west of Ireland. These
regions were mostly ruled over by old Gaelic Irish families – often at
odds with one another as well as the English. One of the most hotly
disputed areas between the English and Irish powers since the twelfth
century was Ulster, with Carrickfergus Castle at its centre. With his
own land flanking the earldom of Ulster, the Gaelic lord Domhnall
O'Neill, king of Tyrone, frequently locked horns with one of the
English-Irish lords, Richard de Burgh, who controlled the earldom
of Ulster itself. With both O'Neill and Bruce holding a shared grudge
against the English, an alliance between these two Gaelic kings was
natural. Ultimately the hope was that through a type of 'pan-Celtic'
brotherhood the Bruce brothers would liberate Ireland from English
sovereignty.[2] In a letter from around 1315, Robert Bruce wrote to 'all
the kings of Ireland, to the prelates and clergy, and to the inhabitants of all Ireland', naming them 'his friends'. The king of Scotland
evoked a shared ancestry, language and culture and, most famously,
used the phrase 'our nation'.[3]

In spring 1315 Edward Bruce had brought with him from Scotland a group of veterans of war: Thomas Randolph, the earl of Moray, John de Soules and Philip Mowbray. The latter was a Scottish noble, formerly loyal to the English as custodian of Stirling Castle, who had become a turncoat following the rout at Bannockburn. Within ten days, Edward Bruce had the support of the most powerful native lords of Ireland; in exchange for helping to oust English nobles he was inaugurated high king of Ireland. This was an ancient title, steeped in Irish mythology and lore. Though Ireland had a select handful of kings in various provinces around the country, there had been no high king to rule over them since the twelfth century.

The campaign in Ireland was ambitious, but it started well. In September 1315 Edward Bruce defeated an army led by Richard de Burgh; in December 1315 he defeated Roger Mortimer of Wigmore at Kells in Meath. Mortimer was an English lord with estates in central Ireland who would, a year later, become the king's lieutenant in Ireland, specifically assigned to the role in order to put down this opposition. His initial defeat was a concerning one. However, by 1317 Edward Bruce was struggling to hold his army together. Famine had spread to Ireland and taken its toll on the Scottish army. As Edward Bruce's men grappled with starvation and disease, the English garrisons in the country were allowed momentary space to gather their strength. When the rain finally ceased and crops began to grow again, Edward Bruce's army filled their bellies with fresh bread and stirred into action. Edward Bruce marched his army out of Ulster for the final time in autumn 1318 to face the English in a decisive battle.

Edmund Butler – the earl of Carrick and the justiciar of Ireland (chief governor) – and the archbishop of Armagh led a vast Anglo-Irish army against Edward Bruce's smaller Gaelic alliance of warriors in what became known as the Battle of Faughart, fought on high ground on 14 October 1318 near Dundalk in County Louth. Edward Bruce, desperate for the fight, refused to wait for reinforcements and marched to battle despite being outnumbered. As a result, 'nearly all these [soldiers] were killed . . . except those who saved themselves by flight'. The distance between the advancing Scottish columns was so great that 'the first was done with before the second came up', and as for Edward Bruce's column of warriors, it 'was routed, just as the two preceding ones had been'. Bruce 'fell at the same time', but in order to make an example of his attempt to overrule English authority in Ireland, he was 'beheaded after death [and] his body being divided into four quarters, which were sent to the four chief towns of Ireland'.[4] Edward Bruce's head was sent as a gift to Edward II.

Two days after Edward Bruce was killed and quartered in Ireland, the English king held parliament at York for the first time in over two years. Edward had been both fortunate and strategic in dealing with the uprising in Ireland. Famine had stopped Edward Bruce as he was gaining strength and winning battles. That crucially bought Edward II time to muster enough men for Mortimer to lead into Ireland and for Edmund Butler to flatten Edward Bruce's inferior force at Faughart. Thanks to the influx of a vast army, Edward II, with the aid of Mortimer on the ground in Ireland, was able to strengthen England's military presence in Ireland sufficiently to prevent any further rebellion taking place.

The joy that emerged from the victory in Ireland was absent from the ongoing domestic situation in England. In January 1316 Thomas, earl of Lancaster, had been promoted to head of the king's council, but in under four months he had given the role up. Lancaster criticised Edward's refusal to adhere to the Ordinances and the influx of new favourites at court. Lancaster's abandonment of his post resulted in another round of infighting and failed negotiations. Relations between the two men soured further when Lancaster refused to allow armed men, travelling to meet the king, to pass through his lands. In response, Edward marched an army past Lancaster's castle at Pontefract, where he 'made his men take up arms as if to appear to besiege the town'.[5] Matters became even more personal when Alice de Lacy, Lancaster's wife, was 'abducted' from her manor in Canford, Dorset, in April 1317 by one of Edward's closest companions, John de Warenne, the earl of Surrey. It is likely that Alice, who was known to be unhappily married to the frequently unfaithful earl of Lancaster, was complicit.[6] Nonetheless, the slight on Lancaster's person and authority was felt deeply and he assumed – fairly or not – that Edward had sanctioned it.

The stalemate between cousins was finally broken in August 1318 when the king, Lancaster and their respective retinues met at Leake, a small village in Nottinghamshire, where they exchanged the kiss of peace – a physical touch, indicating amity – and signed the so-called Treaty of Leake: a settlement to resolve their differences. The Treaty of Leake concluded that there would be a standing royal council of eight bishops and four earls. Lancaster would be a member but would not be present – a banneret of his household would be his representative instead. The council, with its appointed members, would then run for a year, with two bishops, one earl and a baron serving for three months at a time.[7]

In order to appease Lancaster, the king recommitted to the Ordinances, which meant another overhaul of government. To keep him happy, royal allies were given authoritative posts: Bartholomew Badlesmere – the governor of Leeds Castle in Kent – was promoted to steward of the household. This was a prudent appointment: Badlesmere was reasonably neutral, loyal to both Edward II and Lancaster. Less diplomatic and probably pushed for by Edward was Hugh Despenser the Younger's appointment as chamberlain, a role that would place him closer to the king than anybody else. It was agreed that Edward's three remaining favourite friends, William Montagu – later the earl of Salisbury – along with Roger Damory and Hugh Audley, would have to leave court. The country needed the Treaty of Leake to be a success. The unity of the realm was under severe threat, for in April 1318, before the death of his brother, Robert Bruce had successfully besieged the crown jewel of the north, Berwick-upon-Tweed.

With Edward Bruce in Ireland, Robert Bruce continued with his offensive against England. With little sign that the war would reach a peaceful conclusion, the Church intervened: in May 1317, a truce was issued from the papacy in Avignon between 'Edward king of England and Robert Brus, self styled king of Scotland'; the declaration also warned of 'all those who infringe upon the said truce being excommunicated'.[8] Robert Bruce ignored the warning and continued to raid the north of England, eventually capturing Berwick. This blatant rebuff of the pope's order resulted in a papal bull being issued in June 1318 for a 'sentence of excommunication against Robert Brus and his adherents'. According to the Papal Register, Robert Bruce tore up his excommunication notice.[9]

In June 1318 Edward II finally decided to act and asked Lancaster to rally alongside him to retake the castle by force. Despite the urgency of the situation, action did not begin until the following year, when Edward, based in York, began the administrative efforts required to gather a large army, finalising a muster of arms at Newcastle on 22 July 1319.[10]

The king was also in communication with Gascon wine merchants, stipulating that 'wines and other victuals for the maintenance of his lieges, who are going on his service on the said expedition, may be brought in plenty'.[11] As the rules of war dictated, Edward then offered Robert Bruce a chance for peace. The Scottish king replied that 'he did not much care for the King of England's peace'.[12] And so, the battle for Berwick began. At the end of July, an army of around ten thousand soldiers, including mounted knights, light horsemen known as 'hobelars', infantry and archers, marched out of Newcastle towards Berwick with 'trumpets blowing'.[13] Ships, made ready for war, were also dispatched, cutting through the sea bound for the port of Berwick.

As the English made camp on 7 September the night was spent 'in great joy and pleasure [and] music in contempt of their Scottish enemies who were inside the town'.[14] By 8 September the siege was under way. The English launched an offensive against the Scottish barricade at Berwick but were met with fierce opposition. The Scots 'shouted at our people foully and hideously and climbed onto the walls of the town and defended it'. They destroyed an English siege engine, prompting Edward to request that 'all the siege engines at York Castle' be 'shipped with all haste and sent to him' as well as '100 ditchers from Holdernesse'.[15] These siege engines were drawn up to the walls of the town as men stabbed and hacked at each other on the battlements. The ships moored nearby 'delivered a much more vigorous assault than they previously had done' and after a week of hammering Berwick's fortifications, victory looked hopeful for the English.

However, on 14 September shocking news reached the king and the attack on Berwick was terminated. Another battle had taken place without his knowledge. The Scots, led by 'Black Douglas', James Douglas, had covertly moved south, perilously close to York, where the king had not only moved the exchequer in preparation for war in Scotland, but where Isabella, his queen, was waiting. The result was a bloodbath.

The most important strategic and administrative city in northern England, York had been a major centre of recruitment for Edward's campaign. As a result, it had been stripped of its best fighting men. The Scottish counter-attack on York was a clever move. Isabella had been left in the city for her safety and if Douglas could capture her, Edward would be forced to concede defeat.

Fortunately, an English spy had warned the archbishop of York that Douglas was on the move. Isabella was sent to Northampton and a hastily formed plan determined that clerics from York Minster would defend a section of the city wall, with the castle garrisoned by a few seasoned fighters. The archbishop, aided by the bishop of Ely, cobbled together a force consisting of the mayor of York, Nicholas Fleming, remaining able-bodied citizens, peasants, clerics and administrative clerks 'untrained in the art of war'. No knights of the realm, no archers, foot soldiers or experienced warriors were present.[16] This small but brave army left the city gates and marched out towards the River Swale at Myton, fifteen miles from York, where they believed the Scots were camped.

The Scots, aware of the archbishop's offensive, quietly waited for this local militia to walk into their trap. Douglas had created a smoke-screen to confuse and frighten the English; smog filled the air as bales of hay crackled and burned. Order was lost. The Scots formed 'to their custom in a single schiltron and then uttered together a tremendous shout to terrify the English, who straightway began to take to their heels at the sound'.[17] As the desperate English clerics, clerks and peasants fled for their lives, the Scots broke the schiltron, 'mounted their horses and pursued the English, killing both clergy and laymen'.

The mayor was cut down and many others waded into the depths of the River Swale in their flight, drowning in its murky depths. The archbishop and chancellor survived their flight. When they reached York, they barred the gates and in terror awaited a siege that never came, for the Scots turned north. So many clergymen were killed that day, the Scots named the battle the 'Chapter of Myton', a chapter being a gathering of clergy.[18]

At Berwick, the English siege was abandoned and a rumour spread that the earl of Lancaster was responsible for the Scottish foray into York. It was said that he was treasonously in collusion with the Scots and was culpable for both the attempted capture of the queen and the bloodbath at Myton: 'certainly David would not have escaped the hand of King Saul had he not had his friends among the household'. It was suggested that James Douglas not only freely passed through Lancaster's lands on his way back to Scotland but 'the earl [Lancaster] received forty thousand pounds from Robert Bruce to help him and his men secretly'.[19] Hugh Despenser the Younger relayed the rumour to John Inge, sheriff of Glamorgan. In a letter to Inge, Despenser complained that 'the Scots had entered this land of England with the prompting and assistance of the earl of Lancaster'.[20] It was a major accusation of treason, to which Lancaster took great offence, yet it is possible that Lancaster had simply been caught red-handed. As a major magnate in the north, it was notable that his castles were not attacked by Scottish raiding parties and that Lancaster had put up no resistance to their attacks elsewhere. It is also reasonable to assume that Lancaster needed allies against Edward should their dispute tumble into war. However, it is unlikely that Lancaster would sanction the abduction of the queen, which would incur the wrath of the much-feared king of France. Though there is no direct evidence to say Lancaster had betrayed Edward, a secret agreement with Bruce was not outside the realm of possibility, especially since before long we know that they did enter into one (or another one).

After years of bitter arguments and uncomfortable compromise, Edward unsurprisingly had no faith in Lancaster's loyalty to the Crown. Since the murder of Gaveston, Edward had lost all trust and faith in Lancaster, who he saw as a dead weight, hindering him from exercising kingly authority. Edward was no tyrant. As he had shown in his coronation oath, he wished to rule fairly and well, but he would not forgo his relationships in order to do so. Unlike previous Plantagenet kings the hierarchy of power was less important to Edward – if he could rule collaboratively with those he trusted he would. But this alienated nobility like Lancaster, who feared what might happen should Edward's favourites become too powerful, ruling for him rather than being his support network. The fallout between Edward and his cousin had once again run full circle, from hopeful resolution into deadlock. The king would not lift a finger in defence of his cousin. In high dudgeon, the earl of Lancaster withdrew from the siege.[21]

Berwick proved that Lancaster and the king could not, and would not, work together. Edward even forced his cousin to swear on the gospels that he was not in collusion with Robert Bruce.[22]

There was, however, a positive outcome of the siege – a temporary peace agreement with the Scots. The truce was set to last for two years and was confirmed at the parliament held at York in 1320. Even here, though, there was discord. Lancaster refused to attend the parliament, saying it was held '*in cameris*' (in secret); he was still seething from the rebuke at Berwick. Without Lancaster and his men, Edward was paralysed, unable to regain authority in Scotland and secure the northern border. Despite the appearance and expense of a grand campaign, he had achieved nothing. Robert Bruce's grip on Berwick had tightened and Edward had been outsmarted. But it was not Scotland, Bruce or the northern border that would become the greatest problem for Edward II, it was the border between England and Wales: a dispute over the Marcher lands, held by the de Clare family for generations, would bring to a bloody end the rivalry between Edward, Lancaster and the nobility caught up in the maelstrom.

7. Three Sisters

The Welsh Marches were a frontier zone held semi-independently from the Crown by the Marcher lords: the heads of the old families who had been significant players in the region since the eleventh century. The de Clare family, the Mortimers and the de Bohuns were expected to maintain the security of the border between England and Wales through building a series of fortifications and going to war if necessary. The 'king's writ' did not apply here, leaving the lords of these lands with significant power and agency to do as they liked. Of the noble families that had held these lands since the Conquest, the de Clares were the most powerful. The de Clare name carried the prestige of being directly descended from one of the first major landowners after 1066, Richard fitz Gilbert, a Norman knight who fought at Hastings.

In 1290, the de Clares grew closer to the Plantagenet dynasty when the families were united by marriage between the twelve-year-old Joan of Acre, the daughter of Edward I and Eleanor of Castile, and Gilbert de Clare, a man thirty years her senior. At just thirteen, having undergone the unimaginable trauma of conception and birth, Joan delivered her only surviving son, also called Gilbert: the sole heir to the de Clare fortune. Daughters Eleanor, Margaret and Elizabeth followed until the old earl died in 1295.

As tradition dictated, the earldom was handed from father to son. The last earl of Gloucester was Edward II's brave and reckless nephew, Gilbert de Clare, who had been killed at Bannockburn. As Gilbert's bloodied body was brought back from the battlefield, the future of the de Clare inheritance lay in the womb of the countess of Gloucester, Gilbert's young widow, Maud de Burgh.

Maud was the daughter of Richard de Burgh, the earl of Ulster, a politician who played a shrewd game in the marital market and placed his daughters Elizabeth and Maud in advantageous marriages.

Elizabeth was married to Robert Bruce – prior to his uprising against Edward – and Maud was married to the young Gilbert de Clare. It is a tragic irony that Maud's husband would be killed in battle against Elizabeth's.

Following Gilbert's death in June 1314, watchful eyes had been waiting to see whether Maud was carrying the next de Clare heir. A son stood to inherit Gilbert's vast fortune. But the condition of Maud de Burgh between 1314 to 1317 was curious. The countess claimed that she was pregnant, leaving the de Clare inheritance in stasis, with no lord to govern it. Yet Maud never gave birth.

Hugh Despenser had raised the question of Maud's condition at the parliament held at Lincoln in January 1316, arguing the implausibility of her pregnancy and pointing out that 'so much time has passed that if the said countess were pregnant, according to the common course of childbirth she could not be said to have been made pregnant by the aforementioned earl'. An investigation – possibly physical – into the situation was conducted, and its findings were clear. Maud had 'conceived of the aforesaid earl, her late husband, and that from the time of the death of the same earl she felt a living boy in her belly, at the due time and day, and she immediately informed the lord king, the lady queen, and the other magnates of the realm, and furthermore there was and is public knowledge and talk of this almost throughout the whole realm, and especially in those parts where she was then living'.[1]

Despite the biological impossibility of Maud de Clare being pregnant for nearly two years, she appears to have convinced inquisitors and the public, 'especially in those parts where she was then living', that she was with child. These are people who would have seen the countess in person. It is possible that Maud *believed* she was pregnant and it is unlikely that she would not have consulted a physician about her condition. So, what could have caused a pregnancy lasting twenty months and how did Maud appear pregnant? Maud claims to have experienced a 'quickening' – the first moment an expectant mother feels her baby move inside her, like butterflies. This was traditionally treated as a major moment in the gestation period. It is possible that Maud de Clare suffered a rare but real condition, pseudocyesis – known as 'phantom pregnancy'.[2] This psychological disorder mimics multiple symptoms of pregnancy including morning sickness, abdominal bloating and even false contractions.

The term was coined by Hippocrates in 300 BC, yet there are then no documented cases of the condition until the sixteenth century. It is possible that Maud de Burgh was demonstrating symptoms of another illness, ovarian or stomach cancer perhaps, which could also have caused her menstrual cycle to stop and abdominal swelling, but Maud was young to have developed either. What Maud certainly did endure, however, was the immense pressure of providing an heir to secure not only the Gloucester inheritance but her security. Perhaps the weight of expectation, hope, blind optimism and confusion was enough to induce the symptoms of pseudocyesis in Maud de Burgh.

What Maud endured after Gilbert de Clare's death would have been traumatic and stigmatising for a vulnerable widow. There was still no baby a year later – Maud was clearly not with child – and Hugh Despenser was eager to fill the power vacuum that Gilbert de Clare had left.

The de Clare lands were split between Gilbert de Clare's three sisters, the king's nieces, Eleanor, Margaret and Elizabeth. These women were now the wealthiest and most appealing heiresses in the kingdom. At the pleasure, or insistence, of Edward II, two of the sisters were married off to Edward's friends; the eldest, Eleanor, was already married to his favourite, Hugh Despenser the Younger.

Women such as the de Clare sisters were useful assets to the king. They could strengthen ailing alliances, or forge new ones. They could repair old feuds or increase the power, prestige and wealth of noble families by uniting with them. Royal women were important, but they had little choice over their future husband. By 1317 Margaret – the widow of Piers Gaveston – was married to Hugh Audley; and Elizabeth to Roger Damory.

Of all three sisters, Elizabeth had the most turbulent marital history. She had three husbands before she reached twenty-one. Her first was John de Burgh, the son of the earl of Ulster, and brother to Maud de Clare. Elizabeth had a son with John, before her husband was killed in a minor skirmish in 1313, the year before her brother lost his life at Bannockburn. Elizabeth stayed in Ireland, where she met and allegedly became betrothed to Theobald de Verdun. When she returned to England Theobald was accused of 'abducting' Elizabeth from Bristol Castle and marrying her.[3] The legal issue was not that Elizabeth had not consented, but that Theobald had not asked the king's permission. His consent was essential and not requesting it verged on treason. Theobald, probably in the knowledge that marriage to the king's niece would be denied, took the risk anyway. Theobald died in 1316, during the tumult over the legitimacy of the marriage, but Elizabeth was pregnant. As soon as the baby was born, she was considered officially available for remarriage.

Edward did not wait. On 21 March 1317, Elizabeth de Clare gave birth to a baby girl who she named Isabel. Within six weeks of giving birth, the king had pushed Elizabeth to marry Roger Damory. As she went into her third marriage bed, Elizabeth was only six weeks postpartum. As was the norm, her baby was entrusted to the care of a wet nurse and housed separately.

Elizabeth's sister Margaret also had a turbulent marital history. Previously married to Piers Gaveston, Margaret gave birth to a daughter, Joan, only five months before his murder on Blacklow Hill. A fresh marriage to a new favourite of her uncle likely came with its own anxieties. Eleanor de Clare's marriage to Hugh Despenser was her first, though it was not without its own trauma. In 1320 a baby boy, one of many children she carried and gave birth to, passed away; he was possibly stillborn. One of the cruel realities of childbirth in the fourteenth century was the high rate of infant mortality: up to half of newborn babies never survived infancy.[4] The loss was deeply mourned. Edward sent the grieving couple a piece of gold cloth and silk to drape over the tiny coffin.[5]

This was not an unprecedented act of kindness. Though Hugh Despenser was clearly the object of Edward's fraternal affections, of all his nieces Eleanor was his favourite. This prompted speculation that their relationship had become sexual. He paid her expenses, and gave her and her husband land in Scotland and a brooch laden with six emeralds.[6] He bought sugar so he could have sweets made for her, and gifted her a cage filled with goldfinches.[7] Isabella spent time with Eleanor, too, taking Eleanor with her 'to various places on her travels throughout parts of England, sometimes with [three] carts sometimes with two'. Isabella also provided horses for Eleanor when Hugh Despenser took hers away.[8] None of the other noble women in his family or household, with the exception of Queen Isabella and the dowager queen, Margaret of France, received such explicit attention.[9] He even helped Eleanor with medical treatment. As shown in a wardrobe account – a record of purchases, gifts or loans from the king for himself or his household – of around 1319, Edward ordered medicine for himself and for Eleanor to cure an unknown illness.[10]

The direct accusation of a sexual affair has its roots in a chronicle account from Hainault. In it the author stipulates that in December 1325 Eleanor delivered a baby (one of nine she gave birth to over the course of her marriage) at the palace of Sheen, for which the king offered prayers of thanks for its safe delivery.[11] The insinuation, though indirect, is that Eleanor de Clare's baby was fathered not by her husband, but by the king. Though the relationship between Eleanor and Edward could be considered conspicuously close, there is no evidence to prove it went beyond friendship.

Some writers – particularly in the sixteenth and seventeenth centuries – have suggested an alternative to the Eleanor–Edward affair; namely, that the real sexual relationship was between Hugh Despenser and Edward. But, again, there is nothing to prove this. The most likely scenario was that Edward, Despenser and Eleanor spent time in each other's company as confidants and friends. The couple gave the king what he most desired – love and approval. With a father as formidable as Edward I, it is plausible that Edward II, so often called a weak king, was actually a rather sensitive one. What is certain is that, by 1320, Hugh Despenser and his wife were benefiting disproportionately from the king's affections. Edward exercised no restraint or authority over his friend.

By the time Maud de Burgh died in 1320, she was almost in poverty. Her land and wealth had been clawed away by Hugh Despenser the Younger.[12] This granted him further control over the ancestral lands of the earldom of Gloucester, for he was allocated Tewkesbury in Gloucestershire and land and property elsewhere in

England. Despenser now held more power over the Welsh Marches than any other baron. He had acquired the lordship of Glamorgan, including Cardiff and the impressive castle at Caerphilly. But still he wanted more.

In 1320 the shining jewel of the Welsh Marches was the lordship of Gower and its administrative centre, Swansea. Though not on the England–Wales border, this large and fertile portion of land, with its own coastline, was part of the old Norman lordship of Gower. As well as coveting the title 'earl of Gloucester', once held by his brother-in-law, Despenser 'devoted all his energy and thoughts to extending his lordship over the neighbouring lands'.[13] Fortunately for Despenser, Gower was for sale. The current lord of Gower was the elderly but perfidious William de Braose. As most land and title was hereditary his son-in-law, John Mowbray, was the natural and expectant successor. With Despenser now a possible buyer, William de Braose considered Gower effectively up for auction. Other Marcher lords, including Roger Mortimer of Wigmore and Roger Mortimer of Chirk, as well as Humphrey de Bohun, the earl of Hereford, joined the race.

As a powerful noble with influence over the king, Despenser believed Gower would be his. What he had not accounted for was the interests of the old families across the Marches, who feared that if Despenser became too powerful in the region, their own land would be under threat; eventually John Mowbray was appointed lord of Gower, probably with the support of the rest of the Marcher lords.

Despenser took his case to Edward, incensed that he had been deceived by John Mowbray and those who likely supported him. Despenser's greed was thinly veiled and despite his affection for his friend, Edward was still bound by the law. With Lancaster and his Ordinances looming, he had to be careful not to overstep kingly authority and act as a tyrant. Edward may have been ill-advised, easily led and weak, but he was also clever. The pair burrowed away and hatched a plan. Edward concluded that he could only intervene on the grounds that William de Braose had sold important territory without first obtaining a royal licence. By luring William de Braose into an administrative and legal spider's web, claiming the necessity for a royal licence to legitimise the sale, Edward saw to it that Gower was taken into royal hands.

Muffled groans and the sighs of bored men were audible during the October parliament of 1320. Over almost the entire month that parliament was in session more than one hundred and forty petitions were heard. The king, who was robed and seated in majesty, was acting with remarkable focus and care. According to an eyewitness, Edward 'showed prudence in answering the petitions of the poor, and clemency as much as severity in judicial matters, to the amazement of many who were there'.[14] It was perhaps the absence of the earl of Lancaster that caused Edward to act with more grace and duty than usual but this attentiveness towards the dull and laborious task of hearing petitions was more likely because Edward was being conspicuously diligent in his royal duty as he prepared to announce the news that he knew would be inflammatory. At the end of parliament, the king trepidatiously declared that the lordship of Gower, which had been seized by the Crown due to a lawless transaction of sale, would be given directly to Hugh Despenser the Younger.[15] This caused outrage. The Welsh Marcher lords saw Despenser's rise as a threat to their long-standing authority over the region. The earl of Lancaster saw this as another demonstration of favouritism and a rebuff of the Ordinances. Both parties were in opposition to Edward and Hugh Despenser: the announcement not only enraged the lords at Westminster but alienated all those who had landed interests on the Welsh border.

Threatening and deceptive, Despenser could also be violent. At a previous incident during a parliament at Lincoln, he had attacked a knight named Sir John Ros inside the cathedral, 'striking him with his fist until he drew blood'.[16] Vilified as a 'monster' by one account, another calls him 'a most avaricious man . . . [who] . . . contrived by different means and tricks that he alone should possess the lands and revenues [of the earldom of Gloucester]'.[17] He was also said to be 'full of evil and wrongdoing and . . . greedy and covetous whilst in office'.[18] These descriptions are almost caricatures, but in a letter to John Inge, the sheriff of Glamorgan, Despenser evidences their truth. He commands Inge to be vigilant about plots against him so that 'we may be rich and may attain our ends'.[19] Despenser's use of 'we' is telling – he is referring only to himself, using the formal language of an individual from a high social rank above his own, most notably that of a royal.

As the king's favourite, Hugh Despenser was a different beast to Piers Gaveston. He was calculating where Gaveston was pompous but harmless; Despenser was fuelled by greed where Gaveston was foolhardy, believing that his association with the king kept him safe. However, there is a striking similarity between Edward's two favourites' unbending belief that they could do whatever they wished. In the months after the outrage of the October parliament Despenser pushed Margaret de Clare and Hugh Audley to surrender land in exchange for much less valuable property in the south-east of England. A forfeiture of this nature would have been financially crippling for Margaret and Audley, forcing them to rely on funds and support from friends and family. Margaret had been Gaveston's wife (and was Edward's niece) and Audley one of Edward's coterie, but the king now turned his back on them. He appeared to support Hugh Despenser the Younger's relentless land-grabbing. Before 1320 was over, Despenser had also taken the castle and town of Dryslwyn and Cantrefmawr – an important stronghold for the previous princes of Wales – and he had secured control of Lundy Island, a small but important islet in the Bristol Channel. As the darkness of midwinter set in, Edward even paid for candle wax to light Despenser's new properties.[20] No wonder the Welsh Marcher barons felt threatened. Despenser had more control than all of them put together. Over the course of May 1321, they launched an attack on Hugh Despenser, destroying and plundering his existing lands across the Welsh Marches. Determined to hold the king accountable for his actions, rebel Marcher lords entered London on 1 August threatening to both burn the city to the ground and depose Edward if he did not send the Despensers into permanent exile. The author of the *Vita* paints a poignant scene of the anxiety of those caught up in the maelstrom, with the earl of Pembroke pleading with the king, 'take heed of the danger that threatens; neither brother nor sister should be dearer to thee than thyself. Do not therefore for any living soul lose thy kingdom.'[21] It was not at the earl's insistence that Edward backed down, but Queen Isabella's. Heavily pregnant with Joan, her youngest child, Isabella came before the king in appeal. On her knees she begged her determined husband to save the realm and exile the Despensers. Before Edward would accept her plea, he agreed to instead allow the Marcher lords to voice their complaints in person.

At the summer parliament in 1321 Roger Mortimer and his uncle, alongside Humphrey de Bohun, the earl of Hereford, John Mowbray and Edward's two former favourites, Roger Damory and Hugh Audley, along with other landowners on the Welsh Marches made their feelings clear.

Insults were hurled at Hugh Despenser and his father. They had 'dishonoured the king'! They were responsible for the 'destruction of the realm' as well as 'plotting to distance the affection of our lord the king from the peers of the land', and, crucially, conceiving a plan 'to have sole government of the realm between the two of them'.[22] Shouts of 'scheming', 'plotting', 'wickedness' and 'deceit' rang out across Westminster Hall. In a chilling echo of the events preceding Gaveston's fall, it was demanded that both Despenser the Elder and Younger must be: 'disinherited forever, as disinheritors of the crown, and enemies of the king and his people . . . [also that they should be] exiled forever from the realm of England, without returning at any time, unless with the assent of our lord the king, and the assent of the prelates, earls and barons'. In other words, the king would never be permitted to allow his favourites to return.

In accordance with the Ordinances and to keep the peace – and his crown – Edward was forced once more to accept the exile of his favourites. Hugh Despenser the Elder left for France, and Hugh Despenser the Younger went to sea as a sailor of the Cinque Ports, where 'he became a sea monster, lying in wait for merchants'.[23] Yet Edward was frustrated and bitter. In both rage and revenge, he determined that now was his moment to fight back against the nobles who bound him. He would do so by striking their weakest link with remarkable intelligence and guile.

8.   The Battle of the Badlesmeres

Bartholomew Badlesmere was a trusted man. A royal diplomat in negotiations with the Scots, a soldier and custodian of Leeds Castle, Badlesmere was an active member of the royal household who benefited from the king's high opinion of him. After years of service, Edward II had given Badlesmere the idyllic and newly fortified Leeds Castle. A picturesque moated fortification surrounded by fine hunting grounds, with good connections to both London and Dover, Leeds Castle had once been a favourite property of Edward's mother, Eleanor of Castile. This was a munificent gift to the king's steward, who, nonetheless, existed on the periphery of Edward's elite circle of courtiers. From the sidelines, loyal and trusted Badlesmere had watched Edward shower his favourites with lavish gifts. Like Despenser, Audley and Damory, Bartholomew Badlesmere had the good fortune of marrying a distant member of the impressive de Clare family: his wife was a cousin of the three de Clare sisters.

Yet Badlesmere was disgruntled with his lot. He watched as Hugh Despenser the Younger climbed his way into the highest echelons of court. Leeds Castle was no longer enough for Badlesmere. Edward believed he could rely on Badlesmere and in May had dispatched him on a mission north to Sherburn in Yorkshire. There, Thomas of Lancaster had hosted an illegal gathering with the Marcher lords. Badlesmere's job was to persuade the northern lords – including Lancaster – not to join the Marchers in their treasonous quest. Yet Edward failed to recognise that Badlesmere himself was disgruntled, jealous and seeking validation. After Badlesmere reached Sherburn, something, or someone, persuaded him to switch sides against the king and Hugh Despenser. For a man who had carefully and patiently earned his favour, this was an imprudent decision. He and his family would face the consequences.

Shocked that his seemingly loyal steward had defected, Edward decided to lay a trap, to be sprung that autumn. This was intended to punish Badlesmere for his disloyalty, and catch the barons who had sided with Lancaster; it would result in the first major military offensive against the rebel barons. For it to be a success, Edward needed his queen, Isabella.

One of the busiest travel routes in medieval England was the road from London to Canterbury, the site of the shrine of Saint Thomas Becket. In early October 1321, Queen Isabella decided to make the journey to Canterbury; curiously, she decided to go via Leeds Castle – something of a detour. It is possible that Isabella needed somewhere to rest or perhaps she, or a member of her retinue, had fallen sick. Most likely, however, is that Isabella went to Leeds Castle either to interrogate Lady Badlesmere, who was there without her husband, who was holed up in Oxfordshire with the Marcher barons, or to provoke her. In the meantime, Bartholomew Badlesmere had become aware that Edward had discovered he was a turncoat.[1] He wrote to his wife, Lady Margaret Badlesmere, advising her to secure the castle against attack.

Accompanied by a military escort, Isabella rode towards the castle having sent word that her party would arrive shortly. She was expecting hospitality. Lady Badlesmere, however, had been told not to admit anybody and to prepare for a siege. True to the request of her husband, Lady Badlesmere responded to Isabella with a flat refusal of entry. In response, the queen told her men to attempt to enter the castle by force. Instead of submitting, Lady Badlesmere ordered her men to defend the castle with arrows. By this point, Isabella's men were at the walls, with Isabella dispatching orders from a safe distance. When six of her men were killed, she knew her mission was complete.[2] Having treasonously rejected the queen and killed her men, Lady Badlesmere and her husband were confirmed as traitors.

From the Tower of London, Edward dispatched an order, 'directed to all the men of Kent'. He commanded that they meet at Leeds Castle to 'lay siege to the castle . . . which is held against queen Isabella by men of the household of Bartholomew de Badelesmere [*sic*] and others by his command; and they are to come with horses and arms and the *posse* of the county at the king's wages'.[3] The message also went out to multiple counties across the south of England and around Kent: Essex, Hampshire, Sussex and Surrey. Importantly, this summons included the barons Badlesmere had sided with. In one offensive, Edward could reassert his authority and punish his steward. The situation was ridiculous: it did not need so many men to lay siege to a single castle defended by only a small household guard. Remarkably, however, Lady Badlesmere was resolved to put up as fierce an opposition as possible.

The siege of Leeds Castle became more of a society event than a military exercise. All of the major southern lords and those loyal to the king attended. Edward sent for wine and six of his hunting dogs while he was in Kent, presumably to have some sport for the duration of the siege.[4] He also invited his son, the nine-year-old future Edward III, to witness his father's demonstration of power – it would be an easy win.

The Marcher barons were technically allied to Bartholomew Badlesmere and their initial instinct was to aid Lady Badlesmere against the king. The earl of Hereford and the Mortimers marched towards Kent but were intercepted at Kingston-upon-Thames and persuaded against counter-attacking by the archbishop of Canterbury and the earl of Pembroke, who were desperate to keep the peace and find an appropriate resolution to the situation. Curiously, Thomas of Lancaster, the figurehead of resistance against Edward, advised the barons to leave Badlesmere to his fate.[5] Lancaster could see what Edward had planned. The barons would either fight under the royal banner or against it, while unprepared and unequipped to face a royal army. They made a harsh but prudent decision: Leeds Castle was not the hill to die on.

Without the help of the barons, Leeds Castle soon fell to the king. Lady Badlesmere and her children were spared, but incarcerated first at Dover Castle and then at the Tower of London. The men who defended her were not so fortunate. Contrary to normal chivalric practice after surrendering a castle, Edward II had the men hanged, drawn and quartered. Thirteen soldiers were 'hanged for the felony' that day, their land and property taken by the king.[6] Leeds Castle was also seized and Bartholomew Badlesmere declared a traitor. Edward intended all of this to serve as a terrifying example to anyone else inclined to rebel. Lancaster, Badlesmere and the barons went conspicuously quiet, but not for long. To celebrate his victory, Edward re-called Hugh Despenser and his father, much as he had with Piers Gaveston shortly before his murder. History was set to repeat itself – but this time Edward would not go down without a fight, and it was clearly one he thought he could win.

Around this time, the archbishop of Canterbury captured the tension felt across the realm in a message delivered at Saint Paul's Cathedral. Wracked with concern, he announced that the country was 'in danger of shipwreck through civil war'.[7] Hugh Despenser had been granted safe conduct home, clutching letters of protection claiming 'the judgement of exile and disinheritance lately passed upon him by certain magnates contains errors and should be annulled'. The same protection and annulment were extended to his father.[8] While Edward had won the battle against the Badlesmeres, he knew he still had to win the war against Lancaster and the men who were threatening to depose him. Edward was steadfast in his belief that the exile of the Despensers was unjust and he would march to war if he had to. He left London with his remaining loyal nobles, including the earl of Pembroke and the earls of Surrey and Arundel, and rode to Cirencester, where he would spend an anxious Christmas as his army readied themselves to do battle.

With the Despensers back at Edward's side, by January 1322 a rebellion was in motion. The earl of Hereford, Hugh Audley, Roger Damory, John Mowbray, Roger Mortimer and Bartholomew Badlesmere, among others, had stepped over the line from opposition into outright rebellion, determined to carry out their threat of reform and bring Despenser to justice. Badlesmere, in particular, had nowhere to turn and no opportunity to change his mind. Thanks to his defection, which Edward took particularly personally, he was a man with a price on his head whose family were already held captive.

Roger Damory – the husband of Elizabeth de Clare and a former favourite of Edward II – took Worcester by force. Two royal castles were seized, in Gloucester and Bridgnorth. Other rebel barons moved along the River Severn, burning bridges so that Edward and his army could not cross. The earl of Lancaster watched from a distance, refusing to commit himself. Some of the Marcher barons also remained cautious, namely Roger Mortimer of Wigmore. A descendant of one of the original baronial Marcher families, Roger Mortimer, tall and good-looking, was an esteemed military leader, having served the king against Edward Bruce in Ireland. He was also one of the most powerful men on the Welsh Marches and, until now, had always been loyal to Edward II. Like others, Mortimer blamed Hugh Despenser, not Edward, for the dispute so when an olive branch was offered to Mortimer of Wigmore he prudently accepted it.

On a bitingly cold January day, Mortimer along with his uncle, Roger Mortimer of Chirk, who had also loyally served the king as justice of Wales, rode to Shrewsbury. There they met with the king's representatives, the earls of Pembroke, Richmond, Surrey and Arundel. It is unknown exactly what they offered the Mortimers, but it was probably clemency, for at Shrewsbury both Roger Mortimer of Wigmore and his uncle surrendered to Edward II. Perhaps the Mortimers were promised a pardon; if they were, it was an offer that was too good to be true. Demonstrating a new and vindictive side to his character, Edward had both men imprisoned in the Tower of London. The Mortimers were left waiting for news in their cold cells. Mortimer of Wigmore's sons were also imprisoned with those of the earl of Hereford and, within months, his wife and daughters had been split up and sent to monastic houses far from their home. Edward appeared increasingly contrary and unpredictable. Nobody knew what he intended to do with his captives. But their imprisonment ended the possibility that any other rebel baron would accept an offer of peace. Humphrey de Bohun, the earl of Hereford, Badlesmere, Roger Damory and Hugh Audley – all Marcher barons with a grudge against Hugh Despenser – remained defiant. In need of a powerful ally, they fled north to join the earl of Lancaster.

Lancaster had been biding his time, even as he actively prepared for war, securing his main base at Pontefract in the event of a siege. The castle was crenellated, rendering it possible to defend against attackers by shooting arrows and hurling rocks and oil from the partitions along the wall. Lancaster would have been occupied with stocking the armoury with arrows, bows, swords and axes, and ensuring there was enough food and clean water inside the castle. Later petitions to the Crown suggest that Lancaster plundered from the local people in order to do so. A woman by the name of Constance Halliday complained that the earl stripped her of everything, leaving her and her fifteen children starving.[9] These were, of course, petitions directed to a very particular audience. Those complaining of Lancaster's actions were people in need of the king's favour; articulating a grievance against Lancaster meant they were more likely to get it. In times of civil war, neutrality was not an option, even for those most distant from elite politics. Everybody had to find a way to survive.

For Lancaster, survival meant forging the most dangerous and treacherous alliance possible, in case he was forced to fight. Months earlier, he had entered into secret negotiations with Robert Bruce, dispatching letters under the pseudonym King Arthur. Lancaster said he would put up no resistance should the Scots launch a raid into northern England. The condition was that they would come to his aid against Edward. Lancaster was true to his word. In January 1322 – just as the truce signed after the siege of Berwick-upon-Tweed ended – the Scots moved across the border, travelling as far as Richmond in North Yorkshire without facing any resistance.

Collusion with the Scots proved both futile and damning.[10] In March the rebel army marched to Burton-on-Trent in Staffordshire, where they attempted a blockade by burning the bridge, but were overpowered by the king's forces and fled. Lancaster, who had also moved south to aid the resistance on the River Trent, panicked and returned to Pontefract with the rest of the fleeing rebels, leaving Roger Damory mortally wounded from a skirmish with the king's men. Lancaster and his allies had taken up arms; crucially, and even worse, they had unfurled their banners which indicated 'levying war against the king'.[11] This was an act of treason and the beginning of the end.

Fear and bewilderment spread like a virus through the Marcher lords loyal to Lancaster. Some wanted to throw themselves at the mercy of the king, whereas others floated the idea of fleeing to

Northumberland. The expansive landscape of the moors was a tempting prospect for the wayward lords, though they never made it that far.

The Scots were true to their word. They remained in the far north of England as Lancaster brought the rest of his army to meet them. The plan was, presumably, that together they would attack the king's army in the same manner as Bannockburn. Yet Lancaster had not accounted for the English presence across the border in Scotland.

A weatherbeaten and battle-hardened contingent of around four thousand men led by Andrew Harclay were travelling south, their horses stumbling over the uneven moorland around Ripon in North Yorkshire. Harclay was hawk-eyed in his surveillance of the area. He knew that, like his own army, the rebels would need to get across the bridge at Boroughbridge – the crossing over the River Ure – if they were to reach Northumberland. Though the bridge was an essential crossing, it was predominantly a single-file footbridge that could, at most, withstand the weight of a few men and horses. All Harclay had to do was wait.

It is impossible to know whether Lancaster knew his mission was doomed, but he put up a fight nonetheless. In what became known as the Battle of Boroughbridge, on 16 March 1322, Lancaster and Hereford decided to split into two divisions – Hereford would lead one column over the footbridge and Lancaster would take men into the ford over the River Ure. Presumably they intended for Hereford to attack Harclay in a frontal offensive while Lancaster and his men crossed the river on horseback and attacked from behind.

As Hereford led his men across the bridge into battle for full-frontal infantry attack, Harclay instructed his soldiers to cut him off, while his longbow men rained arrows onto those braving the rapid water below. One account describes Hereford's unfortunate death by spear – a soldier had stationed himself below the bridge and with great timing thrust his weapon upward, between Hereford's legs, impaling him and killing the earl in the most painful and igno-minious way imaginable. Gruesome but farcical, it is highly unlikely that this is how Hereford actually died. Another, more accurate account suggests that Hereford was mortally injured elsewhere on his body – though possibly by the same spearman – and that he died in slow agony.[12]

The earl of Lancaster managed to stay alive a little longer than his ally. After his men were pushed back by the barrage of arrows, he fled on foot, only to be captured by Harclay and taken to York Castle. After a week of incarceration in York, Lancaster was moved to his own castle at Pontefract. The next day, Lancaster was brought before the king and Despenser. Both were smug to see the once formidable Lancaster reduced to the role of a humiliated prisoner. Edward had been seeking retribution against Lancaster for a decade following the murder of Gaveston. He likely passed the death sentence against his cousin with satisfaction.

Lancaster was tried and condemned to death. Initially, the sentence was a traitor's death of being hanged, drawn and quartered. But, ultimately, Edward conceded to an appeal from Queen Isabella that Lancaster should be permitted a noble death, by beheading – hardly merciful but considered the most honourable end for a treacherous earl.[13] Much like the execution of Piers Gaveston, the sentence was carried out immediately. In an echo of Blacklow Hill, the earl of Lancaster was taken outside and, 'mounting some worthless beast of burden, was led to the Capitol', a small hill outside Pontefract Castle. Here Lancaster was made to kneel, before being killed with no more than three blows of the sword.[14] A contemporary wall painting in South Newington parish church in Oxfordshire depicts the scene of the earl's death. Lancaster kneels in prayer as the executioner stands behind him poised to strike the final blow. Lancaster's neck is half-severed, with two bloody gashes, alluding to a contemporaneous description of the moment: he 'stretched his head as if in prayer, and the executioner cut off his head with two or three strikes.'[15] From the gore of Lancaster's bloody death to the red cloak he is wearing, this scene is infused with imagery associated with the red rose – the emblem of the House of Lancaster since the thirteenth century.[16] For the first time in Plantagenet history, the greatest lord of the realm, one with royal blood pulsing through his veins, had been executed as a traitor. Lancaster's brutal death preceded a witch hunt, in which the rebels and their families were investigated and punished. The most troubling accounts that haunt the record are the voices of women who suffered appallingly as a consequence of the actions of the rebels, mostly noble women who were left without defence as their husbands were either arrested or killed by the king's men. The most stark account of the fear and punishment inflicted on noble women is from Edward's niece and Roger Damory's widow, Elizabeth de Clare.

Within days of the defeat at Boroughbridge, Elizabeth was arrested and taken with her children to Barking Abbey, a prison in all but name.[17] During her imprisonment she was coerced by Hugh Despenser and her uncle, the king, into signing away the most valuable portion of her inheritance, including her beloved Usk, and Caerleon Castle which she was forced to exchange for the much less personal Gower. The victory at Boroughbridge had not only secured Edward II's kingship – for a time – but allowed Hugh Despenser to take control of the entire Gloucester inheritance by snatching land belonging to Elizabeth and Margaret de Clare.

In a direct order from her uncle, Elizabeth was told that she could not marry again without his permission and was denied any communication with the friends and advisers whose lives depended on her co-operation – when Elizabeth had hesitated in signing her property away, some of her advisers were imprisoned, simply for her delay.[18] Later, in 1326, she compiled a secret document that offers some insight into her experiences during the aftermath of Boroughbridge. She called it a 'protest' against the actions of the Despensers, but more notably in the text itself, the king and the abuse of royal power. In two pages hidden within the *Liber Niger de Wigmore*, a chartulary of the Mortimer estates, Elizabeth delivers a haunting account in which she repeatedly uses the word 'gree' meaning 'will'.[19] Themes of consent, choice and free will course through the statement of Elizabeth de Clare but so does fury and the strong belief that her choice mattered.[20] She writes, *'mon corps et de mes terres'* (my body and my lands) – the stripping and theft of Elizabeth's land, to her, was as physical as her forcible imprisonment. Elizabeth's body as well as her land were no longer her own.

Petitions from other widows of Boroughbridge, such as Alina de Mowbray, and Lancaster's estranged wife, Alice de Lacy, tell a similar story of the legal process being manipulated to strip women across the Welsh Marches of their rightful inheritance, land and property.[21] Alice was forced to 'enter a recognisance' of around twenty thousand pounds, forfeiting her estates. If she failed to comply, Despenser threatened to have her burned alive.[22] Margaret de Clare, the wife of Hugh Audley, was sent to Sempringham Priory in Lincolnshire, where she was forced to live with the nuns for the rest of Edward II's reign.[23]

At his coronation Edward II had sworn to protect exactly this sort of vulnerable woman; by allowing Despenser to cynically enrich himself at their expense, he had comprehensively failed them.

The future for the de Clare sisters was either bleak or uncertain. Elizabeth had lost her third husband in the heat of battle, while Margaret's was taken prisoner at Boroughbridge. Eleanor was the only sister who fared well, thanks to the king and Despenser's victory – for now. Where Eleanor became wealthy and powerful alongside her husband, Margaret and Elizabeth were forced to fight a futile battle for their rightful inheritances. Previously treated with generosity and respect by their uncle the king, as wives of traitors they were now faced with crippling punishment.

Bartholomew Badlesmere was dragged through Canterbury on a pallet before being strung up for hanging. His head was struck from his body and displayed for all to see. England was littered with the heads of traitors and its jails filled with their families. Lady Badlesmere and her children were among many whose cries echoed through dark corridors and cells. Ruination and the threat of the executioner's axe became ever-present spectres. The execution of Lancaster, the king's own cousin, marked a startling new age in royal policy, Plantagenet kingship and Edward's character. Status or royal bloodline was no longer armour the nobility could wear. Anybody could find themselves accused of treason, or condemned as an enemy; nobody was safe. The once generous and warm-spirited king was now suspicious and uncharacteristically severe, hawkishly scouring for signs of deceit or incipient rebellion. Lancaster's insistence that he should control Edward's every decision, as well as who he spent his time with, pushed Edward towards the manipulative Despensers, a far greater threat to the structure of royal power than any of Edward's other companions. The Ordinances achieved the opposite of what they had been created to do. Had Lancaster been willing to negotiate with Edward a decade earlier it is unlikely he would have met such an ugly fate, nor would the Despensers have had the chance to make their precipitous ascent. In the end, Lancaster and the rebel lords underestimated Edward II, a king who eventually proved he was able to think on his feet, act decisively and, when it mattered, prove to the nobility that the king was the greatest power in the realm, able to orchestrate the rise, and fall, of whoever he wished. Those who thought themselves untouchable would inevitably find that fate had other, surprising, plans.

Fortune's Wheel

'What else do tragedies make such woeful outcry over save
the overthrow of kingdoms by the indiscriminate strokes of
Fortune? Didst thou not learn in thy childhood how there stand
at the threshold of Zeus "two jars", "the one full of blessings,
the other of calamities"?'

Boethius, Song I, Book II, 'Fortune's Malice',
On the Consolation of Philosophy.

9. 'Wilful Pleasure of Woman'

Edward II had come out on top. Lancaster was dead, the Ordinances were no longer a brake on his authority and he was able to fill his court and council with men of his own choosing. And yet while Edward had certainly been underestimated by his enemies, neither he nor Hugh Despenser the Younger registered the capability and discomfort of those in their close circle. They failed to recognise the potential of soft power, namely the queen.

As expected of queens in medieval England, Isabella had been both adviser and appellant to the king. She was present at council meetings, and accompanied the king on various expeditions across the realm, resulting in her near capture by the Scots at York in 1319. She interceded on behalf of members of the nobility, seeking aid from the king, and helped set the trap for Lady Badlesmere at the siege of Leeds Castle. She was an architect of Edward's reassertion of power. She had also already carried and delivered four children, including the king's heir presumptive, Edward, as well as John of Eltham, Eleanor and Joan. At only twenty-seven, Queen Isabella had played her part with aplomb.

The execution of Lancaster and the extreme and brutal punishment his followers suffered afterwards revealed a shocking new incarnation of Edward. Isabella, like others, knew that Edward's favourite friend was driving this concerning behaviour. From 1322, however, Isabella found her counsel was no longer needed. The rotting, bird-pecked heads of rebels that leered over London Bridge, drawing anxious glances from passers-by, appeared a symbol of the increasingly autocratic direction that Edward, with Hugh Despenser as his loyal aide, was taking. The rebellion that escalated into a short-lived war appears to have scratched away at Edward's already fragile sense of security and safety. Increasingly suspicious and fearful, Edward was consumed with anxiety and showed no restraint in going after

anyone who acted against his orders. Isabella witnessed the decline in
Edward's reason and humanity as the rule of law gave way to malevo-
lence. One of the first of Edward's loyal men to find themselves in the
firing line was Andrew Harclay.

Charged with the defence of the north, Harclay had doggedly
fought against the constant waves of Scottish invasion by Robert
Bruce, whose power in Scotland continued to grow. Harclay eventually made the prudent decision that the security of the north could
only be achieved through negotiation. Despite his efforts, the frontier had become a wasteland, with settlers forced to flee or exist on
what little sustenance was left after a Scottish raid. Harclay acted
in desperation. At Lochmaben in early January 1323, he agreed to
acknowledge Robert Bruce as king of Scotland. When Edward
found out about this, he had him arrested and tried without a hearing. Harclay was charged with treason and, like those he had defeated
at Boroughbridge, was hanged, drawn and quartered. His head was
set on London Bridge, his body on the walls of Carlisle, Newcastle,
Bristol and Shrewsbury.

Harclay's execution was intended as a warning to those who sought
to override the king's authority, but it was also a deliberate performance of power. Threats and plots against the king were circulating
and Edward became so fearful that his life was in jeopardy he took
to wearing a mail vest beneath his clothes.[1] One such plot involved
a necromancer, an academic named Master John of Nottingham.
He was allegedly employed to kill the king, Hugh Despenser the
Younger and Despenser the Elder by forging wax effigies and stabbing them in the heart. Accusations of necromancy and the use of
dark magic against the elite were not common, but these forces were
deeply feared. People living in the fourteenth century saw necro-
mancers as godless, in commune with the devil, yet also wielding the
power of silent killers. The paranoid Hugh Despenser the Younger
panicked and appealed to Pope John XXII, telling him he was the
victim of 'magical and secret dealings'. The pope did not seem concerned by Despenser's plight and responded from Avignon with the
advice that he should 'turn to God with his whole heart, and make a
good confession'.[2]

More frightening even than black magic was the spectre of Roger Mortimer, one of the Marcher lords who had by some miraculous intervention escaped his imprisonment in the Tower of London. Having fled to France, he was welcomed with open arms by the freshly crowned King Charles IV, Queen Isabella's younger brother. Roger Mortimer's entrance into the French court was a clear rebuff to Edward, who was hunting Mortimer's head. It was not, however, without precedent. By August 1324 the relationship between England and France, so carefully plastered over by the marriage of Edward II and Isabella, was once again beginning to crack.

It was commonplace for all lords who held land in France to pay homage (fealty) to their new king on his accession, as well as at intervals afterwards. Edward II was king in England, prince of Wales and lord of Ireland and (in his mind) Scotland but in France the land he held in Aquitaine was in fief to the French Crown – feudal law recognised that Edward II was subject to the king of France. This meant Edward had to perform a demonstration of homage to the French king, a declaration of his gratitude and subservience. This was a duty that no English king ever relished.

Nevertheless, Edward had always managed to swallow his pride, until now, when he failed to present himself in France in July 1324. Something prevented him from leaving England, most likely his own crippling paranoia, stoked by the admonitions of Hugh Despenser.

Eager to establish his authority, Charles was furious. By August 1324, he had set in motion the confiscation of the Duchy of Aquitaine, which had belonged to English kings in fief to the French Crown since the marriage between Eleanor of Aquitaine and Henry II in the twelfth century. This would remove English laws and customs from France for good.

The vainglorious attitude of Charles IV bolstered his image at court, but he failed to anticipate that this could provoke a drastic response from Edward and compromise his sister's safety in England. Edward's previous behaviour set a clear precedent for how he would respond, and Isabella – like the widows of Boroughbridge – would pay the price.

Over the course of two weeks, Edward II stripped Queen Isabella of her land, including the Duchy of Cornwall, and personal wealth. He ordered the arrest of all French members of her household and, in a particularly petty measure, all French citizens living in England. As compensation, Isabella and her remaining household of a handful of ladies were given an allowance to live off. It was not an insubstantial sum, but the removal of her land stripped her of something more powerful: her agency. Land generated income, from those who paid rent and worked on it. Without the ability to fill her own purse, Isabella was at the mercy of the king. Edward tried to argue that the seizure of Isabella's property in Cornwall was in the country's interests, saying that he feared that 'in the more remote parts of the realm and in lands by the seacoast . . . a fleet of ships could easily touch and perils thereby arise to the king and the realm'. And it was best, he claimed, that Isabella's lands across Somerset, Dorset and Devon 'be in the king's hand for the safe keeping'.[3] The most severe punishment of all came when her three youngest children were taken from her and given into the custody of Eleanor Despenser. The removal of her land and property in 1324 and Edward's petulant refusal to pay homage to her brother made a mockery of Isabella's efforts as queen and prompted a deep resentment. This resentment was aimed not only at her husband, but at Hugh Despenser, whose own paranoia and conspiratorial thinking seemed to blind the king.

In March 1325, Isabella was given a chance to free herself from the chains in which Edward and Despenser had bound her when she was requested to travel to France as part of a diplomatic mission. The sharp-minded Isabella knew this presented an opportunity, but Edward, who saw her as his best hope of improving relations with the French king, ensured she would be watched. The once generous and affable king permitted Hugh Despenser to fill the queen's entourage with Despenser's own spies.

The queen sailed from Dover, carrying with her great hopes for her success. The pope himself had written a personal note, 'rejoicing at her going to France as an angel of peace'.[4] She disembarked at Wissant outside Boulogne and travelled by road to Poissy, an important royal city on the banks of the Seine, north-west of Paris. There she was greeted by three English envoys and her brother Charles IV, who, despite his initially warm and comforting welcome, proved himself over the course of the negotiations to be unyielding. It was only when Isabella managed to speak with him directly, without the presence of English diplomats and papal envoys, that she was able to secure a short truce that would last between April and June that year. The terms, however, were extreme. Charles demanded Edward forfeit all of his lands in Aquitaine. They would only be returned on the condition that he personally travelled to the French court to pay homage to the French king. Isabella's diplomatic efforts were acknowledged in an addendum from Charles stating that he would accept Edward's homage 'through the love of his sister, the queen of England'. Still, Edward would later complain to the pope that he had not expected the French king to refuse his own sister.[5] As part of the French terms, Edward was also expected to cover the costs France incurred over the course of the campaign to confiscate Aquitaine. Further to this, no English military presence would be permitted in Aquitaine, or elsewhere in France, unless locally recruited.

During this time, Isabella seems to have played the same supportive role she had throughout her queenship. In a letter to Edward in spring 1325, Isabella presents herself as a dutiful queen but also a loving wife, referring to Edward on multiple occasions as '*mon tres-doutz cuer*' (my very sweet heart).[6] It is possible that this proud woman with a strong sense of her own regality was dissembling, and that the affection in her letters was more habitual and politic than sincere: there was little value in provoking her husband until she was sure of her own safety.

Her attempts to secure a reasonable solution for England and France came to nothing. Edward and his council could not agree to the terms that Charles offered. But after further envoys were dispatched to France to push for a more reasonable compromise, Edward was forced to accept that he would have to travel himself and pay homage to his brother-in-law by the end of the summer. He never made it. The king got as far as Langdon Abbey near Dover in August 1325, before he wrote to Charles, regretting that he had suddenly been taken ill. It is unclear whether he really was sick – he was undoubtedly unwilling to subjugate himself before his brother-in-law, though the rumour of a coup orchestrated by Roger Mortimer could also have halted his plans; it was said that Hugh Despenser did not want 'anyone to advise the king to cross on account of imminent danger'.[7] Edward agreed that his son and heir, Prince Edward, could travel in his place. At Dover, in order to make the compromise legitimate, he appointed the young Edward duke of Aquitaine, enabling him to perform homage instead of the king. Edward's lands could be restored without his personal safety or ego being compromised; it seemed like the perfect solution to a complex and humiliating situation. What Edward did not account for was that with her son by her side, away from the king, Isabella would find herself in an incredibly powerful position.

Isabella had been in France for six months when in September 1325 she watched her twelve-year-old son perform the ceremonial act of homage for the English-held territories, Aquitaine and Ponthieu. When formalities were completed and the Duchy of Aquitaine was returned to English control, it was assumed that Isabella and Prince Edward would return to England. In anticipation of this, Edward had stopped paying her expenses; Isabella was essentially being coerced into returning.[8] Writing to Walter Stapledon, the royal treasurer who held the purse strings, Isabella expresses rage and appears to threaten him: 'we [I] have promised you that we will keep you from damage and we will cause your body to be well and safely guarded.' Notably, Isabella makes a direct accusation that she can see who pulls the puppet strings at court: 'we see well that you are of the accord of the said Hugh and more obedient to him.'[9] By the end of the year, Isabella had decided not to return to England. She cut a powerful figure in France and was no longer willing to be coerced into submission.[10]

According to chroniclers, bards and playwrights over the coming centuries, Isabella and Edward's relationship was unhappy from the outset, but in reality Isabella turned against her husband over the course of only a few months. In the safe surrounds of the French court, she gained a new perspective on her position. The French queen, her sister-in-law, was a support during this period. They travelled together to Fontainebleau, a country residence that had belonged to French royalty for two hundred years, and dined together on a number of occasions.[11] But it was not the comfort of her brother's court that kept Isabella from England.

In the autumn of 1325 Isabella announced in a proclamation to the court in Paris, 'I feel that marriage is a joining together of man and woman, maintaining the undivided habit of life, and that someone has come between my husband and myself trying to break this bond; I protest that I will not return until this intruder is removed, but discarding my marriage garment, shall assume the robes of widow-hood and mourning until I am avenged of this Pharisee.'[12] Isabella's accusation is almost certainly directed at Hugh Despenser, for she later names him as the initiator of the decision to seize her lands and for mercilessly sequestering her property in England.[13] Isabella intended her decision to stay in France to be a powerful protest against her husband. As she had vowed to do in her speech, she began to propagandise her situation by wearing widow's robes. This 'lady in grief' appeared to have the effect the queen desired, for 'by reason of the anguish that she felt for maintaining peace, the common people greatly pitied her'.[14]

This performance was the beginning of a campaign in which Isabella attempted to rally support as a jilted queen who wished to resume her relationship. By highlighting Edward's loyalty to Despenser above his marriage blessed by God, Isabella not only drew attention to the damage done by Despenser to her relationship with the king, but also the damage done to the king's relationship and oath to the realm, another oath made before God. In early February 1326 she wrote a revealing letter to Walter Reynolds, the archbishop of Canterbury, who had, by order of Edward, pleaded with her to return to England. Reynolds promised that Despenser did not wish to harm Isabella and was not a malevolent character. Unmoved by his plea, Isabella wrote frankly to Reynolds: 'there is no way that we can return to the company of our aforementioned Lord without putting ourselves in danger of death, which we were in greater risk of than we can write about.'[15] Isabella was not only angry, she was terrified. A queen driven from her court was an unconventional situation, but to be so scared that she could not return indicates the lack of power she had as queen in England, weakened into paralysis by Despenser severing her affinity with the king.

Within days of the archbishop's intervention, people across the realm gathered to hear a proclamation ordered by Edward. On 8 February he dispatched a messenger to the sheriff of Northampton, directing him to arrange an announcement that all men-at-arms, the nobility and foot soldiers should ready themselves to defend the realm against 'enemies of the king'.[16]

Messengers were dispatched to Dover where a cold wind blew in from the turbulent Channel. A letter to Ralph Basset, the acting constable of Dover and warden of the Cinque Ports, made clear who these enemies were: the king warned that 'the queen is adopting the counsel of Mortimer, the king's notorious enemy and rebel.'[17]

Isabella had met Roger Mortimer on a number of occasions before they were thrown together in France in December 1325, notably when Mortimer was present at Edward's court. The queen had intervened – along with Eleanor Despenser – against the harsh treatment of Joan, Roger Mortimer's wife, following her imprisonment after Boroughbridge. When Isabella and Mortimer were reunited in France, there was no plot or ulterior motive. Whether the meeting was a chance encounter or carefully arranged, it would alter Isabella's course of action thereafter.

Roger Mortimer had made his way to the French court via Hainault in the Low Countries. When the countess of Hainault, Jeanne, travelled to Paris to attend the funeral of her father, Charles, the count of Valois, Mortimer accompanied her. After reconnecting in these bleak circumstances, Isabella and Mortimer's distant relationship soon developed into something more. Their alliance likely grew out of a mutual loathing of Hugh Despenser and a desire to liberate the realm from his regime. However, the bond created by their shared resentment drew them close and they began a love affair. A bold move for an anointed queen, this reveals much about Isabella's character and the freedom she felt away from the snare of the English court. It also suggests that Isabella truly did consider herself a widow. Isabella was known to be beautiful and her years of courtly experience gave her an assured quality that would have been attractive to a man like Roger Mortimer. He was an esteemed soldier, described as tall and handsome. Mortimer also had the charm and cunning to work a situation to his advantage; he had, after all, escaped from the Tower of London through a broken chimney.

Fearing the inevitable collapse of the holy union between Isabella and Edward, the pope became involved. This was a marriage that carried the security of two realms on its back; no man could be allowed to threaten its stability. The pope had his orders sent to Hugh Despenser advising that 'his participation in the king's government is given by the queen as a reason for her being unable, without personal danger, to return to the king . . . The pope suggests that Hugh should retire, and should devise methods by which the queen may no longer fear to return to her husband.'[18] But this intervention proved futile and Edward became desperate.

By March 1326 Isabella had been in France for a year. Edward was enraged at the lack of control he had over the situation. He dictated a flurry of coercive letters to his son, Edward, and his brother-in-law. The primary theme of his letter to the thirteen-year-old prince was marriage. A marriage contract had not yet been agreed for him, and, as with all royal marriages in the Middle Ages, the union he would eventually enter into would be political. By and large, royalty married for land, allegiance and power. Whatever wife was chosen for the prince, she would bring political, even military, support of her own. As well as providing Prince Edward with a future queen, this marriage was a way for the parties in this dispute to make a powerful ally – would it be arranged by Isabella or Edward II? King Edward was anxious that his son would be coaxed into a marriage without his approval. The letter Edward sent his son reminded the prince of an agreement he had made 'at Dover', presumably before he crossed to France, in which he had promised not to marry without Edward's consent. This was followed by a threat: if he broke his promise, 'he cannot avoid great dishonour and damage to God and all men, and the king's wrath and indignation'.[19] That same day, in a letter steeped in misogyny, Edward wrote to Charles IV, saying Isabella could not truly love the king 'as she ought to love her lord'.[20] He pleaded innocence, saying that at 'no time whilst she was with the king did she receive evil or villainy from the king or from any one else, and the king would not suffer her to do so'. He was silent about the removal of her properties and her household, including her personal doctor and youngest children. He also tried to convince Charles IV that Isabella and Despenser had a 'great and especial friendship', before asking him to see 'reason, good faith, and fraternal affection, without having regard to the wilful pleasure of woman'.[21]

Charles appears to have supported his sister. He was careful not to offer soldiers and arms too readily, but he aided her financially and allowed her to make her own decisions about her future. As he wrote to Edward II: 'the queen has come of her own free will, and may freely return if she wishes. But if she prefers to remain in these parts she is my sister and I refuse to expel her.'[22] Charles also appeared to turn a blind eye to Isabella and Mortimer's unconventional relationship.

The affair between Isabella and Mortimer is often romanticised. Edward certainly suspected they were having sex. He wrote candidly to the king of France that Isabella 'keeps his company in and out of house', suggesting that they engaged as a couple would.[23] Adultery was treason in the eyes of the king and a sin in the eyes of the Church. But this appears to have been the lesser evil, even for Edward. He realised that it was far more than a reckless love affair; Isabella and Mortimer's political union could be incredibly dangerous. As a soldier and leader, Mortimer was an obvious ally for Isabella and, together, with the heir to the throne in their company, they were in a strong position. Isabella and Mortimer began to strategise their return to England, planning to overthrow the Despensers. This time they would return with an army. The Wheel of Fortune had spun in Isabella's favour. Power felt good.

10.   'She-wolf of France'

The approach of Michaelmas traditionally marked the end of the harvest: grain was stored for the winter and grapes were crushed to make wine. Labourers were able to drop the plough and pick up the axe or sword if called into battle. It was a time of new beginnings. On 28 September 1066, William the Conqueror had invaded England and forged a new regime under the Normans.

In September 1326, Isabella of France was intending to do the same. Setting sail from Dordrecht harbour, the fleet comprising one hundred and forty vessels cut through the water in two days, carrying arms, horses, mercenary soldiers and those with a shared hatred for Hugh Despenser.

Edward and Hugh Despenser had been planning the defence of the kingdom since the spring. Warning beacons were readied along the coast and castles were strengthened, particularly those on the northern border in Alnwick, Norham and Wark. Orders were given to remove all 'alien monks, natives of France' from religious houses along the coast and rehouse them elsewhere, 'away from the coastline' – presumably out of fear they would collude with a French invading army. In July, Edward asked the citizens of Bayonne in Aquitaine to 'annoy and injure all subjects of the king of France', an order he reiterated two months later.[1] These panicked instructions show Edward was blind to the real threat.

William I, the count of Hainault, was both a prudent politician and hardened fighter. He had spent his life at war, carving out a handsome portion of the Low Countries that would be ruled by the future counts of Hainault. He knew as well as any that strength was forged in numbers and that allying himself with the future rulers of England would work in his favour. The idea to ask him for support was probably Roger Mortimer's. Mortimer and William I were well acquainted and it was soon agreed that in exchange for one hundred and forty ships and an army of seven hundred seasoned mercenaries, the count of Hainault's daughter Philippa would be betrothed to Prince Edward. With mercenaries from Hainault and a contingent of displaced and disgruntled exiled soldiers from England, Isabella had built a modest army of around one thousand troops. But if she was going to take on Edward and Despenser, she would need to find support within England itself.

On 24 September the queen's army landed in Walton in Suffolk, on the estuary of the River Orwell. She arrived with the intention of putting an end to the political discord that had dominated the country for almost a decade, and was welcomed accordingly. The earl of Kent, Edward II's younger half-brother, had already rallied his men around Isabella. For too long they had been subject to Despenser's threats. As they saw it, England was suspended under a regime of tyranny. Those who rushed to Isabella's side, comforted that she had Prince Edward in her possession, were careful not to act against the king as their counterparts had at Boroughbridge. Isabella was bold but not imprudent and was careful to iterate that the offensive was to remove Despenser, not Edward – whatever the truth of her plans. This had the desired effect of isolating Despenser. Those loyal to the king could still rally behind Isabella without the fear they would be committing treason.

News of the queen's plan travelled fast and Edward panicked. It was likely that Isabella would head for London with her army, so to avoid capture, the king and Despenser the Younger fled from London to Gloucester, where they could gather themselves and an army. All the while, Isabella quickly collected supporters from across the realm. Draped in black robes, she maintained the appearance of a widow, cutting a sorrowful but powerful figure. Isabella's conduct certainly attracted attention but it was also divisive. One account noted that 'there were contradictory rumours in England about the queen, some declaring that she was the betrayer of the king and kingdom, others that she was acting for peace and the common welfare of the kingdom, and for the removal of evil counsellors from the king'.[2] The mood was one of hope but also suspicion. After all, Isabella acted outside the paradigms of femininity as it was understood in the late

Middle Ages. This, along with the allegiance she had formed with Mortimer, was suspect.

Isabella must have known the risk she was taking – women accused of adultery could be tried before the ecclesiastical courts and punished by public whippings or even, in extreme cases, death by burning. Extramarital affairs were condemned by the Church in the strictest terms. However, the justice and morality preached by Christian theologians, enshrined in canon law, also considered women to be the 'property' of men, and men were supposed to be responsible for their property. In cases of infidelity, men were more frequently punished than women – usually fined – because they were thought to be the reasonable sex; as such, they should have control over the marriage. If it went wrong, it was their fault.[3] In a sense, this was how Isabella conducted herself. She did not hide Roger Mortimer from curious eyes, instead presenting herself as the victim of her husband's and Despenser's actions. Perhaps she was willing to publicly acknowledge her relationship with Mortimer to illustrate the ineptitude of her husband.

As her army progressed through Ipswich and Bury St Edmunds, more and more people joined. Roger Mortimer proudly marched at its head – once a fugitive, now a leader. Isabella was hailed as a liberator come to deliver the realm from tyranny. Isabella also gained the support of the bishops of Ely, Durham and Hereford. In a spectacular greeting at Cambridge, they welcomed Isabella, sanctioning her invasion on behalf of the wider Church. This enthusiasm, though genuine, should not be overstated. The country was exhausted by political strife, weakness and corruption; its people were willing to support anybody who would change this.

By October Isabella was ready to target London. She sent a messenger ahead of her arrival. On the 9th, the feast of Saint Denis, the streets around the market cross in Cheapside were thrumming with energy. Before sunrise a letter had been fixed to a stone cross in the heart of the parish community, the location where proclamations were made or civic pageantry took place. By dawn, this letter had drawn a crowd. Further copies were distributed elsewhere across the city bearing the pendant seals of both the queen and her son, Prince

Edward. These letters appealed to the people of London to 'destroy sir Hugh Despenser and other enemies for common profit of all the realm'. Isabella was making a direct appeal to the people to join her and bring down the king's corrupt and conceited coterie. In a copy of the letter published in the *Anonimalle Chronicle*, Isabella proclaimed: 'if the said Hugh Despenser our enemy should come within your power that you should have him taken quickly and kept safely until we have indicated our will with him . . . if you do this, know that we will be always more bound to you.'[4]

The crucible of royal power, London was also the administrative and financial centre of the realm. Edward knew that if he lost London he could lose the fight altogether. As Isabella's proclamation circulated through the various districts of the bustling city, Edward struggled to claw back threads of power through the support of his people by offering the vast sum of one thousand pounds as a reward to anybody who could bring him Mortimer's head, yet his bribe was fruitless.

London had long been a city in which community and co-operation sat uneasily alongside criminality and violence. When Isabella incited rebellion against Hugh Despenser, Londoners rose up in support of the queen. A crowd gathered outside the Guildhall, where Despenser's 'spy', a Londoner called John le Marshall, was dragged from his nearby house – it was believed he was complicit in the corruption at court and was feeding secrets to Hugh Despenser. Without trial he was 'led into Cheapside, stripped, confessed and beheaded'. Similarly, the bishop of Exeter and former treasurer Walter Stapledon, who had withheld Isabella's income when she was in France, was snatched from outside Saint Paul's Cathedral. Stapledon was 'met and seized from all sides and quickly unhorsed'.[5] Dragged from Saint Paul's to Cheapside, Stapledon was beaten savagely before one of his attackers, in an appalling act of brutality, brandished a bread knife and severed the bishop's head from his limp body. Stapledon's head was then delivered as a gift to Isabella.[6] As was often the case in the medieval period, those who existed in the periphery of power, loyal servants to larger political structures, were often the victims of brutal assault, targeted by rebels as scapegoats for the unreachable few who pulled the strings of power from above. With a single spin, advisers, councillors or figureheads, loyal to one regime and opposing another, could find themselves either victorious or the recipient of a grim fate.

The queen had captured the capital. In a short space of time she and her son Edward, who was also eager to see Despenser removed, had achieved the unimaginable. Bishops, abbots, priors, earls, barons and other lords of the land swore loyalty to the queen and her son.[7] In a symbolic gesture, the constable of the Tower of London, John de Weston, released the keys of the Tower into the custody of Isabella's supporters. Those imprisoned inside who had been loyal to the earl of Lancaster's failed cause were released. The next day, Lancaster's plaque, a eulogy to his Ordinances, once ripped down under the orders of Despenser, was reinstated inside Saint Paul's Cathedral.[8] As events in London had shown, the people were by and large supportive of the queen's efforts to destroy Despenser. But they were also aware of the king's role in the rise of his favourite. Lancaster's Ordinances haunted Edward II's every move, highlighting the fact that he had broken his coronation oath to the people of the realm by maintaining favourites to their detriment, allowing the Despensers' outrages to go unchecked. By again putting his few favourites before his many subjects, Edward had unwittingly allowed the traditional and political structures of the realm to unravel. His very position as king was unstable.

London was essential to Isabella's cause in that she had taken Westminster and garnered the support of the City, but her victory over the capital was immaterial if she could not capture Hugh Despenser. Humiliated, Edward and Despenser intended to make their way to Wales, where Despenser had coerced his way to wealth, land and title and where the hapless king, as prince of Wales, hoped he could muster support. They knew they would need significant help to repair the fracturing of their authority. Indeed, their lives depended on it. But this was now a manhunt for Hugh Despenser the Younger, whose only protection was Edward. Isabella was close on their heels. By 18 October she had reached Bristol, but she could not follow Edward into the sea.[9] The king and Despenser had taken a boat from Chepstow to Lundy Island in the Bristol Channel. One contemporary suggests that Edward planned to travel on to Ireland to reinvigorate the Celtic alliance he had defeated at Faughart by forming an Irish-Scottish force with the support of Robert Bruce.[10] Whatever the truth, the panicked Edward's plans were thwarted by the weather. High winds hammered the Bristol Channel for days, forcing him to land at Cardiff and seek refuge in Caerphilly Castle.

Although Hugh Despenser the Younger still eluded Isabella, she managed the next best thing: his father. Hugh Despenser the Elder was a prime target for the queen and Roger Mortimer. He had benefited from, and played an active role in, his son's rise to power. Now, though, Isabella ordered her men to lay siege to Bristol Castle, which Despenser the Elder had been charged with holding. His resistance was brave but Isabella took the castle in only eight days. Bound in chains, Despenser the Elder was dragged before Mortimer and other senior judges. In a show trial meant to mimic Thomas of Lancaster's, Hugh Despenser the Elder was told that since he had introduced a law that prevented a condemned man from speaking in his own defence, he would also be denied that privilege.[11] In the presence of Roger Mortimer, Henry, earl of Lancaster (the younger brother of the executed Thomas), and the earls of Norfolk and Kent, Despenser the Elder was sentenced to death. The first major execution of Isabella's war against the Despenser regime took place at a gallows in Bristol. Hugh Despenser the Elder was hanged, drawn and beheaded. His head was impaled on a spear and sent to Winchester, the seat of his earldom. His body was fed to the dogs.

Around this time, Prince Edward oversaw the summons of parliament to Bristol, ordering the lords and members of the Church to meet in December. The summoning of parliament was usually the king's responsibility, but with Edward II known to have left England, Isabella had the opportunity to place her son in a position of great power. It is unlikely Isabella was planning to depose Edward in favour of her son yet, but she was determined to track down, arrest and execute Despenser. Before leading prelates, it was concluded – possibly by the chancellor – that 'upon the said king going away from his realm of England with Hugh le Despenser, the younger . . . [and] the realm being left without rule . . . the said duke and keeper should rule and govern the realm in the name and right of the king his father, who was thus absent.'[12]

Edward was doggedly loyal to his friend, curiously determined that no harm should come to him. At the same time, the king knew he could not be belittled and controlled again, as he had been by Lancaster and his administrative shackles. Edward was either naive to the possibility that his actions in fleeing with Despenser could cost him his crown, or he panicked and made impulsive decisions in the belief he could regain power with the help of his Welsh and Irish subjects. Edward and Despenser did not stay long at Caerphilly, a sign of how hard they had found it to drum up arms and support in Wales. Even Edward's servants had begun to desert him. In early November they pressed on towards Neath, but somewhere along the road, Edward was discovered by a band of Welshmen led by Henry, earl of Lancaster, who were likely tipped off about the king and his favourite's whereabouts. The fleeing king must have cut a meek figure – drenched by the rain and clutching the Great Seal, a device akin to the monarch's signature and almost the only remaining symbol of his former power. Despenser was discovered in a nearby wood, hiding with Robert Baldock, the last of Edward's government to stay loyal. The despondent trio were handed over to Henry and taken to 'Pant-y-brad' or 'the Vale of Treachery', before being moved on to Monmouth, where Edward was forced to give up the Great Seal.[13] The Great Seal was not a paltry administrative tool, but a physical embodiment of the king's will and power. The act of handing it over symbolised authority changing hands. Although the seal was delivered to Isabella, she did not, and could not – with her son considered a reasonable age for kingship – intend to rule as queen in her own right; over the course of the invasion she had been careful to promote her son as heir. Nevertheless, at thirteen, Edward was too young to govern without the influence of experienced councillors, all of whom were selected by parliament. Edward II was still king but he was rendered powerless. Without the trappings of kingship and with his government against him, Isabella, for now, would effectively become the regent of England. Her first course of action was to deal with Hugh Despenser the Younger.

Edward and Despenser parted ways on a cold mountain path in Wales; they would never see one another again. For Edward it was a stark and harrowing repetition of the trauma of Gaveston. He knew Despenser would be killed. Both Despenser and Baldock were taken to Hereford, where Baldock was handed over to the bishop of Hereford and imprisoned. Despenser was ritually humiliated. Tied to a boisterous horse, he was marched through towns and villages on the road to Hereford where rotting waste and even faeces were thrown at him. When he arrived at Hereford he was put in jail, whereupon he immediately went on hunger strike. He likely wished to take his own life rather than face an execution organised by Isabella and Mortimer. Their intention was to make Despenser's death a public spectacle, having him killed as a traitor in London before a vast crowd. When Isabella was informed of Despenser's hunger strike she feared she would not see justice done in time. The same panel of justices who had tried and sentenced Hugh Despenser the Elder gathered hurriedly on 24 November. Like his father before him, Despenser was forced to remain silent as a roster of grievances was read out, including coercion and theft of land, 'contrary to Magna Carta and the Ordinances'. The pain Despenser had inflicted on women was a major feature of the accusations. The case of Lady Baret, another widow of Boroughbridge, was brought to the judgement: 'simply because you are a tyrant, you had beaten by your scoundrels and shamefully had her arms and legs broken against the order of chivalry and contrary to law and reason'. Despenser was also blamed for the death of Thomas of Lancaster, who he 'martyred and murdered by a hard and piteous death'. He was accused of usurping royal power, specifically in relation to the queen: 'And then, Hugh, you, your father and Robert Baldock had my lady the queen ousted from her lands, which were given and assigned to her by our lord the king, and set her on her journey meanly, against the dignity of her highness and of her estate, abetting and procuring daily, as a false and disloyal traitor, discord between our lord the king and herself by means of your hold on royal power.'[14]

The document listing his appalling behaviour serves as an example of the corruption, deceit and avarice that had become commonplace during Edward's reign. It also reveals the perils that faced a country led by a weak king whose reliance on manipulative and self-interested individuals made him dangerous. In the end, removing Gaveston created a void that proved too easy for Hugh Despenser to fill.

It was decreed that this 'traitor, tyrant and renegade' was to be disembowelled and his entrails burned. On 24 November, at a gallows in Hereford, Hugh Despenser was hanged. Wearing a 'chaplette of sharp nettles' – a kind of crown intended to symbolise his encroachment on royal power – the thin, pale and defeated Despenser was brought before a screaming crowd. His tunic bore a reversed Despenser coat of arms – befitting a traitor – and emblazoned with the Latin text from Psalm 52: 'Why do you glory in malice, you who are mighty in inequity.'[15] Once he had been stripped of his tunic, Despenser's limp, terrified body was hauled into the air, where he was suspended, choking part way to death. Then he was cut open and his entrails were yanked out from his body and cast into a furnace below. Despenser's penis was severed from his body and sent into the flames – a symbolic destruction of his line. Finally, he was beheaded.

On 4 December Despenser's head was 'carried to London through Cheapside accompanied by trumpets, and the head was impaled on London Bridge'.[16] This final act was necessary for Isabella, for Despenser had not, as planned, been executed in London. As a result, something was needed in the capital to mark the end of his control over the king. Shortly after this, every citizen in London was required to swear an oath of loyalty to Isabella and her son. In order to keep the peace, it was also forbidden for citizens to carry weapons. As Hugh Despenser's hollow-eyed head rotted in Cheapside, Isabella celebrated Christmas with her sons, Edward and John of Eltham. As for the king himself, she had arranged that he be moved to Kenilworth Castle in Warwickshire, where he spent Christmas anxiously awaiting his own fate and mourning the death of Despenser. Between Christmas and the new year, a decision was made about Edward's future and also the future of his marriage to Isabella. It was impossible for the union to continue, for doing so would result in Edward's kingship being restored, which would leave Isabella at the mercy of his vengeance following her coup against him. In an extraordinary turn of events, his treatment of Isabella in the removal of her lands and the favouring of Despenser was considered reasonable terms for their separation. Though the marriage was not formally annulled, there was clearly no way Isabella and Edward could resume their previous state as king and queen of England.

In his father's absence, Prince Edward was the natural choice to oversee the first parliament of the year. 'Twenty-four men from north Wales' came to Westminster for the discussion over the future of King Edward II's reign.[17] Edward II had been requested to attend but he would be no more than a prisoner on his own throne. Aware of this, he had refused. What was to be done with the king? The only precedent parliament had to work with was King John, who came close to deposition but conveniently died before he could be forced off the throne. Edward could no longer rule, his doing so would result in civil war – too many members of the nobility and common folk had aided Isabella in her campaign against Despenser. The only way forward would be for Edward to agree to abdicate in favour of his son. For the record, Edward agreed to step down, but whether this was entirely voluntary remains unknown. The abdication of the king, in favour of fourteen-year-old Prince Edward, was formally and finally proclaimed on 24 January 1327. Edward II, a ruined king, would never return to London again. Between January and March 1327, he became known as 'the king's father' and was gifted two tuns of wine by his son, a paltry but perhaps telling present.

At some point in April 1327, he was moved from Kenilworth Castle to Berkeley Castle in Gloucestershire. During this time he is said to have been mistreated – a rumour circulated that he was ignominiously seated 'on a molehill [where a] barbour brought a basin of cold water which he had taken from the ditch' and forcibly shaved; another rumour said Edward was refused sleep and kept in a room next to a pit filled with rotting carcasses.[18] The luxuries Edward enjoyed during his imprisonment would suggest otherwise. He had a household at his disposal including a kitchen and a cook as well as his own personal servant. Accounts show he was allocated cattle for beef, capons (male chickens), cheese, expensive spices, wine and wax – presumably for candles and to seal letters.[19] One contemporaneous chronicle argues that it was the absence of Edward's family that caused him the most grief during his incarceration.[20]

Another account describes the former king as 'despondent', submitting his crown with 'sobs, tears and sighs'.[21] This account is heavily skewed in Edward's favour, but the sorrow attributed to him is also illustrated in an Anglo-Norman poem, *The Lament of Edward II*. The *Lament* chronicles a despondent former king who repents his failures and agonises over his fate.[22] Echoing the chronicles, the *Lament* shows Edward grieving the loss of his family, particularly Isabella: 'God! How much I loved the fair one; but now the spark of true love is gone out, so that my joy is fled.' In his contrition, his sorrow becomes overwhelming, 'Now without delay would it indeed be time to die.' He claims to have 'lost all earthly honour beyond recovery'.[23]

The sobs and wails of the former king echoed through the stony halls of Berkeley Castle. His very existence, however, rendered Isabella and Mortimer's new regime precarious. Edward III's kingship could not be fully legitimised while his father paced the cold corridors of Berkeley. The former king, though incarcerated, cast an uncomfortable shadow over Westminster and it was whispered that something had to be done to be rid of it.

11.   The Society of Craddok

In medieval England a king who inherited his crown too young was in danger – youth was a weakness and necessitated powerful and often ambitious magnates taking on a regency-style government, which was in itself riddled with problems. One way of avoiding argument, or even war, over the young king's legitimacy was to crown him quickly. Thus, in February 1327, within weeks of Edward II's deposition, Edward III was crowned at Westminster Abbey. The lavish ceremony was followed by an elaborate feast in Westminster Hall. The fourteen-year-old king, draped in an ermine-lined 'pure miniver' mantle sat on samite cushions beneath a canopy of gold canvas, festooned with swathes of gold silk.[1] Placed at the centre of the violet and red dais – a raised platform for the royal table – the king looked out over a packed hall, thrumming with the voices of hopeful lords, eager that this celebration should end decades of political discord. The coronation and subsequent feast were costly – the most expensive of his reign and indicative of Isabella's talent for spending money.

But before the festivities could begin, wrongs had to be righted and wounds healed. Under Edward II the country had been divided. Noble families across the realm had had their loved ones accused of treason; some were tortured to death. Even Edward's own cousin had fallen victim to the executioner's axe. The parliament in January 1327 began with great hope for what this young king could do for a fractured kingdom. In a bid to heal some of the torment, it was agreed that Thomas of Lancaster, who had developed a cult following since his death in 1322, should be canonised. This would legitimise those who mourned him and sanctify his Ordinances. It was hoped that Edward III would live by his oath and adhere to the principles of Plantagenet kingship outlined in both Magna Carta and the Ordinances. He would be a king for all his people, not just for his favourites. To demonstrate this, the sentences of treason that were passed against

Lancaster and the other rebel lords were cancelled – including those of Roger Mortimer and his uncle, Roger Mortimer of Chirk, who had died in captivity. These pardons were part of the political reconciliation following the war, but the main reason behind Lancaster's posthumous pardon and exaltation was to gain the loyalty and support of his brother, the influential Henry, the new earl of Lancaster. Henry held as much authority and feudal power as his brother once possessed and his support for the young Edward was essential.

Edward began to sow the seeds of his sapling government, creating a hopeful future with the keen guidance of Mortimer and his mother, but the problem of his father remained. In summer 1327 Edward briefly escaped from Berkeley Castle with the aid of a local gang. Though he was quickly caught, further plots were discovered that promised to liberate Edward from his prison. The problem that now faced Isabella and Mortimer – setting a precedent for the treatment of future deposed monarchs – was that Edward III could not safely hold his throne while Edward II remained alive. In order to strengthen and secure the accession, the former king would have to be killed.

On 22 September 1327, a knight from Somerset in the pay of Roger Mortimer named Thomas Gurney stuffed a crucial message inside his purpose-made leather pouch, sealed it and mounted his horse. He had been tasked with delivering news and he had to make his journey at breakneck speed. Overnight, Gurney galloped to Nottingham in search of the young king and his mother. When he arrived, he was informed that they had already travelled on to Lincoln, where parliament was due to be held. At Lincoln the cathedral was shrouded by darkness and Gurney and his horse were exhausted, having ridden 156 miles in twenty-four hours. In the middle of the night of 23 September, the new king, Edward III, was roused from his sleep and told that his father was dead.[2]

Letters from Lord Berkeley, the custodian of Berkeley Castle, suggest that Edward II died at some time on 21 September 1327, while imprisoned at Berkeley Castle.[3] According to the official record, he died due to a 'fatal happening' – an accident. But this is almost certainly not true.[4] The truth was that Edward II could not be allowed to stay alive. The popular belief is that as Edward slept at Berkeley, men burst into his room and killed him with a white-hot poker. The former king is said to have been pushed down by a 'huge table laid upon his womb', before the poker was thrust up his anus, burning his organs from the inside.[5] The origin of this story is the *Brut* chronicle written around twenty years after Edward's death, which has inspired many popular reimaginings of Edward II's fate. But this story is almost certainly invented, in line with the practice of borrowing narratives from other histories in earlier chronicles to inspire shock and awe.[6] Death by rectal penetration was a trope among medieval chronicles: there was the unfortunate Viking warrior at the Battle of Stamford Bridge in 1066, killed by an Anglo-Saxon spear between his legs; or King Edmund Ironside, who was skewered through the backside by enemies after he went to 'do the duty of nature'.

The myth of Edward II's death is inextricably linked to the rumours around his sexuality. First there had been the relationship with Gaveston, then the relationship with Despenser. A further accusation of sodomy came during a sermon delivered by Adam Orleton, the bishop of Hereford, around the time of Isabella's invasion, in which he branded Edward 'a tyrant and a sodomite'.[7] This, too, should be treated with a degree of scepticism – using influential friends to accuse Edward of sodomy was a means for Isabella to strengthen her campaign.

The whole operation was so clandestine it is impossible to know exactly what took place. How much involvement did Isabella have in the plot, if she knew about it at all? Lack of certainty has led to the suggestion that Edward was not killed and that another body was buried in his place while the real king escaped into exile. The alternative hypothesis is that the former king escaped his prison at Berkeley and fled to Corfe Castle, where he was aided by the custodian Lord Thomas, before moving on to Ireland. The source of the theory is a letter that was pressed into the hands of King Edward III around 1337. It was undated and composed by a Genoese priest named Manuele Fieschi, a senior clerk to Pope John XXII.[8]

Though a tantalising possibility, the full story is far-fetched. The most likely – and most commonly accepted – scenario is that Edward

II was killed under the orders of Roger Mortimer, by men including Thomas Gurney.[9] He may have been smothered to death so that no mark was left on his body.[10] The physical representation of a natural death was important. As a former monarch, Edward was still eligible for an elaborate funeral, during which his corpse would be on show to the realm.

After his death, Edward's body was embalmed and his heart was sent to Isabella, encased in a silver vase, possibly at her request. What would she have made of it? Was this the ultimate, corporeal symbol of absolute power and victory or did Isabella feel grief that the father of her children, a man she had been conditioned to respect and revere, was now dead? As she held his lifeless heart, did Isabella question fate, power and betrayal?

The funerary measures for Edward's internment took place without the usual ceremony that would befit a king. A coffin, shrouded in cloth of gold embroidered with the arms of England, was transported to Saint Peter's Abbey at Gloucester, where he was to be interred in an elaborate and beautiful alabaster and marble tomb. A gilded hearse, flanked with four golden lions, emblazoned with the arms of England, carried Edward's coffin, as well as a wooden effigy of the deceased king, dressed in royal robes and a copper crown – the first record of an effigy of a deceased monarch being used to demonstrate his likeness rather than the corpse lying in state. Usually, a king's funeral and entombment would be at Westminster Abbey, near to Edward I and in the heavenly embrace of Edward the Confessor. Edward II had perhaps imagined he would be buried near to his father and with a telling epitaph about his reign: a single, immortal line that would articulate his character for every mourner or onlooker. He was no 'Hammer' but he may have thought of himself as 'fair', or 'loving', a friend to his people. With no martial prowess to boast of, Edward II has instead faded into ignominy, remembered for his flaws.

In this case, though, a funeral at Westminster Abbey risked drawing too much attention to the murky details of the king's death and fomenting further upheaval. Gloucester Cathedral offered a convenient compromise: Edward's grandfather, Henry III, had been crowned at the abbey in his minority as king, before a later coronation at

Westminster. This connection was tenuous, but, after all, in most aspects Edward's funeral was a compromise. This explains why there is little record of the ceremony. Chroniclers did not see it as a sufficiently momentous event to commit its details to parchment. One thing known for certain is that on 20 December 1327, Edward II was laid to rest, afforded some regal dignity and entombed in the presence of Isabella, who was swathed in black, along with the new King Edward III, who gently knelt before his father's tomb. Questions and fears likely flew through the young man's mind. At fifteen, he may have had his own idea of what it might mean to rule. Edward had watched and learned carefully. He benefited from charisma and popularity and realised, by watching his father tumble from the lofty heights of kingship, that unity was power. He knew that he must set about repairing a realm ruptured by civil war, weak leadership and self-gratification. The only person standing in his way was his mother, her lover and the regime they were beginning to establish.

What was important to Isabella was power. As queen she acted as an adviser to Edward II, and he valued her counsel. Over the past two years this power had shifted in focus. Now she led rather than served and it would be hard to relinquish that sense of authority and strength in service to her teenage son. Initially, Isabella's steps were practical, focused on ensuring her security. When Edward II had stripped Isabella of her independent wealth, she lost all hope of security outside her marriage. On the day of Edward III's coronation, she recovered everything that was taken away. She was not only re-endowed with her original lands in Cornwall and elsewhere, she was granted their worth three times over.

Isabella now held Langley as well as Leeds Castle and Bristol Castle. This was less a case of the teenage Edward gratefully doting on his mother and more that Isabella and Mortimer held a paralysing influence over the young king. Edward III ruled only in name. This is most clearly evidenced in the staggering rise of Mortimer, who enjoyed his newfound position by Isabella's side as her lover and counsel. Though not an earl, Mortimer soon styled himself as one. His three sons had been knighted during Edward's coronation, dressed in cloth of gold and fur, materials only appropriate to the heirs of an earl. Mortimer then acquired lands across the Welsh Marches – those once coveted by Despenser – before being entitled earl of March in October 1328.

Mortimer was rich and powerful but he knew to tread carefully, mastering the inner workings of government from a distance so as not to be accused of the same crimes as the man he had violently deposed. Isabella and Mortimer made sure they could enjoy a regal lifestyle by moving the royal court – an often itinerant body of people, rather than a physical place – to the freedom of Mortimer's castles in the Midlands, and especially to his ancestral seat at Wigmore Castle in Herefordshire. It was common practice for the court to move around the country, castle to castle, following seasonal pursuits like hunting or for various feasts, but Mortimer and Isabella had more freedom away from suspicious eyes in Westminster.

Isabella and Mortimer were able to hold court in a manner that pleased them. Isabella loved storytelling, spectacle and spending money. One of her favourite activities was dressing up: she ordered robes so that she could play 'Guinevere' and Mortimer could play 'Lancelot', re-enacting scenes from Arthurian legend. In 1328, Mortimer held tournaments at Wigmore Castle where Isabella relished the opportunity to indulge her fascination with Arthurian romances, creating games and roleplay. This type of courtly game-playing, romantic storytelling and theatre was a manifestation of the way that the ideals of chivalry were interwoven with noble culture. Isabella's interest in Arthur undoubtedly had a lasting impact on her son, for at fifteen he began to use his legend in his personal politics. While with his mother and Mortimer at Wigmore, Edward formed a fictional society based on Arthurian myth. He called it the 'Society of Craddok'.[11] Adopting a popular myth circulating the Welsh border at the time, Edward ordered green robes for his men and named his company after 'Cradock's mantle', a magic cloak that – in legend – was brought to Arthur's court. The story goes that if the mantle was draped over the shoulders of a lady, it would shrink had she been unfaithful to her husband. In romance literature, Guinevere had a love affair with Lancelot and in this adjunct story, 'Cradock' brought the mantle to Arthur's court, where he presented it to Arthur and Guinevere. Before the aghast Arthur and the rest of the court, Guinevere tried on the mantle, which instantly revealed the queen's infidelity. Shamed, she fled red-faced from the hall: 'Fast with a rudd redd, to her chamber can shee flee.'[12]

Given that Isabella played the part of Guinevere, this play on a local Arthurian myth may have been Edward's way of attacking his mother for her affair with Mortimer, while also conforming to the theatrical courtly games of Isabella's own creation. If so, this was a cunning political game indicative of the fact that Edward was no willing puppet. All the while, he struggled to free himself from their control. Where Isabella and Mortimer enjoyed freedom, Edward had none. Mortimer went everywhere with the king and if he could not be at Edward's side, he ensured that his men would be. Forced into acquiescence, hectored into submission and coddled as if he were an infant, Edward III was powerless.

Clever as Isabella was, she failed to recognise that the security of the realm depended on her releasing the reins and allowing her authority to ebb away. Instead, she made the same mistake as her husband, enabling an ambitious, rapacious man to use her position to enhance his own wealth and status. It was inevitable that cracks would soon begin to appear in the relationship between Isabella, Mortimer and her suffocated son.

In 1328, after years of campaigning, Robert Bruce was on his death-bed. His son David was only four years old and the formidable king of Scotland had to ensure the security of everything he had worked for. Skirmishes between English and Scottish soldiers had continued since the start of the Anglo-Scottish war in 1296. Although various truces were agreed over the course of time, it was only in 1328 that a lasting peace seemed possible. The ailing Robert Bruce was eager to reach an agreement with England now that Isabella and Mortimer held the reins of power, sensing he could bring them to negotiate where Edward never would. Bruce was correct. Isabella and Mortimer were keen to end an expensive war that was draining an already almost exhausted treasury. In March 1328 Edward III formally recognised Scotland as a nation independent from English sovereignty, but he did so unwillingly. Four months later, in July, at the urging of Mortimer, Princess Joan, Isabella's seven-year-old daughter, married David Bruce: a union to help shore up the peace.

These events, after decades of fighting, were an extraordinary development in Anglo-Scottish relations, but they also marked the first time that Edward publicly opposed his mother and her lover. He felt forced into agreeing to a settlement that he believed was unstable from the outset and a shame on his ancestors, notably his grandfather Edward I, whose martial example he was keen to emulate. Edward was not the only opposition: the nobility who had lost land to Bruce called it '*turpis pax*' (a shameful peace) and Henry, earl of Lancaster, considered it a stain on English supremacy. In the end, the peace had only been secured at the battering insistence of Isabella and Mortimer. Edward refused to attend the marriage between his sister and David Bruce.[13]

The tension between Edward and his mother escalated further over the Stone of Scone, the symbol of Scottish kingship that remained wedged beneath Edward's coronation chair at Westminster. According to the terms of peace, Isabella had promised to return the Stone to its rightful place. Edward III dispatched an order to the sheriffs of London to 'receive the Coronation Stone from the Abbot of Westminster, and to convey it to the Queen-Mother in whatever part of the North of England she may happen to be'.[14] The tone is petulant, for Edward never intended to allow the Stone to leave his chair. Instead, he colluded with the abbot of Westminster not to let the Stone leave the abbey. More significant, though, was popular pressure. The people in London were so appalled at the prospect of the Stone being returned to Scotland that it was rumoured they were ready to stage a rebellion. Nervous of Edward's growing belligerence, Isabella and Mortimer backed down. Nonetheless the argument threatened to destabilise all they had worked towards. Edward was trying assert his own authority and the dispute over the 'shameful peace' exposed tensions in the leadership. Isabella and Mortimer had so far managed to avoid the attention of the nobility, but the disagreements over Scotland brought their unconventional self-imposed regency into the spotlight. The first of the nobility who had rallied behind Isabella to question how the realm was now being governed was Henry, earl of Lancaster.

When Henry inherited his brother's lands he also inherited the title steward of England. This made him a protector of the realm, putting him in the position to govern if Edward was unable or overseas. Henry had quietly observed Isabella and Mortimer's theatre from the wings. Though concerned at what he witnessed, he was initially unwilling to launch himself into petty politics – learning, perhaps, from his brother's mistakes. However, by autumn 1328 the new earl of Lancaster could no longer stand to watch the realm financially crippled by Isabella's drastic overspending on a lavish lifestyle and mismanaged by both Isabella and Roger Mortimer – notably the peace they had made with Robert Bruce. But, above all, Henry of Lancaster was appalled that the young Edward III was so bound by their dominance.

In writing to the king and his government, Henry made his wishes known: he wanted the queen to finance her lifestyle through her own dowry rather than through the king's purse; he wanted Edward to be allowed to live on his own with resources to support his household; and he wanted the realm to be governed with greater efficacy. Isabella and Mortimer would have done well to adhere to his wishes – they largely reflected the mood of the rest of government, who were beginning to question why Edward was still controlled by his mother and her lover.

The exact cause of Isabella's anxiety about allowing Edward greater independence is unclear, but she clearly enjoyed the power she was able to exercise in her own right. It is also possible she feared that the young and impressionable Edward could be exploited by others as his father had been: out of her sight, he might develop a network of coercive favourites. At the same time, Edward would turn sixteen in November 1328, he was approaching adulthood, and it was becoming increasingly difficult to justify Isabella and Mortimer's attempts to cling on to power.

By 1329 the situation had become untenable for Lancaster and the king's uncles – Edmund, earl of Kent, and Thomas, earl of Norfolk. They were forced to watch the disempowered Edward dragged around by Roger Mortimer. England was governed by King Mortimer, not by King Edward III, and in all too familiar circumstances the nobility united and began to prepare for war to defend their king against the man who controlled him.

Lancaster and the king's uncles were the first real threat Isabella and Mortimer had faced. Their only shield was the king himself, who they kept with them at all times, as if he were a small child. But events played out in their favour. Lancaster made the first move, marching on London. As he reached the city's outskirts in January he learned that the king's uncles had withdrawn their support for him, opting instead for the safety of neutrality. Lancaster was trapped. Nonetheless he set out to meet the king's party at Bedford. Both sides were decked out for battle, Edward, Mortimer and Lancaster, even Isabella, were all in new suits of armour. And yet no swords were drawn that day. Perhaps the bloody memory of Boroughbridge was still too vivid for both sides. Instead, on a freezing morning in the middle of January, Lancaster knelt before Edward on the sodden ground and begged forgiveness. In doing so he saved his life, lands and title and also, inadvertently, his son Henry's promising future relationship with the young king.

Lancaster's short-lived challenge to their rule weakened Isabella and Mortimer and they became ever more anxious. They tried to exert even tighter control over Edward, which only served to stoke his resentment further. He began to whisper in dark corners with his friends – the knights with whom he had formed the Society of Craddok. Together, they planned how Edward would snatch his freedom from Isabella and Mortimer.

12.   The Coup

Spiritual propaganda was a powerful tool in the fourteenth century. The spiritual conviction of the people could sometimes be enough to set Fortune's Wheel spinning. In 1330, rumours of spectacular miracles occurring at Edward II's tomb in Gloucester precipitated the fall of Isabella and Mortimer's three-year-long regime. As talk grew of the sick being miraculously cured at the foot of Edward's marble tomb, his image in the collective memory began to shift: from tyrant to political martyr. Edward II had emerged from his grave to torment Isabella and Mortimer as they descended into their own paranoid tyranny.

Just like Edward II in the latter years of his reign, Isabella and Mortimer became increasingly suspicious. Their household became smaller, their grip over Edward III tighter and they began to suspect everyone around them of deceit.

In late 1329, wild rumours, emanating from a mysterious source, began to circulate that Edward II was somehow still alive, that he had survived Berkeley and was kept under lock and key at Corfe Castle in Dorset. There was no evidence for this suggestion, but important men believed it, notably William Melton, the archbishop of York, and Edmund, earl of Kent, the former king's younger brother. In January 1330, the archbishop of York put pen to paper regarding an urgent matter. 'To our dear vallet, Simon Swonland,' he wrote, before warning him of the dangers of what he was about to ask him to do.[1] Melton tells Swonland – a respected draper and alderman in London – that he has reliable information that 'Edward of Caernarvon' is alive, well and in want of freedom from his imprisonment. Melton goes on to ask Swonland to procure a roster of garments including miniver caps, six pairs of slippers, girdles and large bed covers. The plan, according to Melton, was for Swonland to deliver these goods to Brother

William de Clyf at Cawood Manor in Yorkshire – William de Clyf was the same man who had brought the letter to Swonland, under the orders of archbishop Melton. Finally, Simon Swonland was required to travel north and procure gold for 'the king', presumably to fund his escape.

Melton had no reason to extort money from Swonland or con him into delivering an abundance of sumptuous clothing, they were kinsmen, with a long-standing financial relationship. As archbishop of York he was already wealthy and well attired. Had his letter been discovered by those loyal to Isabella and Mortimer, the archbishop would be in danger. Melton had to be convinced that the former king lived, and he was not alone: Edmund, earl of Kent, was vehement he had seen his elder brother with his own eyes.

The 28-year-old Edmund is said to have travelled to Rome, charged with persuading Pope John XXII to canonise the late Thomas of Lancaster. The mission failed but on his journey home Edmund encountered Dominican friars who swore the former king was kept at Corfe Castle under the watchful eye of Sir Thomas Gurney.[2] When Edmund travelled to Corfe, he was told that by order of Isabella and Mortimer he was forbidden to see the former king in the flesh. Yet one contemporaneous source claims the earl caught sight of Edward 'sitting royally at supper'.[3] Edmund might well have seen a man who looked like his brother eating a meal, but it could not have been Edward, who was long dead. Nonetheless, convinced by what he believed he had witnessed, around February 1330 Edmund smuggled a letter to his 'brother' assuring him that a plot to rescue him was in motion. It included the lines 'you shall soon come out of prison, and be delivered of that disease in which you find yourself', and, 'you shall be king again as you were before'. This letter was swiftly intercepted and pressed into the palms of Roger Mortimer.

Perhaps the archbishop of York and the earl of Kent were lied to by separate sources. Or perhaps they had fallen into a trap laid by Isabella and Mortimer. The measures taken against Edmund, and the speed with which they were enacted, would indicate the latter. Had

Isabella and Mortimer been sniffing out traitors to their regime, the sentiments expressed in Edmund's letter would be the sort of incriminating evidence they needed.

Its discovery resulted in uproar: Edmund was arrested and brought before Roger Mortimer, who appointed himself prosecutor. The earl was charged with treason for plotting to restore the former king to the throne. White-faced with horror, he had no defence – all he could do was confess and claim he had been seduced by the devil. But this desperate lie could not save him.

Nobody wanted to execute one of the sons of Edward I. Shivering in a thin shirt, Edmund was forced to wait outside the gates of Winchester while someone willing to carry out the merciless task of ending a prince's life was found. Daylight ebbed into darkness as hours went by. Eventually a convicted murderer was found, the only man happy to behead a man of royal blood in exchange for his own life. Edmund was decapitated and his severed head raised before the crowd as that of a traitor. His wife, Margaret, who was around nine months pregnant, and their children were imprisoned and stripped of all their belongings. Meanwhile, Melton managed to escape without punishment by pleading his constant loyalty to the queen.

In their desperation to cling to power and authority, Isabella and Mortimer had been driven to the kind of frenzied cruelty that had characterised the previous reign. A fog of suspicion and fear settled over the court. Spies littered the ports, watchful for foreign enemies or allies of the former king or murdered earl. Edward III was kept under close watch, spies lingering among his household staff, suffocating the young king and his now heavily pregnant young wife, Queen Philippa of Hainault, who was expecting her first baby, the future Edward of Woodstock. This proved to be Isabella and Mortimer's biggest mistake. As time ticked on and the Wheel spun again, Edward III grew more confident. By September 1330, almost eighteen and a new father, he was about to prove what type of king he could and would be by planning a coup of his own.

Edward had begun to quietly plot against his mother and Mortimer since 1329, when William Montagu – a household knight and friend of Edward II – had travelled to the papal city of Avignon to request an audience with Pope John XXII. Montagu informed the pope that Edward was being coerced by Isabella and Mortimer, seeking papal support against them. The pope agreed to help Edward and suggested that in order to distinguish Edward's voice from those of his mother and Mortimer, in letters the king should write 'Pater Sancte' (Holy Father) in his own handwriting so that it was clear that the communication was from Edward. Only four people were aware of the agreement between Edward and the pope: Edward himself, John XXII, Montagu and Richard Bury, keeper of the Privy Seal. Yet by September 1330 Mortimer had smelled a rat.

That autumn the court had moved to Nottingham Castle, where Isabella and Mortimer took up residence. The castle was a magnificent fortress built high on a rocky outcrop, resting above a network of caves and secret passageways known to the townspeople but not to the royal party. On 18 October, Mortimer summoned the king and a number of his household knights, including Montagu, to a meeting. As the fire crackled the atmosphere in the room was tense. Mortimer knew Edward was plotting something, he just did not know what. In a threatening tone, he accused the king of withholding secrets from his mother and himself. He interrogated each of Edward's friends one by one. When he came to Montagu, the young knight vehemently denied the suggestion that Edward would go against his duties as king. Itching for information, but without any real evidence, Mortimer had no choice other than to let them go.

Edward knew that Mortimer was at his most dangerous – paranoid and facing a steadily burning resentment from the nobility across the realm. He had executed the earl of Kent – a royal prince – and though never confirmed, Edward suspected that Mortimer had been the mastermind of his father's murder at Berkeley. He was not to be underestimated, but then neither was Edward, who was about to make his boldest move yet.

As twilight set in on 19 October 1330, Isabella and Mortimer called on their closest advisers to attend an intimate council. As the party kept warm by the fire inside the royal apartment, a contingent of young men gathered quietly at the foot of the castle walls. Feeling their way along the cold stone, through the warren of pitch-black passageways beneath the castle, they shuffled up to a doorway at the top, where the king was waiting. As Isabella and Mortimer continued their meeting, Edward silently admitted around twenty of his men into the belly of the candlelit fortress.

Swords in hand, they hurried to the chamber in which the dowager queen and her lover were conducting their meeting, voices muffled from the other side of the oak door. Bursting in, they overwhelmed Isabella, Mortimer and their guests. In shock, someone screamed out 'Traitors for nought!' while wielding a knife to strike the assailants. But before he could swing, he was knocked back and stabbed by a knight named John Neville, 'through the middle of the body'.[4] The fight become more aggressive and Isabella was roughly pushed to safety while Mortimer was grabbed by Edward's knights. As Mortimer struggled to free himself, Isabella is said to have wailed, 'Fair son, have pity on gentle Mortimer!' Edward had Mortimer dragged from the room to the sound of his mother's screams.[5] Hot-headed and fuelled by adrenaline, he wanted to have Mortimer hanged, but the earl of Lancaster counselled patience: Mortimer should be granted a trial. Once again, Mortimer was incarcerated in the Tower of London, his cell completely sealed so there was no way he could escape.

The principal accusation against Mortimer was that he had usurped the regency, encroached on royal power and kept the king's household in his grip.[6] As a woman, but mostly as the king's mother and a princess of France, Isabella was granted legal immunity and did not face the same charges, despite her active and equal participation in three chaotic years of regency. The outcome was familiar from the last twenty years of political bloodletting: Mortimer was to be executed. In a swift spin of Fortune's Wheel, he had crashed spectacularly and found himself robbed of all kingly pretence. Brought before an expectant crowd at Tyburn gallows, Mortimer was wearing the same black tunic he had worn at the funeral of Edward II. He was then publicly stripped naked and a noose was hung around his pale neck. In his final moments, Mortimer accepted his guilt for his part in the execution of the earl of Kent, a signal of what had finally prompted the young king to snap. Then he was strung up and hanged, the ignominious death of a common thief.

Isabella's fate was very different. After the coup, she was kept within the confines of Berkhamsted Castle where, under close guard, she had time to contemplate her future as a dowager queen. She would doubtlessly have mourned the loss of Mortimer and a relationship built on unity and mutual respect. But Isabella was, above all, a survivor.

The realm needed a leader like Edward III, who could bring stability after almost three decades of civil unrest. Years of infighting had resulted in a dramatic loss of life within the noble classes – a level of bloodshed that was unprecedented since the Norman Conquest. But what was it all for? The power that Edward II and Despenser enjoyed during their supremacy was coupled with a sense of panic and mistrust, so much so the king wore secret body armour beneath his shirt. The same can be said for Isabella and Mortimer. What did their regime achieve? Other than brutality against their enemies – the most shocking of all, the likely murder of the former king himself. Their later treatment of another royal prince, Edward II's younger half-brother Edmund, earl of Kent, evidenced the final collapse of reverence for the noble houses that had helped establish and govern the realm, but also the collapse of morality. Unknowingly, the terrified Isabella and Mortimer became the architects of their own downfall. As Mortimer stood, freezing on the scaffold as Edmund, earl of Kent, had done, he acknowledged his part in that cruelty. Where he had thoughtlessly cast judgement at the top of the Wheel of Fortune, he became a victim of his own making as the Wheel turned and he was crushed beneath it.

The fall of the king and the rise of Isabella and Mortimer is a startling example of how necessary the traditional structures of power were in the fourteenth century. Without a hierarchy in place, power could be snatched. But once it had been snatched, the fear of losing it again obliterated people's consciences. By deposing a king, Isabella and Mortimer created a power vacuum but did not fill it with much more than paranoia and ruthlessness – in their lust for authority and fear of falling they created their own tyranny.

Isabella knew she had lost, but she lived to witness the spectacular growth of her son. Edward III was raised in her image, and his reign, fresh from the shackles of regency, would cast a light over the kingdom as if it were a new dawn, smashing the Wheel of Fortune and beginning an age of unity, chivalry and conquest.

PART THREE

Arthur and Saint George

'For a boar of Cornwall shall give his assistance, and trample
their necks under his feet. The islands of the ocean shall be
subject to his power, and he shall possess the forests of Gaul.
The house of Romulus shall dread his courage, and his
end shall be doubtful.'

Merlin's Prophecy, Cambridge, Corpus Christi College, MS 476

13.   Arthur Redivivus

Edward III was a natural political leader. His modus operandi was to share power, not hoard it. Edward had the remarkable ability to command adoration from his nobility by giving them value and shared incentive as brothers in arms. In doing so he strengthened his own power and that of the realm. For the noble classes, after years of war and the loss of land and loved ones, the age of Edward was like the light at the end of a long and dark tunnel. A king with a natural flair for self-propaganda, he quickly adopted a personal emblem of beams of sunlight bursting through cloud and wind, as if revealing itself as a celestial prophecy – the hidden sun had risen – that symbolised the fact that his reign was a new dawn.

Tall, lean and athletic, naturally well built for the physical lifestyle he enjoyed, Edward had a swaggering charisma, exuding energy and a can-do attitude to kingship. Beloved by his friends, he was already Arthur 'redivivus' – Arthur 'reborn', an idea stemming from the popular Prophecies of Merlin. It was timely that a version of Merlin's Prophecy, *The Last Six Kings of the English* or *The Last Six Kings to Follow John*, appeared around the time he became king. Arthur, the model of kingship is described as the 'boar of Cornwall', the leader who liberated the Britons from the invading Saxons, thus beginning the Arthurian narrative. Edward I was the dragon, Edward II the goat and then, 'after this goat, shall come out of Windsor a Boar, that shall have a head of wit, a lion's heart' and that 'he shall wet his teeth upon the gates of Paris'. It was suggested that Edward III would be this 'boar'.[1]

This type of prophetic propaganda was helpful but Edward had an unimaginably difficult task on his hands. He wanted to reinvigorate the realm, recover authority in Scotland and reinstate England as a major political power on the map of Christendom, just as it had been under his most powerful Plantagenet ancestors.

Edward's natural popularity was helpful. Unlike his father, who was drawn towards scheming favourites, Edward surrounded himself with a variety of loyal young knights with similar values and interests. The ousting of Mortimer shifted the atmosphere at the English court almost overnight: youthful masculine jubilance succeeded dangerous, cold suspicion.

By the end of 1330 Edward III had not only claimed his power, but he had turned eighteen and welcomed a son and heir, a new Plantagenet prince. His son Edward had been born that summer at his and Queen Philippa of Hainault's favourite countryside residence, Woodstock in Oxfordshire. Peaceful, green and quiet, this was a place that felt safe, so much so this palace was selected as the location of the royal nursery. The new prince was named after his father – Edward the Confessor, a patron saint of England, or possibly in the memory of his grandfather. With Mortimer dead and his mother under watchful eyes at Berkhamsted, the king was in the mood to celebrate.

The Christmas festivities held at Guildford were the perfect opportunity for Edward III to put on a spectacle, offering his loyal knights and young new courtiers a chance to enjoy his favourite pastime: the tournament. Jousts were held outside in specially constructed lists – fenced arenas – and indoor sports were played by courtiers in the great hall of the castle, presided over by the young king and queen. Tournaments and jousting were always a major part of medieval court life, but this was particularly true of the reign of Edward III. As a form of training for military combat, they served a dual purpose: enhancing physical skills but also creating unity, sportsmanship, discipline and cohesion. Combatants could enrich themselves by ransoming or capturing horses from their opponents, but above all these tournaments provided an opportunity to boast knightly prowess before an audience.

The first months of Edward's independence were played out against the backdrop of a series of these tournaments. The subtext was rehabilitation. Edward had inherited a realm riven with problems. The nobility that made up the court circle, as well as the main body of parliament, had been ruptured, seemingly beyond repair, with every old noble family scarred. In order to heal old wounds Edward had to become a clarion of hope, a beacon of kingship.

In December 1330, Edward took his queen on a pilgrimage to Glastonbury, the putative site of King Arthur's remains, which had been interred there by his grandfather. Edward must have been impressed at the spectacle of Arthur's vast black marble tomb, balanced on the backs of four crouching lions at the head of the abbey, now glittering with wealth thanks to its prized relics. Yet, despite the Arthurian cult circulating at court, identifying himself *too* closely with Arthur was, Edward knew, problematic. By casting himself as the legendary king, Mortimer had invited criticism. Since childhood Edward had witnessed the fractures of government, civil war and familial murder. He knew that retaining the nobility's support was crucial to the success of his reign. Reinvigorating Arthur in his image through tournaments and pageants, Arthur *reborn*, was something Edward enjoyed but was careful not to over-egg.

In early pageants and tournaments, Edward compared himself more frequently to Sir Lionel, one of Arthur's knights. He placed himself on the same level as his contemporaries, forging a fraternity that was not only unbreakable but aspirational. The efforts Edward made in his early reign would pay off. He demonstrated no clear favouritism and encouraged his nobility to participate in the jubilance and competition of the tournaments. These tournaments were theatres of war, spaces to refine the military skills of the nobility and forge unity on the field. All of this would prove fundamental in Edward's first campaign, against the age-old enemy, the Scots.

The peace in Scotland procured by Isabella and Mortimer was, in the most northern parts of the realm, still considered to be a 'shameful peace'. After three decades of raids, communities across Northumberland, Cumberland and even parts of Yorkshire were left wasted and demoralised. The parchment of chronicles and ballads coming out of the far north, a land desperate for liberation after decades of suffering, was decorated with fragments of the Arthurian fable. Whispers and prophecies spilled across the border, in ink and spoken word, that Arthur was reborn and he would free the north as he once had the Britons. All eyes were on Edward. How would he act? When would he act? In 1332, he was handed the perfect opportunity to restore England's authority.

That year, James Douglas embarked on a personal crusade to the Holy Land, to carry out Robert Bruce's dying wish – to bury his heart at the Holy Sepulchre church in Jerusalem. But James Douglas – together with Robert Bruce's heart – never made it to Jerusalem. On his journey to the Holy Land, Douglas was invited to join Alfonso XI, king of Castile and Léon, in his fight against the Moors in southern Spain. Far from Scotland or Jerusalem, Douglas was killed in a skirmish, with Bruce's heart encased in a silver casket around his neck. Robert Bruce's heir was the six-year-old David II. David was far too young to rule, and without the presence of figures such as James Douglas, who was a major leader in the Scottish resistance, for the first time in decades the Scots were in an incredibly vulnerable position. In late summer 1332, under cover of darkness, waves of English soldiers led by Edward Balliol swam through the depths of the River Earn south-west of Perth. As the son of John Balliol, the disgraced king of Scotland, he had his own claim to the throne. Under the agreement of Edward III, his opportunistic army, known as the 'Disinherited', was made up of the old families pushed out of Scotland by Bruce in 1314.

The Scots were led by Donald, earl of Mar, the hastily appointed guardian. The two opposing armies met at Dupplin Moor in August 1332. Although the Disinherited were completely outnumbered by Scottish infantry, luck was on their side. A series of bad decisions made by the earl of Mar handed them the initiative. English longbows rained arrows onto Scots who had been sent on a reckless charge into battle. As the dead piled up, the Scottish charge became a crush. More Scots suffocated to death than were bloodied by the enemy that day. Victorious, Edward Balliol was crowned at Scone. However, the earl of Mar remained defiant. Skirmishes between the Bruce faction of Scots and the Disinherited took place constantly until a winter truce was agreed. Edward Balliol bedded in at Annan Castle for Christmas festivities but was woken in the middle of the night by Mar's men hammering down its door. Balliol fled into the darkness, wearing only his nightclothes. Desperate for help, he hastened towards England and the aid of Edward III.

The January parliament was held at York, where it was deemed necessary to stress that 'no games' should be played within the vicinity of the proceedings, presumably nobody wanted to be distracted by the sounds of people enjoying themselves.[2] Business was urgent, for developments north of the border demanded action from Edward. The hope was that the Disinherited would be restored and the 'shameful peace' annihilated, but no English army had been victorious in Scotland since the reign of Edward I. If Edward III was to win, he needed counsel and experienced men to guide him. The archbishop of York, the bishop of Norwich, Sir Henry Percy, Sir William Clinton, Sir William of Denum and William of Shareshull, 'enterprising and warlike men, keen to repair their dented prestige'[3] formed a makeshift Scotland-focused counsel and all government administration was shifted from Westminster to York. Abandoned in the reign of Edward II, northern communities were finally front and centre of the royal interest. Edward III's recovery of English territory and overlordship of Scotland would begin with reclaiming the most important – and most contested – garrison town on the Anglo-Scottish border, Berwick-upon-Tweed. The focus on Berwick was not coincidental. After Balliol's successes – which would never have been possible without the sanctioning of his campaign by the English king – he performed homage to Edward III and issued letters outlining what he would offer in thanks. It was agreed that the king would be given land south of the River Forth – an extensive portion of Scotland – along with the castle, town and country of Berwick.[4] With his administration in order, Edward could muster an army. In early April 1333, Edward III marched towards Durham at the head of a large retinue.

Prior to his advance into Northumberland, the king had written to the bishop of Durham likely exaggerating the situation, claiming that 'all the men of the liberty of Durham . . . between the ages of sixteen and sixty years . . . be arrayed [for war] . . . as aforesaid before the said day, because a rumour has reached the king that the Scots intend shortly to invade the kingdom.'[5] The same order was dispatched across Yorkshire, Derby, Nottingham and Lancashire. As Edward reached the gates of Durham, he brought with him the men he had summoned to do battle, a vast horde of young and old, wearing armour if they could afford it. But this was not the full bulk of the army. Thousands of troops were preparing to advance north from the Welsh Marches, Gloucestershire, Shropshire, Leicester and Warwickshire, along with the battle-hardened and eager men of Northumberland, Cumberland, Durham and Westmorland. Packed with skilled longbowmen – wielding England's most deadly weapon – as well as mounted archers, this was a formidable force.

In the middle of May 1333, Edward III arrived at Berwick-upon-Tweed having ensured the security of the newly pregnant Queen Philippa, at Bamburgh Castle in Northumberland. The siege of Berwick was well under way, with Edward Balliol and his men having surrounded the town. Their tents were pitched in the mud, protected by two ditches, the first to specifically enclose the encampment and the second to cut off all supplies to the town.[6] The favourable progress of the siege was partly thanks to the timely recruitment of a Flemish merchant and pirate named John Crabb. Formerly loyal to the Scottish, Crabb had fought against the English at Berwick in 1319, before being captured. Edward saw that Crabb, with his inside knowledge of the town and fortress, was too useful to be locked up or killed. The king set Crabb to work out how to break the defence of the town, commissioning two vast siege engines, manufactured from oak grown in Cowick in Yorkshire. Their production necessitated felling forty trees and employing twenty-four oxen to lug the load to the manor at Cowick, where the engines were built. There a team of carpenters got to work producing two juggernauts designed to smash through stone walls with incredible force. Almost seven hundred stone boulders, cut and chipped into shape by forty stonemasons, provided the ammunition, all loaded onto three ships that sailed from Hull to Berwick.

Clouds of dust and flying rock formed a smog around Berwick as these boulders were hurled into the walls of the town. The town was also hammered by cannons. Soon its church, great hall and tower had been crushed by Edward's siege. The Scots holding the town responded by attempting to destroy the English naval force – which at high tide floated close to its walls. They soaked bundles of dry kindling in tar before lighting them and launching them onto the decks of the ships. But this plan backfired. In late June, the flames turned with the wind, catching wooden ramparts and engulfing parts of Berwick, forcing the defenders to agree that if the town had not been liberated after a two-week truce period, they would surrender. Thomas Seton, the son of the town's governor, Sir Alexander Seton, was handed over to Edward as a hostage to secure the truce.

The siege had been progressing well – the townspeople were exhausted and Berwick itself was crumbling under the constant barrage of rock and fire. But the king was growing impatient and so were his men. Maintaining a large army, one that would dramatically alter the power balance in Scotland, was a near-impossible task. The men, bored by the siege, proved difficult to manage and as the bombardment ran on many deserted. In anticipation of a midsummer Scottish attack, Edward wrote an exasperated letter to the chancellor at York in early June. He said he was 'molt senglement' (completely alone) and that he needed more men urgently.[7] This was likely in anticipation of a Scottish force that had been sent to liberate Berwick.

On 11 July, the last day of the truce period, the Scottish army, led by Archibald Douglas, advanced towards Tweedmouth and came in sight of the English army. The full might of the Scottish force – around twenty thousand men – did not march to Berwick, but a contingent of two hundred mounted troops did. Archibald Douglas informed Edward that this was his relief force and the English king must end the siege or Douglas would attack England with his larger army. Hedging his bets, Edward did not move and told the Scots to do their worst – a bold move considering his pregnant queen was waiting in Bamburgh Castle in Northumberland. According to Edward the truce agreement had been breached: Berwick had not been liberated, nor had the town surrendered. The ultimatum was raised: surrender or hostages would be sacrificed. A tall gallows was erected outside the smoking town walls, blackened by tar and fire. Sir Alexander and Lady Seton were forced to watch as their only surviving son – their other boy, William, had been killed while trying to overcome English ships – was strung up and hanged from the neck. Edward threatened to do the same to every hostage he had taken until Berwick was his. According to the Scottish chronicler Andrew of Wyntoun, Lady Seton counselled her husband that their son had died in honour. It seems unlikely that she was as patriotic and stoic as this story suggests, but the trauma of the appalling situation would have been unbearable. Unable to withstand the threat of further slaughter, the defenders of Berwick soon negotiated. A fresh truce was brokered: if the Scottish force had not defeated the English in pitched battle by 19 July, Berwick would surrender. The defenders of Berwick were aware of the size of Douglas's army, which near doubled Edward's. With Bannockburn being in recent memory, perhaps they thought a Scottish victory was possible. Yet unlike his father at Bannockburn, Edward III was a military mastermind, and a battle was exactly what he hoped for. Fortunately for Edward III, decisive action was about to unfold at nearby Halidon Hill.

On the morning of 19 July 1333, English scouts spotted a large army approaching the north summit of a steep crest known as Witches Knowe. Leaving half of his troops to continue the siege at Berwick, Edward ordered the movement of the other half to meet the Scottish forces head-on. The English arrayed in three formations at the crest of the hill, with archers flanking either side like wings of a bird. Edward III led the central division, with the earl of Norfolk and Edward Balliol commanding the divisions on either side. Rather than launch the traditional line of cavalry into the enemy, Edward ordered his men to dismount.[8] The English lined up on the opposite hill to the Scots, who positioned themselves, also on foot, at the crest of Witches Knowe. Between them was a ditch, the earth sodden with rainwater. The English location was a good one, so long as the Scots were riled up enough to charge towards them. Edward needed a strong position, for the Scottish army was far superior in size, outnumbering the English three to one. Unwilling to flee, he gave a triumphant speech. He 'rode about everywhere among his army and encouraged his men well and nobly, and generously promised them good reward'.[9]

The Scottish army soon caught sight of Edward Balliol, to the left of the English line. Determined to vanquish the man they considered not only a threat but a pretender, the bulk of the army went left, charging straight into a mass of arrows. In a stroke of tactical genius, Edward had arranged his arrows to shoot into the enemy from either side rather than head-on, claiming them in deadly crossfire. Pelted by arrows, the Scottish division aiming for Balliol 'were so grievously wounded in the face and blinded by the host of English archery . . . that they were helpless, and quickly began to turn away their faces from the arrow flights and to fall'.[10] Seeing the rest of their army routed, the surviving Scots fled back to their horses pursued by the king and his English knights, who ran them down. As a result, 'there might men see many a Scotsman cast down onto the earth dead, and their banners displayed, and hacked into pieces, and many a good halberd of steel bathed in their blood.'[11] The victory at Halidon Hill meant that Edward had won back English supremacy, at least south of Edinburgh, and Edward Balliol was temporarily secure on the throne of Scotland, answerable to the king of England as his feudal overlord.

During Edward's reign there would never be permanent peace with Scotland, for rebel armies would continue to revive the spectre of Robert Bruce and fight for independence. However, having achieved respite on the border and placed a Scottish king loyal to the English on the throne, Edward III had achieved an English victory in Scotland, which had not been seen since the Battle of Falkirk in 1298.

During the course of just one campaign, Edward III had overturned decades of Bruce's careful politics and allowed English lords to recover their ancient inheritance, political agency and personal power. Berwick was once again in English hands, its people bruised by siege after siege and homes singed by fire and smoke. Edward considered Scotland pacified, for now at least, but he was not complacent. He knew that his enemies not only lurked across the borderlands that flanked England, but over the Channel too. When Edward III was forced to consider England's relationship with France, which had bullied his father into a subservient feudal role, he saw a glittering opportunity to excel as king and conqueror. Like 'Arthur', he might prove to be the saviour of the realm.

14. The Age of Chivalry

In full plate armour and a surcoat emblazoned with the quartered arms of England and France, Edward III is crowned and enthroned balancing a large sword over his shoulder. His son, Prince Edward, kneels before his father, also wearing a quartered surcoat displaying the French motif, the fleur-de-lis, flanking the leopards of England. It is a purported likeness of Edward III, designed to propagate his image as a chivalrous king: armed, powerful and regal. As a part of a manuscript, this image represents Edward's vision of kingship, all contained inside a small, illuminated initial E for Edward.[1] In this miniature portrait, Edward III projects his main ambition in life from 1337. He sought to forge a united realm with a body of chivalric warriors at its helm: pious, loyal and valorous, these were selected from the finest noblemen England had to offer. With their help, Edward wanted to do what no other English king before him had attempted – conquer France.

Edward's uncle and the last of the Capetian line of kings, Charles IV, had died in 1328, at just thirty-three, leaving no male heir to succeed him. As a result, France was plunged into a succession crisis and Edward III had an arguably promising claim, through his mother, the late king's sister. All that stood between him and the tantalising prospect of ruling both England and France was a piece of ancient bureaucracy: a sixth-century law that forbade the accession of a new monarch through birthright on his mother's side. Instead, the next possible claimant was chosen through the male line. This was Charles's cousin, Philip of Valois, whose reign began a new dynasty in France, the Valois. Edward III reluctantly accepted the new king but found the feudal requirement to perform homage unbearable, missing his deadline for the 'homage' ceremony in 1330. Edward then began to interest himself in the political details of feudal tenure around Gascony, English land in France, rejecting the feudal laws that subjugated English kings to the French.[2] Reflecting on the history of his Plantagenet ancestors, Edward formed the notion that previous kings of France had meddled enough to cause 'damage and dishonour' to the 'nation of England'.[3] By this Edward presumably meant the suzerainty of French kings over the English since King John lost English-held lands to French forces in the early thirteenth century. Edward would no longer bend his knee to a French king – particularly one he considered to be illegitimate. Edward wanted sovereignty over Gascony.

In order to distract the headstrong king of England from his preoccupation with Gascony, and paper over any cracks in their relationship, Philip VI invited Edward to crusade with him to the Holy Land in the early 1330s. It was a clever idea. Edward III had in his possession family crusading memorabilia which included the helmet of Saladin – the former sultan of Egypt and Syria and a leading figure in the Third Crusade – and a knife used against Edward I at Acre. A crusade following in the footsteps of his ancestral giants would have been tempting. Diplomats went back and forth across the Channel, both courts humming with talk of a great fleet bound for Outremer (the four feudal states as established after the First Crusade across the Levant), until the plan to travel east was cancelled in March 1336. The cost had grown untenable, the Ottomans were gaining strength in the east and Edward began to try to barter Philip's desire for him to join the crusade with his granting him sovereignty of Gascony. Philip would not cede his power as feudal overlord in Gascony and Edward had no interest in crusading when it was not on his terms. The added complexity was that France had been loyal allies to the Bruce dynasty in Scotland, which meant Edward III – by placing Balliol back on the throne – had indirectly attacked the French. As relations broke down into the 1330s between England and France, Philip VI sent the very fleet he had prepared for the Holy Land out of France and in the direction of Scotland.

French involvement in Scotland threatened to undermine everything Edward had achieved so far. If Philip aided the Scots, it would mean England was under threat of invasion. Anticipating attack, Edward dispatched eight thousand infantry to patrol the coastline.

During the first parliament of the year in March 1337, the prospect
of war weighed heavily on the minds of the clergy and the nobility. Edward created six earldoms in this session. Land that had been
forfeited to the Crown in the tumultuous years between Despenser's
downfall and Mortimer's execution was divided up among Edward's
closest and most loyal friends.[4] Edward's purpose was not favouritism but was, rather, a pragmatic move: he knew that strengthening
the relationship between the king and the nobility would in turn
strengthen the realm and enable it to withstand the strain of war.
The moment Edward III had been waiting for finally came in May
1337 when Philip VI confiscated Gascony, giving Edward reason to
declare the start of what became known as the Hundred Years War.

A war of succession, the Hundred Years War spanned the reigns of
five generations of kings. In a series of conflicts over trade and territory, European powers such as Flanders and Iberia were also dragged
into the fight, and despite a series of truces and treaties, it raged well
into the fifteenth century. Though the war ended in 1453, threats to
resume the fight between nations lingered on into the sixteenth century. It all began over a trivial incident, but with England and France
a hair's breadth away from conflict it was all that was needed. Edward
III provoked Philip VI by refusing to return a French dissenter
named Robert of Artois, who he had been harbouring in the English
court for the previous two years. Artois, Philip VI's brother-in-law,
had forged his late father's will and rather than attend his summons
by the king, he fled France for England. He feared that if he returned,
he might be imprisoned or worse.

In response, Philip confiscated Gascony, claiming that Edward was
in breach of his obligations. This was Edward's prompt, in September 1337, to finally assert that *he* was the rightful heir to the throne
of France, through his mother. Naturally, Edward sought to demonstrate his new claim through imagery. The English arms – the three
leopards – were quartered with the fleur-de-lis: the leopard and the lily
placed together to represent Edward's kingship. The king's new arms
were displayed across the realm, on banners, flags and on parchment
in manuscripts and administrative records like charters. Establishing
a visual representation of kingship by these means was as essential to

the war as steel and bloodletting. Edward spent the first three years of the war persuading parliament that war was needed to protect England, and travelling across the Low Countries, from Antwerp to Ghent, raising allies and funds. By 1340 he had managed to convince the wealthy Flemish statesman Jacob van Artevelde – who made his money in the English wool trade – to recognise him as the rightful king of France. The proclamation was made in the town square on an ice-cold morning in Ghent before a vast crowd of onlookers. Edward's ambition was shared by his family. Queen Philippa, heavily pregnant, endured the arduous and rough journeying across the Low Countries to join her husband. Over the course of two years, she gave birth twice abroad. First to Lionel, born in Antwerp in 1338, then John of Gaunt, born in Ghent in 1340, shortly before Edward's first major victory of the war.

In late June 1340 the king led a fleet of around one hundred and fifty fishing vessels and cog ships – used for both trade and battle – into the Channel. A naval force of two hundred French vessels blocked access to the port of Sluys situated on the inlet between Zealand and West Flanders, and in order to access the port for trade and connection to his allies, Edward was forced to break through. As both naval forces clashed, English archers picked off the French one by one while soldiers leapt onto enemy vessels, attacking them with swords, axes and even rocks. Just as at Halidon Hill, it was the arrows that won Edward his victory: 'a rain of iron bolts from crossbows and arrows from bows sent thousands to their deaths'.[5] Sea battles in the Middle Ages were a barbaric form of combat, with high levels of mortality. Unable to flee the scene, those overcome by their opponents were most often lost to the depths of the sea. The Battle of Sluys was a devastating outcome for French soldiers. Bloated corpses washed up on the beaches of Flanders, marking the beginning of a new era of terror in France and marking the Channel as English territory.

By 1343 the master of the Royal Mint in London was being kept busy overseeing the process of casting a new line of gold coins that would commemorate the Battle of Sluys. Heating and hammering, shaving and clipping, they cast the molten gold into perfect circles.

On one side of the gold noble glinted the traditional floriated cross flanked by four gold crowns, encircled by 'Edwardus', but on the reverse was a new image, of the king standing inside his warship with his sword drawn. It was hoped that these gold nobles would fill the purses of the great and the good of English society.

In the 1340s, Edward's staggering success on the battlefield was transmuted, through a series of tournaments, into a piece of theatre for the royal court. The tournaments allowed young men to parade their skills before a rapt crowd and make battle look glorious, even appealing – modelling the virtue of chivalry in action. It was entirely propaganda, making the war in France look attractive, but it worked – everybody wanted to be involved. One chronicler from Bohemia observed, 'there came to the king the young sons of certain barons, saying, more out of lightheartedness than earnestness, "Lord king, to spread your fame through tournaments and hastiludes, order a round table in the fashion of King Arthur's court, and the glory of it shall be recorded for all times." '[6] The idea was to mirror the fictional court of Camelot. Edward's political ambition thrummed alongside the Arthurian legends deeply embedded in popular culture. This, and the promise of fame and chivalric glory, rendered the tournaments he held utterly irresistible. The most impressive of them all was the one held in 1344 at Windsor Castle.

A seat of kings since the twelfth century, Windsor perched upon a steep chalk edifice overlooking woodland and marsh with a view stretching out across the River Thames towards London. It was there that under the brown fog of deepest winter in January 1344, Edward decided to throw a tournament.

Invitations were dispatched to 'the ladies of the Southern part of England and to the wives of the citizens of London'.[7] Edward wanted the presence of not only the elite nobility but the wealthiest citizens of London in the growing merchant class. The main focus for the next three days was the joust and the melee. The melee was a 'safe' pitched battle, where all arms were acceptable as long as they were blunted. Fought on foot, fully armoured knights would do battle, swinging their axes, swords or maces, dipping, ducking and dodging. The joust was equally violent, with two fully armoured knights on horseback stationed opposite each other, each with a six-foot lance, blunted by a three-point metal coronal. With the wave of a flag they would launch their horses into full gallop, lower the lance and aim at the face, or more generously the shield, of their opponent.[8] Scores were judged on the location of the blow and the dramatic effect – ideally the lance would splinter into thousands of shards. For Edward, the joust served as a way of both applauding the individual achievements of his nobility, and emphasising the prestige and importance of camaraderie and unity in combat. Jousting had been a mainstay sport among the nobility since the eleventh century and knights would travel across northern Europe to participate, both training for war and building prestige in doing so. Further to this, it was interwoven with the cult around Arthur and his knights. In the thirteenth century, a young knight named Ulrich von Liechtenstein from Styria (now southern Austria) travelled from Venice to Bohemia competing in various tournaments. From a politically influential family, Ulrich had been raised to excel in the art of war. Ulrich later composed an epic autobiographical poem, a combination of romantic fiction and fact, called *Frauendienst* (The Service of Ladies). In the poem, Ulrich boasts of his immense success, breaking over three hundred lances in the space of five weeks and jousting up to eight times a day. Importantly, however, one of the memories Ulrich recounts of his success was his part in a 'round table'.

> Anyone who broke three faultless spears
> Against me in the joust, he is a man
> Who may once have been remote from me
> But now his place at the round table takes.[9]

Ulrich's version of a round table was figurative rather than literal. Knights would form the defence – which they called a round table – against the 'comers' (the attackers). These round-table concept tournaments, interweaving popular romance literature with masculinity, sport and war, gained popularity, peaking in the fourteenth century with Edward and his own knights. But for Edward this Arthurian link went further than sport, it became a part of the fabric of his court, made formal at the Windsor tournament.

On the Thursday morning, near the end of the festivities at Windsor, the king is said to have 'caused himself to be solemnly arrayed in his most royal and festive attire', wearing a velvet mantle and his regalia, including his crown – robes he had made specially for the occasion. The ceremony at the end of Mass in the chapel at Windsor Castle was akin to a coronation. The king left the chapel followed by Henry, earl of Derby, and William Montagu, earl of Salisbury, who both carried the staff of office in their hands. The king carried the royal sceptre. The queen duly followed until everyone in the chapel, intrigued as to what was going on, flooded towards 'the place appointed for the assembly'. The king was then presented with a Bible and, planting his hand firmly on its vellum cover, he swore that, providing he 'had the necessary means', he would begin a round table 'in the same manner and condition as Arthur, formerly king of England, established it'. Promising the inclusion of around three hundred knights in his fraternity, Edward's oath was sealed with the sound of trumpets and drums before the guests 'hastened to a feast, where richness of fare, variety of dishes and overflowing abundance of drinks were all to be found, to their unutterable delight'.[10]

The whole scenario had been cleverly staged by Edward III. He had been careful to send invitations not only to the nobility but also to the increasingly influential and wealthy merchant classes, whose money he needed to endorse and fund his war in France. The reinvigoration of a round table at Windsor Castle in turn reinvigorated Edward's position as 'Arthur Redivivus' – this was a call to arms with the promise of great reward. In evoking Arthur, his knights and the round table, Edward created a sacred military order loyal to the king. People aspired to a place at the king's round table, which contributed to a new and growing sense of nationalism and belonging, with Edward III at its head.[11] This spectacle was politically savvy: Edward was running out of money and he needed to recruit men locally from the realm to build his army. Convincing the nobility and wealthy classes that war in France was essential was one thing, but recruiting laymen, mostly those who manned the ports or worked the land, to put down their scythes and pick up swords, was a monumental administrative effort – he had to offer a wage but also convince them that they were fighting not as feudal vassals, but in defence of their country.

In 1345, Edward decided it was time a new census was taken. Royal officials roamed the country stopping at every town and village to take stock of the landowning population, their interests firmly on the able-bodied men of the realm. In order to procure much-needed funds for his war, Edward turned to the Church and the taxpayer. Clergy were squeezed for their wealth and towns were taxed, assessed on a case-by-case basis. Edward's reasoning was that the war was a national effort.

The tax levied to fund the war helped, but what Edward really needed was men. In early 1346 he and his government made a radical decision. It was ordered that men of the realm would be made to fight not on English soil, but in France, defending the rights of the king, as if France was also his land that needed protecting.[12] All able-bodied men were assembled for war, allocated wages, and those who could not or would not (with due reason) were forced to pay a fine covering their absence. Edward even bent the rules to recruit those who had committed 'trespass' – any crimes – arguing that 'they are now about to set out in the king's service in his present passage, and as he cannot now dispense with their service.'[13]

Medieval kings relied on their nobility to help them recruit their armies. By 1346, Edward III's household had almost one hundred members, split into two groups: the household bannerets and the simple household knights.[14] The bannerets had a superior social status, were awarded a higher rate of pay and had the ability to lead men into battle. They were also entitled to carry a banner emblazoned with their coats of arms, highlighting their station and singling them out from the simple household knights. These household knights played an important part in Edward's feasting and jousts, celebrating Arthur and chivalry, but their position also served another important purpose. Knights were dispatched across the realm to procure fighting men, and 'supervisors of the array' were specifically appointed to ensure these soldiers were mustered in the right location and armed with the appropriate weapons.

By spring 1346, the English government was preparing the largest invasion of the century. Royal residences were used to store supplies, but the Tower of London, as London's military bastion, was the main arsenal. Thousands of arrows were stacked inside the armoury, along with quivers to hold them.

Food enough to feed an army of thousands was a major part of preparation and goods were accrued from as far as Yorkshire. Immense quantities of weapons and foodstuffs such as grain were accumulated as Edward's government busied itself with proclamations reminding the men of the realm of their duty to defend and protect it.

Remarkably, through charisma and careful propaganda, Edward had managed to convince a kingdom and its government to fund a war and fight for their king and country, in the belief that they were defending themselves. This achievement was the result of powerful political rhetoric that endorsed unity and nationhood, enhanced by the romances of Arthur and his knights. To those involved, Edward promised great things: chivalry, glory, triumph in war. In late June, Edward III led a fleet out of Portsmouth, his ships packed with men, horses and thousands upon thousands of arrows.[15] Cutting through the water, the coast of Normandy was soon visible. With his eye on the thin stretch of beach in the distance, Edward was about to begin the most famous invasion of France in medieval history.

15. Ich Dien

As Edward's warships dropped anchor off the beach of Saint-Vaast-la-Hougue on 11 July 1346, men leapt into the rough, grey water of the Channel, beginning the monumental task of unloading the vessels of their weighty cargo. Horses kicked through the deeper water until they reached the safety of the shallows. Small boats made trips between the ships and the shore, where Edward's men amassed. French scouts had been patrolling the coastline until English ships were spied on the horizon. Hearing the news of imminent invasion, the marshal of southern Normandy and captain of the sea frontier, Robert Bertrand, could do little but gather a small but futile resistance using local men.[1] As the first ships landed, the French, hiding behind the dunes, launched a brief attack but were quickly driven off by English arrows. The rest of Bertrand's force fled. Five hundred men were no match against the fourteen thousand troops that began to swarm from English warships onto the beach.

Around midday the king, his surcoat emblazoned with the quartered arms of England and France, disembarked and immediately fell face-first into the wet sand. Horrified, his men stooped to help but Edward was well versed in using an uncomfortable situation to his favour. Laughing off his clumsiness, he called the incident an omen: France had welcomed its king.[2] Edward was au fait with his own history, for William the Conqueror had fallen as he landed in England to claim the throne. It was likely another staged piece of propaganda to install a fatalistic belief that Edward would win.

Following his stumble, Edward climbed a steep, sandy hill overlooking the vast stretch of beach. In his usual public display of chivalry and spectacle he made a point of knighting his first-born son, the Prince of Wales, Edward of Woodstock – later known as the Black Prince.

Kneeling before his father and an audience of thousands of

soldiers, sixteen-year-old Edward was dubbed a knight of the realm. As Edward III's eldest son, the prince was heir to the throne and the king wanted a successor who was his mirror image – both a warrior and a leader. By performing the *adoubement* – the dubbing ceremony – in front of an army of Englishmen, the king was making his son a role model for the other young men of his campaign. The ceremony itself served another purpose. Entering the chivalric order affirmed an individual's obligations before an audience of fellow knights, but it also served as a necessary boost of confidence before the endurance test of a campaign.[3]

With knighthood came immediate responsibility. The king charged his son with leading the vanguard; his division would drive the army through hostile France. In the face of danger, the prince would be expected to fight his way out. That said, he was not expected to learn blindly. Two experienced captains were appointed to guide and protect him if necessary. It was decided that the other two divisions would be led by the king and Thomas Hatfield, a former royal clerk who had recently been promoted to bishop of Durham. But what was unclear was where they would lead them to. Over the next few days Edward III devised a plan that would draw Philip VI into pitched battle, using devastating attacks on horseback against common folk. This was destructive warfare, feared by communities across France, becoming known as the *chevauchée*.

Edward III left the beach of La Hougue in late July with the Black Prince riding ahead in the vanguard. The army burned and pillaged their way inland through Caen towards Paris. In villages such as Valognes, people put up no resistance in exchange for their lives, which were spared, even if their homes fell to flames. At Caen, the wealthy Norman town, strategically important to the defence of the Normandy coastline, the army met armed townspeople supported by Genoese crossbowmen. But such was the strength of Edward's army that even a fortified town such as Caen was taken in a single day.[4]

By mid-August Edward had marched his army to Poissy, so close to the walls of Paris that its terrified citizens could see the smoke from English campfires on the horizon. The invasion had started well. Paris was in uproar, stockpiling small rocks to hurl at English attackers should they attempt to besiege the city. Five hundred soldiers were deployed to try to regain order among the chaos.

Philip VI had not sat idle while Edward torched his country but he was still ill-prepared. Men at arms were scattered across France commanding small garrisons and the main bulk of the army was engaged in besieging the Gascon town of Aiguillon. In order to gather his men quickly Philip had employed the only strategy available to him: slowing down the English in an attempt to prevent further destruction of France. As English soldiers swept through towns and villages outside Paris, turning verdant summer crops grey with ash, Philip mustered his men at Saint-Denis, a town north of Paris, under the sacred battle standard of France, the Oriflamme.

But when the two sides eventually clashed it was not outside Paris but further north, for Edward III, despite his bravado, knew victory sometimes depended on running away.[5] The closer his army drew towards the gates of Paris, the deeper he was moving his men into French territory − closer to French supplies and even French reinforcements. So, as the gates of Paris creaked open and Philip's army rode out, cavalry and men decked out for battle, Edward swung his army round and fled north. The French army chased Edward's tail, their numbers growing in size as they recruited more men from across the realm. The French had around twenty-six thousand soldiers, including the addition of Genoese crossbowmen. Philip ordered that all bridges available to the English should be broken down, trapping Edward between Le Crotoy and Abbeville. With the French marching hard and fast, the gap between the two armies began to close, so much that at Airaines the French army were able to enjoy the hot meal that Edward hadn't had time to eat before he had been forced to flee.

Low on supplies and delirious from weeks of travelling over two hundred miles at great speed, the English army, though strong in number, were significantly weakened by the exhaustion of marching through the heat of summer, laden by weapons and supplies. In late August Edward made the decision to continue north, to the safety of the Low Countries, where allies waited. The great forest of Crécy, however, stood in his way. Moving a large army weighed down by wagons through a wood was impossible. Edward could swing his army west, through marshland, dangerous in its ability to claim wagons, horses and even men, or he could go east and slip past the French at Abbeville. Risking the annihilation of his army and the likely capture of his person, Edward chose the latter and on 26 August 1346 found himself trapped beside the forest of Crécy by an incoming French army.

The English army, with their backs to the forest, were already in a defensive position aided by a 'large wagenburg in front of the forest of all his army's wagons and carts'.[6] They waited. The ground shook as the French rumbled into vision, 'nobly mounted and armoured, their standards blowing in the wind'. On the crest of the hillside, Edward gave the first division to the prince, aided by the earl of Northampton and the earl of Warwick, and took command of the third himself. As Edward had ordered at Halidon Hill, all men would be on foot rather than horseback to allow for maximum use of the English longbow.

Outnumbered by the French army, Edward adopted another strategy from Halidon Hill and arranged his archers in the same fashion – to shoot inwards. Enclosed by baggage carts for extra protection, the swathes of archers were grouped together at the wings of the army. Edward had also been carting barrels of gunpowder across France. Strapped underneath the carts were around one hundred ribalds – an early kind of volley gun that fired clusters of bolts or pellets – designed to injure and bewilder the oncoming enemy. With his men in position, the king undertook the task of readying his inferior army to do battle. For most of Edward's soldiers, used to bloody skirmishes and guerrilla warfare, this would have been their first experience of pitched battle and Edward counselled them 'that a coward became a bold man' before the trumpet sounded.

The French were arrayed in three divisions. The first was made up of crossbowmen and three hundred cavalry and led by John of Bohemia, the king of Luxembourg, recognised by three ostrich plumes protruding from his helmet. John of Bohemia had an impressive military career as a crusader before allying with Philip VI against

Edward. Aged fifty and almost totally blind, his position in the vanguard was a bold – if not a wildly reckless – decision. In the second
division Philip's brother, the count of Alençon, led the flower of
French chivalry: the mounted knights. The king commanded the
third, with the rest of the cavalry and infantry, on the flanks with
the others at the centre.[7] At around 5 p.m. the heavens shuddered
and a deluge of rain fell on the battlefield. Drums boomed as the
French charged. Genoese crossbowmen careered forward releasing
bolts into the English vanguard but were quickly struck down by
arrows from longbows shooting into their flanks on either side. With
most of the English army made up of bowmen, the sky was thick
with arrows plunging into the French line of attack. The French
cavalry followed, the earth shaking with the weight of hundreds
of horses hurtling forward. 'Saint George! For England!' went the
battle cries of the English as Prince Edward, clad in plate armour,
charged into the fray, leading the vanguard. French horses turned and
fled the canon fire and falling arrows. Knights punctured with arrows
were dragged along by their horses as they galloped away. A melee
formed at the centre of the battlefield with the prince slashing and
stabbing his way through the sodden quagmire of men, horses and
mud. Edward watched as his teenage son, eager to do battle, gasping
for breath, desperately clutched his sword. According to the chronicler Jean Froissart, the king refused to send aid, retorting, 'Let the
boy win his spurs.'[8] The story may be apocryphal, but the prince was
in the thick of the fighting. The king's cool head was tested when
his son was struck and he fell to the ground. With waves of French
cavalry launching forward, the prince could easily have been crushed
under the weight of collapsing horses and men were it not for the
quick response of Richard Fitz-Simon, Prince Edward's standard-
bearer, who dragged him to his feet.

Dead men and horses littered the battlefield as what was left of
the French cavalry began to retreat. Philip VI found himself trapped
in the melee. His standard-bearer was killed before his eyes and his
remaining knights counselled him to flee. The king of France ran for
his life leaving the Oriflamme caked in blood and mud, a trampled
mass of cloth. Before the battle was over one final act of bravery on

the French side took place: the suicide charge of John of Bohemia. According to Jean Froissart's florid eulogy, the blind king of Bohemia called out to his men, 'Bring me so far forward that I may strike one stroke with my sword.' His men, agreeing to his request, tied their bridles together and charged forward with a war cry of 'Prague' (the heart of Bohemia), before John of Bohemia was dragged from his horse and killed by English soldiers. The next day his loyal men 'were found in the place about the king, and all their horses tied to each other'. They had all died with the blind king of Bohemia.

When battle was finally over 'darkness had fallen, the king issued instructions that no-one was to pursue the enemy or plunder or dis-turb the dead . . . so their bodies could be better identified in the morning'.[9] A thick fog is said to have descended over the battlefield, shrouding the dead until the first beams of sunlight the following day. Edward III dispatched men to count the fifteen hundred dead French knights. They did not bother to count the additional corpses of four thousand foot soldiers scattered in the surrounding fields. French princes lay lifeless and bloodied, including Philip VI's brother, the count of Alençon. According to their status and the laws of chivalry, Edward arranged their burials to be awarded the same respect and custom as was given to those of his own men who had been killed in battle, totalling around three hundred. The French nobility were laid to rest in holy ground at nearby Montreuil. The remaining bodies of men – fathers, husbands, sons and friends – were hurled into pits.[10]

Legend has it that the prince of Wales, aching from battle, came out to survey the field that morning and spotted the corpse of John of Bohemia. Impressed by his valour, the prince picked up his helmet and plucked the ostrich plumes from it to remember his success at Crécy but also the courage of his opponent. From that moment the prince adopted John of Bohemia's motto: *Ich dien*. I serve. Whether this story is true or not, the prince of Wales had won his spurs on the field of battle.

In the retelling of what had happened at Crécy, fact was often blended with fiction, in order to emphasise chivalry and the glory of victory. Edward had dealt a heavy blow to the French nobility, and his propaganda machine did all it could to exaggerate his achievement over the decades that followed – be that the disparity in the size of the armies, or the valour and grit of the Black Prince. Stories about Crécy were drummed up to invoke patriotism, chivalry and masculinity through chronicles, verse and ballads. It was a battle that made heroes of a few, but this came at the cost of so many lives.

16. Heroes

Despite being one of the most famous battles of the Hundred Years War, Crécy did not achieve a great deal for England. The French army was temporarily overwhelmed but Philip VI fled to safety at Amiens. This left Edward with two options: attempt to overthrow the French king, or continue to plunder his way through France and take control of a region closer to England. The army had been on the march for two months, surviving on bread, oats and pottage – a vegetable and grain stew – if they were fortunate. Edward's decision was largely born out of pragmatism – dragging a tired army, low on supplies, back to Paris in an attempt to besiege the city and core of French royal power would be completely reckless. Instead, Edward and his men would have to endure the drudgery of a protracted siege at Calais.

Calais was the closest port in France to the English coastline – the peaks of Dover's white cliffs being just about visible on a clear day. Whoever held Calais held full control over the narrowest point of the Channel, and benefited from its proximity to the Low Countries. Calais would also be the perfect location to launch major campaigns into France in the future. It had the potential to be a garrison, a port and a secure base. But capturing Calais would not be a simple process. Sited on an island surrounded by boggy marshland, the French city was also heavily fortified. Encased by a double moat, the walls of the city were steep and imposing. The citadel – also inside the city walls – had an additional moat and its own fortifications. Not only this, but the city had access to the sea and thus supplies – its port was also coddled within the confines of its remarkable defence.

On 3 September, Edward had just arrived outside Calais when he wrote a long letter to the northern baron Thomas Lucy, describing the events of his campaign, his victory at Crécy and his current position. He recalls in his letter that after the battle 'we remained there

all night fasting, without eating or drinking', and lists the numerous 'counts and barons and other great lords' who were killed on the
battlefield. The king also stipulates 'we do not expect to depart the
kingdom of France until we have made an end of our war, with
the aid of God.'[1] Edward's chivalric ethos was closely connected to
godliness, and in his letter he refers to self-sacrifice and penance
through fasting. Edward compared himself to the crusading orders
of the past, such as the Knights Templar, and mimicked acts of heroism, piety and self-denial. All of this, however, was about to be
tested, for at Calais, Edward would have to decide between chivalry
and tyranny.

On Wednesday 13 September the king's emissaries, fresh from the
gates of Calais, swept into parliament at Westminster, where they
announced that the king would stay at Calais until the town surrendered; at that point he would 'go after his enemy in pursuit of his
quarrel, without returning to England before he had brought an end
to his war overseas'.[2] This was a big promise to make and indicates
that perhaps Edward had miscalculated the human cost and longevity
of his ambition.

Having surveyed every corner of Calais the English army determined that an immediate attack was impossible; they would have to
prepare for a long siege. Nearby woodland was stripped to build a
new town called Villeneuve-la-Hardie (Brave New Town), a great
wooden settlement of mansions for the king and his commanders, as
well as a viewing gallery from where they could watch the siege as if
it were a tournament.[3] For the soldiers, stables and slums of thatch
and timber were thrown up but the men were also provided with a
market and most likely recreational luxuries such as a public house
and a brothel. As the huge timber complex was hammered and chiselled into place, Henry of Grosmont, the earl of Derby, continued
to raid the north of the country, sacking Poitiers and installing small
English garrisons in towns and villages south-west of Paris. With
Edward III about to launch a siege of Calais and the English also
striking land around Gascony, Philip VI descended into a state of
panic, unsure of where to muster an army and who to attack.[4]

Throughout the autumn more reinforcements, food and weapons

made their way to Villeneuve-la-Hardie from the ports of Sandwich, Orwell and Plymouth. Over the course of the siege the number of men at Edward's disposal almost doubled.[5] Meanwhile, news of another English victory over the Scots reached Calais. Taking the opportunity to attack the north of England in Edward's absence, David II had brought the largest army in decades across the border. However, his attack was a disaster. At Neville's Cross in County Durham his army was routed and any survivors fled. David himself was nearly mortally wounded. Having taken two arrows to the face he was captured and hauled south to the Tower of London, where he would remain Edward's prisoner. With no active rebellion from Scotland to distract Edward from his focus at Calais, he settled into his Brave New Town, joined by the queen and his two daughters, princesses Isabella and Joan, early in 1347.

He watched from his viewing stand as English soldiers stormed Calais from fishing boats. Trebuchets hurled rocks, and cannons blasted into the stone walls, casting debris into the moat. An attack of such a scale should have conquered Calais within weeks, but its sheer impenetrability rendered weapons of siege warfare entirely redundant. Months of repetitive siege action went on, with the English attempting to scale the walls and steer their siege towers through the marshland.

Where winter was harsh and unyielding, the ice-cold wind sweeping in from the Channel, summer brought its own discomforts. In the midsummer heat Calais began to bake. Almost a year had passed since the English arrived and the fortress of Villeneuve-la-Hardie had lost its fresh timber smell and had begun to fester. The sounds of coughing, groaning and vomiting men echoed through the narrow alleyways of the town's rough quarters. Infection had reached Edward's camp, and dysentery, food poisoning and malaria had begun to take hold. The common soldier was not the only victim of disease. Sir Hugh Hastings, who had served Edward in northern France early in the campaign, died of dysentery only weeks in.

Where some soldiers became foul with sickness, others were bilious with boredom and lack of pay. Some were so badly injured participating in wave after wave of assaults on the walls of Calais that

Edward had to pay compensation. John Tony, an archer who was 'maimed in his service near Calais', was awarded lifelong payment due to his injuries.[6]

The soldiers camped in Villeneuve-la-Hardie did not suffer from a shortage of food, unlike the eight thousand citizens of Calais, whose supplies had run out over the course of the year. Mercenary pirates patrolled the coast, preventing supplies reaching the harbour, while the king's army controlled the roads. By summer 1347 the people of Calais were starving. A desperate plea from Jean de Vienne, the commander of the garrison, to Philip VI, intercepted by English scouts, gives some insight into life behind the walls of the town: 'everything is eaten up,' the commander lamented, 'dogs, cats, horses. We have nothing left to subsist on unless we eat each other.' In late July 1347 Philip VI made a feeble attempt to liberate Calais. He drew his army so close to the English camp that he was able to see their flags. Faced by an enormous English army, aided by the Flemish, Philip VI realised he was only willing to negotiate, not fight. When he learned that Edward would not even consider lifting the siege, Philip 'fed his tents to the flames' and marched away. The stricken citizens of Calais were horrified.

Starved into submission, Calais was helpless. Abandoned by their own king they had no choice other than to seek terms with Edward. For his part, Edward III was furious that the siege had lasted the best part of a year, leaving his men ailing and morale low. He knew that at some point the city would crumble from within. Edward directed that six representatives of the town should come before him 'in their shirt sleeves with nooses around their necks carrying the keys of the town and they shall be at my mercy to deal with as I please'.[7] What followed is one of the most famous vignettes of the Hundred Years War. According to chroniclers Geoffrey le Baker and Jean Le Bel, the people were so 'deranged with hunger' that they hurled the French king's standard from the top of the tower and into the ditch below before 'they opened the gates and their captain, John de Vienne . . . came into the presence of the King of England, sitting on a little nag . . . with a halter tied round his neck.[8] He was followed by other knights and townspeople on foot, bare-headed and without shoes, and also with ropes around their necks'.[9] The demoralised Jean de Vienne, followed by five other brave burghers – the wealthiest citizens of Calais – handed Edward a symbolic 'sword of war' in surrender, along with the keys to the town. They had abandoned any attempt at presenting a heroic veneer, choosing instead the lives of the innocent men, women and children of their city. According to Jean Froissart, the heavily pregnant Queen Philippa was so overcome by dejection that she begged her husband to show mercy: 'Ah gentle sir, since I have crossed the sea with great danger to see you, I have never asked you one favour: now I most humbly ask as a gift . . . for your love to me, that you will be merciful to these six men.'[10] As chivalry dictated, the king granted the queen her wish and the burghers of Calais were relieved of their heavy nooses. In posterity, their brave surrender has bathed them in the glow of an affecting, desperate and human heroism.

But Edward III ended his protracted siege in the belief that he was the hero. He had led his men once again to victory and had acted as chivalry dictated, by sparing the citizens of Calais. The rules of siege warfare were clear: if the people of the city surrendered, they must be treated with respect. The starving people of Calais were given bread to fill their hollow bellies, but they were not permitted to stay in their homes. Gathering all the goods they could carry, frail citizens slowly trailed from the city, clutching the morsels of bread the besiegers had given them – the hand that fed them was the same that took everything they had. The people of Calais became refugees, forced to seek a new life in villages and towns across the rest of France. Soon, the city and castle were packed with English and loyal Gascons, a new English colony and mercantile hub. Calais was where Edward and England would generate new wealth. Calais became the centre of the wool trade between England and Flanders. Not only this, but 'tin, lead, worsted and drapes made in England' would now move through the city, the fiscal heart of England's pan-European trading network.[11]

Edward had achieved the unthinkable. He had defeated Philip VI on French soil and taken the most strategic city and port on the French coast, which would remain in English hands for the next three hundred years. Yet he had not taken the crown and had not been able to claim Gascony as a sovereign state. Edward had begun a war that remained entirely unfinished. As he returned to England for the first time in well over a year, his grand plan was to memorialise his victories at Crécy and Calais through the creation of an elite new chivalric institution: the Order of the Garter.

From 1347 the secular order of chivalry, the Order of the Round Table, planned by Edward in 1344, was replaced by a new, slicker system, steeped in chivalric ethos and visually bound by the emblem of a blue garter that was worn by all its members. It became known as the Order of the Garter, an exclusive ensemble of royalty and knights of the realm. It was a fraternity – that permitted some women – meant to represent an honourable band of brothers, bound by battle, chivalry and devotion to God and their patron saint, Saint George. Based at the newly founded Saint George's Chapel at Windsor, each of the garter knights was allocated an individual stall in the chapel. This was Edward's version of a holy order, inspired perhaps by the Knights Templar of the thirteenth century and certainly by Arthur's knights of the Round Table. Edward believed he was evoking great deeds of history, overseen spiritually by the Order's patron saint, another warrior and hero, Saint George. In hagiography – the record of saints' lives – Saint George is the most revered of all military saints. A Cappadocian Greek turned Roman guard, he was martyred as a hero for refusing to recant his Christian faith in the fourth century AD. Throughout the medieval period Saint George was celebrated across Christian Europe but also in Muslim countries: Syria, Lebanon and Palestine, where he was said to have had healing powers. By adopting Saint George as the Order of the Garter's patron, Edward III cast him as an icon of war, as well as a traditionally Christian English saint. By association, Saint George provided a spiritual endorsement for Edward and his ambition to rule both England and France. His motto for the Order of the Garter, *honi soit qui mal y pense* ('shame on he who thinks evil of it'), was devised to commend Edward's war against France. Edward celebrated Saint George as a hero, just as he saw himself and his men as heroes for their ongoing efforts to attack the country that had demanded their subservience. One of the major points of the Order of the Garter was to reward that heroism.

For the first cohort of Garter knights Edward III had selected his closest brothers in arms – those who had served loyally over the course of his reign, from that dark night in the tunnels beneath Nottingham Castle to the days lingering in the mud outside Calais. Henry of Derby, now earl of Lancaster, and the earls of Warwick and Salisbury were joined by lower orders, bannerets and knights of the household, such as Miles Stapleton and John Chandos, who fought with the Black Prince at Crécy.

Women were an important part of the cult of courtly love and the chivalric ethos and Edward was keen to include them in his new chivalric order. Queen Philippa was allocated a 'corset' – a tunic – of red velvet embroidered with eagles and gold trees. While Philippa of Hainault had not wielded a sword on the battlefield, her importance on both the political and chivalric stage of fourteenth-century England is clear. Meanwhile, Princess Isabella – Edward's eldest daughter – was given robes embellished with the king's insignia and the fleur-de-lis of France. In years to come she would be allocated a formal ceremonial role that placed her on a level with the Garter knights. Based on the bonds of war, heroism and piety, the Order also represented familial power and unity.[12] It would become the most revered order of chivalry in the history of England, lasting centuries. All of this would be celebrated thereafter, annually, on the Garter feast day, 23 April, known as Saint George's Day.

Edward III's career reached its pinnacle with the creation of the Order of the Garter. From his emergence as Arthur Redivivus to the king who conquered Calais, he seemed unstoppable. The English court in spring 1348 was jubilant. Feasting and dancing, Edward and his knights dressed in elaborate costumes, the king as pheasant, others as swans, peacocks and even dragons.[13] Yet as they congratulated each other, praising the king, a greater danger had emerged in the east. One that would threaten Europe more than any earthly army. It was an enemy that no hero could defend his people from, a hostile faceless invader who did not abide by the laws of humanity. It did not know mercy. This enemy became known as the Black Death.

PART FOUR

The Age of Apocalypse

' "LISTEN, the last stroke of death's noon has struck –
The plague is come," a gnashing Madman said,
And laid him down straightaway upon his bed.
His writhèd hands did at the linen pluck;
Then all is over. With a careless chuck
Among his fellows he is cast. How sped.
His spirit matters little: many dead
Make men hard-hearted. – "Place him on the truck.
Go forth into the burial-ground and find
Room at so much a pitiful for many.
One thing is to be done; one thing is clear:
Keep thou back from the hot unwholesome wind,
That not infect thee." Say, is there any
Who mourneth for the multitude of death here?'

Christina Rossetti, 'The Plague', *Bouts-Rimés Sonnets*

17.   The Princess and the Plague

'You will find this present work has a painful and unpleasant beginning as the sad memory of the deaths in the recent plague, which my
book carries at its forefront, is universally horrible to all who saw it
or otherwise knew of it . . . as if forced by necessity, I have brought
myself to write what follows.'[1]

These words, written in the fourteenth century, come from
Giovanni Boccaccio's collection of short stories, *The Decameron*,
in which a group of men and women seek comfort in storytelling.
They cluster together in the countryside, having escaped Florence,
a city teeming with sickness, and together they cast a new future
from the ashes of the world they have lost. Fictional though these
characters were, their experience is grounded in fact: a near-global
pandemic had begun around 1346, reaching its deathly peak in 1348.
It was known by many names, 'the Great Death', '*the* Death', 'the
Great Plague' or 'the Pestilence', but it was later, and most famously,
named 'the Black Death'. This was a human tragedy of immense
proportions, spreading from the east to the west, from around the
Black Sea to the Mediterranean, halving entire populations as it
rapidly escalated. It remains the greatest biological catastrophe in
known history.

Many feared it had been inflicted by God, but the real cause was
more mundane: bacteria called *Yersinia pestis*. Once absorbed into the
bloodstream, usually by a flea bite or contact with infected tissue,
the bacteria spread rapidly through the body until they killed their
host. There were three variations of the plague – bubonic, pneumonic
and septicaemic. The latter two variants killed quickly, within a day
or two of infection, by attacking the respiratory system or causing
bacteria to collect in the bloodstream, eventually leading to blood
poisoning. It took around a week for the bubonic plague's symptoms

to develop; these took the form of lumps known as buboes. Autopsies carried out by scholars in Avignon, by order of the pope, demonstrate that medical research was conducted in haste to learn about this silent killer: 'many dead bodies were cut up and opened, and it was found that all who die so suddenly have an infection of the lungs and spit up blood . . . [the pneumonic plague] . . . certain apostemes suddenly appear on both armpits . . . [bubonic plague] . . . from which men die without delay . . . that people from both sexes are stricken in the groin.'[2]

Having witnessed the onset of the plague in Florence, Boccaccio describes the buboes as 'certain swellings [that] appeared on both men and women, either on the groin or under the armpits and some of these swellings grew as big as an ordinary apple, others like an egg . . . the common people called these "plague boils".'[3] The boils turned black and blotches of livid contagion spread over the arms and thighs, 'an unmistakable token of coming death'. Some recovered but the general rule was that within three days of swellings appearing, there was almost certain death.

The source of the deadly bacteria was unknown, but a contemporary Syrian scholar named Ibn al-Wardi claimed that 'it began in a land of darkness'.[4] Where this land of darkness actually was remains a mystery, for like so many others, plague eventually claimed Ibn al-Wardi's life too. Before the disease consumed his body, he managed to document the trauma of the sickness on parchment. 'An Essay on the Report of the Pestilence' was his account of the impact of plague on the city of Aleppo in Syria. Lamenting the cruelty of the disease, he wrote, 'It swore not to leave the houses without its inhabitants. It searched for them with a lamp.' He also speaks of the desperate attempts to cure the victims: 'Oh, if you could see the nobles of Aleppo studying their books of medicine. They follow its remedies by eating dried and sour foods. The buboes which disturb men's lives are smeared with Armenian clay . . . They perfumed their homes with camphor, flowers, and sandal. They wore ruby rings and put onions, vinegar, and sardines together with the daily meal.' And, with death approaching, he recounts the anguished preparations of the people of Aleppo:

One man begs another to take care of his children, one says goodbye to his neighbours.

A third perfects his works, and another prepares his shroud.

A fifth is reconciled with his enemies, and another treats his friends with kindness.

One is very generous; another makes friends with those who have betrayed him.

Another man puts aside his property; one frees his servants.

One man changes his character while another mends his ways.

For this plague has captured all people and is about to send its ultimate destruction.[5]

By the time the plague reached Florence the virulent bacteria had already travelled extensively and erratically, springing up in pockets across western Christendom, from small hamlets and villages to cities. The plague was without prejudice. According to the fourteenth-century scholar Nicephorus Gregoras, who lived in Constantinople, 'the calamity attacked men as well as women, rich and poor, old and young. To put matters simply it did not spare those of any age or fortune.'[6]

It is impossible to account for the exact spread of *Yersinia pestis* but it emerged around 1345–6 before becoming particularly virulent in 1348. The bacteria were mostly carried by rodents, and had origins in marmots found in present-day Kyrgyzstan.[7] Traditionally, these large rodents existed well away from human habitation, but in the late Middle Ages the largest land empire in history, the Mongol empire, was spreading. Marmots became food, fur and leather for itinerant Mongol hordes as, in the thirteenth century, they spilled out of Mongolia into the Tian Shan mountain range. The Mongols repeatedly exposed themselves to *Yersinia pestis* and carried it thousands of miles. But marmot meat was not the only source of food for rampaging Mongol armies; they also gathered and carried sacks of millet grain (a staple of the Tian Shan region) to sustain them as they besieged cities such as Baghdad in Persia and Caffa, a Genoese colony in what we now know as the Crimea. These sacks often carried rats and other rodents now infected with the bacteria.[8] Another possibility is that the bacteria were spread by camel caravans carrying *Yersinia pestis* from the mountain range of Tian Shan to the Volga region of Russia and its major trading city, Kazan.[9]

What *is* known is that the bacteria entered Europe from the Volga region via sacks carried by merchants across the Black Sea into the Mediterranean. Plague landed in Genoa in 1347 before reaching Venice, Florence and Marseilles in advance of the spring of 1348. A musician named Louis Sanctus in Avignon describes how three galleys filled with infected sailors were marooned outside Genoa before they were finally allowed to drop anchor at Marseilles and infect the locale.[10] Plague leapt from Marseilles into Languedoc and Bordeaux then Paris, Burgundy and Normandy. But just before the Black Death reached England, Edward III and his family had already suffered a personal tragedy: the loss of Princess Joan.

After his success in France, Edward was eager to expand his influence and – in the knowledge that the French were regrouping rather than retreating – his network of allegiance in Europe. He had his sights set on Castile and Léon, the superpower of Iberia which made up most of contemporary Spain. Castile was the heart of Iberia, a large mass of land enclosed by Portugal and Galicia to the west, Granada to the south and Aragon and Navarre to the east. Domestically, despite his military successes in France, Edward III was approaching a stalemate with parliament over another tax on the realm, designed to fund the war effort but also support Edward's diplomatic plans. Alfonso XI, king of Castile, was, for the moment, a bystander to the war between England and France. But if one of the two combatants was able to persuade Castile to join his cause, he would gain access to one of the best naval fleets in Christendom.

As the Black Death crept through southern Europe in the first months of 1348, Edward III was busy attempting to broker a marriage agreement between his daughter Joan and Alfonso's son Pedro. Born in Woodstock around 1333, Joan was described by her father as his 'dearest daughter . . . distinguished, notwithstanding her youth, by gravity of manners and by the comeliness of fitting grace'; she was also said to be 'the favourite of her mother'.[11]

Joan was around fourteen when she prepared to leave England.

Her marriage was above all a diplomatic mission that would take her across the Channel, through Gascony, over the Pyrenees and into northern Spain. Joan, a princess who had travelled across most of northern Europe before she was five, was used to such extensive journeys. But she bore a huge weight of expectation: everything about her needed to reflect the wealth, power and taste of the English court, a court that Edward III wanted to appear cosmopolitan, affluent and educated.

In preparation for Joan's new life in Castile a beautiful and carefully considered trousseau was compiled and packed in chests.[12] Thomas de Baddeby, Joan's treasurer, was placed in charge of the organisation of the trousseau; with the scratch of ink on parchment, he itemised every beautiful detail. There were vestments for Joan's personal chapel, including richly embroidered cloth from Reims and two tapestries, one woven with images of popinjays and the other decorated with details of roses and wild flowers. Other items included a gold-embroidered black gown, decorated with a gold circle and a recumbent lion detailed inside it, 'the robe . . . powdered throughout the field with gold leaves'. Joan was also provided with a beautiful new bed, embroidered in silk and gold, displaying two fighting dragons. She was given silk curtains (for her bed), a bath, a copper warming pan and a looking glass. For riding she had a saddle made of scarlet and purple velvet, embroidered and powdered with pearls; four saddles for her ladies were also included, as well as ermine robes for her loyal entourage. Though the most important and symbolic items of all her luxurious belongings were, of course, her wedding robes: a long white tunic and a silk cloak. It is reasonable to assume that Joan was daunted by the prospect of her impending marriage and thrilled by these beautiful new clothes, but she would never wear them.

It was well known that Alfonso XI of Castile led a double life, his attention split between a loveless but dutiful marriage to his queen, Maria of Portugal, and his loving but charged relationship with his mistress, Eleanor de Guzmán. It was rumoured that Eleanor was trying to sabotage the marriage between Pedro and Joan, possibly in order to further the interests of her own son by Alfonso, Enrique Trastámara. In early February, Edward wrote to the lord chancellor,

Robert Bourchier, who had been tasked with taking Joan on her journey to Castile. Edward asked Bourchier to 'obtain security that if the infante Peter and the king's daughter [Joan] have a son, he shall be King of Castile after his father's death'.[13] Edward wanted to be certain that Eleanor could not place her son in the line of succession. Concerned by the dynastic threat Joan might face in Castile, Edward failed to recognise the real danger facing his daughter on her journey to Spain. Joan travelled from Westminster to Surrey with her parents, where they kissed her goodbye. She went on to Exeter, where she stayed at the expense of the bishop of Exeter, before travelling to the monastery at Buckfastleigh in Devon. Next she moved on to Plymouth, where she would set sail. Every step of her journey brought Joan closer to the peril coming in the opposite direction.

On 31 March 1348 Princess Joan and her household arrived at Bordeaux.[14] There were at least four ladies-in-waiting to serve the princess, and her safety was ensured by the presence of an armed guard of fifty men including knights and thirty archers.[15] Around the same time that Joan and her entourage arrived in France, people were starting to fall ill in towns and cities across the south of the country. Though there is no surviving account of exactly what happened to Joan in Bordeaux, it is possible to piece together an idea of her final weeks. Bordeaux was the most important port city in Gascony; situated on the Garonne estuary, it was widely used for English travel and trade. The princess stayed in the city, likely the castle, for the next three months – probably in quarantine. In May, the guard charged with escorting the princess, led by Henry, earl of Lancaster's man, Stephen de Cusington, left the princess in the safe confines of the castle at Bordeaux. Protecting a princess was comparatively dull, so these warriors were quick to take up the orders of the seneschal of Aquitaine and travel to the Dordogne, where they expected to find fighting. The same month the lord chancellor, Robert Bouchier, left at 'the assent of the lady [Joan]', detouring via Bayonne to confirm final arrangements with Alfonso's ambassadors, eventually arriving back in England in late July.[16] By the time his party arrived home, the princess was dead. In an account of his expenses for the journey, Stephen de Cusington noted that he had returned from France on 6 July, 'returning from parts of Gascony into England after the death of the same lady on the first day of July 1348'.[17] It is worth asking why the princess was left with a small entourage when plague was rife across the Mediterranean. It is certainly possible that these men fled to save their own lives, but also unlikely that they would abandon the daughter of Edward III to meet her end alone. The only reasonable conclusion was that people did not know what this strange and potent pestilence was or where it had come from, or how much danger Joan was in.

Though it is impossible to know exactly what the princess's experience of plague in Bordeaux was, testimony from elsewhere in France offers some evidence of its impact in spring 1348. In Avignon, it was estimated that seven thousand homes lay empty within the walls of the city and 'in Marseilles all the gates of the city save for two posterns were closed' in order to try to quarantine the city. The same account could 'tell you similar things about every city and settlement in Provence'.[18] With the citizens of Bordeaux either dying, fleeing or hiding, the most likely scenario for Princess Joan was that she died having been infected while quarantining in Bordeaux Castle – for even a fortress was unable to keep out the unwelcome intruder of the Black Death. After the princess's death, the surviving members of her household left Bordeaux. They either came to the conclusion that the city was unsafe, or found they were no longer welcome in the castle without the princess. By the end of July, they had travelled three miles outside of Bordeaux to Loremo, where they stayed until 3 September. Here the household account comes to an abrupt end. Princess Joan was given a respectful but swift burial at the cathedral of Saint-André in Bordeaux and laid to rest in the quire – the heart of the cathedral. Years later, in memory of Joan, her younger brother John of Gaunt, who had only been eight at the time of her death, endowed an obit for her there – an annual, intimate service of remembrance.[19] Joan's memory was preserved by the flickering of candles and the mellow hums of priests.

On 15 September, Edward III wrote again to Alfonso XI, Queen Maria and Pedro in Castile.[20] The letter was likely composed by a clerk, probably dictated, and through it we gather a sense that the news of Joan's death had been received recently. This fragment of the past illustrates the universality of the family's unbearable grief. 'But see (with what intense bitterness of heart we have to tell you this) destructive Death who seizes young and old alike, sparing no one, and reducing rich and poor to the same level has lamentably snatched from both of us our dearest daughter (whom we loved best of all, as her virtues demanded). No fellow human being could be surprised if we were inwardly desolated by the sting of this bitter grief, for we are human too . . . but . . . [Joan] . . . whom we have loved with pure love has been sent ahead to heaven to reign among the choirs of virgins.'[21]

Even the greatest of kings, conquerors and heroes were not safe from either the Black Death or the unbearable grief it brought. Joan died without the comfort of her family around her, but before long Edward III and the realm would have to face the pestilence themselves. It had moved across the Channel.

At ports in northern France, merchants and sailors loaded their wares onto ships ready to embark on the short journey across the Channel. Bristol, Southampton, Plymouth, and Melcombe in Dorset, were all typical destinations. The chronicles vary over where exactly the first outbreak of the plague was in England but all point towards the south-west. The *Anonimalle* chronicler notes that the infection was brought to the shores of England by merchant ships, that 'it lasted in the south country around Bristol through August and all winter . . . with the result that the living were hardly able to bury the dead.'[22] Another claims that the plague arrived in Bristol as early as June 1348. The Franciscan monks of King's Lynn in East Anglia name Dorset in 'midsummer' as one of the early hotbeds of plague and offer precious details that other accounts lack. They claim, 'two ships, one of them from Bristol, landed in Melcombe in Dorset . . . in them were sailors from Gascony who were infected with an unheard of epidemic illness called pestilence'. Within three days, people of Melcombe had succumbed to the plague.[23] The truth is likely that the plague entered around the same time across multiple ports along the south of England.

Once it had arrived, the plague spread unevenly through the

summer of 1348. In Wiltshire a morbid account describes women dying while in labour and bishops forced to consecrate new ground for lack of space in burial grounds.[24] In London, 'more than two hundred corpses were buried almost every day' and in Saint Albans, according to Thomas Walsingham, a monk living at the abbey there, 'the living were hardly able to bury the dead'.[25] Most of the accounts coming out of England were from monks witnessing the devastation in their enclosed communities as well as the outside world. One account, from Meaux Abbey in the East Riding of Yorkshire, tells of how Hugh the abbot had recently ordered a new crucifix. During the process the craftsman completing this important duty fasted, eating only bread and water, working from a nude model 'standing before him'.[26] When plague hit Meaux Abbey, Hugh, like many others, began to develop buboes and died within a few days. He was buried 'before the crucifix he had put up'. These accounts, read closely, give a fractional glimpse into the experiences of people living through the Black Death and how they might have felt about it. Following Hugh's death, survivors carefully considered where to bury him. He was not tossed into a pit, filled with corpses, but was buried before a material representation of what he had held dear in life, his faith, visible in the wooden crucifix he had so thoughtfully commissioned.

Some who had been able to prepare for death managed to legally submit their will in the London courts.[27] Like today, people took great care over the welfare of their loved ones and their material possessions. In the wills of those living in London there is a pattern of 'charitable donation'. Adam, the son of a London pepperer (spice dealer), wished to have an 'iron bound chest' filled with 'forty pounds sterling' to be placed in the church of Saint Mary Bothaw (close to what is now Cannon Street), where he wished to be buried. The purpose of the money was 'to be lent to poor parishioners' in the area. A similar specific donation to the poor is seen in the will of Hugh, a glover from London, who requested that his wealth be 'divided among those who, having been reduced from affluence to poverty, are ashamed to get a livelihood by begging'.[28] Repeated requests for chantries and the 'pious uses' for remaining wealth can be found in the wills enrolled at the Court of Hustings in 1349, the peak plague year in the city. Living in close communities, bound to the parish they lived in, people were deeply and closely connected to their neighbours. Working together, celebrating feast days together and worshipping together, these communities were as close as families and as a result were intensely emotionally invested in their preservation. In the wills that were written, people were mostly concerned for the welfare of their souls, but they also considered the welfare of their communities. Where people displayed empathy and consideration for the living and the dead, structural measures were also necessary to slow the speed of infection, for people learned fast that plague spread with the movement of people. Edward III and his government cancelled parliament and sanctioned the closure of courts across the country. He requested that the clergy perform rites to protect the realm, before escaping Westminster shortly after Christmas, so he and his family could quarantine themselves in the peaceful palace of King's Langley in Hertfordshire.[29] The Black Death did not discriminate, but wealth did enable a degree of safety. The nobility with castles and grand houses across the countryside were able to quarantine in comfort.

But most people did not have the luxury of high walls and verdant landscapes. Without country residences to flee to, people instead had to be resourceful, seeking various forms of medicinal cures, or the security of spiritual redemption. Herbs were burned in the home to ward off plague, cold food was prescribed in the heat of the summer to balance the four humours – blood, yellow bile, black bile and phlegm. This system of four bodily fluids was how people considered their physical and mental health – ideally they should all be in balance with each other. Doctors were usually clerics who worked to treat the sick and, according to the cleric Father Dom Theophilus, a Benedictine priest from Milan, in the case of imminent death, spiritual medicines were administered: 'let him first gather as much as he can of bitter loathing towards the sins committed by him, and the same quantity of true contrition of heart, and mix the two into an ointment with the water of tears. Then make him a vomit of frank and honest confession, by which he shall be purged of the pestilential poison of sin and the boil of his vices shall be totally liquified and melt away.'[30] This obscure language, combining the physical with the spiritual, is curious. It is extremely penitential, speaking of sin, guilt and regret but framed as though it were a physical purge.

As acts of contrition, these 'spiritual medicines' align closely with other alternative means of spiritual cleansing that were popular in England and across Europe during the plague years. In September 1349, 'about Michaelmas', the flagellants arrived in England from Flanders. Naked but for a small loincloth and a hood, painted with a red cross front and back, they carried a whip in their right hand. The whip 'had three thongs. Each thong had a knot in it, with something sharp like a needle, stuck through the middle of the knot so that it stuck out on each side, and as they walked one after the other they struck themselves with these whips on their naked bloody bodies.' Three times during the procession the men would prostrate themselves on the ground and make the shape of the cross with their bodies as another walked over them, lashing their backs with his own whip. 'It was said that they performed a similar penance every night.'[31] This sort of ritualised self-flagellation became popular across Europe, particularly in Italy where the flagellants were known as the 'Bianchi' for the white robes they wore. The wrath of God became a theme in Europe, in the belief that He was responsible for this biblical sickness, and various scholars and clerics attempted to find reason for His punishment.

An anonymous poem from the time suggests human immorality was the root cause: 'plague is killing men and beasts. Why? Because vices rule unchallenged here. Alas! The whole world is now given over to spite. Where can a kind heart be found among the people? No one thinks on the crucified Christ, and therefore the people perish as a token of vengeance.'[32]

The disobedience of children was blamed, using scripture as evidence, 'for in the old law children who were rebellious and disobedient to their fathers and mothers were punished by death'.[33] Even hedonism was considered a cause, for 'in this way they spent and wasted their goods, and . . . abused their bodies in wantonness and scurrilous licentiousness'. The royal court was at the centre of such celebration and consumption of goods and as a result choice of clothing was another thing to blame. According to one source: 'the whole of England was thrown into madness and excitement by a rage for bodily adornments . . . they also possess shoes with pointed toes as long as a finger . . . these are more like devils' talons than apparel . . . because the people squander the gifts of God on pride, lechery and greed . . . it is only to be expected that the Lord's vengeance will follow'.[34] Without the medical knowledge necessary to explain the origins and reasons for plague, blaming humanity, even children, was a desperate attempt to find reason in ruin. The criticism of how people lived, experienced joy or even misbehaved (as children do) smacks of anger, guilt, fear and shame – all powerful human emotions felt alongside the inevitable grief of losing so many. It is tragic that as well as the appalling experience of plague, the limitations of human knowledge in the period meant that people either pointed the finger of blame at others, or inflicted further misery upon themselves.

In 1349 the king's chancery wrote to bishops across the realm that 'God who has been offended by their guilt, is pacified by the performance of penance for sin and by the prayers of the faithful'.[35] In a year of unimaginable loss, pain and fear, repentance and piety were some of the only means people had to make sense of the devastation.

When Edward left quarantine in the summer of 1349 and went on a hunting tour across his lands in the west of the country, he saw for himself the impact of the plague on the people. Homes were entirely abandoned, fields unsown and unploughed, crops laid to waste and livestock left to wander. It is impossible to know exactly how the king felt at the shock of it all, but likely panic at the prospect of trying to rebuild a country that had endured such loss, and grief for all those who had not survived.

Around the same time, Princess Joan's trousseau arrived back in England. Cloth of gold, saddles worked with pearls, embroidered scarlet, gilded spoons, her candelabra, coffers and her capes – all of it was returned to the Crown.[36] The ornate saddles went back to the royal armoury but some items were deemed so personal that they had to be returned to Joan's parents. Philippa was given her daughter's beautiful bed. Edward received a velvet missal (a book dedicated to

Mass) shrouded in purple velvet with four silver tassels. These surviving fragments of the princess were a personal, tangible memory of a daughter lost to the most devastating pandemic in human history. The survivors of the first wave of Black Death now carried the grief and memory of those loved and lost, as well as immense trauma and a stark sense of their own mortality.

18. New Beginnings

The Italian humanist scholar Francis Petrarch experienced the horrors of the Black Death when living in Parma. Traumatised by all he had witnessed he wrote to his brother, Gherardo, a monk living at the Monastery of Montrieux in the foothills of the Sainte-Baume mountain ridge in southern France. Gherardo carried his own shock and grief, having watched as all thirty-five of his brethren had died. Gherardo, remarkably, was the sole survivor and continued to live in the silence of the monastery, surrounded by picturesque woodland with only the company of his dog. In the letter to Gherardo, Petrarch captures a sense of, What now? The collective and communal feeling of grief and the haplessness in navigating a new world, scourged by death. He writes, 'what are we to do now, brother? Now that we have lost almost everything and found no rest. When can we expect it? Where shall we look for it? Time, as they say, has slipped through our fingers. Our former hopes are buried with our friends . . . last losses are beyond recovery, and death's wound beyond cure.'[1]

Across Christendom people began to navigate a new world while trying to pay respect to the many souls that had been lost. In 1352 masons in Cambridge began to cut the stones that would eventually form Corpus Christi College, established by the local community specifically to commemorate the souls of the dead. The guild of Corpus Christi had already been formed three years earlier at the height of plague in the city. Overwhelmed by death, two parish guilds had merged to establish a new college for scholars and priests with the purpose of burial and commemoration. The idea was that living fellows of Corpus Christi would be charged with performing the spiritual salvation of those deceased. Rough-handed labourers stacked freshly cut stones, building the college through which a path was created that scholars would tread for centuries to come. This path passed Saint Bene't's Church and over the mass burial pit of

Cambridge plague victims, intended to act as a constant reminder of those lost. Passing over the dead was a binding of the spiritual world to the physical, by prayer, earth and stone. This acceptance of death, living with it and, in some ways, revering it, inspired an artistic and literary movement known as memento mori, meaning 'remember you will die'.

The idea of the dead coexisting with the living was far from new. In *Historia*, the twelfth-century chronicler William of Newburgh describes revenants – a spirit or corpse, revived from the dead – moving among the living, rising from their graves, before being cut 'limb from limb, [to] reduce it into food and fuel for the flames'.[2] This image of a corpse was a powerful religious symbol, representing sin and the human body. People believed that the stench of a rotting corpse could and would infect the living with plague. This image of the corrupted body became a potent visual symbol of memento mori, prefiguring the inevitable decay of death. The *danse macabre* (the dance of death) became an iconic image – skeletons dancing together with the living, and transi tombs – the peaceful effigy of a deceased person, above a worm-eaten, decomposing corpse – all became a visual and deeply evocative reminder: 'remember you will die'. Where memento mori art offers valuable insight into some of the human emotions of those living in the fourteenth and even fifteenth centuries, there is little that has survived in the written record that directly evidences grief.

One poem, however, written in English in the late fourteenth century by an anonymous author stands out in its sorrow and anguish over the loss of a beloved one: *Pearl*.[3]

> But I lost my pearl in a garden of herbs;
> she slipped from me grass to ground,
> and I mourn now, with a broken heart,
> for that priceless pearl without a spot.[4]

In this fragment of the poem the reader is told that the speaker has lost something dear to him, in the grass of a beautiful garden, abundant with herbs and flowers. It, or she, appears to be both an object – a physical pearl and the pride and joy of the jeweller (the speaker) – and also a person. It becomes clearer over the course of the poem that Pearl is his daughter who has died around the age of two and is buried in this green garden. Stricken by 'the coldness of sorrow', he falls into the flowers and, 'swamped by scent', drifts off to sleep. The poem progresses into a dream vision where over a stretch of unfordable water he is reunited with his Pearl – 'what person could hope for a pleasure more pure than to hear and see their ornament?' She is older, a maiden around her early teens, and they speak to one another as if she were alive. She soothes him by saying that she is in heaven at the side of Christ. She goes on to explain the beauty of heaven, its chambers and the unearthly citadel, schooling him to think of his place there and encouraging him to be with her. But as he tries to cross the water, to join her in Paradise, he is abruptly woken, finding himself in the green garden once again, the site of his bereavement. Over the course of his time at the opening of heaven – 'the ornamented dazzle of downs and dales, of wood and water and splendid meadows' – the speaker, now a visionary, understands that what decays and is lost on earth is transformed in heaven. He has bridged the space between life and death and touched the edge of blissful infinity. But like the unfordable water he is trapped behind, he remains encased in life until his time comes.

Written in response to the loss of a child, 'Pearl' is also a poem that offers hope in the depths of sorrow – after death and the earthly decay of the physical body there is bliss, an extraordinary paradise in which the departed exist un-tormented by the prison of the corporeal body. This too is a kind of memento mori. Lines such as 'when our flesh and bones turn foul in the grave', or 'your cold corpse must sink through the soil', remind the reader that death is inevitable but also that a life of piety will ensure a place in heaven, a place with Pearl.

Alongside the insights into the speaker's grief, 'Pearl' contains a more sinister undercurrent: plague. From the first stanza the term 'spot' is used in relation to the pearl's appearance. Black spots and dark lesions on an otherwise flawless surface suggest a cause for the speaker's bereavement – 'oh black soil you blot and spoil my precious pearl without a spot'. The imagery of pestilence persists throughout the poem, suggesting that Pearl was a young casualty of the Black Death.[5]

Where there was immense grief there was also a sense of rebirth. In the fourteenth century people lived their lives with circularity, largely dictated by the seasons in farming and the harvest. The death phase of autumn, the absence of life in winter, the promise of rebirth with spring and the abundance of summer. As people began to emerge from their homes, like green shoots bursting from the cold ground following the blackness of the major plague years, there was now the light of a so-called golden age.[6]

Although half the population had died, life had to keep moving – crops had to be harvested and trade continued. While the 1340s had ended in tragedy, the 1350s started in prosperity as survivors of the Black Death were faced with opportunity for self-betterment. With so few people demanding goods, prices of food, drink, clothing and non-essential items plummeted while the value of skilled labour peaked. With people being paid higher wages for want of their labour, demand for luxury items like spices, silks, furs and wax surged. The world after the plague was marked by a boom in technological advancement. People flocked from the countryside to towns and cities, the hubs of commerce, trade and artistry. Of them all, London was the most popular destination.

With more people living in London the city became even dirtier. A conglomeration of filth – blood, bones, food waste and cinders – made public hygiene a problem and the foul smell contributed to the overall sensory overload of the city.[7] The smells of smoke, cooking, incense, offal and faeces wafted through the streets of London. Animals snuffled and barked. Carts rumbled over cobbled pavements carrying wares and waste to and from the walled city. Water trickled from the roofs of houses and down into the Thames along with rainwater and liquid waste from chamber pots. The sounds of shouting and clattering rang out alongside the tolling of bells. After the Black Death, however, these bells were joined by urban clocks. Placed opposite churches, these clocks were symbolic of a growing industrial working world. An *horlogeur*, or clockmaker, became a new occupation in the second part of the fourteenth century and many specialist craftsmen found work in cathedrals across England.[8] With so many dead, new opportunities sprang up around the country to learn skills such as brewing, armoury and masonry, or to work in administration as scribes. Young men and women enrolled as apprentices – before the plague this type of training was usually kept within a family – learning new skills and contributing to a recovering realm. The cloth industry and the iron trade flourished with people buying cloth rather than making it themselves, laboriously spinning wool and flax.[9] Wind power was harnessed and the advent of the water mill enabled food production to flourish, for people were able to progress from grinding grain themselves to using the power of water to make flour. Unlike before, when bread could be scarce, daily bread was produced in abundance.

Just as people started to work more, they started to drink more, with ale being produced in vast quantities. From the peasant poor to the elite, ale was in high demand across England as a major part of the average person's daily diet, consumed at breakfast, lunch and dinner. The act of brewing was typically the work of women. Known as 'brewsters' they had, up until 1348, brewed ale in the home and sold it from the home, mostly serving their local community, but after 1348 these skilled women moved from the home to a place of work – the brew house, mass-producing ale to cater to a thirsty populace.[10]

With fewer men alive to work, women juggled domestic duties with labour outside the home, not only in brewing but in traditionally male roles as spicers, vintners, masons and even as armourers.[11] When farm labourers were not working the land during seasonal periods like sowing or the harvest, they migrated, hiring themselves out, sometimes on a transnational scale, travelling thousands of miles overseas.[12] These workers moonlighted as drovers, whalers, miners and even mercenary soldiers. They had portfolio careers and earned as they travelled, moving together in crews that were known to be violent and unpredictable, drinking heavily and engaging in knife fights for sport. Such emigration increased income, but it did not necessarily lead to people working *more*. In fact, the opposite was often true. Thanks to the advancement of technology like the water mill, people had more time to rest. Men particularly enjoyed football, wrestling and cockfighting and people enjoyed a better diet: fresh meat, fish and higher-quality bread became part of daily meals, even for the lower classes.

Perhaps unsurprisingly, it was not long before the elite felt threatened by the sudden elevation of their social inferiors and tried to re-enforce the pre-plague status quo.[13] 'Labourers that have no land to live on but their hands . . . May no penny ale please them, nor no piece of bacon, only fresh flesh or fish, fried, roast, or baked,' wrote the poet William Langland in his narrative poem *Piers Plowman*. In his allegorical exploration of England's post-plague society, Langland complains that labourers had become accustomed to finer food and drink and that created an economic problem: 'He must be hired at a high rate, else will he chide, And wail at the time.' Wage inflation had become untenable and it was not long before action was taken.

A new law was introduced to keep down labour costs and regulate the labour force. It was called the Ordinance of Labourers, and aimed at those who 'will not serve unless they may receive excessive wages'.[14] Those targeted were 'all able bodied men under sixty who were not tradesmen or artisans and who did not own or till land'. They were forced, by threat of imprisonment, to work for the same wages accepted 'before 1346'. The same rules applied for skilled workers such as 'saddlers, skinners, tailors, smiths and carpenters'.

By 1351 the Ordinance was ratified as the Statute of Labourers. Though capitalising on the need for labour remained a punishable offence, local justices struggled to enforce the law due to repeated waves of plague. More and more workers were needed to replace those who were dying and as a result wages continued to rise. As wages increased, prices began to inflate again as popular goods were bought cheaply and sold for multiple times their original value.

Some goods, jewels and gold, that remained unaffordable and too luxurious for the layman were copied and fakes proliferated. Subsequently, the elite became even more protective over their status and the luxury items they had always enjoyed exclusively. The ultimate defence of their social station came in the form of sumptuary laws – legislation intended to limit luxury and extravagance. This gave the lords control over the sartorial ambitions of the lower classes, a means of limiting labourers who had advanced themselves as a consequence of plague. The lower classes were banned from wearing certain furs or cloth colours, even the length of their shoes was restricted – the fashion of the time being exceptionally long shoes. The longer the shoe, the higher status the individual.

None of this, even allied to other measures such as controlling the price of grain or wine, or capping the pay of masons and butchers, could return a changed world to its former state, nor would it bring back the workforce that existed before 1348. The complexity of the post-plague era means it can't simply be described as a golden age.[15] Those who were once very poor, but had survived the worst epidemiological disaster in known history, certainly gained more opportunity than they had before the Black Death, but they largely continued to exist in relative poverty and at the mercy of further waves of disease. Yet, with such loss of life, serfdom was ended and survivors were able to move up the social ladder by demanding better pay and capitalising on the opportunities made available to them. Those who were able to afford better food, buy cloth rather than make it, and build lives in the burgeoning cities like London became a growing demographic of people. What the plague did create was a new 'middle class', who believed that it was possible to better their lives.

The first wave of plague – many more would follow – slowed down by 1351. In this strange new world, the absence of people was sorely felt, with homes left empty, half-eaten food rotten and livestock left to roam, untended. Petrarch asked the question 'what are we to do now?', and what followed was an interesting study of humanity in the face of catastrophe. The cult of memento mori evidenced an emotional response: fear that was imbued with hope as well as a macabre acceptance of death. New opportunities engendered new ambitions up and down the social scale, which led to immigration and a boom in technological innovation. Ultimately, people were freed from the shackles of a fatalistic belief that the condition they were born into would necessarily dictate their future, but this freedom was not without its problems. As the king and his government had struggled to implement strategies to keep the people safe from plague, increasing sanitation and preventing movement, they now used their power against the people to try to hinder social progression. The king and his government relied on the urban elite for vast loans to fund the war, yet they could not accept their ambitions. This power struggle and the closing gap between the noble classes and those who became wealthier and more influential in the second part of the century unsettled the traditional and accepted hierarchy. Tension was palpable and the consequences of this would reverberate for years to come.

19.   Winner and Waster

In early January 1355, Queen Philippa of Hainault laboured for one final time at Woodstock Palace. Twenty-five years after she had given birth to her first son, Edward, she gave birth to her last, Thomas.

Thomas was born into a large family, with three older sisters and four brothers – Edward (the Black Prince), Lionel, duke of Clarence, John of Gaunt and Edmund of Langley – all already out of the royal nursery. Edward was already the battle-hardened hero of Crécy, Lionel was married to Elizabeth de Burgh, the wealthy daughter of the earl of Ulster, and John of Gaunt would soon marry Blanche of Lancaster, the daughter of Henry, the newly entitled 'duke' of Lancaster. These brothers formed part of Edward III's vision of a new Plantagenet empire. Where Thomas was allocated a wet nurse, a rocker and installed in the royal nursery at Woodstock, his brothers were adorned with land and titles and formed their own adult house-holds. These households were like miniature courts for prospective kings, packed with loyal friends, servants and men they would take to war.

Aside from government, the household was the most important secular institution of the second half of the fourteenth century.[1] It shaped the lives of the Plantagenet family and the fates of those who served them. Members of a royal household lived together, ate together, washed together, wore the same clothing and moved together. The household was a living, breathing body, an amorphous space and collective unit, tasked with serving those at the top. The purpose was both practical and for show. Hierarchical by nature, the most esteemed members served the head of the household directly, as a lady-in-waiting or a chief officer. Others were responsible for day-to-day functions, such as managing the pantry and kitchen, which involved various tasks, such as tending to the larder, the cellar or spices. The day was laid out around prayer and meal times. Time was spent hunting and hawking, and the king would also be heavily engaged with his council.

The environment of the king's household was glamorous, sumptuous, hedonistic and sometimes suffocating. Richly decorated with tapestries, silks and plate, it was loud, fragrant and busy – intended to emulate Camelot. Lit by numerous candles, interior spaces were expected to be clean and sweet-smelling. Herbs and spices were used to promote a sense of cleanliness, and personal hygiene was considered a mark of gentility. People living and working within the household washed on waking, before and after each meal and before going to bed for the night. They had baths regularly, much more than the average person – in wooden vats of hot water scented by rosewater and spices. Hair was brushed with ivory combs and toothpicks were used. Laundry was another of the tasks that fell to household staff. Bed linen and linen clothing were regularly washed and dried. Wool and thicker clothing was brushed clean or beaten. Waste was flushed from latrines into a cesspit and some of the wealthiest households, such as the king's, had running water, hot and cold. The fourteenth-century royal household was far from dirty and basic, it was glittering, full of gossip, sex and scandal, and one of the most thrilling places to exist. Many of those employed in one of the prince's households saw their lives progress in dramatic ways. The most famous of all to do so was Geoffrey Chaucer. Around the same time that Thomas of Woodstock was born, Chaucer left his childhood home in the Vintry ward of the City of London and entered the service of Elizabeth de Burgh and Lionel of Antwerp. The couple were only around twenty and seventeen respectively, and their household was steeped in high fashion and fun.[2] Employed as a page, Chaucer's role was diverse. He ran errands, served as an attendant and was expected to take on minor responsibilities like delivering messages and cleaning armour. In this role he would have also experienced some of the best parts of life in the household: hunting, riding, ball sports, archery, dancing and reading as well as storytelling.[3] Chaucer would have travelled with the household across the country. In spring 1357, Elizabeth and Lionel went to London, where Chaucer probably witnessed one of the most exciting events of the age: the Black Prince riding into London with a remarkable prisoner, the king of France.

In 1357 a scholar from Oxford predicted that after a wave of pestilence, tempest and war, the kingdom of France would be destroyed and the king of England would reign supreme.[4] This hypothesis tied in nicely with Edward III's planned conquest of France, for on 21 September 1356, King Jean II of France, who had succeeded Philip VI in 1350, was captured at the Battle of Poitiers. It was the defining achievement of the Black Prince's life and one that the English court would celebrate for the next three years. Although, according to one source, the capture was a happy accident.[5] After the exhausted English army, who had been significantly outnumbered, had defeated the French force and chased them from the field, they were aghast when the French king arrived late to the battle with reinforcements. Jean II, spotting the Black Prince with only a few men, directed his attack that way. Yet, to Jean's horror, the earl of Warwick returned from pursuing French soldiers and 'took the French army in the flank, and fought them fiercely'.[6] Caught up in the melee, Jean II and his younger son Philip were captured, along with a number of other French nobility. Their collective ransom would be enough to bankrupt France and weaken the morale of the country.

The Black Prince first took Jean II and the other captives to Bordeaux, before returning to England in spring 1357, shortly after Edward's traditional Garter feast. In May they landed at Plymouth and from there the spectacular procession towards London began. People brought out 'quantities of bows and arrows and of every kind of arms', for the French king to see.[7] The message they meant to convey was clear: England was the superior power. When the procession arrived in London in late May, the crowds erupted. People pushed and shoved, bustling to get the best glimpse of the path the Black Prince and his captive would take. The mood was merry. Wine was handed out freely, a rare luxury for those who would normally only consume ale. The guilds were dressed in full livery and marched through the streets to greet the prince and the French king, escorting them to the cheers and whistles of the crowd.[8] Silver- and gold-plate confetti rained over the advancing party, scattered by maidens from low-hanging windows. The Black Prince is said to have ridden behind Jean II, entering the city on a black hackney, a simple riding horse.[9] The king of France was offered a far superior white horse, commensurate with the laws of chivalry. The festivities that followed the Battle of Poitiers and the capture of Jean II were described by the prince's contemporaneous biographer, Chandos Herald (the herald of Sir John Chandos), in his verse *Life of the Black Prince*. He recounts the court dancing, hunting, hawking, jousting and feasting, 'just as in King Arthur's time'.[10] Culminating with the massive Garter feast of 1358, this was a celebration not only of the victory over France, but the prestige of England's sacred military order founded by Edward a decade earlier, before the eruption of plague. Where the original foundation feast was haunted by the fear of the Black Death, its ten-year anniversary was pregnant with prosperity.

Edward's plans were ambitious: 'In the year of grace 1358 the king made a proclamation in all parts of the kingdom that all aliens, from whatsoever part of the world, who wished to attend the festival of Saint George would have safe conduct to enter the kingdom of England.'[11] This celebration of the Order of the Garter and of Saint George was going to be a major event. Before the capture of Jean II at Poitiers, the Garter feast had been ceremonial by nature and only important within the context of court life. However, with Jean II a guest in England, housed comfortably at the Savoy Palace on the Strand, the celebrations served as a piece of political theatre intended to impress the king of France but also to make a statement to the whole of Christendom. Heralds were sent across Europe to announce that jousting was expected to take place around 23 April. The duke of Luxembourg and knights from Gascony were all in attendance, as was the queen of Scotland, Edward's younger sister, whose husband, David II, was Edward's other kingly prisoner, brought out along-side Jean II to prove Edward's supremacy. All of Edward's children were present, including Lionel of Antwerp and his wife, Elizabeth de Burgh; by association Geoffrey Chaucer was also fortunate enough to witness the type of spectacle that made Edward III stand out in comparison to his forebears on the throne.[12]

For the members of the Order of the Garter this was also a dazzling opportunity to demonstrate their fame, as they draped themselves in the ceremonial blue and white robes, trimmed with ermine and decorated with garters.[13] Queen Philippa is said to have worn a blue coronet, blue being the colour associated with the Order, with bright gold woven throughout. Edward III also wore blue and gold, his robes decorated with shining gold falcons and a blue girdle that hung around his waist.[14]

With Windsor emulating Camelot, symbolic references to Arthur were part of the celebrations.[15] A piece of music composed within Saint George's Chapel, 'Sub Arturo plebs', is a reflection on divine favour imposed on those who live under the rule of Arthur.[16] Like much of the connections to the mystical court of King Arthur previously played out at Edward's court, roleplay, costume, tales and riddles were a large part of the tournament, most notably evidenced in a series of letters written around the height of the Order of the Garter celebrations, and intended to be read aloud and performed. Known as the 'Jousting Letters', five have survived and they offer a rare glimpse into the fantastical, hedonistic world of the court during this period.[17] Each letter is written as if from an imaginary queen, 'Pantesilia, Queen of Persia', 'Judith, Empress of Egypt and Arabia', 'Niolas, Queen of Nubia', 'Emely, Empress of Europe and Judea' and finally, a real queen, Philippa Queen of Albion – clearly Queen Philippa of England. Each queen suggests a worthy combatant for the joust to the lady presiding over the tournament. In the letter from 'Pantesilia', the suggested contender is 'a huntsman in our neighbouring forests and deserts, who knows little or nothing of anything except dogs and hunting . . .' Having selected an opponent she directs the huntsman to 'give him six blows with the lance, seated in low saddles, in your presence, this very day immediately after meal time'. These letters show women played a role within the tournament and the chivalric camaraderie of the court. They may not have physically participated in the joust, but they were the organisers, the presiding figures and, importantly, they had fun. In these fictive dialogues, powerful women converse as if they were the rulers of exotic courts. They organise men and their activities, they flirt and tease. In

'Judith', the woman is the dominant sexual figure in an encounter, imposing flirtatious 'penalties' on the contending knight should his performance be poor. More than anything, the letters shed light on the joy of the court, the pleasure taken in performance in a unique social space, shifting between fantasy and reality. This was a space for self-expression and fluid identity; there was no more exciting time to be a member of the English court than at the time of the Garter celebrations.

As England's elite arrived at Windsor, the chronicler Henry Knighton gushed that 'the splendour of the festival was richly varied and it is not within our powers to do it justice'. The excess of Edward III's court had not gone unnoticed and the contrast between haves and have-nots was dramatised in a poem known as *Wynnere and Wastoure*. The unknown poet remarked that the king dined on gold and silver plate but paid for it all on credit.[18] True to the style of much poetry of the period, *Wynnere and Wastoure* begins as a dream, the narrator having fallen asleep in a woodland. In his dream state he finds himself outdoors in front of a pavilion, dazzled by imagery of the Order of the Garter:

> The roof and sides all arrayed with red,
> Adorned with English bezants embossed with gold
> Girdled about with garters of dark blue;
> And every garter glittered richly with gold.[19]

The king is seated in state inside the pavilion, dressed in elaborate and expensive robes, with the garter symbol emblazoned across them. He is undoubtedly Edward III. The dreamer finds out that the king is trying to resolve a problem between two men, Wynnere and Wastoure, present at what appears to be a tournament. When called forward, the men each present their argument. Wynnere's point is that the best course of managing wealth is to save and not squander money on frivolity, but Wastoure believes that wealth should be enjoyed and spread out within the community. Wynnere argues that Wastoure spends beyond his means, to the detriment of the realm.[20] Edward III's Garter feast of 1358 provided inspiration for the poem, but the poem also emphasises the discontentment of the rising wealthy merchant classes, the wasteful attitudes of the elite who relied on borrowing from Italian banks and wealthy merchants, and the ongoing cost of war. It captures the mood of the late 1350s, of jubilance and frivolity, but also of the unresolved conflict with France. Although Jean II had been captured, there was still no peace agreement, and Edward III was yet to achieve his ambition of ruling over France. The poem closes with a hint of what was to come when the king counsels Wynnere:

> And look to me, Wynnere, if you want to gain wealth,
> When I go to the wars to lead my men;
> For in the proud palace in the rich city of Paris
> I plan to have it done, and dub you to knight.[21]

The Garter feast was a flagrant display of power – a space for the English court to play out their most elaborate fantasies. Yet in April 1358, as Edward and his court celebrated, there was an undercurrent of uncertainty and intrigue over his plan to resume war. The cost was great, and to pay for it the king was indebted to lenders across England as well as in the Low Countries and Italy – a debt that Edward's own subjects were liable for should the king fail to pay it back. But, with Jean II captive, the realm was also eager to see what this unstoppable king could do given the chance and with the support of his eldest sons. Swathed in cloth of gold and blue garter insignia, Edward III basked in the glory of victory. Yet to be the ultimate winner and claim the crown of France, Edward would have to double down on a country already destroyed by war. This was a moral conundrum: was it really winning to stare out from his new throne at a country blackened and wasted by a war of his own creation?

20. Lions and Leopards

France was in tatters. After the plague had left the English arrived and took their king. This was followed by two weeks of violent uprisings. Centred around northern France and Paris, a bitter rebellion known as the Jacquerie consumed the country in early summer 1358. The poor and labouring classes rose up in their thousands, wasted by war, discrimination between the classes and a sense of fury at the Crown for having failed to protect the people from the horrors of war. Mercenary soldiers, left to linger by the English army after the Crécy campaign, wreaked havoc on the countryside, inflicting appalling brutality on common people, who in turn took out their rage on the wealthier citizens and nobility, such as the French knight who was captured by peasants and forced to watch his family be massacred before he was murdered and his castle burned.[1] France was on its knees; it was an obvious time for Edward III to strike. He decided to take his three eldest sons, the Black Prince, Lionel of Antwerp and John of Gaunt, with him. The objective was to travel to Reims, the spiritual capital of French kings, where he would be crowned, and then take Paris, the political capital. This would be his largest and most ambitious campaign to date, fuelled by previous victories and the pro-war rhetoric he had spent decades carefully promoting, and funded by steep loans. The campaign would be for England, for Arthur and Saint George, but most of all it would be for Edward.

While Edward III presented a vision of himself steeped in Arthurian symbolism – and with Saint George as the patron of his new order – the French had their own means of projecting power. The sons of King Jean II – Louis I of Anjou; Jean, duke of Berry; Philip, duke of Burgundy; Louis, duke of Bourbon; and the future King Charles V – invested heavily in the arts. One of the most prestigious and coveted art forms of all were the elaborate and intricate tapestries produced in France in the late fourteenth century. As a son of the French king and a wealthy patron, Louis I of Anjou commissioned the largest surviving narrative representation of the Book of Revelation, its scenes all intricately depicted on a series of woven panels. The tapestry was so immense that Louis could not fit his magnum opus on the walls of his home, the Château d'Angers, so its panels had to be rolled up and kept in a cupboard.[2] He only brought them out when the weather allowed them to be displayed outside.

The scale of the tapestries, telling the story of the Book of Revelation, meant the best way for people to see them was to walk around them. The scenes depicting the Apocalypse offered a physical and immersive experience. Within the narrative is a cluster of horsemen clad in the same armour as the average English soldier. One man, centre frame, stands out, wearing a distinctive mark of the English: a single pheasant feather worn in his helmet, as was common for English and Scottish soldiers in the fourteenth century.[3] In another scene a dragon passes a gold sceptre topped with the French motif of a fleur-de-lis to a sea beast, grotesque and terrifying, rising from the waves to snatch the sceptre.[4] If this is the Apocalypse, it has arrived with the English. The soldiers are the demonic cavalry and the sea beast is the monster arriving at the shore of France to consume the country in its gnashing fangs. The clearest indication that this was a terror campaign is the depiction of the horsemen of the Apocalypse as Edward III and his sons in the moment they descend on France.

The army that crossed the Channel in 1359 was the largest force of Edward III's reign. It was also probably the largest army, up to that point in history, ever to leave the shores of England. A high proportion of the ten thousand men Edward had recruited from England and Wales were volunteers. Years of propaganda, the insatiable appetite for Arthurian legend and the glamorisation of war had paid off. Most of these men were mounted archers, trained to shoot both the crossbow and the longbow, the deadliest weapon of the Hundred Years War.[5]

At the end of October 1359, soldiers spilled into the port at Calais.

Sundry goods, horses and thousands of arrowheads had been bundled into barrels that littered the town and garrison, waiting to be heaved onto the carts that would form Edward's baggage train. Finally, in three columns, Edward III, the Black Prince and Henry, duke of Lancaster, led troops out of Calais towards Reims.

The duke of Lancaster was one of the most experienced military leaders of the Hundred Years War and Edward III's closest friend and ally. The pair were also cousins, enjoying a far better relationship than their forebears. Lancaster was immensely rich, inheriting vast lands from his father and his uncle, the executed Thomas of Lancaster. Henry had allotted much of his personal wealth and loyalty to Edward's wars in France and was certainly well rewarded. Earlier in the year Edward had married his third son, John of Gaunt, to Henry's daughter, Blanche of Lancaster, at Reading Abbey – Lancaster was now bound to Edward by marriage as well as blood. His devotion also produced a new title. Shortly after the foundation of the Order of the Garter, Edward made Lancaster a founding member of the Order, and gave him the title of duke. The first dukedom of Lancaster: this was a distinct and notable privilege.

Young and newly married, Gaunt was itching for the same military prestige as his older brother. The Black Prince travelled with Lionel, duke of Clarence, and his own company of men, including Geoffrey Chaucer.

According to one source, the three columns travelled through France, 'riding and destroying the land', though the worst of the attacks came when the army were reunited thirty miles outside of Reims.[6] Around 4 December, Edward III reached his destination. Situated in the Champagne province, Reims was the city where French kings had been crowned for centuries. According to legend, the pagan chieftain Clovis was both baptised and crowned at Reims in 496. A white dove – an image of the Holy Spirit – fluttered down from heaven carrying in its feet a precious ampula of holy oil, dropping it into the hands of Archbishop Remigius. This oil, given by God, thereafter marked French kings as spiritually superior to all others, adding impetus to Edward's reason for wanting to be formally crowned at Reims in the traditional manner of French kings – doing so would give spiritual legitimisation to his claim.

Edward's intention was to be peacefully accepted and crowned but the actions of his army in the vicinity around Reims were far from peaceful. Thomas Gray, a northern baron and author of *Scalacronica*, served as a captain in the Black Prince's column. He wrote of his time on campaign near Reims that 'the town of Cormicy was taken by escalade and the castle won, the keep being mined and thrown down by the Prince's men.' Elsewhere, Lancaster's division, along with John of Gaunt, also captured Autry and Cernay, two fortified towns on the border of Lorraine; Cernay was taken under cover of darkness, after which English soldiers reduced the town to ashes. The king's division led their own raid 'from Reims nearly to Paris', where 'they set themselves in ambush and sent their scouts up to the gates of the city. They made such an uproar in the suburbs that those within the city did not have the courage to come forth.'[7]

Raids and attacks were carried out across the countryside in the hope of lowering morale and making people believe the Valois monarchy could not or would not protect them. Letters of remission and tax accounts show a country destroyed by localised attacks.[8] Refugees were common, streaming into towns and cities seeking help and protection from English soldiers. The chronicler and Parisian Carmelite friar Jean de Venette was an eyewitness to the ruin, offering a deeply affecting portrayal of the destruction of his home village, Venette, near Compiègne in northern France. 'The English destroyed, burned and plundered many little towns . . . capturing or even killing the inhabitants . . . Houses and churches no longer presented a smiling appearance with newly repaired roofs but rather the lamentable spectacle of scattered, smoking ruins to which they had been reduced by devouring flames.'[9]

While Edward III succeeded in attacking the surroundings of Reims, he could not break the morale of those inside the city. The resistance was spearheaded by the enigmatic captain of the city, Gaucher de Châtillon, a nobleman from Champagne who had the nous to prepare for a protracted siege.[10] De Châtillon built a vast wall, complete with towers, between the cathedral and the Porte de Mars – an ancient monument in the city. An additional defensive circuit of ditches was dug around the city. The immediate surroundings were torched so the English could take no shelter, arms were stored and a citizen's watch was arranged. To pay for the city's defence he taxed both the citizens of Reims and the refugees who were flooding in from surrounding towns and villages. Drawbridges were dismantled and gates firmly closed. Masses of chains were stored inside the city so the people could hold back the English forces with an additional chain wall in the event that they broke the defence.[11]

Reims would not capitulate. Edward was forced to station himself ten miles away, at the Benedictine monastery at the summit of the Montagne de Reims. As Edward knew from Calais twelve years earlier, a siege could last a very long time indeed. The difference between then and now was that time was a luxury that Edward could not afford. Initially he was gentle in his approach. He commanded his men to cease plundering while he negotiated a temporary truce. It elapsed, and yet Reims still did not fall. So it was that in late December 1359 Edward began to use force. Groups of men swarmed to the city walls and began a blockade.

The citizens of Reims would likely have known about the Siege of Calais in 1346, when people faced starvation due to the English blockade. Though Reims had ample food and water, it was still possible that the English would eventually starve them to death, or enter the city by force, bringing a quicker but bloodier end. The laws of war at the time were based in part on a passage from the Bible's book of Deuteronomy, which stated that if a city fell to a besieging army having resisted attack, the defenders had no right to mercy: 'When the Lord your God delivers it into your hand, put to the sword all the men in it.'[12] One citizen of Reims encapsulated in song the sense of terror that pervaded the city. The French composer and poet Guillaume de Machaut served as one of many men who performed guard duty – his job was to patrol the high walls and keep watch on the

English encamped on the horizon.[13] When Machaut was not guard-
ing the city he wrote a motet – a vocal composition – based on the
biblical story of Daniel in the lion's den. Machaut begs God to come
to their aid:

> our enemies surround us
> Even our countrymen have been changed into brigands
> Leopards and lions.
> Wolves, birds of prey and eagles
> Snatch away every creeping thing.[14]

Leopards and lions were vivid symbols of the English; eventually,
with no agreement brokered, Edward III began to roar. Three
divisions attacked the walls of the city, launching thousands upon
thousands of arrows into Reims. Defenders countered by hurling
rocks onto the archers below. In an attempt to try to scale the walls,
the English nailed together wood felled in the local forest to make
siege towers. The people of Reims fought back by setting alight any
timber in the ditches around the walls, which prevented the English
from moving their engines closer. The Black Prince's division –
including both Geoffrey Chaucer and Lionel of Antwerp – were
the only ones to make progress towards the walls.[15] The assault was
doomed. After seven weeks outside Reims, Edward conceded defeat
and turned his attention to Paris.[16]

Edward dragged his army through the sleet and mud of a freezing
winter until finally, in late winter 1360, they reached Beauce on the
south side of Paris, a lush region that had been largely abandoned by
the local people, who carried what they could, then streamed with
other refugees into Paris's packed streets. The English army moved in,
devouring food and stealing possessions that had been left behind.[17]
After wasting the town, the army marched on to Paris and camped
in Chanteloup, twenty miles away. Having failed in Reims, Edward's
aim was to intimidate Charles, the king's eldest son and dauphin of
France, into making a favourable deal: more land and full sovereignty
over Gascony. The best way to do so was to inflict terror upon the
surroundings of the city.

In the village of Orly, local people were cornered inside their parish church and massacred.[18] At a Benedictine priory-turned-makeshift garrison in Arpajon, terrified clerics and local refugees surrendered to the English after being abandoned by the defenders of the garrison, following days of being brutally besieged. Before they fled Arpajon, French soldiers who were meant to protect the people instead turned on them in punishment for their surrender, setting fire to a church where people had gathered for safety. Nine hundred were engulfed in the flames and those who tried to escape were cut down by the English.[19]

Unable to lure the dauphin to fight in pitched battle, Edward departed Paris. As he marched away, he left with blood and soot on his hands; less Arthur, saviour of the Britons, and far more the leading horseman of the Apocalypse returning to hell.

In May 1360, Edward got some of what he desired – not the crown of France, but a generous portion of the country – via the Treaty of Brétigny, a peace agreement that brought the first phase of the Hundred Years War to a close. In return for renouncing his claim to the French crown, Edward was granted an enlarged and sovereign Aquitaine, which included the disputed Gascony.[20] This vast territory, comprising a third of the entire kingdom of France, would not be held in fief to the French Crown, but ruled as an independent duchy. The title 'duke of Aquitaine' was replaced by the superior 'lord' and no English sovereign would have to perform homage for these lands. The enormous sum of three million écus was agreed for the full ransom payment of Jean II.[21] In preparation for his return to France, Edward gave his rival a gift of a long cloth of 'blu', a blue suit swathed in an extraordinary amount of squirrel fur.[22] After a decorous ceremony, perhaps wearing his blue suit, Jean II was taken back to Calais in early July 1360. From there he was to travel further into France in order to raise the money for his ransom. Forty French noblemen remained in captivity, acting as security in case Jean failed to provide the promised fee. Their ranks included the dukes of Berry and Orléans, and Jean's reluctant and capricious son Louis, duke of Anjou, who was hauled from his comfortable Château d'Angers to serve as hostage to the English in Calais.[23]

In a letter to the French people Jean offered an explanation for his decision to abandon the fight. The people were told that:

> because of the said wars many mortal battles have been fought, people slaughtered, churches pillaged, bodies destroyed and souls lost, maids and virgins deflowered, respectable wives and widows dishonoured, towns, manors and buildings burnt, and robberies, oppressions and ambushes on the roads and highways committed. Justice has failed because of them . . . it seemed in truth that greater [evils] could have followed . . . in order to put an end to the wars and the evils and sorrows spoken of above . . . we have consented and do consent to, ratify, will and approve [this treaty of peace].[24]

That same July, Pope Innocent VI personally wrote to Edward and Jean II, congratulating the former on bringing negotiations to an affable conclusion, as the pope called it, '*mutatis mutandis*' (with things changed that should be changed).[25]

Writing later, Geoffrey Chaucer reflected on his experience campaigning with Edward in France, where he witnessed, and participated, in the horrors inflicted on the French people. In 'The Knight's Tale', the first story in his *The Canterbury Tales*, the knight speaks of thousands slain, a tyrant using force to get what he wants, giving voice to the inhumanity of war. There is no chivalry, only cruelty. It was hoped that the Treaty of Brétigny would finally free France from the onslaught of the English. But it was riddled with problems, and would be ineffective should two important clauses not be met: the French needed to hand over an enlarged Aquitaine plus all other promised territory – including Calais, Ponthieu and Guyenne – and the English had to withdraw from northern France. It took years for the French to surrender Aquitaine and the English never upheld their part of the deal. Still, at least for a short time, the war between England and France was over.

Edward's greatest victory was also, in some respects, a failure. If Edward had persevered, noted one contemporary commentator, 'the captains and their men could easily have conquered the kingdom of France, to the advantage of the King of England and his heirs'.[26] Edward III had spent years of hosting tournaments and festooning Windsor with symbols of France. He had styled himself as king of France and identified himself with national heroes such as Arthur and Saint George, yet the pervading feeling across the realm was: what was the point? For those who had given their hearts and souls and even their lives to Edward, the Treaty of Brétigny was the ultimate betrayal.

The Treaty of Brétigny left Edward III in control of a similar amount of territory, and able to command a similar level of respect, as Henry II and Eleanor of Aquitaine in the twelfth century – before King John lost his lands to the French in 1204. England, Wales and Ireland were his and he had overlordships of both Scotland and Aquitaine as well as portions of France including Calais. English territory was no longer confined to England and the Isles; it was becoming a continental empire.

Edward III could not rule Aquitaine in person, as Eleanor had done for much of her life. He was first and foremost king of England and his presence was required in England, where his government was based. At almost fifty, Edward was getting older and a quieter existence at Windsor or his castle in Sheen (Richmond) was increasingly appealing. Without the king himself to rule Aquitaine what was needed was a royal figure beloved by the people but who would govern with strength in the king's image. Aquitaine needed the Black Prince.

With his formidable war record, the prince of Wales was the most eligible bachelor in Europe. As the future ruler of Aquitaine and future king of England, he was expected to marry a European princess, one who would bring land, wealth and a European political alliance. But when he announced his clandestine betrothal to his cousin, Joan of Kent, in summer 1361, he broke with a long-standing Plantagenet tradition. This was the first time that the heir to the English throne had married an English noblewoman.

Joan of Kent was the daughter of Edward III's uncle, Edmund, earl of Kent, and following the death of Joan's father on the scaffold in 1330, Philippa of Hainault had raised her in her own household and ensured that she received an education befitting her status. When Joan's brother died in 1352, she inherited the earldom of Kent in her own right, elevating her to the title of countess. Joan was not a stranger to court gossip and scandal. At the age of twelve she was noticed by Thomas Holland, a knight of the royal household almost fifteen years her senior. Joan was persuaded by Holland to enter into marriage in 1340, albeit in secret – there was no reading or publishing of banns and no blessing by a priest. But when Holland returned from a military campaign in Prussia he was crestfallen to discover that his wife was now married to someone else: William Montagu, the earl of Salisbury. When Holland built up enough wealth to reclaim his wife, the matter was taken to the papal court in Rome and eventually Joan's marriage to William Montagu was declared void.[1] Naive and still incredibly young, Joan was given the mocking nickname the 'Virgin of Kent', a cruel comment on her duplicitous love life.

In December 1360, Thomas Holland died suddenly in Normandy; within six months, Joan and the Black Prince were married. Though it is unlikely Edward was eager for his son to marry Joan, there is no contemporary evidence that proves the couple were not supported. The match between Edward and Joan resembled French royal unions. It was regular practice for both French royal houses, the Capetians and the Valois, to marry a member of the French nobility rather than looking beyond the realm.[2] England had just won the first phase of the Hundred Years War and a foreign match for political stability was not as important as it might once have been. Equally, at a time when fertility was of great importance in a royal marriage, the fact that Joan had already given birth to five children was probably considered an auspicious sign by the Black Prince.

Remarriage for widows in the fourteenth century was not uncommon, nor was it unlawful. The most famous of all Chaucer's characters from *The Canterbury Tales* is Alison, the Wife of Bath. Alison married five times, with her first wedding coming when she was twelve. Widows were important and highly respected, largely due to the fact that many, like Joan, were incredibly wealthy.[3] Remarriage, according to English law, allowed women to maintain their lands and titles while also moving up the social ladder, like Joan had. At thirty-three, Joan was still relatively young and had been described by contemporaries as 'the most beautiful lady in England'.[4]

The only real problem with the marriage was that they were related. Consanguinity – the fact of being descended from the same ancestor – was a serious legal consideration that could not be bypassed, even in medieval Church law. A special papal licence was needed if one wanted one's marriage to a cousin to be acknowledged in the eyes of the church. Fortunately for the Black Prince and Joan, the problem was not unprecedented. In 1359 the royal family had to obtain the same licence for John of Gaunt and Blanche of Lancaster, both technically descended from the same patrilineal ancestor, Henry III. The Black Prince and Joan were even more closely linked, both descending from a shared great-grandfather, Edward I. The administrative back-and-forth lasted for much of the summer until finally, in September, a papal bull of dispensation was issued.[5] The couple were officially wed in October 1361 at a ceremony held at Lambeth Palace and conducted by the archbishop of Canterbury, Simon Islip, before festivities at Windsor Castle.

The marriage was a glimmer of hope in another period of great loss. In 1361 a second brutal wave of plague claimed more lives across northern Europe. Known as the 'Second Plague', this strain, a mutation of the first, was particularly virulent against 'young people and children'.[6] Two more of Edward and Philippa's daughters were killed in the Second Plague: Mary, countess of Brittany, and Margaret, countess of Pembroke. They were sixteen and fourteen years old respectively. It is also likely the same plague killed another important and beloved member of the family, Henry, duke of Lancaster. His funeral was held in April, attended by Edward III, Queen Philippa, their sons and their wives. Gold cloth was delicately laid over the bier of their dear friend and 'noble' cousin.[7]

Lancaster represented the old guard; he was personally responsible for much of the king's military successes in France and was an ally Edward had relied on heavily. With Lancaster's death his great wealth, amounting to around twelve thousand pounds per year, streamed into the purse of Edward's son, John of Gaunt (the new duke of Lancaster), through his wife, Blanche, Lancaster's daughter. This inheritance was to be shared with Blanche's sister, Maud, countess of Holland and Zeeland. But Maud died soon after her father, leaving the whole

Lancastrian inheritance to Gaunt. To some, the luck was suspect, 'vulgar repute that she had been poisoned to reunite the inheritance'.[8] In reality, Maud had probably been another victim of the plague.

Only in their early twenties, the new duke and duchess of Lancaster became the richest and most powerful young couple in the realm. The Black Prince, however, bore the greatest responsibility during this time. On 19 July, he knelt in full armour before Edward III to pay homage as prince of Aquitaine, holding the principality independently but under the overlordship of his father. The plan was that the Black Prince and Joan of Kent would set up a court in Aquitaine and rule there on the king's behalf.

The enlarged Aquitaine was a vast body of land bordering Spain in south-west France. The prince controlled territory from Poitiers in the north to Toulouse in the south. In the middle were the important French settlements of Limoges, Angoulême and Périgueux. Up until the prince's arrival in summer 1363, Sir John Chandos had been acting as Edward's lieutenant. He had been given the complicated task of overseeing the surrender of French towns and villages across Aquitaine per the terms laid out in the Treaty of Brétigny.[9] Since the war began, the constant harrying of towns and villages across France, by a private army of men named the Free Companies, was considered to be worse than the plague.

The Free Companies were bands of mercenary soldiers – Bretons, Gascons, Germans and English – that had stayed in France after the formal exodus of the English armies. Tired of wages being paid late or not at all, they pillaged their way across the country. Jean Froissart lamented that they would 'destroy the noble kingdom of France' through plundering and murdering as they went.[10]

One group calling itself the Latecomers is even said to have threatened the papacy at Avignon: 'hordes of bandits and robbers wasting the land – Englishmen and others – and they still had possession of a huge number of castles and fortresses that few people dared travel across the country'.[11] The captain of the Latecomers embraced their notoriety, signing his letters 'God's Friend and the World's Enemy'. As the Free Companies' strength and size grew, they began occupying castles and garrisons across France. Even a 'crusade' against them, launched from Avignon by the pope, was unsuccessful. Those who enlisted in this papal army soon realised they were better off switching sides, so joined the mercenaries.[12]

Though the Free Companies answered to nobody, they did – by and large – respect the territory controlled by their own sovereigns.[13] This meant that while English or Gascon gangs avoided targeting areas possessed by the English Crown, such as Aquitaine, others, such as the Bretons, saw these areas as fair game. In particular, Breton companies terrorised the regions of Limousin and Rouergue. One of John Chandos's first tasks from 1361 had been to push them out. These early years smoothing out the cracks that had been left in Aquitaine by years of warfare were bloody and required grit. By spring 1362, the Free Companies, led by the notorious Gascon thug Hélie Meschin, otherwise known as 'Petit', decamped to Burgundy. They were now the problem of the lieutenant of Burgundy, Jean de Tancarville. The path was cleared for the Black Prince's grand entry.

While Chandos was trying to make Aquitaine a comfortable and peaceful royal territory, the Black Prince was working on recruiting men from his lands in Cheshire and Cornwall to join him. This was a considerable opportunity for soldiers who sought to advance their position. Men who enlisted as archers were granted money, land and the promise of minor office in Aquitaine. Criminals were offered pardons if they joined the prince.[14] The Black Prince arrived in Aquitaine in July 1363 and received homage from local lords and dignitaries at the cathedral of Saint-André in Bordeaux. Kneeling lords kissed the Bible and pledged fealty to the prince of Aquitaine. These ceremonies were an important part of the prince's initiation into his new life and they were followed by an extensive tour of the region. The prince and princess took in their lot, visiting Cognac, which would become the administrative centre of the prince's rule, and trying various residences. The castle at Angoulême, with its lush landscape, idyllic polygonal keep and large tower, became a favourite.

As well as travelling around Aquitaine, the prince was also occupied with finessing the aesthetics of his new court, mainly stationed in Bordeaux. Their household was expected to be an expression of their power, demonstrated through hospitality, conspicuous consumption and exhibitions of chivalry. In Aquitaine, this type of display and opulence had direct links to the region's own cultural fabric.[15] Celebration and romance were the distinguishing features of the Occitan culture of southern France. Eleanor of Aquitaine's grandfather was Duke William IX, otherwise known as the 'Troubador Duke', a songwriter and poet. Aquitaine produced popular troubadour poetry and a habit of immense spending on the trappings of luxurious ducal life; the lifestyle the Black Prince and Joan were walking into suited them well. Joan became a sartorial icon. She introduced the trend for corsets, slit at the sides and trimmed with ermine. She wore colourful shimmering fabrics and silk belts with enamelled panels and had more silk imported from Aleppo and Alexandria.[16] Joan literally glittered with jewels and pearls woven into her hair, dripping in gold and precious stones. She wore tight-fitting silk dresses with a plunging, suggestive neckline edged with ermine. A Breton lord called Jean de Beaumanoir was appalled by the new trends, commenting that Joan had 'adopted the fashions of the English or the Free Companies' and that 'he was disgusted by those women'.[17]

Governing Aquitaine was an exciting opportunity for the Black Prince. He had a beautiful new wife, who became pregnant with a son in the spring of 1364, a loyal coterie of English and local Gascon knights, and the French were occupied trying to raise enough money to pay for King Jean II's ransom, leaving the prince free to establish himself without torment. Two unexpected events conspired to unsettle this happy equilibrium. First, Jean's son, the duke of Anjou, who had been held hostage in Calais, escaped his captivity. This forced Jean to save face by returning to England to fulfil his chivalric promise and see through the end of his ransom. The second unexpected event was that in April 1364 the convivial but ill-fated Jean fell sick and died.

Jean II had not been a formidable opponent, but he was succeeded by Charles V, who was no sword-wielding monarch but had a formidable and strategic mind. Physical might was outsourced to the constable of France, Bertrand du Guesclin, a man who achieved the same military renown as the Black Prince – who envied his French competitor. Du Guesclin was an experienced warrior and with Charles's backing he intended to remove the Free Companies altogether by pushing them into Spain in the guise of a crusade, sanctioned by the papacy in Avignon, against the Moors in Granada.[18]

In 1365 hordes of mercenaries belonging to various Free Companies moved through the French countryside towards Aquitaine. They marched with the ostensible aim of crossing the Pyrenees for Spain. Some mercenaries were perhaps tempted by the spiritual benefits such a crusade would offer, but their incentives were largely financial. The papacy in Avignon and the French Crown had to raise a sum large enough to tempt the Free Companies into mercenary service; whether they pillaged and murdered their way across Spain was unlikely a concern of the French or the Black Prince and his people in Aquitaine. A motley crew of fierce and lawless mercenary warriors trickled over the border. France was finally free of the fear of the Free Companies. Sir Hugh Calveley, an experienced English knight from Cheshire – who had some experience as a mercenary himself – helped supervise the exodus of the Free Companies, working alongside Bertrand du Guesclin to move men over the border through Navarre and into Spain.[19]

Though the intention was that the mercenaries would fight in Granada, they instead became involved in a conflict gripping Castile, one that would eventually draw both Bertrand du Guesclin and the Black Prince to the battlefield. It was a war between brothers: the Spanish king, Pedro I, and his half-brother, Enrique Trastámara.

Pedro was wildly unpopular. After the death of his father, Alfonso XI, Pedro had his father's mistress, Eleanor de Guzmán, murdered, along with her children. The only survivor was her son, Enrique Trastámara, who fled to the court of Charles V. The French king had his own axe to grind with Pedro, who had married his cousin Blanche of Bourbon. It was a loveless marriage, with Pedro favouring his mistress María de Padilla and locking Blanche away. She died in captivity in mysterious circumstances, likely murdered at Pedro's command.

Perhaps unsurprisingly, the Spanish king was dubbed Pedro the Cruel. When Enrique enlisted French aid, Charles was more than happy to help. The Free Companies could be used to fight the Moors, but they could also aid Enrique and oust the loathed Pedro. As mercenaries began to spill over the border into Navarre, Pedro panicked and beseeched Edward III for aid.

An alliance between England and Castile had been formalised at Saint Paul's Cathedral shortly before the Black Prince left for Aquitaine. The agreement had a specific clause that now appeared immensely useful to Pedro I: English soldiers would come to the aid of Castile if the French invaded.[20] Given the French were supporting Enrique with a collection of paid mercenaries, this clause was now active.

In early 1366, Enrique's army, with soldiers from France under the command of du Guesclin, and neighbouring Aragon, as well as the Free Company mercenaries, took the whole of Castile in fifty days.[21] Pedro fled with his daughters, Constance and Isabella, and a few chests hurriedly stuffed with personal wealth. His destination was the court of his only ally, the Black Prince.[22]

As Pedro stepped from the large carrack that had brought him to the port at Bayonne, he cut a miserable figure. A desperate king displaced from his throne was not what the Black Prince wanted or needed. But it remained a matter of both English interest and honour to help Pedro, for a Castile controlled by Enrique, a French puppet, was a threat. Castile boasted the best navy in Europe, with influence across the Mediterranean and eastern trade routes. The Black Prince, however, may also have had his own priorities. The chronicler Jean Froissart was at the prince's court at the time of Pedro's arrival. He noted that the prince, despite objections from his counsel, wished to adhere to the treaty but also confirmed the existence of a rivalry between the Black Prince and Bertrand du Guesclin. Whispers circulated at court that 'the Prince was making this expedition through pride and presumption, and that he was jealous of the prestige that Bertrand du Guesclin had gained in helping to put Enrique on the throne.'[23] There is likely some truth in Froissart's suggestion. The prince's reputation was built on military prestige. An opportunity to beat the French military commander was probably too tempting to refuse. The problem was the expense. An army would have to be mustered and paid for by the English on credit. They would only be reimbursed by Pedro I when he had reclaimed his throne. For the prince, still in his relative infancy as ruler of Aquitaine, the whole operation was an incredible risk and he proceeded with caution.

The plan was to muster an army out of Aquitaine and cross the Pyrenees, entering Spain through Navarre. England had long-standing ties with the country but it was now ruled by Charles of Navarre, a duplicitous and shady individual whose loyalty could not be relied on. Charles had previously allowed the Free Companies and the French passage through his territory but he was a man who hedged his bets. Generally considered to be one of the most scheming characters of the Middle Ages, Charles may have also been the most prudent.

Border regions like Navarre were hugely important during this period. They were essential to the movement of large armies but they were also porous spaces of linguistic and cultural exchange. The population of Navarre were a combination of Castilian, Basque, Aragonese and Navarrese. It had a uniquely mixed religious group of Christians, Jews and Muslims, who intermingled and worked across a variety of trades.[24] In 1290 Jews had been expelled from England so Edward I could gain wealth from their assets, and elsewhere in Europe Jews were still persecuted. But Charles of Navarre offered Jews the ability to own land and property. Equally, Charles ensured the security of his Muslim subjects; in 1357 he organised for three families who wished to make pilgrimage to Mecca to travel under 'safe royal conduct, protection and custody', on both their outbound and inbound journeys.[25]

Navarre may have been a haven to some, but it was an irritant to the English and French, because the capricious Charles of Navarre controlled the Pyrenees passes, the only routes into Spain. The arrival of the Free Companies across the Pyrenees meant that Charles of Navarre had already received thousands of soldiers.[26] If Charles were to switch sides by allowing more soldiers access to Navarre, he wanted something in return. Charles laid out the cost of the crossing: money as well as territory in Castile, including castles lining the country's eastern march. Pedro, by this point, was willing to agree to anything. With Charles having sanctioned passage through Navarre, the Black Prince began recruiting soldiers from among the Gascons and dispatched his loyal friend John Chandos to try to hire the few Free Companies who remained in France, floating around the Saône valley and Auvergne.

The Black Prince's army was swelled by those of his subjects who had served under Bertrand du Guesclin to oust Pedro in the first place and were trickling back into France. In addition to this, John of Gaunt – who had been preparing to join his brother from England – had mustered a company of around five hundred trained archers and was sailing for Bordeaux.

The Black Prince, John of Gaunt and their army of Gascons, mercenaries and English archers gathered in the foothills of the Pyrenees, ready to cross the mountain range. They would be taking the Roncesvalles Pass, a popular pilgrim route that led, ultimately, to the holy city of Santiago de Compostela. The pass was riddled with danger. Violent gangs lingered in the hills and would attack the army's stragglers if given the chance. If they did not attack them, wolves might. But the main danger was the weather. The Black Prince made the crossing in February 1367, when the mountain range was covered in snow and ice. Strong winds hammered his men, the cold air biting their faces and numbing their hands. Progress was slow in this hostile environment and it took the army over a week to finally reach the other side, where they based themselves in a small village on the frontier of Navarre called Navarrette, before marching deeper into Spain.

In late February Enrique Trastámara received a candid letter from Charles V of France, relaying his father's and grandfather's experience of facing an English army. Charles counselled Enrique to exhaust the English. Make them move around the countryside until they tire, run out of supplies, force them to withdraw. Enrique, however, chose to ignore this advice. So it was that on a dusty plain outside the town of Nájera, a lesser-known battle of the Hundred Years War took place.

At dawn on 3 April 1367, Enrique – or as Chandos names him, the Bastard, born to his father's mistress – and his army stood in battle formation on a slope that led down to a stream called the Yalde. The men soon spotted the standard of Saint George in the distance, the flag rippling in the breeze before the mass of the English army appeared only a few hundred yards away.

The English arrived on horseback, but as their tactics had dictated since 1330, they dismounted to prepare to fight. In the vanguard of the English army was John of Gaunt, yet to experience pitched battle.[27] Close to him was the fierce John Chandos. The prince placed himself in the next line, perhaps wanting his younger brother to have the same chance to achieve glory in battle as he had been given at Crécy. Before the battle began, the prince rallied his men, announcing: 'We must conquer them with blow of lance and sword. Now let us so act this day that we may depart in honour.'[28]

As his men cheered, 'Saint George!' the prince turned to Pedro and said, 'Sire king, today will you know if ever you will have Castile again. Have firm faith in God.'[29]

The vanguard heaved forward, charging full pelt towards the enemy line, and in his recollection of the battle, Chandos Herald commented on the dust and sand whisked into the fray as 'archers shoot thicker than rain falls'.[30] Thousands of arrows streamed through the clear sky, over the heads of the charging English and into the Spanish line, who were covering themselves with shields. Among their ranks, 'spears fell to the ground: and body upon body followed'.The Spanish responded with crossbow bolts, hammering into approaching English, before they made their own charge: 'one held lance in hand, and they made fierce onslaught to attack their enemies . . . great was the din and reek. There was neither banner nor pennon that was not cast down.'[31]

The melee was thick with steel and blood and an account of John Chandos being briefly crushed by a Spanish soldier, 'great in stature', named Martín Fernández, offers a startlingly clear description of the brutality of the battle. The men scrapped on the ground, punching and ripping each other before Chandos was 'wounded in the vizor'. Snatching a dagger from his belt, Chandos dealt a mortal blow to Fernández, stabbing him in the side. 'The Castilian stretched himself out dead and Chandos leapt to his feet. He grasped his sword with both hands and plunged into the fray.'[32] Just as the Black Prince brought his own line forward, Enrique's cavalry also charged, but, again, their horses were struck with arrows, crashing to the ground and crushing those around them. Picked off by English arrows, soldiers fighting for Enrique began to abandon hope and those who could fled across the Najerilla river. But some were crushed in the flight, others drowning in the crossing. Around five thousand men fighting for Enrique were killed at the Battle of Nájera.[33] Enrique Trastámara had escaped on the horse of one of his squires and Bertrand du Guesclin fled to safety, eventually making his way back to France. Both French and Castilian prisoners were taken that day and according to Pero López de Ayala, a chronicler and prisoner, Pedro personally murdered five Castilian men, including Enrique's chamberlain, who he had pulled from a hurdle before slitting his throat.[34] The Black Prince flatly refused a mass slaughter of the other prisoners, stating that his men 'had fought for honour and the prisoners were theirs' – a reminder to the Castilian king of the meaning and importance of chivalric practice in war.[35]

The Battle of Nájera was an emphatic victory. Pedro had his throne back, and the prince had defeated his military rival Bertrand du Guesclin on the field – a great boost to his ego. Yet this battle precipitated financial disaster, for Pedro soon made it clear he had no intention of repaying the Prince for the money he spent accruing men and supplies to fight for Pedro. Furious, the prince and his army returned to Gascony.[36] The Black Prince spent the next two years trying to exact revenge for the time, money and effort he had wasted. Before he could do so, Enrique Trastámara intervened. In another invasion of Castile supported by the French, Enrique captured his half-brother before killing him in one-on-one combat. This was even worse for the Black Prince. The French now had an ally on Castilian soil and the prince had no chance of claiming back his expenses. In order to rescue Aquitaine's perilous finances and pay for the Spanish adventure, the government was forced to impose a *fouage* (property tax) on the people. Though the prince had introduced a series of *fouages* since 1363, none was as permanent as the one he now proposed.

This left the nobility in Aquitaine – particularly the counts of Armagnac and Albret – furious, raging that 'when they were under the vassalage of the king of France, they were not oppressed by any such tax or subsidy'.[37] Adding to this, the prince became unwell, suffering the early signs of a long degenerative gastric illness that would eventually take his life.

Before long, enraged local lords appealed to Charles V for aid against the punitive *fouage* and turned against the Black Prince, favouring the French king as a feudal overlord. By 1368 Charles V was in luck: disgruntled Gascon nobles 'went to France to lay their complaints before the court of the king of France . . . they said they were under the jurisdiction of the king of France, and that they were bound to return to him as their sovereign lord.'[38] Charles found a loophole in the peace agreement between England and France that allowed him to act against the Black Prince in Aquitaine. Because Edward III had failed to remove *all* his men from northern France, the Treaty of Brétigny was redundant and Charles now had a valid reason to resume war against the English. By the end of the year, French troops moved towards the border of Aquitaine and 'thus this country began its rebellion against the Prince'.[39] 'Since Christmas,' a member of his household wrote, 'the Prince is ill, our men shut up in their castles and the danger from the enemy is all around us. More money and men are desperately needed. If they do not arrive soon, the French may deal such a blow to our principality that we shall not be able to recover.'[40] A year later, the situation became much worse.

Shortly after Christmas in 1369, Aquitaine was bitingly cold. Small rivers and lakes froze over, frost coated the bare trees and the roads were perilous. John Chandos prepared to ambush a French raiding party on the bridge at Lussac that stretched across the Vienne river. As the French approached, the knight leapt from his horse, sword in hand, and declared, 'I am John Chandos: look at me well; and, if God please, we will now put to the proof your great deeds of arms which are so renowned.' Bursting with enthusiasm for the fight, but ill attired for it, Chandos was wearing a 'large robe'. With the road slick with ice, Chandos, tangled in his robs, slipped and crashed to the ground, only to be impaled by a lance, 'below the eye, between the nose and forehead', by an opportunistic squire named James de St Martin.[41] This was an ignominious end for such a renowned warrior.

Even the French believed 'it was a great pity he was slain . . . he was so wise and full of devices'.[42] The greatest knights were often dedicated a *chanson*, a song narrating the life of its subject, sometimes set to music. Though the *Life of the Black Prince* was written by Chandos's herald, it interwove both their adventures, showing them as brothers in arms.

The Black Prince had a bleak future ahead of him, painted with the cruel veneer of loss. In September 1370 Edward of Angoulême, the eldest son and heir of the Black Prince, died at Bordeaux. He was just five years old and his parents were undone with grief.[43] The death of his son was the final blow after an appalling run of bad luck. In a formal ceremony at Bordeaux, the prince's brother John of Gaunt received the homage of the barons of Aquitaine. He was appointed duke of Aquitaine and left to try to repair the last two years of disorder and war. In January 1371, the Black Prince and Princess Joan, along with his second son, Richard, now three, left Aquitaine for Southampton. The prince of Aquitaine, carried in a litter, returned home, never to set foot in France again.[44]

22. A Parliament of Rats

The Black Prince returned to a country in mourning. In 1368 Edward and Philippa's second surviving son, Lionel of Antwerp, had died in Italy, shortly after he'd been married for the second time to Violante Visconti, the daughter of the wealthy duke of Pavia and Milan; it was rumoured he was either poisoned or that he overate at his wedding feast. On his deathbed, Lionel allegedly requested that his 'flesh and entrails be buried in Pavia near the tomb of Saint Augustine of Hippo', but he was later buried in Suffolk, next to his first wife, Elizabeth de Burgh.[1] In early 1369 the nobility of England were summoned to attend masses for Lionel's soul, and the king and queen mourned the loss of another child. In September 1368 Blanche of Lancaster died following the birth of an infant named Isabel, who did not survive either. The heaviest blow to Edward III came a year later, when Queen Philippa of Hainault died at Windsor.

Philippa had been a permanent source of support to Edward III, described as 'a most noble woman and most constant lover of the English'.[2] Five months after her death, the funeral procession began from Windsor. Candles burned around the coffin, bathing it in warmth and light, before it was taken along the Thames to Saint Paul's Cathedral. From there it was moved to the queen's final resting place at Westminster Abbey. A monk in Westminster gave a florid lament: 'While she flourished she was full of grace to the English. The people were not in want; neither was her country in need of grain . . . But her own goodness would have come to the supreme joys [of heaven].'[3]

The relationship between Philippa and Edward seems to have been close and loving. The delay of her funeral until January was possibly due to another outbreak of plague that summer. It might equally have been the result of Edward's grief and his desire not only to preserve the mortal existence of his beloved wife but also to inter her around their wedding anniversary in January. Queen Philippa's death marked the end of a long and loving marriage, but it also presaged political trouble. Without her steady presence and careful advice, Edward's hold over the realm began to unravel.

In the early 1370s Edward himself became unwell. His illness was another major turning point, marking the beginning of the end. In the winter of 1371–2, he was suddenly taken ill at the village of Everleigh near Marlborough Castle, prompting an emergency summoning of five doctors from Oxford.[4] John of Gaunt, who had returned from Aquitaine having negotiated a truce with Charles V to cease fighting for two years, along with his new wife, Constance – the daughter (and heir) of the former king of Castile, Pedro I – was thrust into de facto leadership, one he neither expected nor wanted. It is possible that Edward had suffered the first of a series of strokes.[5] Over the course of the next few years, systems in and around government began to crumble as an increasingly infirm Edward III made a number of terrible decisions that led to widespread corruption. A cabal had emerged that enjoyed increasing indulgences from the king. This included William Latimer, the chamberlain of the king's household, and his son-in-law John Neville, the king's steward and lord of Raby Castle in Northumberland. In 1372 they were given ermine-lined Garter robes, a privilege usually reserved for princes of the blood and titled nobility.[6] But the most notable beneficiary of the king's generosity was Alice Perrers, his mistress – or, as Thomas Walsingham called her, his 'unspeakable whore'. Walsingham added that she was a 'shameless, impudent harlot . . . of low birth', and that 'blind fortune elevated this woman to such heights and promoted her to a greater intimacy with the king than was proper.'[7] Having been in the queen's service when she and the king began a relationship in the mid-1360s, Alice Perrers became an immediate beneficiary after Philippa's death. The mother of at least three of Edward's illegitimate children, she was granted by the king the deeds of land in Northumberland and the borders, including Branxton, Lowick, Carham and the Cheviots.[8] In 1373 Alice was gifted 'certain jewels and goods of the queen's' and in 1374 he even named a royal barge, *La Alice*, after her.[9] Clearly he was infatuated.[10]

The image Walsingham paints of Alice Perrers is steeped in suspicion and misogyny. A woman like Alice represented the ultimate female sinner to a monk like Walsingham; to him she was a temptress who bewitched the king with her sexual powers. While some of the slanders have a basis in truth, Walsingham – unlikely to have even met Alice – was overly critical. His criticism was partly rooted in snobbery. After the Black Death, the merchant class had continued to develop as a powerful social group in England and Alice was an example of their increasing influence. London, more than anywhere else in the realm, had a growing oligarchy of merchants, representing new money in a way that staunch royalists and the nobility found galling.

As courtiers, many of these merchants profited from Edward's purse in addition to their various covert financial schemes and deceits. A major merchant exporter named Richard Lyons, along with the nobleman William Latimer, bought up Crown debt at ludicrously cheap prices, but loaned his own money to the Crown with impossibly high interest. Lyons also engineered a way for his exports to pass through ports other than Calais, therefore avoiding the tax he'd have paid had he conducted his business through official routes. Both men had connections to Alice Perrers, who, along with her generous land grants, was given vast quantities of gold and silver by Edward. This climate of corruption from those around the king's bed came to a head in 1376 at the first parliament in three years.

In *Piers Plowman*, William Langland uses allegory to comment on the moral decay and weakness of government. In one memorable scene, a group of rats and mice convene, concerned about a cat who has been tormenting them. One rat suggests attaching a bell to the cat's collar, but no rodent is brave enough to do the deed. The plan is fruitless, one mouse declares. The rodents will only prevail if they can rule together – only that way can order and stability be established. The gathering, in the end, achieves nothing. It is possible that this fable was used by Langland to comment on what soon became known as the 'Good Parliament',[11] named for how it attempted to reform the governance of the realm.

In late April 1376, parliament gathered inside the Painted Chamber at Westminster Palace. Members of both houses were squashed together in the long and narrow room, which was decorated by scenes from the Old Testament.[12] Colour leapt from the walls, scarlet red and vivid green, gold and ochre, set against a background of brilliant pale blue.[13] The floor was laid out with black and yellow tiles and there was a vast canopied state bed, in place since the reign of Henry III.[14]

Voices hushed as the chancellor, Sir John Knyvet, announced the three reasons for parliament being held: 'The first and principal reason was to make an ordinance by their good advice for the good governing of the country of his realm of England; the second was to ordain for the defence and salvation on the frontiers of the same realm, by land as well as by sea, against the enemies, of whom he has a great plenty, as they know well; and the third was to ordain for the maintenance of the war.'[15] The Lords and Commons then separated, to discuss the business of parliament before the next session. The lords – noble members of the realm – remained in the Painted Chamber and the commons – elected knights of the shires, merchants and country gentry – moved to the chapter house in Westminster Abbey. Already ailing, the king soon retreated, unable to cope with the pressure of the gathering. With the Black Prince almost entirely incapacitated by his illness, John of Gaunt was the only representative of the Crown.

Rumbles of discontent were felt within the commons as its members used their platform to air their concerns. These were largely to do with the king requesting a further tax to support the war in France, and the profiteering of William Latimer and Richard Lyons from private loans to the crown. What the commons proposed was incendiary, but reflected the anger of the common folk of the realm. They sought to revolutionise the government and correct the moral character of the king's rule. They began by collaborating on a long petition that they hoped would move the king to act on their behalf.

However, to do so, they first needed to find someone who would be able to articulate these issues with strength and clarity. Of those gathered, Peter de la Mare, a knight from Herefordshire, appeared to be the best man for the job.[16]

De la Mare's appointment marked him as the first elected speaker of the House of Commons. His role was to plant the authority and voice of the commons at the centre of proceedings, to refuse a grant of taxation and to request reform. Before John of Gaunt and the lords present, he made accusations of corruption against William Latimer, Richard Lyons and Alice Perrers, as well as Lord Neville of Raby and three more merchants embroiled in the murky double-dealings of their inner circle. When asked to be more specific, a few days later he laid out the charges in four points: the staple – the port through which all imports and exports out of England went through – had been removed from Calais without the permission of parliament; Latimer and Lyons had orchestrated loans to the Crown with injuriously high interest and bought Crown debt at the lowest possible rate; and Alice Perrers was squandering Crown assets.[17] John of Gaunt had little choice other than to allow the commons to express their grievances. Two weeks later, Peter de la Mare informed Gaunt that the commons would proceed no further without the removal of the king's evil councillors.[18] As a result, Richard Lyons 'was impeached and accused by the said commons of many deceits, extortions and other evil deeds done by him to our lord the king and his people'. William Latimer was also 'impeached and accused by the charge of the said commons of various deceits, extortions, grievances and other evil deeds', and Alice Perrers was accused of 'maintenance, bribing and influencing the parties', on penalty for which, 'Alice can [be] banished from the realm'.[19] Unlike the others, Alice was not impeached. She never formally faced allegations from her peers but, in absentia, was subject to an injunction – a legal restriction against her interfering with the management of the realm.[20] Parliament had no power to exact banishment against Alice; that lay only in the hands of the king. At some stage, it is likely that he was persuaded to exile Alice, and that for the good of the realm and his reputation he should consent to the demands of the commons. In doing so he could retain the dignity and respect he had so carefully cultivated throughout his earlier reign.[21]

The image of Edward had morphed from a chivalrous king – Arthur Redivivus – to that of a lecherous old man – giddy and foolish over a much younger woman. As the poet John Gower aptly wrote around 1376: 'No king will ever be feared who prefers to give up his shield and wage battle in bed.'[22] And yet many of the claims made against Alice Perrers feed into the trope of the 'problem woman'. Withered by contemporaneous accounts of her character, unable to defend herself during the Good Parliament, voiceless in the record, Alice has long been considered self-interested and Machiavellian. By her actions and association with the king, Alice had carefully – often ruthlessly – guaranteed her own security after his death. She had over the course of her career become a businesswoman – lending money and accruing property and wealth. She was clearly a capable, clever human being who had recognised both her vulnerabilities as a mistress of the king, but also the opportunities this position brought her.

A break in proceedings of the Good Parliament came when the Black Prince's health took a dramatic turn for the worse. By early June, as he lay in Westminster Palace, unable to be moved to Kennington – his usual residence – it was clear he was dying. On 7 June the prince called his clerks to his chamber to draft his will. This determined his wish to be buried at Canterbury Cathedral and for his belongings to be dispatched to Princess Joan and his son, Richard. Exceptional detail was given to both his funeral cortège and his tomb – if the prince was not able to die a war hero, he would at least be remembered as one.[23]

Throughout this period, the prospect of Richard's accession lingered over everything. With the death of the Black Prince imminent, and the fast decline of the king, the realm was about to fall into the hands of a much-coddled nine-year-old boy unable to govern independently. Overseeing his succession and early kingship would be a task for John of Gaunt. In a moving deathbed scene, the Black Prince 'called the king and duke of Lancaster his brother, he commended them to his wife and son, whom he greatly loved and begged that each should help them. Each swore on the Holy Book, and freely

promised to aid his child and maintain him in his right.'[24] The Black
Prince died on 8 June at Westminster Palace aged forty-five. The
grief felt by the family is described as 'lamentation and sighing, of
crying aloud and sorrowing. There [was] so great a noise.'[25]

A series of florid eulogies were penned by chroniclers after the
event. Compared to a warrior of Greek myth, the Black Prince was
dubbed 'a second Hector . . . when he died, all the hopes of the
English died with him . . . he attacked no nation he did not conquer.
He besieged no city that he did not capture.'[26] To others he was 'a
wellspring of courage', and 'the flower of the world's chivalry'.[27]
The Black Prince was an undoubted military mastermind and would
likely have continued his father's pursuits with the same gusto he had
shown in his earlier career – perhaps even exceeded them to claim
France in its entirety. The unfortunate death of the Black Prince, a
popular and seemingly fair ruler, ended the years of domestic peace
and martial glory that Edward III and his sons had enjoyed for nearly
fifty years.

In his immense sadness over the death of this beloved eldest son and
heir, Edward III retreated to his quiet country residence at Havering,
where he could mourn without the disturbances inevitable at Westminster. John of Gaunt was not permitted the same luxury. Though
he was devastated, he returned to parliament to carry out his duty as
the king's eldest surviving son.[28]

The funeral and commemoration of the Black Prince were exactly
as his will requested. The whole event was a lament for England's
greatest hero. Two warhorses, decorated with the prince's coat of
arms, rode ahead of his coffin as it progressed into Canterbury. With
it came the prince's armour and the 'equipment' he used in battle,
brought by men with robes emblazoned in the prince's insignia and
others carrying 'a black pennant of ostrich plumes'.[29] In life the
prince had travelled to Canterbury to visit the shrine of Thomas
Becket. As a result, the cathedral clearly became a sacred space to
both the prince and Joan of Kent – now a bereft widow – the couple
having endowed two chantry chapels in the south transept of the
crypt.[30] The tomb the prince specifically requested was given impec-
cable attention to detail. Cast in hollowed-out metal, it went against

funerary tradition – normally an armoured figure would be chiselled from alabaster or wood.[31] Cast 'fully armed in plate of war', it is possible that the prince wanted his tomb to serve as a second skin, a physical impression of his armour, bound to his body in death. The effigy itself was even designed as a faithful impression of a suit of armour, each link, each plate, the same as in life.[32] The prince wished to have the quartered arms of England and France blazoned over his amour while his head rested upon his helmet topped with the royal crest, a leopard or lion, and his hands firmly pressed together in prayer. Around him was the armour he wore in battle, still scratched and dented from years of combat. In an echo of early medieval burial practice, the prince was quite literally laid to rest as if he had fallen in battle. But his final, perhaps more pointed, message was that death comes to us all. With over half his life spent in a world marked by plague, his tomb epitaph was a memento mori: 'Such as you are, I used to be: You will become such as I am: On death I did not ponder: So much while I was alive . . . But now I am poor and wretched: deep in the ground I lie . . . For God's sake pray to the celestial King to have mercy on my soul.'[33]

The Black Prince's death precipitated a rapid decline in the health of Edward III, a new interest in Prince Richard and a heavy burden for John of Gaunt. On 10 July, the Good Parliament finally closed. Months later, however, in January 1377, summons were released for lords and commons to attend another session, which would become known as the Bad Parliament. Under John of Gaunt, Alice Perrers returned to the king, 'like a dog returning to its vomit', as Thomas Walsingham sneered, quoting Proverbs. Peter de la Mare was imprisoned, Latimer was reinstated. Piece by piece, the work of the Good Parliament was undone by John of Gaunt. Negating the will of the people was the greatest mistake of his career.

Over the course of Richard's minority, Gaunt became an enemy to the people of London and an enemy of the Church. In 1376 the preachings and beliefs of a new religious reformer, John Wycliffe, had caught the attention of John of Gaunt, who, according to his clerical critics, was looking for ways to reduce the Church's authority and pressure the Church to fund more of the war effort (both these

accusations were probably true).[34] Wycliffe's ideas were revolution-
ary and a key influence on the later Reformation.[35] They were also
timely. The atmosphere in England was friendly to reform, something
exemplified by the Good Parliament. As Langland had questioned
the order of things with *Piers Plowman*, Wycliffe attempted to form
his own conclusions about doctrine. This made him another target
of Thomas Walsingham, who claimed that Wycliffe's writings contained 'a particularly poisonous tirade against monks and other
property-owning people in religious orders'. He goes on to say that
Wycliffe's followers 'from among his associates at Oxford and elsewhere . . . [dressed] in ankle-length garments of russet, as a sign of
their greater perfection'.[36] Wycliffe's followers adopted a uniform of
dark red robes and carried a staff, a symbol of their pastoral calling.
These were not designed to symbolise 'perfection' or moral superior-
ity, however, but rather simplicity and an absence of clerical wealth.
These followers became known as the Lollards. They argued against
the church having temporal land and power,[37] that priests should be
able to marry and that confession was simply a method of imposing clerical power over the people.[38] They believed that the Church
should place Christ at the centre of faith, not the adoration of relics
or the amassing of excessive wealth by collecting money from the
laity. Charity should be shown to the poor and worship should be
based on knowledge of scripture rather than ritual. In keeping with
this, one of Wycliffe's lasting legacies was his role in the translation
of the Bible from Latin into the vernacular, so that it was accessible
to the great mass of people.[39]

Gaunt's support for Wycliffe planted him in the middle of a clerical
feud. In February 1377 John Wycliffe was summoned to Saint Paul's
Cathedral to face the archbishop of Canterbury, Simon Sudbury, and
William Courtenay, the bishop of London, to answer accusations of
heresy.

Wycliffe arrived with John of Gaunt and the marshal of England,
Henry Percy. A northern lord, Percy was warden of the Scottish
Marches and it's likely his presence was intended to intimidate. When
the bishop of London refused to let Wycliffe be seated, an argument
broke out and Gaunt threatened to drag the bishop from the cathedral

by his hair.[40] The people of London were protective of their cathedral and their bishop and soon a small angry rebellion started in the city. Gaunt was forced to seek protection from the mob in Kennington Palace with Joan of Kent.

It is unclear why the archbishop and bishop ceased to press charges against Wycliffe. He continued to preach, which left the pope furious. In May 1377 he dispatched a series of bulls to Simon Sudbury, the archbishop of Canterbury, spitting with rage that Wycliffe had, in effect, got away with it: 'For shame! – they [the English Church] have been negligent . . . the bishops – singly or jointly – are to determine if these are Wycliffe's teachings. If so, they should have him imprisoned by papal authority.'[41] And then, in a letter the same day, 'theologians [must] bring these matters to the attention of King Edward III, his noble sons as well as other magnates of England and councillors of the king, showing them how much shame is being brought to the realm.'[42] Wycliffe was summoned again following the pope's outburst, but once more he managed to evade imprisonment or death, perhaps slipping away under Gaunt's protection.

As the papal bulls condemning Wycliffe travelled across the Channel, King Edward III lay dying.[43]

In the twilight hours of 21 June, he finally passed. Thomas Walsingham paints an apocryphal picture of Alice Perrers slipping the rings off the king's fingers as he gasped his last breath.[44] Alice went on to remarry William Windsor, the king's lieutenant in Ireland – likely an agreement that had been reached with John of Gaunt to both secure her safety and remove her from court life.[45]

The king's death threw the realm into a state of 'deep mourning'.[46] Though Edward's final years had been a marked contrast to what had preceded them, the country had enjoyed fifty years of steady authority. The news had to be kept within England: 'Immediately all the passes were shut, so that no one could get out of the country; for they did not wish the death of the king should be known in France, until they had settled the government of the kingdom'.[47] The question of succession, and how it was to be managed, was urgent, because the existing truce between England and France was set to expire and the new king of England was a child. For the first time since the beginning of the war, England was in a vulnerable position; this would be the optimum time for the French to capitalise on that weakness.

Once Edward's body had been eviscerated and embalmed it was laid out at Sheen Palace. The chamber was draped in swathes of black cloth.[48] Sometime before the dead king was moved towards his final resting place, his face was studied in detail so that a mannequin could be made for the funeral. The body was made from wood and straw but the face was moulded from a plaster death mask, taken from Edward's flesh and bone.[49] His eyes stare coldly and his nose is long, straight and regal, but his mouth tells the final story. Distorted and tilting downward, the cause of Edward's death – a series of ultimately fatal strokes – is unmistakable.[50]

Henry Knighton captured the mood of the realm at the death of Edward III, lamenting the loss of 'the flower of this world's knighthood, for whom to do battle was to reign, to contend was to triumph'.[51] The epitaph on his tomb at Westminster paints a similar portrait: 'Here is the glory of the English . . . the unconquered leopard, he was a powerful Maccabeus in his wars . . . He ruled mightily in arms; now in heaven may he be a heavenly king'.[52] Edward III was a king who led with his sword and he had been loved by his people, but by the end of his reign he was morally defeated. The figure slumped on the throne surveying his knights at the final Garter feast in April 1377 was a different man to the king who overthrew the regime of Mortimer and Isabella, took Calais and regained Scotland and Aquitaine, building the largest English empire since Henry II.

As Edward had declined, the age of chivalry declined with him. Passion for war and the glory of conquest became a thing of the past, held dear only by the veterans of Edward's wars in the 1350s and 1360s. Richard II took the throne as a ten-year-old boy, quivering in the shadow of his father's legacy. Merlin's Prophecy had likened Edward III to a boar who would rain terror on France but the beast to follow was an ass. Where Edward III was a king who had invested his life and kingship in expanding English influence across Christendom, Richard – entirely unprepared to rule – was destined to do the opposite.

PART FIVE

The Age of Revolution

'Vox populi de civitate vox de templo vox Domini
reddentis retributionem inimicis suis.'
(A voice of the people from the city, a voice from
the temple, the voice of the Lord that rendereth
recompense to his enemies.)

Isaiah 66:6

23.   Vox Clamantis

Around midsummer in 1377 fifty ships were spotted crossing the Channel. These were not fishing vessels or merchant traders but French warships threatening death and destruction. They were heading for one of the leading ship-building towns in England, Rye, a place that had contributed generations of mariners and ships to the Plantagenet war machine.

The French docked away from the beach and released hundreds of soldiers, who splashed through the waves to storm the town, scaling the walls and breaking through the defences. Raids were a part of life on the coast and the people of Rye were accustomed to French attacks. A cacophony of warning bells echoed over the town. It was of little use. The French looted the church and burned Rye to the ground. Only the stone wall, its gate and tower and a few stone houses remained standing. They even took the bell.

Shortly before the coronation of King Richard II the temporary truce negotiated by Gaunt between England and France had expired and the attack on Rye was part of a two-week assault on the English coastline led by the French admiral Jean de Vienne. Vienne hit not only Rye but Rottingdean, Weymouth, Dartmouth, Plymouth, Southampton, Poole and the Isle of Wight, where he managed to extract a six-hundred-pound ransom from its residents.[1]

The people of Rye made a special appeal to the new king. 'In view of the destruction of their town', they begged 'for a certain sum of money . . . to provide the town with walls and other fortifications to protect it in future.'[2] They offered to build the king more boats in return. The offer was meagre but necessary. English strength had dwindled.

The French weren't the only ones attracted by England's vulnerability at the start of Richard's reign. In June 1377 the Scots began to pressurise the border, trying to tease the English into conflict. Though they were unsuccessful it became clear that both France and Scotland were watching for their next opportunity to strike.

In the Middle Ages, the vulnerability created by a child king increased the possibility of war, disrupting the hierarchy of leadership because there was no adult at the top of the government. After the death of King John in 1216, his son Henry III was crowned so quickly he could not even make it to Westminster in time for the ceremony – Gloucester Cathedral had to suffice. And although there was no serious threat to Richard's succession, rumours circulated that John of Gaunt might stage a coup and claim the crown for himself. There was no evidence Gaunt was planning to overthrow Richard – it was far more likely that John of Gaunt intended to vigorously uphold the succession, as he had promised the Black Prince on his deathbed. As the eldest surviving son of Edward III, John of Gaunt should have been a beacon of strength and hope during Richard's fragile early years as king. The problem was that John of Gaunt's actions the previous year had made him wildly unpopular in London and with the commons – a Gaunt regency would result in anarchy. With threats on the coastline and the border, it was essential John of Gaunt swallowed his pride and made a display of loyalty to Richard while also cementing his nephew as the rightful king of England. There was no better opportunity than Richard's coronation.

The coronation of a new king was always laden with religious and political symbolism. In an elaborate ceremony Richard left the Tower of London and rode towards Westminster to be crowned. The commons, knights and lords preceded him, all dressed in white robes.[3] In front of Richard rode his uncles, John of Gaunt, Edmund of Langley and Thomas of Woodstock, and finally came Richard, his small frame covered in white cloth. As he rode through Cheapside, the streets were packed with revellers, many of whom had travelled miles to witness the event: this was a once-in-a-lifetime opportunity.

The official coronation was the following day. Richard was bathedand dressed in sacred coronation regalia, including a pair of slippers that were too big for his child feet. He was then led from Westminster Palace to the Abbey. As with Edward II's and Edward III's coronations, the nobility played a vital role in the ceremony, relative to their rank. John of Gaunt ensured he was front and centre in order to demonstrate his loyalty to Richard and the Crown.

Under a canopy of cloth of gold, Richard was carried into Westminster Abbey and placed before the choir on a chair his ancestor had prepared for Edward II's coronation. The Stone of Scone was still jammed beneath it, representing his authority over Scotland. To the sound of singing and chanting and the smell of incense, Richard II was crowned. He 'swore that he would allow the Church to enjoy her liberties, that he would keep to the true faith and that he would put a stop to plunder and all acts of injustice in all classes of people . . . ensure the good laws of the land and judge fairly between man and man'.[4] The people submitted to their new ruler, 'with a mighty shout' that they would uphold and obey him. After the service Richard, perhaps overwhelmed by the experience and pressure, was 'gathered up' into the arms of his tutor, Simon Burley.[5] In the process one of his sacred slippers fell off and was lost in the throng.

Propaganda was a powerful tool during the coronation. John of Gaunt and the councillors around Richard knew they could not project an image of strength and power in his accession, so instead they used Richard's age to their advantage. The ceremony was couched in innocence – the abundance of white robes stood for youthful purity and virtue. It was made clear that Richard was a king divinely appointed. This sense of divine right, so deeply instilled at Richard's coronation, became the principle he would rule by.

The coronation was a theatre of royal power but in truth the realm was vulnerable. The current king was a child, the country was crippled by the cost of the previous king's war, and the post-plague generation were no longer bound by punitive feudalism but had entered into a class system that now included growing numbers of merchants and skilled labourers. People began to push the boundaries of social hierarchy. Though social mobility was still limited, the fatalistic sentiment of the pre-plague age had shifted. The problem for Richard, Gaunt and the government was that they did not see the change coming. A clash between the people, the king and his government became inevitable and it began over taxes for the defence of the realm.

The poll tax was introduced in 1379 as a tax of 4d per person at a graduated rate of pay, depending on personal wealth and status. Although this appears to have been an effective and fair way to collect funds from the populace, wealthier people began to look for ways of paying less tax, such as concealing the presence of women in the household – every female over sixteen was expected to pay her share – from tax collectors.[6] When what they received was deeply under the estimate, the sheriffs and exchequer knew there was something awry and a more effective system would have to be imposed if the Crown was able to sustain the war in France and protect the realm.

In November 1380 rain battered the windows and roof of Saint Andrew's priory in Northampton, the chosen location for Richard's late autumn parliament. Summons had been released to the lords and commons but a violent storm raging in the Midlands prohibited travel in the area. John of Gaunt was not present for the opening of the Northampton parliament, where the issue of tax was to be raised. Though historically blamed for its increase, he was otherwise occupied in the Scottish borders – he had been called away to broker a truce with the Scots following a particularly aggressive Scottish raid on Penrith.[7] As Gaunt was absent, the chancellor and archbishop of Canterbury, Simon Sudbury, broke the news to the lords and commons that the amount that the government needed to sustain the country was around one hundred and sixty thousand pounds, a sum the speaker of the commons scoffed to be 'outrageous'. After much discussion between the two houses the commons agreed they could meet one hundred thousand and the rest would have to be provided by the clergy. The final decision was 'three groats from every lay person . . . from males as well as females, of whatsoever status or condition they be, who are over fifteen years of age, except for genuine beggars who will be charged nothing'.[8] This third poll tax in four years was triple the cost of the tax imposed in 1379 and it was quite simply unaffordable, punitively impacting the poor, who were expected to pay the same tax as the rich.

The Peasants' Revolt – a name that has been imposed on the events of summer 1381 by posterity – was the largest, most violent and most impactful rebellion in England in the Middle Ages, and the first against the Crown. It was a response to several factors: the aggressive assertion of regal power, the negation of rights, the influence of the king's councillors on his person and an influx of foreign immigrants, as well as punishingly high taxes. But the trigger for the rebellion of summer 1381 was the introduction of the poll tax intended to fund the defence of the realm but which instead caused anarchy.

Contemporary records refer to it as a 'rising', led by the general populace, not just pitchfork-wielding peasants. Peasants made up some of the coalition of rebels, but they were joined by soldiers, merchants, clerics, tanners, smiths, tilers, artisans. There were women and children, young and old. People across the realm were desperate, taxed beyond their capacity to pay for a war that never seemed to end.

The collectors were relentless in their pursuit of taxes and it was arguably the methods they used to extract the tax, rather than the tax itself, that led to trouble. Contemporary sources claimed that 'actions of the investigators greatly provoked the people'.[9] Most notable was a sergeant at arms and tax collector, John Legge.[10] His tyrannical behaviour included virginity checks designed to identify young married women who were avoiding payment: 'he would assemble the men and women before him, and horrible to relate, would shamelessly raise the young girls' skirts to discover whether they were corrupted by intercourse with men.' If he believed these girls to be sexually active, he 'would compel their friends and parents to pay the tax for them, for many would rather choose to pay than to see their daughters shamefully mistreated'. People in Kent could no longer bear the 'intolerable burdens incessantly laid upon them' and began to consider their options.

In late May 1381 the collector John Bampton travelled to Brentwood in Essex to investigate unpaid taxes. When he pushed for payment, local people become violent and forced him out of the village. The violence quickly escalated as local jurors – blamed for exacting the taxes and punishing those who could not or would not pay it – were captured and beheaded, their heads carried on poles for days, 'as an example to others'.[11] On 10 June the treasurer, Sir Robert Hales, had his home in Essex sacked. The commons 'arrived at this manor, ate the food, drank three casks of good wine and threw the building to the ground'.[12] In Kent, Rochester Castle came under siege; the constable Sir John Newton was arrested and used as a messenger/prisoner by the Kent faction of rebels. Around this time a number of leaders emerged from the damage and destruction. A craftsman named Wat Tyler stepped forward from the Kent rebels, there was John Ball – a radical priest – and the name Jack Straw also appears, though he was probably a fictitious champion meant to represent the masses.

A pattern of destruction took the growing number of rebels towards London. En route they emptied prisons, entered Canterbury Cathedral 'with one voice asking [the monks] to elect a monk to be archbishop of Canterbury to replace the chancellor Simon Sudbury, "for he who is archbishop now is a traitor and will be beheaded for his inequity"'.[13] As the rebels reached the walled city of London the band of around sixty thousand incited fear and panic. The Feast of Corpus Christi was due to be held in the middle of June. Traditionally it was meant to celebrate the corporeal body of Christ in the Eucharist, and people would normally witness a solemn and holy procession through the streets, with Masses and the tolling of bells across the city. In 1381, London was not brimming with festivity but in grave crisis. The feast marked the climax of the rebellion. The best account of what took place over the course of three days comes from the *Anonimalle Chronicle*, whose author was probably an eyewitness, possibly placed within the king's entourage.[14]

On 12 June, 'before the hour of Vespers', sixty thousand rebels from Kent gathered in Southwark. Some burst into the Marshalsea prison and released the prisoners.[15] Others targeted Lambeth Palace, the home of the archbishop of Canterbury, destroying official records and burning goods. The following day, they all crossed London Bridge. Although the drawbridge was raised as the rebels approached the gate, the mayor was forced by citizens inside London to lower it again. Waves of people flocked into the city shouting and chanting. The din would have been terrifying. Local people joined in with what became a frenzy of looting, burning and, often, killing. Prisons were stormed and criminals released. Shops were burned, houses were destroyed and officials were beheaded. Clerks and scribes were targeted and multiple books were burned at the offices of Temple – evidencing a mistrust of scribal culture and how information was recorded.[16]

Foreign workers were also targeted. A brothel on London Bridge, run by Flemish women, was destroyed out of malice and on the same day a group of Flemings were murdered outside the London wall.[17] The following day saw unprecedented levels of violence against people from immigrant communities. On 14 June, the *Anonimalle* chronicler records the rebels shouting, ' "whoever could catch any Fleming or other aliens of the nation, might cut off their heads"; and so they did accordingly'. From Saint Martin's Church in the Vintry, a popular home for immigrant weavers in the city, thirty-five Flemings were 'dragged outside and beheaded on the street . . . it went on for all that day and the night following with hideous cries and horrible tumult'. Around one hundred and fifty people were murdered, their bodes left piled up in the streets.[18]

Violence on this scale rocked the fabric of the community to the core.[19] Chaucer, who had grown up on Vintry Ward, revisited the scene of the massacre in 'The Nun's Priest's Tale':

> So hideous was the noise, ah *ben'dic'te*,
> Certes, he Jacke Straw and his mainee
> Ne made never shoutes half so shrille
> Whan that they wolden any Fleming kille.[20]

When the rebels reached London, Richard and his immediate councillors had fled to the Tower of London for safety. Fourteen-year-old Richard scanned the horizon. Many of London's great houses were up in flames, most shockingly, perhaps, his uncle's Savoy Palace. John of Gaunt was in Berwick at the time, attending another series of peace talks with Scottish lords. The Savoy had passed down the

Lancastrian line over one hundred years; it represented Gaunt's importance, wealth and lineage. By the end of 13 June, it was a crumbled wreckage.

It was agreed that Richard should meet with the rebels and on 14 June he left the Tower on horseback for Mile End with a small army of nobility. After he rode away a contingent of rebels gained entry to the Tower – how is a mystery but it is possible that they managed to break inside this supposedly impenetrable fortress, for the clerk of the works was later paid for 'repairing and constructing' the door that had been hammered at by the rebels.[21]

A woman named Johanna Ferrour led the group of insurgents into the Tower that day and was later put on trial for her actions.[22] The archbishop and treasurer were dragged from the Tower of London and up Tower Hill. There they were beheaded, their heads wedged on pikes and displayed on London Bridge in the manner of traitors.

When Richard returned from Mile End having achieved little by reconciliation with the rebels, he was shocked to discover the murder of his most senior officials. The remaining councillors urged peace, suggesting Richard should give the people what they wanted and end the violence ripping apart the realm, for rebellions were popping up around England, in East Anglia, Worcester, Chester and Beverley in Yorkshire. Another meeting was arranged at Smithfield, away from the city on a flat open plain, normally a space for jousts and tournaments that on Fridays served as a horse market.[23] On 15 June it would become the place the Peasants' Revolt ended.

Thousands of rebels made their way to Smithfield where the mayor of London, William Walworth, asked for their 'chieftain' to present himself.[24] 'Wat Tyghler of Maidstone' made himself known, 'mounted on a little horse' and carrying a small dagger. On greeting the king, Tyler was enthusiastic. He bent his knee and quickly stated he wished for a charter stipulating a series of laws, including that 'no lord should have lordship in future, but it should be divided among all men, except the king's own lordship'. He also asked that clerical wealth be 'divided among the people of the parish . . . that there be no more villeins in England, and no serfdom or villeinage . . . but that all men should be free and of one condition'.[25]

What Tyler requested was extreme by fourteenth-century stand-ards, perhaps an attempt to create a version of Magna Carta that benefited common folk. Richard duly agreed to his wishes: he wanted the rebels to disband so he could deal with the problem later. But at this point a fight broke out. Tyler was hot and thirsty in the June sun and asked for a jug of water. As soon as he was given water he 'rinsed out his mouth in a very rude and villainous manner before the king', before then drinking a 'great draught of ale'.[26] As he was preparing to leave, one of the king's valet's spat that Tyler was 'the greatest thief and robber in all Kent', prompting a brawl. William Walworth intervened and Tyler mashed his dagger into the mayor's armour. In response, the mayor drew his dagger and 'ran Wat two or three times through the body, mortally wounding him'.[27] With Tyler dead and thousands of rebels waiting for his return the situ-ation appeared incendiary – certain death for the king's retinue and possible death for the king himself. The *Anonimalle* chronicler claims that Walworth 'rode as hastily as he could back to the city and com-manded those who were in charge of the twenty-four wards to have it cried . . . every man should arm himself . . . and come to the king's aid in St John's Fields'.[28] This suggests that the king's men thought civil war was imminent.

Richard's response was more measured. He rode to the rebels and commanded them to follow him to Clerkenwell Fields, only a few hundred yards north of Smithfield. There they were shown the head of Wat Tyler and surrounded by English soldiers, 'just as sheep are enclosed within a fold'. Richard immediately released a proclama-tion, pardoning 'our said liege men and subjects for all felonies, acts of treason and transgressions and extortions . . . and we hereby grant our complete peace'.[29] The rebels had their pardon, the king and his men had the head of Tyler, the transaction appeared simple and, remarkably, the rebellion was over. With this, the rebels dispersed back to their homes in the hope that some justice had been done. In reality, what followed was a manhunt.

Richard may have appeared magnanimous but London was on fire, the archbishop and treasurer slaughtered and innocent people had been attacked, robbed and murdered. Order would have to be restored. Over the course of the next year and beyond, the king's courts were packed with rebels. Although some managed to escape soon after the events, many others were caught and forced to face the law. For instance, Matilda Bremobole, her husband and daughter, who were accused of joining the riot and burning the Savoy and the Priory of Clerkenwell.[30] Johanna Ferrour, who broke into the Tower and ordered the deaths of Sudbury and Hales, was also captured – though her punishment remains unclear.[31]

The rebellion escalated elsewhere in the realm and in Norwich two men 'came to the Priory of Carrow, greatly threatened the life and limb of Lady Margaret de Engys, prioress . . . if she did not release to them her charters, muniments and court rolls'.[32] The terrified Margaret gave the rebels what they wanted but later sought retribution in the courts. The bishop of Norwich, Henry Despenser, the grandson of Hugh Despenser the Younger, had taken it upon himself during the rebellion to exact his own justice in the area, and cut such an intimidating figure Thomas Walsingham describes him as a 'warlike priest, like a wild boar gnashing its teeth . . . [fought] . . . where the danger was greatest, stabbing one man, knocking down another and wounding the third'.[33]

It is no surprise the rebellion escalated as quickly as it did, but idealism and the genuine desire to make the world anew were accompanied by shocking acts of violence, fuelled by bigotry and misinformation. Where the rebellion did not achieve the reform people wanted, it did send shockwaves through the realm, most of all through the royal court. Those who enjoyed the trappings of a luxury existence were forced to acknowledge, for the first time, that their world could burn too. John of Gaunt, so distraught by the loss of the Savoy Palace that he never rebuilt it, started to take precautions every time he visited London, going as far as to wear a breastplate beneath his clothes in anticipation of attack.

Most significant of all was the impact the rebellion had on Richard. That warm June day would be etched onto Richard's memory and identity as marking the moment he stepped into his kingship with aplomb. With Gaunt away in Scotland and his closest advisers falling over themselves with anxiety, it was Richard who had the nous to approach the rebels in person, speak and be heard. His understanding of kingship had always privileged his belief that he ruled by divine right over the more prosaic virtues of responsibility and accountability. Now, at fourteen, by medieval standards he had reached adolescence and could, as a young adult, govern the country as he saw fit. For better or for worse.[34]

24. Milky Way

Midway through Richard II's reign, Geoffrey Chaucer began writing *A Treatise on the Astrolabe*, a kind of medieval instruction manual for mapping and reading the stars.[1]

The astrolabe or 'star catcher' was a portable device resembling a sundial, with moveable plates and a dial to calculate astronomical position by utilising lines of altitude. Small enough to lie flat in the palm of one's hand, the idea was, 'thou maist turnen [it] up and doun as thyself liketh' (you may turn it up and down however you like).[2] Chaucer understood that to make sense of the world it is often necessary to look up, and *A Treatise on the Astrolabe* suggests that Chaucer knew exactly how to consult the galaxy.[3]

Fourteenth-century star gazers were fascinated by constellations and celestial movement and the study of the universe soon became popular at courts across Europe. By the 1380s, Richard had become obsessed with astronomy and the occult.

In the later fourteenth century, ownership of astrological books, astrolabes and horary quadrants was commonplace among the high nobility. John of Gaunt commissioned books on astronomy and Joan of Kent commissioned John Somer's *Kalendarium*, which predicted solar eclipses into the fifteenth century.[4] Richard's particular fascination may have been piqued by his mother but also Geoffrey Chaucer, whose career had brushed the peripheries of the royal court since his military service during the first phase of the Hundred Years War.

It is no surprise that the stars attracted Richard. Since childhood he had been told that the stars had literally aligned on the day of his birth – the Feast of the Epiphany on 6 January. In the Bible, this was the day the Magi arrived in Bethlehem to greet the infant Christ with gifts of gold, frankincense and myrrh. The date, and its symbolism, was woven into Richard's life and kingship. The Magi were effectively astronomers, led by a star to the place of Christ's birth, but they were also kings and Richard symbolically identified himself with them throughout his reign. Every year on his birthday Richard gave offerings of gold, frankincense and myrrh, and Epiphany became the most celebrated holy day in his court.[5]

He was a king who also saw himself as a mage, an expert in symbols, astral readings, alchemy and possibly, if more critical chroniclers are to be believed, the more sinister aspects of the occult.[6] Richard owned an astrolabe as well as horary quadrants, conical-shaped instruments used to work out the time of day by the sun's altitude, his obsession only increasing over the course of his reign.

But astronomy was not the only thing on his mind. In 1381, after years of negotiation, Richard was finally married to Anne of Bohemia, the daughter of the Holy Roman Emperor, Charles IV, a marriage that forged an alliance between England and Bohemia, two of the major states in northern Europe.

The new queen sailed into Dover in December 1381. Her ship managed to dock and Anne of Bohemia, a petite fifteen-year-old princess, stepped from the vessel, at which point 'there suddenly followed a disturbance of the sea greater than any that had been seen for a long time . . . the ships which were anchored in the harbour . . . were suddenly driven into collision with each other, and the ship, in which a moment ago the princess had been sitting, came apart and was dreadfully smashed into many pieces.'[7] To superstitious eyes Anne's arrival was an omen.

Richard and Anne made a strange, perhaps endearing couple. Anne was timid and small. The Westminster chronicler sarcastically commented that Anne was 'a tiny portion of meat', a reference both to Anne's small frame and also the tiny dowry she brought with her. Richard's appearance was still notably childlike, with a mop of golden curls and a round face that sometimes flushed red.[8]

The marriage appears to have developed into a genuinely loving relationship, albeit one that became a fiscal nightmare. Richard's government soon realised that Anne had cost the realm a fortune as her brother King Wenceslaus IV not only failed to pay her promised dowry in full, but borrowed an extravagant sum from Richard, who was over-eager to hand out cash and favours to his new brother-in-law as well as to Anne's counterparts and servants.

Anne's coronation in 1382 gave Richard a further opportunity to show his devotion to her. The *Liber Regalis*, or 'Royal Book', was probably commissioned by Richard as a gift for Anne. The book serves as a guide, a 'how to' for coronations. Anne herself is depicted in gold leaf and lapis blue enthroned and seated opposite (and slightly below) Richard. She is surrounded by bishops, dripping in cloth of gold. Her long yellow hair trails down her back and she is dressed in flowing robes. Richard and Anne lean gently towards one another; it is as if he is guiding his nervous queen as her crown is lowered steadily onto her head. Painted in gold, pink and deep blue, Anne is Marian in appearance. This idealised comparison was a familiar trope in depictions of medieval queens, just as they were regularly celebrated as childbearers and interceders. In the years to come, as trouble began to stir at Richard's court, Anne would play an active part in trying to keep the peace and keep her husband from making grave mistakes.

Richard did not identify with the legacy of the military-minded Edward III and deliberately avoided casting himself in the image of his father. He was an aesthete, gazing inwards, at himself and his court rather than outwards to European politics. Strikingly, in the 1380s Richard began to show alarming parallels with his great-grandfather, particularly in his dangerous decision to allow favourites to dominate his court circle. The old servants of the Black Prince who had protected Richard in his minority began to disappear from government. The most notable addition to Richard's inner throng was Robert de Vere, the debonair earl of Oxford, who was five years older than Richard and held the young king in the palm of his hand by extracting favours from the king and alienating older members of court. Their relationship began to echo the old affair of Edward and Gaveston, and Thomas Walsingham later suggested that de Vere used 'magic spells' on Richard to bring him into his favour and control him.[9] The rise of figures like de Vere led to a power struggle among the elite and the marginalisation of major political players, including the king's uncles. Tensions were high and as a result, when in the 1384 Salisbury parliament, Richard's actions were questioned by Richard, earl of Arundel, the king allegedly spat back, 'You can go to the Devil!' But it was during that parliament that something far more disquieting had begun to develop out of the sour atmosphere.

The Salisbury parliament was held in the great hall of the bishop's palace in spring 1384. A large, crenellated manor, the palace had a central courtyard flanked by four outbuildings and a moat. It was close to Salisbury Cathedral and Old Sarum, the site of the first English cathedral and subsequently a space infused with poignant early Christian mythology and meaning. Richard was staying at the palace when he took part in an intimate Mass in the chamber of Robert de Vere and was informed of a plot against his life. The celebrant was an Irish Carmelite friar named John Latimer. At the end of the service, as the king got up to leave, Latimer grabbed Richard and nervously whispered that John of Gaunt, the duke of Lancaster, planned to have Richard murdered. Furious and betrayed, Richard acted rashly: 'without deliberation, [he] ordered the aforementioned duke to be killed'. But his advisers flatly refused, 'asserting that it would be unjust for anyone to be condemned without a trial'. Richard's initial rage cooled and he conceded that propriety was needed in dealing with the issue. When Latimer was pressed further, the cleric revealed that a nobleman, Lord Zouche of Harringworth, head of one of the oldest houses in the realm, had 'full knowledge' of the plot. Panicking, the bewildered friar 'shammed insanity . . . stripping off his cope and shoes and pitching them out the window and generally producing the behaviour characteristic of a madman'. On witnessing the spectacle Richard ordered that the friar be kept in custody while the claims were investigated. Richard did not need proof to suspect his uncle of plotting against him. The accusation made by the monk, however ridiculous and unfounded, would be treated as if it were gravely serious.

The episode was the culmination of the mistrust that had been growing between the king and his three uncles, a situation that had been exacerbated by the behaviour of Robert de Vere, who saw Gaunt, Edmund and Thomas as obstacles in the way of his climb up the ranks of the nobility. It was no coincidence that Richard had been taking Mass in Robert de Vere's rooms, nor that the accusation took place during parliament, away from court. Perhaps de Vere did suspect something, or whispers had become rumour, and rumour became fact, but John of Gaunt's response when questioned about the accusations is telling. Gaunt let out a great sigh, as if exhausted by the stupidity of his nephew, and lamented, 'Oh why, my Lord, do you trust such informers? Am I not your uncle? Am I not your protector? Am I not the chief man in the realm after you? What could influence me to betray or even kill you, when I would gain nothing from your death?' Gaunt's tired plea to the king feels convincing.[10] After all, he had spent nearly a decade after the death of the Black Prince protecting Richard and overseeing his accession. The problem was that Gaunt and Richard were men cut from very different cloths.

John of Gaunt was a product of his father's reign, bound by chivalry and loyalty to his family. Unlike Richard, he was also unbending in following his father's ambition to expand Plantagenet rule. He had been hankering to invade Castile and seize its throne since his marriage to Constance, the daughter of Pedro I, in 1371. But more than ten years later, he still found himself pandering to the whims of his spoiled and impetuous nephew. Arrogant and often conceited though he was, Gaunt was no fool. In response to this new accusation, Gaunt did what he was accustomed to and played the role of the chivalrous knight. Before the assembled lords, he loudly challenged any man who accused him of treason. This, however, was not enough to quell suspicion. Riddled with gout, Lord Zouche was summoned from his bed to face questioning about what he was alleged to have known about the plot. Suffering pain as well as the ignominy of being 'unbelted and with an uncovered head, like a thief or a traitor', Zouche was eventually released after expressing genuine bafflement over the accusation and there being no real evidence for his involvement.

Friar John Latimer was left to the devices of Richard's bullish half-brother John Holland, who inflicted appalling torture: 'a lead of great weight was fixed to his genitals, and similarly to both his feet, and a great fire was lit under the soles of his feet'.[11] A rope strung about the friar's neck 'suffocated him in his throat and broke his spinal cord'.[12] Latimer's treatment was unbearably cruel and unjust, but also motivated, in part, by fear. During the process, Latimer's persecutors kept him shackled, reportedly because they were afraid that he might use witchcraft against them.[13]

Latimer was murdered by awful torture on the grounds that he should be considered a traitor for accusing another of the same. His mutilated and battered body was dragged through Salisbury on a pallet and then buried at Saint Martin's, an old Saxon church at the centre of the town. As the body was pulled through the streets, a common warning against treachery, it is claimed by Walsingham that the 'wickerwork crate on which the monk's body was carried actually became green again and put forth flowers and leaves'.[14] The sight of a blind man who was passed by the grisly procession was said to have suddenly returned to him. Others also claim that a bright light shone over Saint Martin's churchyard after the friar was buried.[15] The stories are apocryphal but served the authors of the chronicles as portent signs for what was to come.

Those who feared portent symbols looked to the sky for omens and in the late summer of 1384 a storm raged over England. Thunder boomed across the heavens and flashes of lightning 'dreadfully scared mortal men'. After the rumbling had stopped there was 'an eclipse of the sun lasting about an hour'. Astronomers would have been able to understand the movement of the planets by using an almanac – a kind of booklet strung on the belt that could predict the movements of the tide and the stars. People living and working on the land, however, were mostly illiterate, without access to this knowledge. For them, the darkening of the sky was a sign that Doomsday was approaching. The eclipse was, of course, no omen, but Richard's mood at court was growing as dark and unpredictable as the skies.

In late November 1384, preparations were being made in Westminster for a high-profile duel. The duel was planned for the middle of parliament, usually a welcome burst of entertainment for the lords and commons, weighed down by petitions from across the realm and discussions about defence. But this was a matter of life or death, glory or treason. In a rare but not-unheard-of situation, a duel became a trial by combat, an ancient custom that had been introduced into common law since the Conquest to settle matters if no witnesses or a confession could be obtained. It followed an accusation of treason from Martlet de Villeneuve, from Navarre, against John Walsh, the king's victualler, or wine-seller. It was claimed that Villeneuve really sought revenge for Walsh having raped his wife. At some point during the day the king, his uncles and the rest of parliament took to the lists – the jousting arena – to watch the duel play out.

Fully armoured and clutching a lance over six-feet long, Martlet de Villeneuve stared down his opponent at the end of the arena. The most powerful men of the realm watched in silence from the stand, draped in finery, as the armoured horses below scuffed the ground, ready to charge into action. At the signal, Villeneuve and Walsh dug in their spurs and burst forward, levelling their lances at one another. Seconds later, John Walsh overcame Martlet de Villeneuve. As far as Richard, parliament and John Walsh were concerned, justice had been served. The righteous man had won. Martlet de Villeneuve was posthumously hanged, drawn and beheaded and John Walsh made a knight 'enriched with many gifts, both by the king and the duke [of Lancaster]'.[16]

This duel – however brutal by nature – appeared to bring Richard and his uncles together. Yet the reality was very different. Richard was sour following the execution of Friar Latimer and remained suspicious of Gaunt. By 1385 it is possible that Richard was ruminating on ways to get rid of his meddling uncle.

In February John of Gaunt travelled by boat to visit his nephew at Sheen wearing a breastplate concealed beneath his clothes. Only weeks earlier Gaunt had received a warning that his life was in danger, that Richard had planned to arrest him during a great council meeting in Waltham in Lincolnshire.[17] Gaunt excused himself from the meeting and fled to Pontefract, where he could gather himself and think of a plan. Gaunt's decision to run speaks volumes. Richard was already unsafe, untrustworthy and unpredictable but Gaunt could not hide for ever. Gaunt's plan was to surprise Richard and confront him about the plot on his life.[18] He asked his men to wait with his boat and went into the palace alone. As expected, Richard 'protested on oath that he had known nothing of these plots', but the fact was, the gulf in interest that divided the king and his uncles had never been greater. Richard's uncles wanted him to focus on strengthening the realm by concentrating on war with France, but Richard's self-interest and disregard for authority rendered this impossible. Richard was hot-headed and frequently lashed out; John of Gaunt was not the only recipient of his fury. Shortly after Richard's altercation with Gaunt he came up against the archbishop of Canterbury, William Courtenay, who effectively accused Richard of not listening to the advice of his council. Accounts describe Richard as being so incensed with rage that his uncle Thomas of Woodstock had to intervene else 'he would have struck the archbishop'.[19] Instead, 'he shouted many foul words', resulting in the archbishop storming off in a rage.

Richard's behaviour had pushed his councillors to the edge. In the end, it was his mother who had to lay down the law. Princess Joan was suffering from ill health. She had gained so much weight that she found it difficult to move around. It is possible she had dropsy, the same swelling disease that took Philippa of Hainaut's life. What Joan did still have, even nearing the end of her life, was influence over Richard. After time with his mother, Richard emerged penitent. He must have known that one way he could appear eager to co-operate would be to appease his uncles and do what his grandfather and father had done before him: go to war.

Over the course of Richard's reign, war in France had trundled on, to the detriment of the English. A meagre portion of Gascony and Calais remained in England's hands, far from the empire Edward III had built — part of which some of the older statesmen at Richard's court, including his uncles, had personally fought for. Where the French coastline once lay vulnerable to English attacks, coastal towns across England now anxiously scanned the horizon for hostile ships. The French, aware of the unstable political situation in England and knowing that your enemy's enemy is your friend, turned to the Scots. With a new, young French king on the throne in the form of Charles VI, following the death of his father in 1380, the French were empowered to strike England on their own soil.

In early summer 1385 the competent but brash French admiral Jean de Vienne had landed his forces in Scotland and forged an alliance with 'those haters of peace and concord'.[20] Together they planned to burn the borderlands in a manner that had not been seen since the worst years of Edward II's reign. For Richard, this was an opportunity to look kingly. His uncles saw this as a chance for Richard to prove himself as a ruler, finally showing his strength as king with sword in hand. In July an alleged (but likely overestimated by contemporary chroniclers) one hundred thousand men crossed into Scotland.[21] Encamped just over the border with his standard blowing in the breeze, Richard knighted over three hundred men with a sword to mark the beginning of the campaign. He endowed his uncle Edmund as duke of York and Thomas as duke of Gloucester, exactly the sort of regal behaviour that would have impressed John of Gaunt. However, this good feeling was undermined when Richard endowed Robert de Vere as marquess of Dublin. The title was at the level of dukedom, and had only recently been introduced by Edward III. It was only given to royalty or family, and so Richard's elevation of de Vere made him practically royal.[22] The news was met with fury. This anger was exacerbated by the frustration caused by Richard's army's subsequent failure to engage with either the Scots or the French, despite their superior numbers.

The more nimble enemy avoided battle, moving fast and disappearing into the expanse of the Scottish landscape. The French had managed to inflict some damage on the borderlands with the help of the Scots, whose knowledge of the terrain was essential, but the English army now remained largely in hiding. The English moved towards the Firth of Forth where they 'burnt to ashes their [Scots] woods and houses . . . reducing corn and hay to almost nothing'.[23] They burned everything in their path, including Holyrood Abbey outside Edinburgh. But, crucially, they were running out of food. Tired of repetitive conflict with Scotland and the drudgery of this campaign, Richard's mood grew dark. Gaunt wanted to push on and chase down the Scottish and French forces who were lying just across the Forth, defeating them in a single blow. Richard had a different idea. Having run out of supplies for the army, he wanted to turn around and march home, abandoning the campaign altogether. The result was an argument, uncle pitted against nephew against a back-drop of driving rain and grey clouds. Richard got his way and the army moved out of Scotland having achieved nothing. The French also returned home, having given up the attack because they were unable to collaborate with the Scots or navigate the terrain of the country. The whole exercise was a waste of time for both sides.

Though the chroniclers sneered at Richard's retreat, his reasons for doing so were astute. Richard knew that driving a fractured, hungry army into unknown enemy territory could invite disaster. Gaunt may have been an excellent diplomat and statesman, but he was a terrible military leader: his numerous failures in Aquitaine were testament to this. This desperate campaign into Scotland, an attempt to rekindle the Edwardian glory days, was ill-conceived and badly-led, the best option probably was to end it before it descended from farce into calamity.

Another factor that likely pushed Richard to return to West-minster was the news that he received while marching through Scotland. His beloved mother, Joan of Kent, had collapsed and died on 8 August. This news would have impacted Richard enormously, for Joan had been a gentle presence in his life. He returned to London in early autumn in mourning for his mother. Gaunt, furi-ous with his petulant nephew, remained in the north of England, but he would also have been crushed by the death of his sister-in-law, who had been a lifelong ally and friend.

There was, however, a glimmer of light for Gaunt in a terrible year. After nearly a decade of strife and tension in England, he was finally to have his opportunity to take back Castile, claiming it for his wife, Constance, as the heir to the former king, Pedro I. While the English had been unsuccessful in Scotland, there had been a great battle in the Iberian Peninsula. The Portuguese had won a crushing victory against the Castilian army, resulting in the loss of 'almost all the flower of the nobility in Spain'. With Castile militarily weak-ened, now was the time to strike. He would be able to put distance between himself and Richard, while serving England's interests by controlling the most effective naval force in the Mediterranean. To Gaunt's surprise, Richard sanctioned the campaign – less because he cared what happened, or believed his uncle was capable of pulling off such an ambitious enterprise, and more because he was keen to be rid of Gaunt, whose power and authority choked Richard's own.

Once John of Gaunt had sailed out of Plymouth bound for Spain, taking his family and a large army with him, Richard considered himself free. He was answerable to nobody, or as Richard had put it in a previous parliament: 'The king will do as he chooses.'[24] Richard was filled with blind optimism and remarkable ego. To a gathering parliament in 1386, he announced, 'Just as the sky is rendered clear and bright by the stars, so dignity makes not only kingdoms but kingly diadems shine with its light.'[25] But the kingdom was far from shining with light, it was on the cusp of something difficult and dark. With Gaunt gone, Richard was without the guidance he sorely needed. The king had moved through adolescence swelling not only with self-importance but also with the desire for independence. Gaunt faced the impossible and exasperating task of trying to get Richard to take responsibility and rule in the manner of Edward III. Yet, though uncle and nephew had locked horns many times, Gaunt was never a threat to Richard. The danger to the king, as it had been for so many other kings before him, came from the nobility.

Where Richard saw a wonderful future, Thomas Walsingham read the stars and warned of 'the greatest upheaval'.[26]

25. A Mirror for Kings

In summer 1386 two large French ships were captured outside the port of Calais. After English seamen climbed onto their decks they began to investigate what hefty cargo was contained inside the bellies of these two maritime juggernauts. On one vessel they found the master carpenter for the French king, who had been tasked with accompanying his work – a large defensive wooden wall. The other boat was packed with 'machines, guns and powder, and other weapons of war'.[1] These vessels had been bound for the port of Sluys, the site of the massive English victory that had taken place at the start of the Hundred Years War almost fifty years earlier. This was also where the French army mustered an armada that they hoped would end it. The plan was to launch the largest ever invasion of England.

Charles VI was now seventeen. Bolstered by youthful optimism and the support of his uncles, he hoped to succeed where his ancestors had failed. With John of Gaunt absent, now launching his own invasion in Castile, England was steered by weak leadership. With the admiral Jean de Vienne at the helm of the French fleet, it was the perfect time to strike.[2]

John of Gaunt's absence was felt almost as soon as he had sailed out of Plymouth. As rumours of an imminent invasion from French forces began to circulate, people across the realm began to panic: 'like frightened rabbits and anxious mice [Londoners] sought secluded spots and searched carefully for hiding places . . . as though the city would soon be captured . . . they rushed like drunkards, to the walls . . . and in great terror did everything they were accustomed to do in times of dire necessity'.[3] The lord mayor of London, Nicholas Brembre, weeks away from the end of his term in office, took the situation into his own hands by releasing a series of orders to secure the city. Travellers were recalled, people were told they could not leave due to 'expected attack' and provisions were pooled.[4] Across the country, people did what they could. Fortifications were hastily thrown up, a hodgepodge fleet of merchant vessels and shipping boats muddled together in the Thames and the citizens of coastal towns were ordered to 'save and defend' the coast 'as stoutly as they can'.[5] Of the nobility, it was the practically minded Henry Bolingbroke, John of Gaunt's son, who led the largest muster of arms around London.[6] The impression that endures is of panic. Richard II and his government were not in control of the situation: a radical parliament was urgently needed.

In the end, the panic was for nothing. Much to the frustration of the hopeful French, appalling weather and unfavourable wind stopped the armada from departing. Better to abort the mission than endure an entire fleet of ships being cracked and splintered by rough waves. In England, however, panic and discord remained. What the threat had exposed was an unprecedented absence of governance over the realm. Edward II was weakened by infighting and petty politics, but Thomas of Lancaster snatched the reins when he had to, becoming the driving power in the realm. Edward III had proved that attacking one's enemies before being attacked by them, by and large, kept England powerful and its borders safe. John of Gaunt represented the traditional hierarchy of feudal power and authority, but he was absent. Unable to look beyond Westminster and his useless government, Richard was paralysed by his own lack of experience. The precedent had been set for the commons to wield their own authority over how the realm was governed during the Good Parliament in 1376. As the stability of the realm crumbled, Richard was faced with another power struggle – not against Lancaster or the king of France, but against his own people.

In October 1386, parliament was opened at Westminster by the chancellor, Michael de la Pole, who was responsible for the management of Richard's government. De la Pole was an unpopular man, who had already requested defence funds. Despite this the country was still terrifyingly vulnerable. Michael de la Pole stood before the lords and commons and requested a sum five times greater than he had before – the largest request for funds ever. He had manifestly failed to read the room.[7] Both the lords and commons were tired of sanctioning taxes for no visible benefit to the realm and now the chancellor had the gumption to ask for more. United in their rage, the lords and commons, 'with one mind . . . complaining grievously', decided that the chancellor, having failed to spend funds appropriately, should be impeached.[8]

The Good Parliament had set a precedent for the commons' power, particularly over the appointment or impeachment of royal government officials. At the time, Gaunt had been troubled by this demonstration of power against royal authority. A decade later, Richard took the exercise of this power as a personal affront. Incandescent with rage, Richard refused to attend further sittings until the commons complied with his wishes and raised the tax that de la Pole had requested.[9] The commons refused and dispatched Thomas, the duke of Gloucester, Richard's uncle, to persuade the king to act accordingly. When Gloucester threatened deposition should Richard not comply, he had no choice other than to return, pink-cheeked, with his chin in the air.

In what became known as the 'Wonderful Parliament', the lords and commons had united in an attempt to repair a realm fractured by poor governance and cronyism. Michael de la Pole was impeached and fourteen lords were appointed as a 'commission' for one year.[10] At nineteen years old, Richard still had the same amount of power as when he was a child – a situation he was acutely aware of. Richard took his household, including the newly elevated Robert de Vere, the smug and self-important duke of Ireland, to the Midlands to contemplate his next steps.

Between 1386 and 1387 the situation in the realm improved. In March 1387, in a particularly successful mission, a French fleet was ambushed by Richard, earl of Arundel, who had been appointed admiral of England. Thousands of barrels of wine were acquired by Arundel and over one hundred French ships were captured in the process.[11] Compared to major battles fought by Edward III, it was a relatively small victory but one that was sorely needed, even if Richard probably would not have taken the news well. Ousted from court at Westminster, he occupied himself by touring the realm with Robert de Vere and the unpopular Michael de la Pole, surveying the country for pockets of support should he need it. All the while, following the counsel of his most loyal friends, Richard began to find ways to pick holes in the Wonderful Parliament. While the king was preparing his next course of action against a growing body of malcontented lords, Robert de Vere found a new way of angering Richard's uncles.

Robert de Vere had been unhappily married for ten years to Philippa de Coucy – the daughter of Princess Isabella (Richard's aunt and the eldest daughter of Edward III and Philippa of Hainault). After a decade, they remained childless. With Richard's support, de Vere appealed to the pope for an annulment. Part of his urgency was down to the fact he had developed a relationship with Agnes Lancerona, one of Anne of Bohemia's ladies-in-waiting. Expecting the pope's approval, de Vere married her anyway. The result was not only a scandal but a deep insult to the royal family, leaving a grand-daughter of Edward III jilted by her husband for a woman, 'said to be a saddler's daughter – certainly not noble – and ugly too'.[12] It was suggested that de Vere used false evidence in the case he put to the pope, but it was less about the way he conducted the annulment and more that he dared request it at all.[13]

With John of Gaunt away, Thomas, duke of Gloucester, represented the old guard of the Edwardian era. Gloucester took particular offence to de Vere's snub against his niece, but it was Richard's actions in summer 1387 that marked the beginning of a new bloody feud.

In August six judges from the courts of the King's Bench and the Common Pleas travelled to Shrewsbury to meet with the king. Richard was accompanied by Anne, Robert de Vere and his former tutor and now close adviser Simon Burley, as well as Michael de la Pole, the former lord mayor of London, Nicholas Brembre and the archbishop of York, Alexander Neville. Richard wanted to understand in what respects the constraints against his power as monarch were legal, or, more importantly for his cause, illegal. The chief justice of the King's Bench, a bullish authoritarian called Robert Tresilian, gave the judges ten questions to answer, but the outcome was inevitable. Richard had them threatened with death if they did not come to the unanimous conclusion that 'the king should have control . . . in

respect of all other articles touching parliament until the end of parliament. And if anyone acted contrary to the king's will, as though
he were in parliament, he is to be punished as if he were a traitor.'[14]

Richard had the answers he needed and he was now able to legally
challenge the actions taken against him in the Wonderful Parliament.
By manipulating the law to his advantage he could accuse his enemies
of treason. But this would not be simple. As Richard accumulated
legislative ammunition, those who opposed him and de Vere were
also ready to fight. The result was a mirror image of a not-so-distant
past: a king protecting his favourite; a court of corruption, treason,
deceit and murder.

On 17 November 1387, Richard sat in state in Westminster Hall.
Three men quietly knelt before him with their heads bowed, awaiting an answer to their plight.[15] Richard glowered at them: his
uncle, Thomas, duke of Gloucester; Richard, earl of Arundel; and
Thomas, earl of Warwick. They came before him as Lords Appellant
and they wanted him to remove the treacherous advisers from his
company, namely Robert de Vere.

For Gloucester, the main issues were the snub against his niece,
Philippa de Coucy, as well as de Vere's rise in wealth and power,
which had elevated him to the same social level as Gloucester himself. The earls of Arundel and Warwick also felt that their interests
were threatened by Robert de Vere. One further issue was the war in
France. These men had constantly pushed to continue the conflict in
order to retain England's territory on that side of the Channel and so
keep the coastline of England relatively safe. Richard, however – on
the advice of his own advisers such as Michael de la Pole and Simon
Burley – sought a negotiated end to the war in France. He would not
invade or show military strength as his grandfather might have. As
a result, England was weakened by the near-constant threat of invasion. The three nobles had made their grievances known during the
Wonderful Parliament, identifying themselves to Richard as potential threats to his authority. A year later, they were making a final
appeal for resolution.

In what appeared to be a moment of hopeful reconciliation,

Richard told the Appellants to bring their formal appeal to parliament in the new year, where they would be heard.[16] As the lords thanked the king and returned to their army, Richard sent news to his friends of danger. Michael de la Pole fled to Calais in disguise: he 'shaved off his hair and beard and dressed as a Flemish poulterer'.[17] He even carried a basket of chickens for effect. Robert de Vere did not go to such extremes. He allegedly dressed as a soldier 'with a quiver of arrows' and rushed north to Chester, to its constable Thomas Molineux. When he arrived, he handed a letter of great importance to the constable, a commission to 'gather their people and with every safeguard to convey the king's kinsman and most particular friend to the king's presence, sparing neither trouble nor expense'.[18] It was a call to arms, for both de Vere and Molineux to muster an army out of Chester – a city that would be steadfast in its support for Richard throughout his life; that would be loyal to the king and the king alone.

Only weeks later, Robert de Vere led four to five thousand men out of the gates of Chester: this was a private army promised generous pay for their services. De Vere quietly wove through the countryside, hushing his men as they marched along roads that were fraught with danger. Civil war was brewing and many would take up arms against him if they were given the chance. As Robert de Vere hastened along the road for London, he may have pondered the fate of Piers Gaveston, whose head was taken on Blacklow Hill all those years ago.

By the time de Vere reached Oxfordshire, the Lords Appellant were not only aware of his movements but had gained allies. Thomas Mowbray, the son-in-law of the earl of Arundel and former childhood friend of Richard, had become disaffected by de Vere's prominence at court. After jostling with de Vere for the king's attention, Mowbray gave up hope, but remained bitter. In December 1387 he joined the Appellants as they marched to intercept de Vere's army before he could reach the king. In a further boost to the cause, Gaunt's son Henry Bolingbroke had joined his uncle, the duke of Gloucester. The plot to assassinate his father in the early 1380s must have played on his mind as he marched against the wayward favourite. But aside from the affront to Gaunt, there was no obvious reason why Henry had decided to throw his lot into the fight, for until now he had been a peripheral force, acting according to his father's wishes and largely staying out of politics. This sudden change of heart was, like others, probably due to the unsettling rise of Robert de Vere. Henry most likely understood that de Vere was a man who had dangerously high ambitions and could only be stopped by force.

At twenty years old, Henry Bolingbroke was a crucial ally. It was not just that Gaunt had left the entire Duchy of Lancaster under his protection, Henry was also a skilled warrior, possessing the martial flair that Richard lacked. Tall and handsome, with the angular Plantagenet features of his father, he was popular. And there was one more thing that Bolingbroke possessed and Richard did not: a son. Henry's decision to join the Lords Appellant changed the course of his life. From 1387 onwards, his fate would be intertwined with Richard's.

As Robert de Vere marched towards London through Oxfordshire, the Appellant army tried to engage his force. The result was a collection of skirmishes that ultimately resulted in a short battle. On 20 December 1387 Robert de Vere wove his army through thick fog towards Radcot Bridge, just outside Chipping Norton, an essential crossing for anyone who wanted to meet the road to London. Knowing this, Henry Bolingbroke had stationed his men at the foot of the bridge.[19]

Radcot Bridge was a large stone crossing that would enable even mounted horsemen to ford the River Thames that gushed beneath it. As Robert de Vere approached, the fog obfuscated his view, until, quite clearly, Henry Bolingbroke and a large army appeared from the murk. De Vere immediately unfurled the royal banner, ordering trumpets and readying his men to do battle. Bolingbroke's men had already been at work. They had dismantled the bridge, moving the stones and rendering it impassable. Robert de Vere was trapped. 'We have been tricked!' he announced in a panic. With his men refusing to fight, de Vere 'jumped off the horse he had been riding, and mounted another courser, hoping to flee from his adversaries along the bank of the River Thames'. But Gloucester was waiting for him. De Vere was penned in, Henry Bolingbroke on one side and the duke of Gloucester on the other. Preferring to risk drowning than be captured, he made a bold move and used the confusion of the fog to his advantage. Momentarily out of sight, de Vere 'threw away his gauntlets and sword and other equipment . . . and jumped into the River Thames'. Against the odds, Robert de Vere managed to swim through freezing water to safety.

He had avoided the fate of the other royal favourites and escaped. The same could not be said for much of de Vere's army. Many 'drowned in the marsh'. Thomas Walsingham gives a detailed account of the bitter end met by the constable of Chester, Thomas Molineux.[20] Having worn himself out by swinging his sword, fighting in defence of his person, Molineux leapt into the river, pursued by Thomas Mortimer, a knight and illegitimate son of Roger Mortimer, the second earl of March. Mortimer ordered the constable to come out, or he would be chased by a flurry of arrows. ' "If I come out," pleaded Molineux, "will you spare my life?" ' Mortimer responded, ' "I am making no promises . . . but you must either climb out or else soon be killed." ' The drenched constable gave himself up but Mortimer showed no mercy. He murdered the man while he was still trying to clamber out of the river.

The Appellants were victorious. De Vere had escaped but would never return – he later died in a hunting accident having fled to Flanders. Richard was weakened and would now be forced to comply with the wishes of both the lords and the commons. The Wonderful Parliament was succeeded by another, held in February 1388, that would be known as the Merciless Parliament. More trial than parliament, judgement would be dealt upon those who, it was believed, had corrupted the young king for long enough.

Richard was a child on his accession, and his boyish appearance, lack of an heir and impulsive behaviour kept him locked in a state of eternal youth. Bad governance could not be laid at the feet of the boy-king who was too young to rule, too young to understand what he was doing wrong. Others would have to shoulder the blame.

As Richard had requested, the Lords Appellant attended parliament in February 1388 with a petition outlining their appeal.[21] Since Radcot Bridge, Richard had spent the Christmas period and following feasts holed up in the Tower of London. He did not even celebrate his Epiphany birthday.[22] As parliament opened at Westminster on 3 February, Richard was forced to sit and listen.

The five victorious Lords Appellant – Thomas, duke of Gloucester, Henry Bolingbroke, Thomas Mowbray, the earls of Warwick and Arundel – wearing golden robes, all proudly strode into the White Chamber of Westminster Palace on the first day of parliament. Richard squirmed in his throne as they arrived with their arms linked. As before, the leading Appellants were Gloucester, Warwick and Arundel, described by Thomas Favent, a clerk of the Salisbury diocese, as 'indivisa trinitas' – the undivided trinity.[23] Gloucester wanted to clarify his position before proceedings could continue. Kneeling before Richard, 'he understood that our said lord the king had been informed that the said duke was about to depose our lord the king and make himself king'.[24] Gloucester was eager to make clear that his opposition to Richard's favourite courtiers was not also a step to ascending the throne himself. In a public display of acceptance and seeming forgiveness – perhaps rehearsed in the Tower – Richard acknowledged his uncle's gesture, stating 'that he considered the said duke guilty of nothing, and fully excused him'. It would soon become clear that this was not what Richard actually thought.

The new chancellor, Thomas Arundel, the bishop of Ely – the brother of the earl of Arundel – opened parliament and after the regular pattern of proceedings got to the point of the session: the consequences for the circle of Richard's advisers who the Appellants considered to be guilty of treason. Michael de la Pole and Robert de Vere, who both lingered in exile, were in their absence formally confirmed as traitors to the realm and sentenced to a traitor's death. It took two hours for the clerk to read the full thirty-nine articles of treason in full, indicting not only the escapees but Alexander Neville, the archbishop of York; Nicholas Brembre, the former lord mayor of London; and the chief justice of the King's Bench, Robert Tresilian. They were accused of manipulating Richard, a king 'of tender age' and 'innocence'.[25] In doing so they had lined their own pockets while watching the realm crumble into financial difficulty, badly advised the king in relation to the war with France and alienated the king from not only his subjects but other members of his government. The main culprit was Robert de Vere; in his absence, others would pay the price.

Due to his status as archbishop of York, Neville's life was spared but he was stripped of all his temporalities – the immense land and wealth that came with his position. Brembre and Tresilian were condemned to die as traitors.[26] Judge Tresilian, however, was in hiding. This left Brembre, who was unwilling to go without a fight. When brought from the Tower before parliament in the White Chamber, Brembre maintained his innocence and said that his guilt could only be proved in a trial by combat. Brembre wanted to prove his innocence, or die by the sword, anything but a traitor's death. He was refused the honour. When Richard briefly piped up, hoping to come to his ally's defence, all five Lords Appellant stripped off their gauntlets and threw them down – a symbolic action marking readiness to fight.

The problem for the Appellants was that a committee of twelve noblemen, led by the level-headed Edmund of Langley, Richard's elder uncle after John of Gaunt, could not find sufficient justification to take Brembre's life. The appearance of legality was important, no matter how exasperating this might be for the Appellants. Partway through the argument, however, proceedings were interrupted: the hiding place of Robert Tresilian had been discovered. Judge Robert Tresilian had imposed death penalties throughout his career; in February 1388 it was his turn to meet the same grisly fate. The duke of Gloucester personally led a contingent of guards to the belly of Westminster Abbey, where Tresilian had sought sanctuary. To the sound of a loud protest from the abbot of Westminster, Judge Tresilian was dragged from his hiding place. He cut a sad and unkempt figure, 'wearing the garb of a hermit'.[27] That same day, he was tied to a wooden hurdle and dragged by horses through the streets from the Tower of London to Tyburn, where he was stripped naked and hanged by the neck until he was dead.

Despite Brembre's bold defence, he could not avoid the same fate. In the end, it was agreed that although it was hard to prove that he had personally committed treason, it was easier to show that he was aware of treason *being* committed and had taken steps to conceal it.[28]

Brembre received the same treatment as Judge Tresilian. He was dragged through the streets on a hurdle and taken to Tyburn, where he was hanged.

Parliament lasted an achingly long four months, during which time other members of Richard's household were accused of manipulating the young king for their own gain during his minority. Of these household knights a particular example was made of Sir Simon Burley, Richard's friend, former tutor and father figure. Burley had been the fortunate recipient of grants and generous gifts, had arranged the marriage between Richard and Anne of Bohemia and acted as warden of the Cinque Ports – a role that rendered him vulnerable to criticism regarding the constant invasion threats. His loyalty was unquestionable and the charges levelled against him evidence that the Lords Appellants' desire for revenge had gone too far. Edmund of Langley, the duke of York, stood his ground against his brother, the duke of Gloucester, insisting that Burley was loyal to Richard out of love, not for personal gain.

In late April, the tensions that these arguments provoked came to a head before parliament when Gloucester threatened to prove Burley's guilt 'with his sword-arm', prompting the duke of York, usually the calmest, most measured of the brothers, to 'turn white with anger' and call his brother a liar. The two Plantagenet princes glowered at each other across the room, as if readying themselves to leap upon each other. Richard was said to be the one who stopped them.[29]

Henry Bolingbroke and Thomas Mowbray counselled against executing Burley, and Queen Anne also attempted to intervene, falling to her knees before the three leading Appellants, begging for his life. Despite 'the humble prayers upon her knees', Simon Burley was condemned to death in early May.[30] With his hands tied behind his back, Burley was made to walk 'along the king's highway through the middle of the city of London to Tower Hill'. There 'he was beheaded on flat ground'.[31] Simon Burley had cradled the ten-year-old Richard on his coronation day, carried the sleeping boy to bed when the day became too much for him; Richard, powerless for now, would neither forget nor ever forgive his execution.

The following May, a year after the death of Simon Burley, Richard

summoned his council and began coolly, 'I have spent some years
under your counsel and rule . . . now however by God's care, we
have attained the age of our majority, and indeed are already in
our twenty-second year. Therefore we desire and will the freedom
to rule and regulate our person and our inheritance . . . to choose
and appoint to their posts our officers and ministers, and so freely
to remove those who are now in office'.[32] Without either, rage or
obvious delight, Richard removed his uncle the duke of Gloucester from his council, along with the earl of Warwick and the earl of
Arundel. The 'undivided trinity' were quietly replaced in a blood-
less coup with men of Richard's choosing. For his part, Thomas
Mowbray grovelled to Richard, and Henry Bolingbroke distanced
himself. Curiously Richard did not punish either of them. It is likely
Richard feared Gaunt's reaction if he had, as well as valuing Mowbray's repentance.

In the most symbolic act of reclaiming his kingly authority, the
chancellor, Thomas Arundel, now archbishop of York, was summoned to Richard and requested to hand over the Great Seal. Richard
delicately wrapped the precious crucible of royal authority in his
robes. Pausing for thought he then handed it to the bishop of Winchester, William Wykeham.[33]

Despite the crushing defeat and death of all those close to him,
Richard had somehow, peacefully, managed to regain his power.
By passing the Great Seal to Wykeham he was not choosing a man
he necessarily thought would navigate the role of chancellor with
aplomb, but he was selecting his own government, rather than
government selecting for him. At twenty-two, Richard was still
considered incapable and innocent, coddled into adulthood with his
wings clipped for his own safety. Richard could never escape the
image of him as a boy-king in oversized white robes, for he was never
allowed – or would not allow himself – to grow up.

In conflict with his own sense of identity, moving into the 1390s
Richard channelled his time and money into convincing others that
he was who he thought he was: a king at the cutting edge of Europe's
artistic and literary rebirth, otherwise known as the Renaissance.

26. Renaissance

In late fourteenth-century Europe a new cultural movement had emerged from Italy. It was a flowering of literature and art and architecture influenced by classical scholarship and antiquity. Though England was on the edge of these developments, its cultural output was already moving in the same direction and Richard was keen to be the one leading it.

Sometime in the early 1390s, Richard was presented with a portrait of himself, later called the Wilton Diptych, named after Wilton House in Salisbury, where it was kept until the early twentieth century. In the two-panel portable painting, Richard is portrayed as blushing and wide-eyed with golden curls – the little boy he was so determined to prove he was not.

It is unknown who made or commissioned the Wilton Diptych, only that it was created with extraordinary skill by an artist possibly trained in Italy during the flowering of the Renaissance. With a wash of bright gold and lapis blue, no expense had been spared in its creation. Richard is front and centre, on his knees before the Virgin Mary, his hands clasped in prayer. Behind him stand the three patron saints of England: Edmund the Martyr (holding the arrow); Edward the Confessor, who holds his ring; and John the Baptist holding a lamb. Richard is shown to be England's ultimate champion, as one of the angels, draped in ultramarine, leans forward to hand him the standard of Saint George. As if they were members of his own personal devotional army, each angel wears Richard's badge, the emblem of the white hart, which is also seen adorning Richard's cloak and on the reverse of the altarpiece. In a touching and poignant nod to Anne of Bohemia, the hart on the reverse of the panel rests in a grassy meadow, on a bed of rosemary – the herb being her emblem. In an intertwining of holy and personal symbolism, Richard wears a necklace of broom seedpods around his neck as he looks up into the eyes of the holy family. Broom blossom, *planta genista* in Latin, was the origin of the Plantagenet name. In a nod to his ancestors Richard recovers the memory of generations of kings before him.

The Diptych is a vivid representation of Richard's kingship and character as he moved into the final decade of his reign and his life. It is an intimate portrayal of a young man who is washed in his own sense of divinity and self-importance. This could be a narcissistic depiction of selfhood, staring into the Diptych as Narcissus stares at his own reflection in the pool of water, or it could be considered a visual gambit designed to convince Richard of his own importance and his station as king. If his own council and government could not, or would not, support him then the angels adorned in his emblem would. In this reading, the Wilton Diptych is a lament to a king who, above all, lacked the confidence that kingship required.[1]

Richard was insecure. He was overshadowed by his famous father and grandfather, to whom he was constantly compared. His reluctance to go to war was perhaps because he feared that he would fail where they had been victorious. The only place that Richard could truly exercise some level of individuality and agency was in his artistic patronage. As a result, the early 1390s ushered in an extraordinary literary and visual culture. Through art, architecture and literature Richard promoted his own style of kingship in a more self-conscious fashion than his predecessors.[2]

One of the most famous alliterative poems of the period, *Gawain and the Green Knight*, was composed around 1390 and offers a glimpse into England's enduring fascination with Arthurian legend. *Gawain* would have originally been orated to a rapt audience, told around Christmas time, its verse spoken out loud to the backdrop of a flicker of flames in the hearth, candles, ivy and holly adorning the hall. It is the story of a mystical Green Knight visiting the court of King Arthur at Camelot during the Christmas feast. There he makes a challenge to the brave and restless Sir Gawain, seated at the Round Table. The Arthurian court in *Gawain and the Green Knight* is represented as youthful and peaceful – more a Ricardian court than the martial incarnations inhabited by Edward III.[3]

Elsewhere the scholar John Gower, author of *Vox Clamantis*, was commissioned by Richard to compose his epic poem *Confessio Amantis*. It is a love story in which an ageing lover confesses to the chaplain of Venus. The poem became so popular it survived for centuries, rewritten into over forty different manuscripts.[4] The early versions of the *Confessio* included dedications in the epilogue to both Richard and Geoffrey Chaucer. It is certain that John Gower and Chaucer knew each other and it is possible that within the heady atmosphere of Richard's artistic court they spent time with each other and perhaps even inspired one another. This was also a time when Chaucer was particularly active, for around the early 1390s he began his most famous work, *The Canterbury Tales*.[5]

Set in the Tabard Inn in Southwark, Chaucer brings together some of the most famous figures of literature in the grittiest part of London's outskirts. Southwark was the location of ale houses, inns and brothels, a marked contrast to the lofty and elegant delights of Richard's court. As the pilgrims in Chaucer's *Canterbury Tales* demonstrate, Londoners were a wonderful sprawl of different characters. Where there was lechery, theft, drunkenness and xenophobia, there was also community. Richard relied on the support of these Londoners. Mercantile loans had provided the royal court for decades and this urban community held more power than the royal family of England liked to admit. Yet Richard was not a man of the people. His focus was ultimately his self-image and his grandiose idea of kingship.

In October 1390, Richard hosted the most spectacular event seen in Europe in the later Middle Ages: a lavish tournament at Smithfield where the great and good of European chivalry were invited to show off their skill.

An elaborate procession took place on the afternoon of 10 October, from the Tower of London to Smithfield, where 'the queen of England and her ladies and damsels had already arrived and were installed in chambers handsomely decorated'.[6] As part of the carefully curated spectacle there were 'sixty armed warhorses ornamented for the tournament, each ridden by a squire at walking pace; then came sixty high ranking ladies, mounted on palfreys, most elegantly and richly dressed, each leading by a silver chain a knight armed for tilting . . . in this procession they moved through the streets of London, attended by numbers of minstrels and trumpeters to Smithfield'. Londoners lined up to watch this dazzling array of knights and ladies. Where previous royal parades had been a joy to observe – the entry of King Jean II of France into London, or the coronation of Richard II – this particular event left a sour taste. Following a bad harvest and another wave of plague, people were starving. Sources claimed that 'the dearth bore very hard upon the people, and especially the commons and the poor, for you might see babies and children on the roads and in their houses crying and clamouring with hunger, begging for bread, and their mothers with none to break for them'.[7] Preoccupied with his own majesty and the more attractive activities of casting himself as a Renaissance man and hosting lavish feasts during his Smithfield tournament, Richard had forgotten about the people.

In London, measures were taken by the mayor and aldermen to protect citizens from starvation. Items were sold at a fixed price to those in need and as a result people were just able to endure the ache of hunger until the harvest recovered and grain once again filled barns across England. Though necessary, this was expensive and the mercantile classes of London were no longer willing to dole out loans to the Crown, prioritising the situation in the city, which left little remaining in the coffers.[8]

When Richard's requests for loans from both individual merchants and civic bodies were refused time and time again, he began to consider their refusal a demonstration of disloyalty and dislike of his person. In December 1391, Richard's suspicions were confirmed: the people of London were disaffected with their king, enough to treasonously criticise him, as evidenced in a court case held in the Court of Chancery. One William Mildenhale of London was accused of failing to report his late father for criticising Richard's kingship (the father was claimed to have said that 'the king was not able to govern any realm, wishing that he were in his gong [toilet] where he might stay forever without further governing').[9] A further slight on Richard's authority in London came with a dispute in January 1392 over the administration of London's legal rights. John Hende, the lord mayor of London, proclaimed that royal officials would have to obtain his permission if they wanted to arrest a London, citizen. Richard responded by ordering the mayor to appear before him and his council every day for a week or be fined a thousand pounds. The mayor represented the people of London – by demanding such a steep fine the king was either forcing the citizens of London into submission or exhorting money from them. With the atmosphere so febrile it is no wonder a riot broke out in Fleet Street, over something as small as a loaf of bread. In February 'a baker's man was carrying a basket full of horse loaves [a large and cheap loaf of bread] [when] along came a yeoman of the bishop of Salisbury [who was also the treasurer] . . . who took a horse loaf out of the baker's basket and . . . broke the baker's head.'[10] The offending yeoman then dashed into the bishop of Salisbury's palace and had the gates sealed behind him. A riot ensued outside, with threats to burn the palace to the ground.

Richard considered this riot a grave offence against the Crown. He set about dismantling London as the commercial capital by moving the Court of Common Pleas to York. The Chancery followed. Richard summoned London officials to his castle at Nottingham, where he found them guilty of allowing rioting and discord to take place in London and grievous error in the city's government. The lord mayor, aldermen and sheriffs of London were stripped of office and a hefty one-hundred-thousand-pound fine landed upon the capital – notably the same amount Richard had demanded in the first place. The king had dismantled London's privileges and reasserted royal authority in only two months; the only option Londoners had to redeem any sense of self-governance was to show grovelling remorse. The way to Richard's heart was through his ego.

Though it made him feel powerful, it did not serve Richard to have the Chancery or the Court based in York. Financially it was far more sensible for them to remain in London. Once Richard felt the balance of authority weighed in his favour, he re-established normal practice. In gratitude, the Londoners put on a jubilant spectacle they knew he would relish. The leading aldermen and representatives of the city's trades and guilds rode out to meet the king and escorted him to London Bridge. There he was presented with 'a milk white steed saddled and bridled wearing trappings of white-cloth-of-gold and red together . . . the queen they gave a pure white palfrey . . . and the conduits of London ran with white and red wine . . . a high stage was erected on which were many angels [singing] various melodies and songs . . . an angel came down from the high stage, by a device, and set a crown of gold, precious stones and pearls upon the king's head and another on the queen's.'[11] At Westminster the couple were offered further lavish gifts and an appeal for his 'mercy, lordship and special grace'. If this appeared to be another coronation, it was meant to. Despite Richard's protestations and his bid to take control, the pure, white innocence of youth would not leave him. Nor, it seemed, did he truly want it to.

Showered with adoration and reverence, Richard had reached the pinnacle of his kingship. He had cooled his temper and battled his own insecurities during the early 1390s. This was made possible by a series of small victories – patronising the arts, spending elaborately on self-promotion, seizing back power. But Richard's narcissism had a habit of rearing its head when life did not go according to plan.

In June 1394, Queen Anne of Bohemia died at Sheen aged twenty-seven from a fast and unknown illness, possibly a victim of a wave of plague that summer.[12] The couple never had children, but it appears not for want of trying. The apothecary bills of Anne of Bohemia from the final year of her life suggest she was concerned for her fertility. *Trifera magna*, which contained opium and various herbs, was one method prescribed in the *Trotula* – a collection of texts on women's health, likely written by a woman – to help women conceive.[13]

Anne was to be buried in Westminster Abbey in a tomb specially commissioned to eventually encase Richard's body alongside hers. This was the first royal couple's tomb of its kind, with their hands clasped together in bronze, a loving and infinite union. As to be expected, the imagery Richard had carefully chosen to be chiselled into the tomb was laden with symbolism. Anne's hair is long and flowing, there are sprigs of broom blossom – *planta genista* – an A and

R intertwined together and Richard's [1]
Her personal inscription read:

> When she lived in the world she was th
> She was devoted to Christ and v.
> was ever inclined to give her gifts to th
> and relieved the pregnant. She was [1]
> was gentle and pretty. She provid.
> to the sick.

Richard's efforts in commemo.
devoted side. If he had been anxious a.
did not openly blame Anne. She had se
interceding on behalf of Rich.
cool to his heat, offering a mindful w.
the same manner as his mother. With
pered. Without her, he was dang

Up until Anne's death, Richard had s
The country was at peace, the tumult
to be buried and forgotten. Howe
ster Abbey, cracks began to show in Ri.
of Arundel, a constant source of irri.
He was nowhere to be seen when h.
in ceremony from Saint Paul's Cathe
later on, Arundel attempted to leav
into a fury. An eyewitness recalled h.
and hit him [Arundel] so violently or
ground and his blood flowed copio.
not been stopped, Richard would ha,
there and then. Richard's behaviour h
next year.

Fire and smoke consumed walls, wind
and shadows of the flames danced
cloud of black smog could be seen a.
Sheen was on fire. This was no accid
of King Richard II. The king ha.

to the ground' while 'glass, tiles, stone and timber' be salvaged and stored.[15] It is likely that Richard wished to use the material on future building projects, busying himself with the renovation of his properties. Yet this was also the home that he and Anne had developed together, a space he had been happy – and so it is also possible that he could no longer, in his grief, bear this palace humming with her memory to stand.

The dismantling of Sheen was followed by a strange fascination with the corpse of his old friend Robert de Vere. After he had been killed hunting boar in autumn 1395, de Vere's body had been embalmed before being returned to England from the Louvain (a region in what is now Belgium), at Richard's request. An elaborate service to formally inter his dearest friend was held at Cole Priory in Essex with Richard, the archbishop of Canterbury and de Vere's mother in attendance. The funeral was 'magnificent', but Richard's behaviour was disturbing. In front of those gathered he lifted the top of the cypress-wood coffin to gaze at de Vere's embalmed body, 'to touch the fingers' and 'publicly demonstrate his affection for the dead man which earlier he had lavished upon the living'.[16]

The year 1395 appears to have been when Richard pondered on life, death and memory. He razed Sheen and saw to the burial of his former friend. But Richard ruminated most particularly on his own posthumous reputation, specifically how he and the roster of Plantagenet kings that had come before him would be remembered. He appealed to the pope to canonise his great-grandfather Edward II. This was not Richard's first attempt, and it would not be his last. On a mission to Florence, royal emissaries, Peter Merk and James Monald, were tasked with delivering into the hands of the pope a 'gold cup and a gold ring set with a ruby, also the *Book of Miracles of Edward Late King of England, whose body was buried at the town of Gloucester*'.[17] Richard's obsession with the canonisation of his ancestor was multifaceted. In one sense, he saw Edward II as a mirror of himself – a king who did not identify with the military-minded monarchs that came before him, but who through his friendships had loved and lost. In another, he sought to legitimise and sanctify Edward's memory in opposition to Thomas of Lancaster, the man who had challenged him in life before being canonised himself – just as Richard felt threatened by the Lancastrians in his reign, namely his uncle John of Gaunt.

Gaunt had returned from Spain dejected but rich, having failed in his attempt to conquer Castile. Never the military strategist his father and brother had been, Gaunt watched his men slowly perish in the dusty plains of Castile. Gaunt's rival, Juan I, cut him a deal: if he abandoned his claim he would be generously paid off, and his daughter Catherine married to the heir to the Castilian throne. With little option, Gaunt took the deal and returned to England a different man. Tired of war, in want of peace and without the emotional energy needed to deal with Richard's highly volatile state, Gaunt was haunted by the lingering animosity between Richard and the Lords Appellant.[18] In his final years he saw his role as protecting his family and securing their inheritance. In 1396, following the death of his wife, Constance of Castile, Gaunt married his long-term mistress, Katherine Swynford. In a remarkable demonstration of affability, Richard permitted Gaunt's request to have their four children legitimised, taking the name Beaufort.[19] This might have been motivated by kindness, though was more likely a means to keep him on side.

Gaunt had been working for Richard using his diplomatic skills to conclude a peace agreement with France. In 1389 Gaunt had been part of a delegation sent to Leulinghem, outside Calais, where representatives of England and France met to discuss terms of a truce. That truce was finally sealed at Ardres, also near Calais, in November 1396 at a meeting of the two kings, Richard II and Charles VI.

The French were not in the hopeful position they had been a decade before. On a particularly hot day in 1392, while riding through Le Mans, Charles VI had gone mad and killed a number of his own entourage.[20] This was possibly the first episode of his psychosis, triggering what appears to have been a long and debilitating mental illness – likely paranoid schizophrenia. He later famously believed that he was made of glass. By 1395 war no longer benefited either side.[21] A truce for the English would leave the kings of England with de facto sovereignty over Gascony and Calais – regions Richard's representatives in France had clung on to. A truce would allow coastal communities in England to relax after the near-constant threat of

French invasion throughout Richard's reign. Closer to home, a truce would also remove the threat from Scotland, stabilising the northern border. With no allies at their heels, the Scots would have to accept the new status quo and cease large-scale raiding and border warfare. The benefit for the Valois was that no further lands would be the subject of challenges by the English and the people of France could live without fear. But for both parties the major incentive to end the war was financial. War was costly; it demanded higher taxes and often led to rebellion.

The truce was confirmed with a marriage alliance, the first Anglo-French union since Edward II and Isabella of France in 1308. Charles VI offered the widowed Richard the hand of his daughter Isabella of Valois, who at the time was a week away from her seventh birthday. The marriage could not be consummated for up to a decade, so Richard's acceptance of his bride is puzzling. It appears to have been a short-term political decision, driven by a genuine desire to be rid of the perpetual problem of war with France, rather than a long-term dynastic one, for there was no possibility of producing an heir quickly. The hope expressed was that 'the numerous, great and widespread outrages, evils, enormities, wrongs and shedding of human blood occasioned by the war should cease . . . that friendship and co-operation of an exemplary kind should be fostered between their kingdoms and their subjects.'[22] What better way to demonstrate solidarity than a wedding? Isabella's dowry would also have been tempting to Richard, who loved money. The eight hundred thousand francs was a helpful addition to the Crown purse and made some headway in compensating the English for never receiving the agreed ransom for Jean II following his capture at Poitiers. Sixty years of near-constant war had been brought to an end, or so it seemed. Richard left France with Isabella of Valois and a sense of relief.

In the last decade of his reign, Richard invested in another portrait of himself, which could not have been more different from the child-like image in the Wilton Diptych. In a remarkably rare depiction of a fourteenth-century king, Richard is seated on the coronation chair, crowned with his sceptre in his arms. He is surrounded by bright gold and wearing a green tunic emblazoned with the letter R. His robe is crimson; ermine is draped over his shoulders. Where the Wilton Diptych was personal and private, this was public. Richard is older. His beard is slightly forked and he is seated on his throne in majesty. It was on these terms that Richard liked to be considered – high and mighty, majestic. In the 1390s he even began to change the language of kingship to adhere to his vision. 'My lord' had been the normative term in addressing the king, but Richard, for the first time in history, requested to be addressed as 'your majesty', or 'your highness'. The Westminster Portrait is probably an accurate depiction of Richard at the height of his power – by the late 1390s he had pacified the citizens of London, ended the war with France and amassed a vast fortune. He had dealt with domestic and overseas problems. He had grieved for his wife and best friend and laid both to rest. That said, one major rupture to his ego was still festering in his mind: his personal revenge against the Lords Appellant.

27. The Last Plantagenets

On an early evening in midsummer 1397, the earl of Warwick made his way down the Thames by boat to Coldharbour, where he had been invited to dine with the king. Warwick was not the only guest summoned to the king's table. The earl of Arundel and the duke of Gloucester were also asked. Warwick, however, was the only one to attend; Arundel made his excuses, while Gloucester claimed to be unwell. As Warwick dined with Richard, all seemed well and the king was in an amiable mood, but Warwick had been fooled. Richard had harboured resentment against the Lords Appellant for a decade, and that evening, as he watched Warwick eat his meal and drink his wine, Richard knew he was about to get his revenge. The earl of Warwick was arrested as soon as he finished his meal, thrown onto another boat and sent downriver to the Tower of London, the place where traitors were sent to await their sentence.[1]

With Warwick safely bundled away, Richard made his way to Pleshey in Essex, the home of the duke of Gloucester. In the darkness the household were woken by bangs and shouts as the king and an armed guard demanded entry. Sweating and pale, Gloucester greeted his nephew half-dressed, having had no time to prepare himself – no armour, no sword. 'In the quiet of the night he [Richard] personally arrested Thomas duke of Gloucester . . . disregarding the grief, tears and prayers with which the duchess his wife and the whole household entreated him.'[2] To prevent his other uncles from staging a coup to rescue Gloucester, Richard had his loathed uncle dispatched to Dover. He was then sent across the Channel to be imprisoned in Calais. There, Gloucester would remain under the watchful eye of Thomas Mowbray, his fellow Appellant, who had spent the last decade attempting to crawl back into Richard's favour. Richard then sent the archbishop of York, Thomas Arundel, to persuade his brother, the earl of Arundel, to give himself up. Despite protestations from the earl that 'he was only too well aware of the king's deceits and evil designs', he could see he had no choice.³ As an armed guard marched to his home at Reigate, Arundel presented himself for arrest. He was then spirited away to Carisbrooke Castle on the Isle of Wight. Suspicious of the loyalty of the archbishop of York, Richard had him exiled from the realm, likely so he would not interfere with the forthcoming trial of the arrested Lords Appellant.

Within days, Richard began to dismantle the structures of power that each of these lords had built over the course of their careers as courtiers and landowners. On 15 July, 'under pain of forfeiture of life and limb', Richard released an order to arrest the personal retinues of the duke of Gloucester and the earls of Arundel and Warwick.⁴ There would be nobody within their households or employ to rally support. Richard's carefully considered coup had so far gone to plan.

That September, parliament was held in a vast, makeshift tent, a temporary space to house the lords and commons of the realm as the renovation of Westminster Hall was under way – Richard's grandest building project to date. Masons and carpenters were working to create a new hammerbeam roof, overseen by the most in-demand architect in the realm, Henry Yevele, famed for his royal tomb commissions. To the sound of hammering and the shouts of workmen, the chancellor, the bishop of Exeter, opened proceedings, forced to raise his voice over the din of construction. 'There shall be one king for all,' he announced, as a theme to his opening. The address was a warning that those who went against Richard would be punished for their treachery. The atmosphere in the commons would have been one of intense nervousness. Richard was seated on a temporary throne, elevated on a platform enabling him to look down in majesty and 'deliver his judgements . . . presiding in greater splendour and solemnity than any king of this realm ever had before'.⁵ It was not Richard who made those present nervous, but the thousands of Cheshire archers that surrounded Westminster, each with a quiver full of arrows and Richard's white hart symbol emblazoned on their breast. These were Richard's men, loyal to him alone, and they would enact whatever command he gave them. They even reportedly addressed Richard with jocularity, affectionately calling him

'Dycun'.[6] With this armed guard surrounding Westminster and the three Appellants in Richard's custody, this parliament would become known as the 'Revenge Parliament'.[7]

The primary concern was the trial of the Lords Appellant who Richard had held prisoner since their arrests in July. Within weeks of their incarceration, a body of lords came to Richard at a council held in Nottingham Castle. These lords wished to lodge what can only be described as a counter-appeal against the 'undivided trinity' of the Merciless Parliament. It was called the Appeal of Treason, directed against the 'trinity', Gloucester, Arundel and Warwick, and argued that these three lords were traitors to the Crown for threatening Richard with deposition. These lords, or counter-appellants, were the earls of Rutland, Kent, Huntingdon, Nottingham, Somerset and Salisbury, Thomas Despenser and the king's chamberlain, William Scrope. Their appeal to the king was most likely a demonstration of absolute loyalty designed to save their skins.

Thomas Mowbray and Henry Bolingbroke's names were notably absent from the accusations. Mowbray was back in favour and Henry had carefully stayed away from Richard, avoiding his gaze at all costs and following his father's advice to remain loyal. But as the charges of treason were brought against the three most dogmatic of the Lords Appellant it is reasonable to assume that Mowbray and Henry Bolingbroke were secretly terrified. Having been brought back from custody in Carisbrooke Castle to face trial, a determined-looking Arundel, according to an eyewitness, wearing a red hood, was brought before parliament, where he was expected to answer for his crimes.[8] The earl of Arundel's quick temper and rash decision-making had led him to this situation, but he defended himself before parliament with admirable gusto.

John of Gaunt, as steward of England, presided over the trial, an awkward role considering his brother was accused of treason and his son had only narrowly avoided arrest. Whatever Gaunt's anxieties about his brother and son, he was no friend to the earl of Arundel, whose rude manner had irked him in the past. On this occasion, Arundel reminded Gaunt that he had been pardoned for his actions in 1387, to which Gaunt responded, 'that pardon has been revoked, traitor'. John Bussy – loyal to Richard and speaker of the commons – joined in, supporting Gaunt to point out the commons, as well as the king and the lords, had also revoked the pardon. 'Where are those faithful commons?' spat Arundel. 'I know all about you and your crew, and how you have got here: not to act faithfully, but to shed my blood. The faithful commons of the kingdom are not here . . . while you, I know, have always been false.' Later, Henry Boling-broke leapt to his feet (and his own defence) and announced that the earl had tried to seize the king. Arundel was inflamed: 'You, Henry, earl of Derby, you lie in your teeth! I never said anything to you or to anyone else about my lord the king except what was to his welfare and honour.' Boiling with rage and the desire for revenge, Richard interjected, reminding Arundel of Burley. His dear Burley who he and Anne had tried to save. Burley who was sent to the gallows in spite. This was enough for Richard. 'Pass the sentence,' he demanded of Gaunt. Arundel was to be killed as a traitor, spared the ignominy of hanging, drawing and quartering only due to his noble birth. But he was to be beheaded immediately. Marched to Tower Hill (where Simon Burley lost his life), the earl of Arundel was executed with little ceremony.

The same day, parliament received news that the earl of Glouces-ter could not attend his trial. After being taken in custody to Calais, under the supervision of Thomas Mowbray, 'there, in that same prison, he died.'[9] Later it was discovered that the duke of Gloucester had been murdered in the underbelly of a hostel in Calais. It was convenient for Richard that Gloucester left a confession to William Rickhill, one of the king's justices from the common bench: 'I had done wrong . . . I have by my disloyalty and unkindness offended my lord and, as I have said before, acted against him . . . and so will I answer before God at the day of judgement.'[10] Gloucester's death did not save him from a posthumous conviction of treason, a sentence that John of Gaunt was forced to pass against his youngest brother. The days of chivalry, honour, brotherhood and loyalty that had char-acterised Gaunt's youth were long gone.

With both Arundel and Gloucester dead, the attention was turned to the earl of Warwick, who had been contemplating how to save his head. Where Arundel went to the block fighting, Warwick appeared before Gaunt a snivelling, terrified wreck. He 'foolishly, wretchedly and pusillanimously' broke down and blamed Gloucester and Arundel, saying that he had 'trusted in the wisdom of the duke and the earl'.[11] Weeping and sobbing, Warwick begged for mercy. Richard's main enemies were Arundel and Gloucester; having defeated them both, Richard was satisfied with Warwick's contrition and showed the earl mercy. Warwick's life had been spared, but he was stripped of his lands and his title, and exiled to the Isle of Man for the rest of his life.

As parliament closed, Richard was magisterial. He rewarded those who had been loyal to him in crushing his political enemies. The two remaining Appellants were among those who received new accolades. Henry Bolingbroke was elevated from earl of Derby to duke of Hereford, and Thomas Mowbray became duke of Norfolk.

It was not unlike Richard to offer a gift, a pardon or an act of generosity and then revoke it. After the Peasants' Revolt, he issued charters of manumission – legal documents freeing a person from bondage – to the rebels which he went on to cancel, instead exacting bloody revenge. He pardoned the three Appellants in 1387 then punished them a decade later. In 1398, then, it was no surprise when Richard turned on Mowbray and Bolingbroke. But it was the beginning of his end.

Richard was the architect of the falls of Arundel, Gloucester and Warwick, but when it came to Henry Bolingbroke and Thomas Mowbray he had little to do other than watch them both unravel. The spectre of the murdered earl of Gloucester came back to haunt Thomas Mowbray as rumours circulated that he had murdered the prince and would be punished for the crime. Sick with anxiety and fear, Mowbray looked for an ally and, naturally, turned to his fellow surviving Appellant, Henry Bolingbroke. Thomas Mowbray intercepted Henry on a road near Brentford in December 1397. Charging up to Henry on horseback, Thomas Mowbray announced: 'We are about to be undone . . . because of what was done at Radcot Bridge.' Mowbray claimed that he had heard a rumour that the king plotted to seize them and also murder Gaunt and one of his other sons, John Beaufort. The plot was part of Richard's desire to take revenge on 'the judgement concerning earl Thomas of Lancaster', namely his subsequent reverence and canonisation. The suggestion was that Richard planned on stealing the Lancastrian inheritance.

Henry was in conflict over what to do, but, as expected, went straight to his father. They were surrounded by an atmosphere that was dense with suspicion and intrigue; it was difficult to know who, if anybody, could be trusted. Gaunt drew on his own experience of Richard's deviance and counselled that the king should be informed. In the past, the act of bringing dark plans into the light had left Richard exposed and penitent. But this time, when Henry told Richard what had happened between himself and Mowbray, he appeared to know nothing about the plot. Either there was no truth in the rumours, or he was playing a remarkably astute hand by allowing Mowbray and Bolingbroke to turn against each other over hearsay.

The two men were called before the king to deliver their versions of the story in January 1398. Henry offered the king an explanation 'to the best of his memory' about what had happened. Mowbray was incensed, for Henry had thrown him to the wolves at a time when he was already anxious for his future.[12] Henry now believed that Mowbray had murdered his uncle at Calais and suspected Mowbray was also trying to draw him into his own political machinations. Richard watched as the two men at his feet hurled accusations at one another. He decided the only way to resolve the situation was through a trial by combat.

On Monday 16 September, the two remaining Lords Appellant strode into an arena at Coventry ready to joust and, if necessary, fight man-to-man with whatever weapon was available to them. By the end of the day either Henry Bolingbroke, the duke of Hereford, or Thomas Mowbray, the duke of Norfolk, would be dead. It was the most thrilling and unnerving spectacle of the age, presided over by the king and the great and good of the realm. John of Gaunt, weakened with age and anxiety, could not bear to watch, and stayed away.

Spectators had come from as far away as Scotland, Germany and France, packing the purpose-built stands to witness this showdown between two major English noblemen, one the son and heir of the wealthiest man in the realm. Henry of Bolingbroke was seen as the favourite. He was famous for his skill, winning tournament after tournament, and only a few years earlier he had spent time fighting with the Teutonic Knights in Lithuania. Decked out in brand-new armour sent specifically as a gift from the wealthy duke of Milan, Gian Galeazzo Visconti, he cut a fine figure.

But then Thomas Mowbray was no stranger to fierce combat either. He had served Richard in Ireland, and now marched into the arena dressed in neat-fitting German armour, ready to do battle. At around 9 a.m., Bolingbroke emerged and announced to the hushed crowd: 'I am Henry of Lancaster, duke of Hereford . . . and I have come here to do my duty in combat with Thomas Mowbray, duke of Norfolk, a false and disloyal traitor to God, the king, his kingdom and myself.'[13] He then raised his shield, which bore the cross of Saint George, before closing his visor and riding to his seat, which was adorned with red flowers, symbolising Lancaster. The two men's lances were then measured and their seconds were ordered to remove the horses' restraints. Bolingbroke lowered his lance and spurred his horse forward.

Richard gazed down at his cousin and old friend as their lances were pointed at one another. As Henry began to charge forward the king suddenly stood and cried out. Such an intervention was unprecedented and the crowd gasped in shock; Richard then demanded that both men return to their places, before he retired for two hours to decide what to do. Once he had made his decision, the king asked the speaker of the commons, John Bussy, to deliver his verdict. Both men had been honourable, so much so that surely one could not be killed and therefore be dishonoured in death. Instead, he chose exile. The crowd groaned with disappointment. Henry Bolingbroke, it was declared, would be banished from the realm for ten years. Thomas Mowbray, for ever. In Richard's mind, this decision was final.

Perhaps Richard was moved by the honour displayed by the two men before him. But just as likely was that Richard, the most insecure king ever to sit on England's throne, liked to feel powerful – to hold supreme authority over life and death. Another, more urgent impulse might have been his fear that if Henry Bolingbroke were to die a hero's death he would become another Lancastrian immortalised in his plight; for ever remembered as a greater man than Richard. A victory for Bolingbroke, and the glory that came with it, would present Richard with a similar problem. Banishment was the only way to marginalise and belittle his enemy and rival.

Mowbray had no choice but to accept his fate and exile. Richard suggested he go on crusade. Henry was permitted five weeks to prepare himself. He spent most of that time in the company of his father, who he feared he would never see again. Gaunt counselled that Henry should go to Iberia, for his sister Philippa had married Juan of Portugal, and his half-sister Catherine was married to the king of Castile. Paris, where Gaunt had allies and connections, was another option, which Henry, in the end, took up.

In February 1399, within months of Henry's departure for Paris, John of Gaunt died from an unknown illness. He was exhausted and dejected, having watched his family, once unbreakable in unity, shatter in acrimony. Chroniclers later suggested that Gaunt died riddled with venereal disease following his excessive fornication outside of wedlock. Thomas Gascoigne, the author of the *Liber de Veritatibus*, went as far to claim that Gaunt died of 'a petrification of the genitals due to carnal copulation'. Wretched with the disease, Gaunt is alleged to have exposed his rotting penis to Richard, counselling his nephew never to commit adultery – a darkly amusing, if likely apocryphal, story.

John of Gaunt was laid out for the unusual length of forty days – in penitence for his earthly sins, most likely adultery – before being interred beside his first wife, Blanche of Lancaster, in Saint Paul's Cathedral. A week before Gaunt's funeral, Richard took possession of the Duchy of Lancaster and revoked Henry's ten-year exile. Bolingbroke was now to be banished for life. The news reached Henry in Paris in a letter from one of Richard's closest men, William Bagot, who was troubled by Richard's growing tyranny. Bagot risked his life in contacting Henry but his message was clear: he told the duke to 'help himself with manhood'. In other words, take back what was rightfully his.[14]

Overthrowing a king was not easy. It involved gaining the support of the majority of the realm, but also the ability to overcome conscience. Kingship was God-given, the divine right that Richard lived by. It was not a right that could be removed if there was no direct heir to take on the responsibility. Yet Richard had abused his power and in doing so had lost the trust of the people he had promised to protect in his coronation oath. As Henry, duke of Lancaster, crossed the North Sea and landed at Ravenspurn in Yorkshire, he returned to England with a litany of pledges of support, notably from those loyal to the House of Lancaster.

Over the course of the fourteenth century, the Lancastrian affinity had grown and matured. Thomas of Lancaster had gained land, fortune and men. His dogmatic pursuit of righteousness had earned him a cult following. His brother Henry, earl of Lancaster, had fostered Leicester as a power base, quietly and carefully building local loyalty and popularity, sentiments that spread across Lancastrian estates. Thomas's son, Henry, the first duke of Lancaster, was equally popular. He helped to overthrow the Mortimer regime and bring further wealth and glory to the Lancastrian name. When John of Gaunt, a Plantagenet, married Blanche of Lancaster, two great houses were united; Henry Bolingbroke was a direct consequence of that unity.

By July 1399, Henry had an army of several thousand, its ranks filled with Lancastrian retainers, landowners and workers, loyal men seeking change from an unpredictable and dangerous king. The lords Roos, Willoughby and Greystoke all rode out to meet Henry and offered him their men and steel. The cities of York and Hull gave money and Lancastrian castles across the north gave safety.

As Henry moved south, his forces continued to multiply until, in late July, he reached Berkeley Castle – the prison of the last deposed king, Edward II. There, he came face to face with his uncle, Edmund, duke of York – caught between his nephews and forced to choose who to support. Edmund, ever the diplomat, considerate and careful, chose not to try to stop Henry. He did not actively join his cause, but neither did he counsel him against it.

By late summer, Henry had most of the country behind him and even took Chester, the city that had been most loyal to Richard.[15] As the whole of England appeared to flock behind Henry, as though he were a messiah, Richard was in Ireland, where he had travelled to deal with civil unrest. On his return he found himself on the run. Other than his collection of Cheshire archers, who were effectively Richard's personal thugs, Richard had few men at his command. One of the members of his diminished retinue was Jean Creton, a French servant of Charles VI who had accompanied Richard to Ireland. Creton later composed *La Prinse et Mort du Roy Richart d'Angleterre* (The Capture and Death of King Richard of England), which offers an account of what happened.[16] In a stark repetition of the events of 1326, Richard fled to Wales, as had Edward II before him. In August 1399, Richard took refuge behind the fortified walls of Conway Castle, along with a cluster of loyalists, where eventually he was captured. There are different versions of the same story. Some suggest that Richard offered to abdicate while at Conway; Creton argues that he was tricked into submitting himself with the promise he would retain his kingship.[17] Nonetheless, Richard found himself in the Tower of London by September 1399, a figure so dejected his own dog did not even recognise him.

Adam of Usk talked of how Richard became maudlin in his imprisonment. 'My God this is a strange and fickle land . . . which has destroyed and ruined so many kings, so many rulers, so many great men . . .'[18] As if in a dream, Richard began to ruminate on all those who came before him. The Plantagenet kings whose statues lined Westminster Hall, who he had gazed upon from his own throne, perhaps wondering if he would join them in the roster of great kings.

As Richard pondered on his fate and legacy, others looked to familiar legends to make sense of the situation. For the author of the *Traison et Mort*, a French chronicle, Merlin's Prophecy that 'a king will be betrayed' by someone close to him, 'after he has reigned for twenty-two years' had come true.[19] Henry had in some ways betrayed

Richard but then he had little choice. Either he lost everything, or fought for justice and faced the consequences. It is unlikely that Henry had been plotting to take the throne for himself. Henry possessed the same sense of royal duty as his father. It is more plausible that he knew he had to act if he wanted to recover his inheritance, probably hoping that Richard would be repentant and they could come to an administrative agreement, much like the deal Thomas of Lancaster and Edward II had reached over his Ordinances. But there could be no peaceful resolution between the cousins and so Henry of Lancaster was forced to contemplate a step his ancestor would undoubtedly have taken in 1322 had he defeated Edward II at Boroughbridge. He had to depose the king.

Richard and Henry faced one another in Richard's room in the Tower of London. Richard, assailed by the reality of the situation, was characteristically petulant. He clutched his crown, his last talisman of kingship, close to himself, clearly unwilling to face delivering it into Henry's hands. Finally, reluctantly, instead he chose to 'place it upon the ground'.[20]

In an official document known as the 'Record and Process', the formalities of Richard's deposition are clearly detailed. Almost by definition a pro-Lancaster text, it claims that Richard was compliant in his abdication, which by all other accounts is unlikely. The Record also highlights the reasons for Richard's deposition in a litany of thirty-three formal complaints.[21] He was accused of 'evil government', and of having imposed 'needlessly grievous and intolerable burdens upon the people' and 'coerced justices of the realm with threats of life and limb'. The document stated that Richard was responsible for the murder of the duke of Gloucester, who was 'secretly suffocated, strangled and barbarously and cruelly murdered'. Another part of the indictment focused on Richard's tyrannical use of his private army. His Cheshire archers were accused of 'beating and wounding others, plundering the goods of the people, refusing to pay for their provisions, and raping and ravishing both married and unmarried women'. When it was put to the floor in parliament whether King Richard II should be deposed the unanimous cry was 'Yes, yes, yes!'[22]

Henry's formal claim to the Crown was recorded in a charter at the Tower of London in early October. It marked the dawn of a new era. For the first time in history this declaration was made and recorded in the vernacular, rather than clerical Latin or courtly French. This evidenced the shift in English identity, as a nation in itself, with its own language and customs. This claim was for all to hear and understand, in English, offering a remarkable, almost phonetic, understanding of voice at the end of the fourteenth century:

> In the name of the fadir, son, and holy gost, I, Henry of Lancaster, chalenge this rewme of Yngland . . . I that am disendit be right Lyne of the blode coming fro the gude kynge Henry therde, and thorgh that right that god of his grace hath sent me.[23]

Henry IV's coronation on Monday 13 October 1399 was a gratifying nod to his ancestry – the feast day of the Translation of Edward the Confessor, the saint most appropriately associated with English kingship. But though Henry IV had Plantagenet blood running thick through his veins, he was the first Lancastrian king. His reign marked the end of a long, unbroken line of Plantagenets.

Epilogue

Mortal Remains

Merlin's Prophecy, *Six Kings to Follow John*, was remarkably accurate in its anthropomorphic portrayal of the kings who reigned over the course of the fourteenth century. The fierce dragon, Edward I, was followed by his son Edward II – the pliable goat. Then England became stronger under the determined boar, Edward III, subsequently weakened by the tyrannical king, Richard – the ass. The final king was Henry IV, the moldwarp – a mole with rough skin, possibly alluding to a skin condition that Henry later suffered (perhaps psoriasis).

These creatures represent the unique personalities that governed the kingdoms of England, Wales, Ireland and even Scotland. They were human beings with their own interests and fallibilities, carried by the ebb and flow of royal power and foreign and domestic intervention. This ebb and flow of power also applies to the century they governed in – the fourteenth century – which is multifaceted and riddled with opposing themes. Where there was glittering spectacle and developing national culture, there was also famine, plague, war and immense sorrow.

The first part of the fourteenth century was rife with both internal conflict and the greatest threat from Scotland in English history. Edward II inherited a kingdom from his father, the Hammer of Scots, but he did not inherit his fierce conviction. The son of a bully, Edward II lacked the political confidence of leadership and as a result was drawn to those who did possess it. But the problem Edward II faced was what to do with his power. As king, he was expected to be the one to wield it, and yet he continued to share it with his closest companions, whatever the cost, destabilising the very concept of divine kingship and alienating those who revered it: the nobility. By giving his power to Piers Gaveston and Hugh

Despenser the Younger, through remarkably myopic acts such as displaying Gaveston's arms alongside the king's at his coronation, and allowing Despenser to cherry-pick whatever land he liked, Edward II dismantled God-given hierarchy: the idea of rule by one king, not, as the *Vita* chronicler described, 'two kings'. With the nobility of England confused and inflamed by Edward II's style of kingship, Robert Bruce, a king who was an exemplar of leadership, became the first Scottish king in history to weaken England's power. Defeat at Bannockburn was followed by constant cross-border raiding and demand for tribute payments, and the north of England was effectively detached from the rest of the realm.

Edward II's infatuation with his favourite courtiers meant he overlooked another powerful figure who lived under his nose: his own wife. Isabella was dutiful but she also had a sure sense of her own worth and when Edward would not support his own queen against Hugh Despenser the Younger's avarice, she was quick to act. Isabella was briefly a heroine but soon she, blindsided by her own ambition, developed a taste for power. She and Roger Mortimer had deposed Edward II and taken the throne for her son. And yet instead of ceding power to Edward III when he came of age, they hugged it more closely, unable to let it go. Their regime, once glittering with the prospect of peace and unity, became, with one spin of Fortune's Wheel, a shocking demonstration of paranoia and cruelty that ended on the scaffold.

Edward III's symbol of an eruption of light emerging from behind a cloud was appropriate following an age of such darkness. The moment he charged through the door at Nottingham Castle and arrested Mortimer was also the moment he burst confidently into his kingship, a confidence that defined the first part of his reign. Edward successfully recovered English authority in Scotland, winning a decisive victory at Halidon Hill, but what established his reputation was his claim over France – a claim that would obsess English kings for the following two centuries. The greatest and most eulogised of Edward's battles on French soil was Crécy, which cemented the status of his son Edward, prince of Wales, as the formidable 'Black Prince', the epitome of the chivalric hero. The reign of Edward III brought about a reinvigoration of chivalric culture. Edward III made the legendary King Arthur part of the fabric of court life, and, more importantly, wove the myths into England's national identity. The same is true for Saint George, a Christian martial icon who Edward adopted as the spiritual idol of chivalry and unity in the Order of the Garter, but whose status as patron saint of England has endured.

Edward III was good at making war appealing, but the reality of his invasions of France was less glamorous. Destructive raids through French communities – Edward never actually reached Paris, the crucible of French kingship – were brutal, punitive campaigns pitted against common folk rather than the kings. As the scholar Petrarch observed when travelling through France, following one of Edward's sallies, the once verdant landscape was now blackened with the stain of fire and human suffering. Edward III won a handful of victories and eventually signed the Treaty of Brétigny, which mostly just meant that Edward no longer had to bend his knee to the king of France. It is difficult, now, not to be struck by the futility and waste of it all. Edward achieved his desire to be remembered as a hero, but there were other, perhaps more fitting, candidates for immortality among those who suffered as a result of his actions. *The Burghers of Calais*, barefoot and weighed down by hunger, were cast in bronze by Auguste Rodin more than five hundred years later as a eulogy to their heroism in the face of adversity.

The Black Death was the greatest killer of the fourteenth century and beyond. Yet from loss there was also gain. Labour shortages meant that common people suddenly found themselves with new freedom and power. They could work in new places and new trades. Most significantly, they could demand more money. Although the very poor remained poor and the very rich remained rich, a large and bountiful middle class of working people emerged who, after burying their loved ones, were no longer shackled by a fatalistic existence.

The so-called 'Peasants' Revolt' was the clearest example of the way society had shifted after the plague, but also of the tensions that followed. People marched for a better life, but the old institutions used their power and authority to try to inhibit these ambitions. At the helm of all of this was the young king Richard II, whose extraordinary bravery during the rising showed a king who was either blindly naive or convinced that he was a demi-god divinely chosen to rule, or, most likely, both.

As Richard moved into adulthood, his mental state deteriorated; it is possible that he had borderline personality disorder. Deeply sensitive and vulnerable, Richard was also cold and calculating and obsessed with his own identity. The art that came out of his reign represents a king with two sides to his kingship: the fresh-faced innocent boy kissed by angels; and the powerful enthroned man, a king with mighty purpose but with the cold stare of a tyrant. Richard saw himself in his great-grandfather, Edward II, and both were afflicted by an inability to get on with their peers. But where Edward was affable and easily manipulated, Richard was a different beast altogether. The last Plantagenet king was a despot; when he could not command respect, he ruled with fear.

When Henry Bolingbroke usurped his cousin, he did so with a respectable claim to the throne, but he would spend the rest of his reign fighting to keep the crown on his head. Richard was eventually killed – probably around 14 February 1400. It was rumoured that he had been starved to death after being imprisoned in Pontefract Castle.

Henry had quickly learned that his cousin could not be allowed to live: to rule effectively meant to rule ruthlessly. Soon after his death, Richard was interred at dawn, buried with no real ornament or ceremony at King's Langley in Hertfordshire, Piers Gaveston's resting place. Henry IV did not want the spectacle Richard's status would have traditionally demanded to attract attention to his cousin's corpse. Richard's body remained inconspicuously at King's Langley until Henry V finally exhumed it and transferred it to the tomb that Richard had designed for himself. He had been a despicable king but his tomb gives another impression, one of proud Plantagenet lineage and royal power. *Planta genista* was embossed into the metalwork – the symbol of the Plantagenets, the symbol of generations of kings – a line of kings descending from 'Arthur'.

In 1871 the tomb of Richard II was wedged open and his bones were studied, just as his great-great-grandfather Edward I's decayed remains had been inspected almost a century earlier. The antiquarian historians who carried out their investigations were fascinated by the idea that these bones had once carried flesh; that these bodies had once walked this Sceptred Isle, carrying with them their own thoughts and feelings about the world they inhabited. Cracking open the tombs and gasping at the mortal remains of kings tells of a fascination with human beings, those makers of tales and myth.

It is these narratives, details and legends about the fourteenth century that persist, told by generations of historians through many different lenses; the facts often interwoven with mythology, in turn absorbed into history. Shocking and salacious, glittering and glorious; in the end, they are all human stories.

Acknowledgements

When I sat down to discuss the final manuscript for this book with my new editor, James Pulford, he asked me how I had conjured the sheer quantity of information on the fourteenth century that he was then faced with deconstructing and turning into an actual book. Thank you so much to James, for meticulously battling through my jam-packed draft manuscript to help me shape it into what it is now. I am so grateful for your calm and clear-eyed approach to the tumultuous fourteenth century.

Though I am indebted to James for the chopping and commenting, I also could not be more grateful to the team at Hutchinson Heinemann, Anna Argenio and Helen Conford, for both commissioning the book and welcoming me into the family. Thank you, Anna, for the hysterical laughter and for being a supportive and patient editor, and for becoming a great friend.

It generally takes a long time to produce a book, and as my dear PhD supervisor, Miri Rubin, once told me, 'life happens around it'. Life really did happen during the three years it took me to write this one. I became a mother for a second time and ran the gauntlet of raising two young children while also trying to 'be in the book'. I had a notepad wedged under my pram in case of an unexpected long nap, and I pondered the fourteenth century during *many* sleepless nights. Life has never been so busy or so full thanks to my two wonderful children. I can still feel the hopeful tug on my sleeve as I inch away into my office to write. Babies, though you have never really had *all* of me, I hope you will also be proud of what I have achieved and let it serve as inspiration to follow your own hopes and dreams – I will always wave your flag.

Where life has happened there has also been death. While I was writing this book, my family suffered the tragic and sudden loss of my darling brother, Tom. In my sadness I turned to words and wrote down my plague chapters. It felt timely. In those dark days I was closer to my sources than I ever have been, sitting with the grief of those living in 1348 as it touched my own 'sting of grief', as described by Edward III when reflecting on the loss of his daughter Joan. Time really can be transcended by such powerful human feelings, and it was those characters and this book that gave me great comfort during such sadness.

I cannot forget the support of my contemporaries over the last few years, particularly this year. Thank you to My Women – Hannah Dawson, Rebecca Rideal, Sophie Ambler, Joanne Paul, Mary Wellesley, Amy Jeffs, Hallie Rubenhold, Kelcey Wilson-Lee, Kate Williams and the rest of the Clio Club – and all of my beloved friends for being there to talk, and those who shared thoughts on sections of the book or helped navigate some tricky material. Thank you so much to Dan J, for reading chapters, making me lol and for your immense kindness. Thank you to Denise Roland for being a great reader and friend: you have been a saving grace in so many ways. Thank you, Suzie, for being a tiger mom, big sister and dear friend – I will for ever admire you. Thank you to Helen Castor for being my guiding light during a tricky time with the manuscript and feeding me the perfect line: you are an inspiration and wonderful. Thank you to Seb Falk for introducing me to the magic of the medieval cosmos and to Callum Watson for reading and commenting on my Bannockburn chapter, and to Andrew Spencer for tea in Corpus Christi College, Cambridge, and sharing observations on Edward I. Thank you to Miri for your endless patience and understanding; I am so grateful to you for pushing me to think harder and for your cakes when I didn't have time to eat. Thank you to Lyndsay, for everything – you are a gift. Thank you to the giant support network of both medieval and wider historians and writers, who I now call friends. There are too many of you to name, but by the smile on my face when I see you, know you are in my thoughts as I write this.

A huge and special thanks to Paul Dryburgh for everything you have done for me in the process of writing this book – from reading tricky texts (including the whole draft), to generally being there to discuss the fourteenth century. You are my walking, talking encyclopedia and I feel blessed to have had such thoughtful and interesting discussions with you. Thank you to Romily McNulty for all of your support and valuable thoughts on translations; I am grateful for your wonderful mind.

A huge thank you to Helen Purvis and the team at Knight Ayton for keeping me organised as I wrote the book. Thank you particularly to Rachel Mills and everyone at RML for all your amazing work in getting me to where I am now (!): what a wonderful near-ten years it has been in your care.

Lastly, thank you to the friends and family I have largely ignored this year, for loving me anyway. Above all, thank you to Henry. There are many men in this story who thought they were heroes, but I have the good fortune to be married to a real one. As I was writing this book, my husband saved the life of a stranger who was being attacked and as a result he was badly injured himself. Henry, with immense courage you have still found the resolve to be my strength and stay, a lighthouse in rough seas, co-parent *and* my first reader. It is only appropriate that every word in this book is lovingly dedicated to you.

Illustration Credits

1. Edward I. Public domain.
2. Edward II. Public domain.
3. The charter granting Piers Gaveston the earldom of Cornwall. Photograph © Helen Carr.
4. Edward III and the Black Prince. incamerastock/Alamy Stock Photo.
5. Richard II. Heritage Image Partnership Ltd/Alamy Stock Photo.
6. Detail from the Angers Apocalypse Tapestry. Bridgeman Images.
7. The Angers Apocalypse Tapestry. Public domain.
8. Isabella of France. Public domain.
9. Tomb effigy of Philippa of Hainault. Angelo Hornak/Alamy Stock Photo.
10. The Stone of Scone. Farm Images/Contributor/Getty.
11. A fourteenth-century astrolabe. © Giancarlo Costa/Bridgeman Images.
12. Tomb of Edward, the Black Prince. Michael Freeman/Alamy Stock Photo.
13. The Wilton Diptych. Public domain.
14. Coronation Chair. parkerphotography/Alamy Stock Photo.
15. Wheel of Fortune. From the British Library archive/Bridgeman Images.
16. Victims of bubonic plague. Public domain.
17. The execution of Hugh Despenser. Bridgeman Images.
18. The Battle of Crécy. Public domain.

Notes

CCR: *Calendar of Close Rolls*
CDS: *Calendar of Documents Relating to Scotland*

CPR: *Calendar of Patent Rolls*

PROME: *Parliament Rolls of Medieval England*
TNA: The National Archives

Introduction

1 Barbara Tuchman, *A Distant Mirror: The Calamitous 14th Century* (New York: Alfred A. Knopf, 1978); the book's title was intended to suggest that the suffering of the twentieth century, with global war and the Spanish flu epidemic, reflected the suffering of the second part of the fourteenth century.
2 'Reading against the grain' is to closely read against the purpose of a text, to reveal clues or details that offer an alternative perspective. This is a technique and term coined by the late David Bartholomae and Anthony Petrosky and popularised in regard to women's histories by the late historian Natalie Zemon Davis.

Prologue: Avalon

1 J. Ayloffe, 'XLIII. An Account of the Body of King Edward the First, as It Appeared on Opening His Tomb in the Year 1774. By Sir Joseph Ayloffe, Bart. V.P.S.A. and F.R.S.', *Archaeologia*, vol. 3 (1775), p. 381.

Part One

1 Raphael Holinshed, *Chronicles of England, Scotland and Ireland*, vol. 6 (1587), ed. Henry Ellis (London: J. Johnson et al., 1807), p. 318.

1. The King Is Dead

1 Matthew Paris, *Flores Historiarum*, vol. 3 (London: Eyre & Spottiswoode, 1890), p. 324; *Calendar of Documents Relating to Scotland Preserved in Her Majesty's Public Record Office, London*, vols. 2–4, ed. Joseph Bain (Edinburgh: H. M. General Register House, 1881–8), p. 495.

2 *The Chronicle of Lanercost, 1272–1346*, ed. and trans. Henry Maxwell (Glasgow: J. Maclehose, 1913), p. 180.

3 Thomas Wright (ed.), *The Chronicle of Pierre de Langtoft: In French Verse from the Earliest Period to the Death of King Edward I*, 2 vols. (London: Longmans, Green, Reader and Dyer, 1866), vol. 2, p. 463.

4 *Calendar of Documents relating to Scotland*, vol. 3, no. 1851, p. 495.

5 Paris, *Flores Historiarum*, vol. 3, p. 495.

6 *Calendar of Documents relating to Scotland*, vol. 3, nos. 1790, 1791, pp. 480–81.

7 Michael Prestwich, *Edward I* (London: Methuen, 1988), p. 556.

8 ibid.

9 Constance Bullock-Davies, 'Lanval and Avalon', *The Bulletin of the Board of Celtic Studies*, vol. 23, no. 2 (1969), 128–42; *A Companion to Marie de France*, ed. Logan E. Whalen (Leiden: Brill, 2011), p. 33; for Avalon and Aballava as the Roman fortress at Burgh by Sands, see Nicholas J. Higham, *King Arthur the Making of a Legend* (New Haven: Yale University Press, 2018), pp. 108–9.

10 Jean Froissart, *Chronicles of England and France*, trans. Thomas Johnes, vol. I (London: W. Smith, 1844), p. 38.

11 'EDWARDVS PRIMVS SCOTORVM MALLEVS HIC EST. PACTVM SERVA', J. Ayloffe, 'XLIII. An Account of the Body of King Edward the First, as It Appeared on Opening His Tomb in the Year 1774. By Sir Joseph Ayloffe, Bart. V.P.S.A. and F.R.S.', *Archaeologia*, vol. 3 (1775), p. 379.

12 *The Anonimalle Chronicle 1307 to 1334: From Brotherton Collection MS 29*, ed. Wendy R. Childs and John Taylor (Cambridge: Cambridge University Press, 2013).

13 Seymour Phillips, *Edward II* (New Haven: Yale University Press, 2010), pp. 72–3; Kathryn Warner, 'Edward II Digs Ditches' (12 March 2016), *Edward II Blog*, edwardthesecond.blogspot.com [accessed July 2024].

14 *Flores Historiarum*, p. 173, quoted in Phillips, *Edward II*, p. 8.

15 *The Chronicle of Geoffrey le Baker*, trans. David Preest, intro. and notes Richard Barber (Woodbridge: Boydell & Brewer, 2018), p. 3.

16 Walter de Guisborough, quoted in Marc Morris, *A Great and Terrible King: Edward I and the Forging of Britain* (London: Windmill Books, 2008), p. 359.

17 Friedrich W. D. Brie (ed.), *The Brut, or, The Chronicles of England* (London: Kegan Paul, Paul, Trench, Trübner, for the Early English Text Society, 1906), pp. 196 and 203.

18 G. L. Haskins, 'A Chronicle of the Civil Wars of Edward II', *Speculum*, vol. 14 (1939), quoted in Phillips, *Edward II*, p. 97.

19 Justin Bengry, 'Can and Should We Queer the Past?', in Helen Carr and Suzannah Lipscomb (eds.), *What Is History, Now?* (London: W&N, 2021), p. 49.

20 Wendy R. Childs (ed. and trans.), *Vita Edwardi Secundi* (Oxford: Clarendon Press, 2005), pp. xl, 5; Haskins, 'A Chronicle of the Civil Wars of Edward II'.

21 I am grateful to Dr Savannah Pine for sharing her work on ritual brotherhood and biblical representation; see S. Pine, '"Comme Nostre Frere"': Knightly Ritual Brotherhood Reconsidered', *Cultural and Social History*, vol. 19, no. 3 (2022), 227–45.

22 BL Add. 54180, f.107r.23 Bnf fran, 119, f.344v.

24 T. Rymer (ed.), *Rymer's Foedera* (London, 1739–45), *British History Online*, british-history.ac.uk/rymer-foedera, vol. 1, p. 145.

25 TNA, E 41/460.

26 'duos reges in uno regno, istum verbaliter, istum realiter conregnare Annales Paulini', in William Stubbs (ed.), *Chronicles of the Reigns of Edward I and Edward II*, vol. 1, *Annales Londonienses and Annales Paulini* (London: Longman, 1882), p. 259.

27 *Vita Edwardi Secundi*, p. 7.

28 *CPR*, Edward II, vol. 1, 1307–13, *British History Online*.

29 *Vita Edwardi Secundi*, p. 9.

2. Two Kings

1 H. M. Colvin (ed.), *The History of the King's Works, Middle Ages*, vol. 1 (London: Her Majesty's Stationery Office, 1963), p. 505.

2   TNA, E 101/468/21, f.1v.

3   Colvin, *The History of the King's Works*, p. 505.

4   TNA, SC 8/318/E322.

5   Colvin, *The History of the King's Works*, p. 506.

6   Warwick Rodwell, *The Coronation Chair and Stone of Scone: History, Archaeology and Conservation* (Oxford: Oxbow, 2013), p. 47.

7   Paul Binski, *Westminster Abbey and the Plantagenets: Kingship and the Representation of Power, 1200–1400* (New Haven: Yale University Press, 1995), p. 138; Rodwell, *The Coronation Chair and Stone of Scone*, p. 50.

8   William Stubbs (ed.), *Chronicles of the Reigns of Edward I and Edward II*, vol. 1, *Annales Londonienses and Annales Paulini* (London: Longman, 1882), p. 262.

9   *The Chronicle of Geoffrey le Baker*, trans. David Preest, intro. and notes Richard Barber (Woodbridge: Boydell & Brewer, 2018), p. 4.

10 On 8 February 1308, Philip IV, king of France, wrote to Edward II to inform him that he was sending a royal party to the coronation with instructions to the new king 'by mouth', TNA, SC 1/34/7; Stubbs, *Annales Paulini*, p. 262.

11 T. Rymer (ed.), *Rymer's Foedera* (London, 1739–45), *British History Online*, british-history.ac.uk/rymer-foedera, vol. 1, p. 150; Seymour Phillips, *Edward II* (New Haven: Yale University Press, 2010), p. 141.

12 Wendy R. Childs (ed. and trans.), *Vita Edwardi Secundi* (Oxford: Clarendon Press, 2005), p. 9.

13 ibid., p. 11.

14 *CCR,* Edward II, vol. 1, 1307–13, *British History Online.*

15 *PROME*, Edward II, April 1308.

16 Stubbs, 'Annales Paulini', p. 268.

17 *PROME*, Edward II, April 1308.

18 ibid.; 'Adoptivi fratis', Stubbs, *Annales Paulini*, p. 273.

19 From D. Lincoln, and C. Muniments, D. ii/56/1, no. 42., in J. R. Maddicott, *Thomas of Lancaster, 1307–1322: A Study in the Reign of Edward II* (Oxford: Oxford University Press, 1970), p. 83.

20 *Vita Edwardi Secundi*, p. 13.

21 Maddicott, *Thomas of Lancaster*, p. 92.

22 *Vita Edwardi Secundi*, p. 17.

23 After Gaveston's death, Edward II made payments to his household staff. In 1313 he paid four shillings and three pence to Richard White-flesh. TNA, E 101/375/8, f.27r, Wardrobe Accounts Edward II.

3. Blacklow Hill

1 Wendy R. Childs (ed. and trans.), *Vita Edwardi Secundi* (Oxford: Clarendon Press, 2005), p. 19.
2 *PROME*, Edward II, August 1311.
3 British Library, Add Ch 11241.
4 *PROME*, Edward II, August 1311.
5 *Vita Edwardi Secundi*, p. 33.
6 ibid., p. 41.
7 ibid., p. 45.
8 ibid.
9 ibid.
10 ibid.
11 ibid.
12 ibid., p. 47.
13 ibid., p. 49.
14 TNA, E 101/375/8, fo.26r.
15 *Vita Edwardi Secundi*, p. 53.
16 TNA, DL 25/ 1900.
17 Elizabeth A. R. Brown and Nancy Freeman Regaldo, 'Universitas et communitas: The Parade of the Parisians at the Pentecost Feast of 1313', in Kathleen Ashley (ed.), *Moving Objects: Processional Performance in the Middle Ages and the Renaissance* (Amsterdam: Rodopi, 2001).
18 TNA, E 101/375/9, fo.24r, fo.24v.
19 *CPR*, Edward II, vol, 2, 1313–17, *British History Online*.
20 *Vita Edwardi Secundi*, p. 75.

4. The Road to Bannockburn

1 British Library, Cotton Titus X XIX fo.87r.
2 *The Chronicle of Lanercost, 1272–1346*, ed. and trans. Henry Maxwell (Glasgow: J. Maclehose, 1913), p. 200.

3 TNA, SC 8/306/15251.

4 TNA, SC 8/263/13134.

5 TNA, SC 8/283/14119.

6 It is unclear exactly how large Edward's army was, as chroniclers like to create a large disparity. It was probably around fifteen to twenty thousand men.

7 Wendy R. Childs (ed. and trans.), *Vita Edwardi Secundi* (Oxford: Clarendon Press, 2005), p. 89.

8 Thomas Gray, *Scalacronica* (Cambridge, Corpus Christi College, MS 133), Algorism; for more on *Scalacronica*, see Andy King, *Sir Thomas Gray: Scalacronica (1272–1363)*, Publications of the Surtees Society, 209 (Woodbridge: Boydell Press, 2005).

9 *Vita Edwardi Secundi*, p. 91

10 ibid.

11 *The Chronicle of Lanercost*, p. 210.

12 TNA, SC 8/82/4051.

5. The Third Apocalypse

1 John de Trokelowe and Henry Blaneforde, *Chronica et Annales*, ed. Henry T. Riley (London: Longmans, Green, Reader and Dyer, 1866), p. 95.

2 Ian Kershaw, 'The Great Famine and Agrarian Crisis in England 1315–22', *Past & Present*, no. 59 (1973), p. 22.

3 *The Chronicle of Lanercost, 1272–1346*, ed. and trans. Henry Maxwell (Glasgow: J. Maclehose, 1913), p. 210.

4 ibid.

5 James Halliwell-Phillips (ed.), *The Chronicle of William de Rishanger of the Barons' War: The Miracles of Simon de Montfort* (London: Printed for the Camden Society by J. B. Nichols and Son, 1840); Matthew Paris, *Flores Historiarum* (London: Eyre & Spottiswoode, 1890), vol. 3, pp. 123, 321.

6 Jean Scammel, 'Robert I and the North of England', *English Historical Review*, vol. 73, no. 288 (1958), p. 402.

7 29 September.

8 Wendy R. Childs (ed. and trans.), *Vita Edwardi Secundi* (Oxford: Clarendon Press, 2005), p. 103

9 *PROME*, Edward II, January 1315.

10 TNA, SC 8/170/8494.

11 TNA, SC 8/142/7085; SC8/171/8520.

12 TNA, SC 8/147/7319.

13 *Vita Edwardi Secundi*, p. 107.

14 ibid., p. 97.

6. *A Song of Steel*

1 John de Trokelowe and Henry Blaneforde, *Chronica et Annales*, ed. Henry T. Riley (London: Longmans, Green, Reader and Dyer, 1866), p. 98.

2 Colm McNamee, *The Wars of the Bruces: Scotland, England and Ireland 1306–1328* (East Linton: Tuckwell Press, 1997), p. 166.

3 Robert Bruce, quoted in McNamee, *The Wars of the Bruces*, p. 166.

4 *The Chronicle of Lanercost, 1272–1346*, ed. and trans. Henry Maxwell (Glasgow: J. Maclehose, 1913), pp. 225–6.

5 Wendy R. Childs (ed. and trans.), *Vita Edwardi Secundi* (Oxford: Clarendon Press, 2005), p. 141.

6 ibid., p. 151.

7 *PROME*, Edward II, October 1318.

8 'Regesta 67: 1317–1318', in W. H. Bliss (ed.), *Calendar of Papal Registers Relating to Great Britain and Ireland*, vol. 2, *1305–1342* (London, 1895), pp. 165–70.

9 'Regesta 109: 1334', in Bliss, *Calendar of Papal Registers Relating to Great Britain and Ireland*, pp. 414–23.

10 *Vita Edwardi Secundi*, p. 161.

11 '1319, membranes 10, 9, 8, 7, 6, 5, 4, 3, 2, 1', in H.C. Maxwell Lyte (ed.), *Calendar of Patent Rolls, Edward II: Volume 3, 1317–1321* (London, 1903), pp. 337–57; Membrane 1. 24 June, York.

12 *Vita Edwardi Secundi*, p. 161.

13 *The Anonimalle Chronicle 1307 to 1334: From Brotherton Collection MS 29*, ed. Wendy R. Childs and John Taylor (Cambridge: Cambridge University Press, 2013), p. 97.

14 ibid.

15 *Calendar of Documents Relating to Scotland Preserved in Her Majesty's Public Record Office, London*, vols. 2–4, ed. Joseph Bain (Edinburgh: H. M. General Register House, 1881–8), vol. 3, no. 663, p. 124.

16 *Vita Edwardi Secundi*, p. 167

17 *The Chronicle of Lanercost*, p. 227

18 Seymour Phillips, *Edward II* (New Haven: Yale University Press, 2010), p. 348.

19 *Vita Edwardi Secundi*, p. 167.

20 Translation in J. R. Maddicott, *Thomas of Lancaster, 1307–1322: A Study in the Reign of Edward II* (Oxford: Oxford University Press, 1970), p. 249.

21 Maddicott, *Thomas of Lancaster*, p. 249.

22 *Vita Edwardi Secundi*, p. xiv.

7. Three Sisters

1 *PROME*, Edward II, January 1316.

2 This hypothesis is my own, based on the experiences of other women living with the same condition and the evidence available in the record. This was not uncommon for women under duress. It is believed that in the sixteenth century both Anne Boleyn and Mary Tudor developed pseudocyesis.

3 *PROME*, Edward II, October 1320.

4 Rachel Podd, 'Reconsidering Maternal Mortality in Medieval England: Aristocratic Englishwomen, *c.*1236–1503', *Continuity and Change*, vol. 35, no. 2 (2020), 115–37.

5 Kathryn Warner, *Edward II's Nieces: The Clare Sisters: Powerful Pawns of the Crown* (Yorkshire: Pen & Sword History, 2020), p. 76.

6 TNA, E 101/376/7, f.99r.

7 TNA, E 40/15216; Michael Prestwich, 'The Court of Edward II', in Gwilym Dodd and Anthony Musson (eds.), *The Reign of Edward II: New Perspectives* (York: York University Press, 2006), p. 71.

8 F. D. Blackley and G. Hermansen (eds.), *The Household Book of Queen Isabella of England, for the Fifth Regnal Year of Edward II, 8th July 1311 to 7th July 1312*, The University of Alberta, Classical and Historical Studies, vol. 1 (Edmonton: University of Alberta Press, 1971), pp. 127–9.

9   Edward gifted the queen, the dowager queen Margaret and Eleanor Despenser the same gold brooch studded with six emeralds; TNA, E 101/376/7, f.99r.

10 Prestwich, 'The Court of Edward II', p. 71; British Library, MS Add.17362.

11 Warner, *Edward II's Nieces*, p. 110.

12 Natalie Fryde, *The Tyranny and Fall of Edward II: 1321–1326* (Cambridge: Cambridge University Press, 1979), p. 33.

13 Wendy R. Childs (ed. and trans.), *Vita Edwardi Secundi* (Oxford: Clarendon Press, 2005), p. 185.

14 Register of Thomas de Cobham, Bishop of Worcester, 1317–27, pp. 97–8, https://archive.org/details/registerofthomas00cath/page/n5/mode/2up; British Library, Cotton Mss., Nero D.X, f.110v. in *PROME*, Edward II, October 1320.

15 *PROME*, Edward II, October 1320.

16 *PROME*, Edward II, January 1316.

17 *The Chronicle of Lanercost, 1272–1346*, ed. and trans. Henry Maxwell (Glasgow: J. Maclehose, 1913), p. 230.

18 *The Anonimalle Chronicle 1307 to 1334: From Brotherton Collection MS 29*, ed. Wendy R. Childs and John Taylor (Cambridge: Cambridge University Press, 2013), p. 93.

19 TNA, SC 1/49/143; Seymour Phillips, *Edward II* (New Haven: Yale University Press, 2010), p. 367.

20 'par comand le Roi pur faire ent Torches tortz priketz et chaundell pur seruir loustel monsire Hugh le Despenser le fiz', in James Conway Davies, 'The First Journal of Edward II's Chamber', *English Historical Review*, vol. 30, no. 120 (1915), p. 676.

21 *Vita Edwardi Secundi*, p. 165.

22 *PROME*, Edward II, July 1321.

23 *Vita Edwardi Secundi* , p. 197.

8. The Battle of Badlesmeres

1   *Calendar of the Fine Rolls Preserved in the Public Record Office*, vol. 3, *Edward II A.D. 1319–1327* (London: Her Majesty's Stationery Office, 1911), p. 71.

2 William Stubbs (ed.), *Chronicles of the Reigns of Edward I and Edward II*, vol. 1, *Annales Londonienses and Annales Paulini* (London: Longman, 1882), p. 299.

3 *Calendar of Patent Rolls*, 1321–24, British History Online

4 TNA, E 403/196, m.8; E 403/197, m.8.

5 *The Anonimalle Chronicle 1307 to 1334: From Brotherton Collection MS 29*, ed. Wendy R. Childs and John Taylor (Cambridge: Cambridge University Press, 2013), p. 103.

6 *Calendar of the Fine Rolls*, p. 76; *Anonimalle Chronicle*, p. 103.

7 Seymour Phillips, *Edward II* (New Haven: Yale University Press, 2010), p. 400.

8 *Calendar of Patent Rolls*, 1321–24,British History Online.

9 TNA, SC 8/7/336.

10 *CCR*, Edward II, vol. 2, 1318–23, *British History Online*.

11 Wendy R. Childs (ed. and trans.), *Vita Edwardi Secundi* (Oxford: Clarendon Press, 2005), p. 211.

12 ibid.

13 Lisa Benz St John, 'In the Queen's Best Interest: Isabella, Edward II and the Image of a Functional Relationship', in Jeffrey S. Hamilton (ed.), *Fourteenth Century England*, vol. 8 (Woodbridge: Boydell & Brewer, 2014), pp. 29–32; Phillips, *Edward II*, p. 408.

14 *Anonimalle Chronicle*, p. 109; *Vita Edwardi Secundi*, pp. 213–15; Phillips, *Edward II*, p. 409.

15 *Vita Edwardi Secundi*, p. 215.

16 The red rose became associated with the earls of Lancaster with Edmund Crouchback adopting the motif; see Mrs Bury Palliser, *Historic Devices, Badges, and War-cries* (London: Sampson Low, Son & Marston, 1870), p. 370.

17 *CCR*, Edward II, vol. 2, 1318–23, *British History Online*.

18 British Library, Harley 1240 ff.86v-87.

19 ibid.; with thanks to Romily McNulty for an important discussion around these particular points and constructs in Elizabeth's protest.

20 With the greatest of thanks to Rhiannon Cox for discussing with me her PhD thesis on the treatment of noble women under Edward I and Edward II and sharing her forthcoming paper, 'Women on the Edge: The de Clare sisters and the Marches of Wales in the Early Fourteenth Century' (University of Bristol); G. A. Holmes, 'A Protest against the Despensers, 1326', *Speculum*, vol. 30, no. 2 (1955), pp. 207–12.

21 TNA, SC 8/173/8631.

22 Louise Wilkinson, 'Alice de Lacy', in *Oxford Dictionary of National Biography*, 2022.

23 TNA, SC 8/95/4719; for the exact details of Despenser's illegal land exchanges, see Rhiannon Cox, 'Women on the Edge'.

Part Two

9. *'Wilful Pleasure of Women'*

1 'Secresia harness' (secret harness), TNA, E 403/196, m.8; E 403/197, m.8.

2 'Regesta 112: 1323–1324', in W. H. Bliss (ed.), *Calendar of Papal Registers Relating to Great Britain and Ireland*, vol. 2, *1305–1342* (London, 1895), f.50.

3 *Calendar of the Fine Rolls*, 1319–27, p. 300.

4 'pur lamer et la contemplacion de sa soer, la roigne Dengleterre' in W. H. Bliss (ed.), *Calendar of Papal Registers Relating to Great Britain and Ireland*, vol. 2, *1305–1342* (London, 1895); Seymour Phillips, *Edward II* (New Haven: Yale University Press, 2010), p. 472; Wendy R. Childs (ed. and trans.), *Vita Edwardi Secundi* (Oxford: Clarendon Press, 2005), p. 229.

5 Bliss, *Calendar of Papal Registers Relating to Great Britain and Ireland*, p. 468.

6 *Vita Edwardi Secundi*, p. 235.

7 Pierre Chaplais (ed.), *The War of Saint-Sardos (1323–1325): Gascon Correspondence, and Diplomatic Documents* (London: Offices of the Royal Historical Society, 1954), pp. 199–200.

8 TNA, SC 1/49/106.

9 TNA, SC 1/49/188.

10 Phillips, *Edward II*, pp. 480–81; TNA, SC 1/49/106.

11 Chaplais, *The War of Saint-Sardos*, pp. 267–70.

12 *Vita Edwardi Secundi*, p. 143.

13 G. A. Holmes, 'Judgement on the Younger Despenser, 1326', *English Historical Review*, vol. 70, no. 275 (1955), p. 264.

14 'The French Chronicle of London: Edward II', in Henry T. Riley (ed.), *Chronicles of the Mayors and Sheriffs of London 1188–1274* (London: Trübner, 1863), pp. 248–67.

15 Roger Twysden (ed.), *Historiae Anglicanae Scriptores X* (London, 1652), col. 2767–8.

16 *CCR*, Edward II, vol. 4, 1323–27, *British History Online*.

17 *The Chronicle of Geoffrey le Baker*, trans. David Preest, intro. and notes Richard Barber (Woodbridge: Boydell & Brewer, 2018), pp. 29–32.

18 'Regesta 113: 1324–1326', in Bliss, *Calendar of Papal Registers Relating to Great Britain and Ireland*, f.50, f.261d.

19 Friedrich W. D. Brie (ed.), *The Brut, or, The Chronicles of England* (London: Kegan Paul, Paul, Trench, Trübner, for the Early English Text Society, 1906), pp. 252–3.

20 *The Chronicle of Geoffrey le Baker*, p. 27.

21 *CCR*, Edward II, vol. 4, 1323–27, *British History Online*.

22 Quoted in Helen Castor, *She-Wolves: The Women Who Ruled England Before Elizabeth* (London: Faber & Faber, 2011), p. 287.

23 *CCR*, Edward II, vol. 4, 1323–27, *British History Online*.

10. 'She-wolf of France'

1 T. Rymer (ed.), *Rymer's Foedera* (London, 1739–45), *British History Online*, british-history.ac.uk/rymer-foedera, vol. I, pp. 234–6.

2 *The Chronicle of Lanercost, 1272–1346*, ed. and trans. Henry Maxwell (Glasgow: J. Maclehose, 1913), p. 250.

3 Sarah McDougall, 'The Opposite of the Double Standard: Gender, Marriage, and Adultery Prosecution in Late Medieval France', *Journal of the History of Sexuality*, vol. 23, no. 2 (2014), 206–25

4 *The Anonimalle Chronicle 1307 to 1334: From Brotherton Collection MS 29*, ed. Wendy R. Childs and John Taylor (Cambridge: Cambridge University Press, 2013), pp. 123–7.

5 ibid., p. 129.

6 *The Chronicle of Geoffrey le Baker*, trans. David Preest, intro. and notes Richard Barber (Woodbridge: Boydell & Brewer, 2018), p. 23.

7 *Anonimalle Chronicle*, p. 129; 'The French Chronicle of London: Edward II', in Henry T. Riley (ed.), *Chronicles of the Mayors and Sheriffs of London 1188–1274* (London: Trübner, 1863), pp. 248–67.

8 ibid.

9 Adam of Murimuth, *Continuatio Chronicarum: Robertus de Avesbury de Gestis Mirabilibus Regis Edwardi Tertii*, (Cambridge: Cambridge University Press, 2012), pp. 48–9.

10 *The Chronicle of Lanercost*, p. 253.

11 Seymour Phillips, *Edward II* (New Haven: Yale University Press, 2010), p. 513.

12 *CCR*, Edward II, vol. 4, 1323–27, *British History Online*.

13 Phillips, *Edward II*, p. 515.

14 G. A. Holmes, 'Judgement on the Younger Despenser, 1326', *English Historical Review*, vol. 70, no. 275 (1955).

15 *Anonimalle Chronicle*, p. 131.

16 ibid.

17 *Rymer's Foedera*, p. 238.

18 *The Chronicle of Geoffrey le Baker*, p. 30.

19 Phillips, *Edward II*, p. 288.

20 Friedrich W. D. Brie (ed.), *The Brut, or, The Chronicles of England* (London: Kegan Paul, Paul, Trench, Trübner, for the Early English Text Society, 1906), pp. 252–3.

21 *The Chronicle of Geoffrey le Baker*, pp. 26–30.

22 Phillips, *Edward II*, p. 291.

23 British Library Royal MS 20, A II. c 1307-c 1327, 11r-146v; Claire Valente, 'The "Lament of Edward II": Religious Lyric, Political Propaganda', *Speculum*, vol. 77, no. 2 (2002), p. 433.

11. The Society of Craddok

1 TNA, E 361/3, rot.m.1.

2 TNA, DL 10/ 253.

3 James Bothwell and Gwilym Dodd (eds.), *Fourteenth Century England*, vol. 9, (Woodbridge: Boydell Press, 2016), p. 3.

4 James Raine (ed.), *Historical Papers and Letters from the Northern Registers* (London: Longman, 1873), p. 355.

5 *The Chronicle of Geoffrey le Baker*, trans. David Preest, intro. and notes Richard Barber (Woodbridge: Boydell & Brewer, 2018), p. 32.

6 Kit Heyam, *The Reputation of Edward II, 1307–1697* (Amsterdam: Amsterdam University Press, 2019), pp. 242–68.

7 Ian Mortimer, 'Sermons of Sodomy: A Reconsideration of Edward II's Sodomitical Reputation', in Gwilym Dodd and Anthony Musson (eds.), *The Reign of Edward II: New Perspectives* (York: York University Press, 2006), pp. 48–60.

8 Archives départementales de l'Hérault, France, G 1123.

9 Dr Ian Mortimer offers a rattlingly good argument for the survival of Edward II in his 'The Death of Edward II in Berkeley Castle', *English Historical Review*, vol. 120, no. 489 (2005), 1175–1214.

10 Seymour Phillips, *Edward II* (New Haven: Yale University Press, 2010), p. 298.

11 TNA, E 361/3 rot 12, m2.

12 Richard Barber, 'Edward III's Arthurianisms Re-visited: Perceforest in the Context of Philippa of Hainault and the Round Table Feast of 1344', in Elizabeth Archibald and David F. Johnson (eds.), *Arthurian Literature* (Woodbridge: Boydell & Brewer, 2013), p. 65.

13 Paul Doherty, *Isabella and the Strange Death of Edward II* (London: Constable and Robinson, 2003), p. 142.

14 'Roll A 1b: (ii) Nov 1327–July 1328', in *Calendar of the Plea and Memoranda Rolls of the City of London*, vol. 1, *1323–1364*, ed. A. H. Thomas (London, 1926), *British History Online*.

12. The Coup

1 Roy Martin Haines, 'Sumptuous Apparel for a Royal Prisoner: Archbishop Melton's Letter, 14 January 1330', *English Historical Review*, vol. 124, no. 509 (2009), 885–94.

2 *CCR*, Edward III, vol. 1, 1327–30, *British History Online*.

3 *The Chronicle of Geoffrey le Baker*, trans. David Preest, intro. and notes Richard Barber (Woodbridge: Boydell & Brewer, 2018), p. 39.

4 Andy King, *Sir Thomas Gray: Scalacronica (1272–1363)*, Publications of the Surtees Society, 209 (Woodbridge: Boydell Press, 2005), pp. 106–7

5 *The Chronicle of Geoffrey le Baker*, p. 47.

6 Paul Dryburgh, 'The Career of Roger Mortimer, First Earl of March (c.1287–1330)' (PhD thesis, University of Bristol, 2002), p. 152.

Part Three

13. Arthur Redivivus

1 Friedrich W. D. Brie (ed.), *The Brut, or, The Chronicles of England* (London: Kegan Paul, Paul, Trench, Trübner, for the Early English Text Society, 1906), p. 74.

2 *PROME*, Edward III, January 1333.

3 ibid.

4 Ranald Nicholson, 'The Siege of Berwick, 1333', *Scottish Historical Review*, 1961, vol. 40, no.129 (1961), 19–42.

5 TNA, SC 8/296/14794.

6 For the siege of Berwick, see Nicholson, 'The Siege of Berwick, 1333'.

7 *Calendar of Documents Relating to Scotland Preserved in Her Majesty's Public Record Office, London*, vols. 2–4, ed. Joseph Bain (Edinburgh: H. M. General Register House, 1881–8), vol. 3, no. 663, p. 124, p. 195.

8 Brie, *The Brut*, p. 285.

9 *The Anonimalle Chronicle 1307 to 1334: From Brotherton Collection MS 29*, ed. Wendy R. Childs and John Taylor (Cambridge: Cambridge University Press, 2013), p. 163.

10 *The Chronicle of Lanercost, 1272–1346*, ed. and trans. Henry Maxwell (Glasgow: J. Maclehose, 1913), p. 289.

11 Brie, *The Brut*, p. 285.

14. The Age of Chivalry

1 British Library, Cotton MS Nero D VI, f.31r.

2 W. Mark Ormrod, *Edward III* (New Haven: Yale University Press, 2013), p. 186.

3 ibid.

4 Matt Raven, 'The Earldom Endowments of 1337: Political Thought and the Practice of Kingship in Late Medieval England', *English Historical Review*, vol. 136, no. 580 (2021), 498–529.

5 Jean Froissart, *Chronicles of England and France*, trans. Thomas Johnes, vol. 1 (London: W. Smith, 1844).

6 'Bohemian Chronicle', *Die Königssaaler Geschichtsquellen*, ed. Johann Loserth, in *Fontes herum Austricarum, Scriptores VIII* (Vienna, 1875); Richard Barber, 'The Round Table Feast of 1344', in Julian Munby, Richard Barber and Richard Brown (eds.), *Edward III's Round Table at Windsor* (Woodbridge: Boydell Press, 2007), p. 38.

7 Adam of Murimuth in Barber, 'The Round Table Feast of 1344', p. 39.

8 For jousting, see Tobias Capwell, *The Arms and Armour of the Medieval Joust* (Leeds: Royal Armouries Museum, 2018).

9 Ulrich von Liechtenstein, *Frauendienst*, trans. J. W. Thomas, intro. Kelly DeVries (Woodbridge: Boydell Press, 2004), stanza 1429.

10 Adam of Murimuth, quoted in Munby et al., *Edward III's Round Table at Windsor*, pp. 38–43.

11 In 2006 an excavation that took place at Windsor Castle showed that Edward III had begun an elaborate building project to create a physical building known as the 'House of the Round Table'. The project was eventually abandoned and pulled down in the 1360s. For a detailed account of the building project, context, and the excavation work in 2006, see Munby et al., *Edward III's Round Table at Windsor*.

12 Jonathan Sumption, *The Hundred Years* War, vol. 1, *Trial by Battle* (London: Faber & Faber, 1990), pp. 489–90.

13 *CCR*, Edward III, vol. 5, 1340–43, *British History Online*.

14 On Edward III's household knights, see Matthew Heffran, 'Edward III's Household Knights and the Crécy Campaign of 1346', *Historical Research*, vol. 92, no. 255 (2019), 24–49; Matthew Heffran, *The Household Knights of Edward III: Warfare, Politics and Kingship in Fourteenth-Century England* (Woodbridge: Boydell Press, 2021).

15 T. Rymer (ed.), *Rymer's Foedera* (London, 1739–45), *British History Online*, british-history.ac.uk/rymer-foedera, vol. I, p. 350.

15. Ich Dien

1 Jonathan Sumption, *The Hundred Years* War, vol. 1, *Trial by Battle* (London: Faber & Faber, 1990), p. 500.

2 Michael Jones, *The Black Prince* (London: Head of Zeus, 2017), p. 82.

3 Craig Taylor, *Chivalry and the Ideals of Knighthood in France During the Hundred Years War* (Cambridge: Cambridge University Press, 2013), pp. 162–3.

4 For details on the Battle of Crécy, see Michael Livingstone and Kelly DeVries (eds.), *The Battle of Crécy: A Casebook* (Liverpool: Liverpool University Press, 2015).

5 See Michael Livingstone, 'Losses Uncountable: The Context of Crécy', in Livingstone and DeVries, *The Battle of Crécy*, pp. 1–13.

6 *The True Chronicles of Jean Le Bel, 1290–1360*, trans. Nigel Bryant (Woodbridge: Boydell Press, 2011), p. 180.

7 Sumption, *Trial by Battle*, p. 526.

8 Jean Froissart, *Chronicles of England and France*, trans. Thomas Johnes, vol. 1 (London: W. Smith, 1844), pp. 164–5.

9 *The True Chronicles of Jean Le Bel*, p. 182.

10 Jean Froissart, *Chronicles, in Lord Berners' Translation*, sel., ed. and intro. Gillian and William Anderson (London: Centaur Press, 1963), p. 99.

16. Heroes

1 'Edward III Letter to Thomas Lucy', in Michael Livingstone and Kelly DeVries (eds.), *The Battle of Crécy: A Casebook* (Liverpool: Liverpool University Press, 2015), pp. 55–9.

2 *PROME*, Edward III, September 1346.

3 W. Mark Ormrod, *Edward III* (New Haven: Yale University Press, 2013), p. 288

4 ibid., p. 286.

5 ibid., p. 290.

6 CPR, *Edward III*, vol. 7, 1343–46, *British History Online*.

7 *The True Chronicles of Jean Le Bel, 1290–1360*, trans. Nigel Bryant (Woodbridge: Boydell Press, 2011), p. 201.

8 ibid., p. 202; *The Chronicle of Geoffrey le Baker*, trans. David Preest, intro. and notes Richard Barber (Woodbridge: Boydell & Brewer, 2018), p. 80.

9 *The Chronicle of Geoffrey le Baker*, p. 80.

10 Jean Froissart, *Chronicles of England and France*, trans. Thomas Johnes, vol. 1 (London: W. Smith, 1844), p. 188.

11 TNA, SC 8/229/11401.

12 For women in the Order of the Garter, see Shelagh Mitchell, 'Ladies of the Garter: Edward III; Richard II; Elizabeth II', *Court Historian*, vol. 22, no. 2 (2017), 151–67.

13 Juliet Vale, *Edward III and Chivalry: Chivalric Society and Its Context 1270–1350* (Woodbridge: Boydell Press, 1982), pp. 69–71.

Part Four

17. The Princess and the Plague

1 Giovanni Boccaccio, *Decameron*, a new English version by Cormac Ó Cuilleanáin, based on John Payne's 1886 translation (Hertfordshire: Wordsworth Classics of World Literature, 2004), p. 4.

2 Louis Sanctus, 'Letter', 27 April 1348, in John Aberth (ed.), *The Black Death: The Great Mortality of 1348–1350: A Brief History with Documents* (London: St Martin's Press, 2005), p. 33.

3 Boccaccio, *Decameron*, p. 6.

4 Aberth, *The Black Death*, p. 11.

5 Michael Dols, '"Ibn al-Wardī's Risālah al-naba' 'an al-waba": A translation of a major source for the history of the Black Death in the Middle East', in *Near Eastern Numismatics, Iconography, Epigraphy and History: Studies in Honor of George C. Miles*, ed. Dickran K. Kouymjian (American University of Beirut, 1974), p. 448.

6 Nicephorus Gregorus, 'Byzantine History, ca. 1359', in Aberth, *The Black Death*, p. 15.

7 James Belich, *The World the Plague Made: The Black Death and the Rise of Europe* (Princeton: Princeton University Press, 2022), p. 54.

8 Monica Green, 'The Four Black Deaths', *American Historical Review*, vol. 125, no. 5 (2020), 1601–31.

9 Belich, *The World the Plague Made*, pp. 60–63.

10 Sanctus, 'Letter', p. 22.

11 Mary Anne Everett Green, *Lives of the Princesses of England*, vol. 3 (London: Longman, 1857), p. 248.

12 Joan's trousseau is transcribed in 'Observations on the Most Noble Order of the Garter; Illustrated by the Accounts of the Great Wardrobe of King Edward the Third', in *Archaeologia* (1844), p. 52.

13 T. Rymer (ed.), *Rymer's Foedera* (London, 1739–45), *British History Online*, british-history.ac.uk/rymer-foedera, vol. 1, p. 1061.

14 TNA, E 101/391/16.

15 TNA, E 101/391/17; Jonathan Sumption, *The Hundred Years War*, vol. 2, *Trial by Fire* (London: Faber & Faber, 2001), pp. 49–50.

16 Bourchier travelled on a ship called *La Katerine*, possibly loaned by the Castilians from Bayonne, where Joan was meant to travel to meet Pedro of Castile. The length of time (eight weeks) it took him to arrive back in England suggests that he went to Bayonne to confirm the arrangements after leaving Joan and travelled back to England from there. TNA, E 101/312/32.

17 TNA, E 101/391/17.

18 Rosemary Horrox (ed. and trans.), *The Black Death* (Manchester: Manchester University Press, 1994), pp. 41–61.

19 *Inventaire sommaire des archives départementales antérieures à 1790, Gironde, Archives ecclésiastiques, Série G (Nos 1 à 920): Inventaire des Fonds de l'Archevêché et du chapitre métropolitain de Bordeaux*, vol. 1 (Bordeaux : G. Gounouilhou, 1892), G, C317; the *Inventaire sommaire* suggests an alternative date, that Joan died on 3 August, and that was the date that the constable of Bordeaux wassummoned to ensure that the Mass was being carried out as ordered by Gaunt in 1389.

20 *Rymer's Foedera*, p. 1068.

21 Horrox, *The Black Death*, p. 250.

22 *Anonimalle Chronicle*, in Horrox, *The Black Death*, p. 62.

23 *Anonimalle Chronicle*, *Polychronicon* and *Grey Friars at Lynn*, in Horrox, *The Black Death*, pp. 62–3.

24 *Eulogium Chronicle*, in Horrox, *The Black Death*, pp. 63–4.

25 Thomas Walsingham, quoted in Horrox, *The Black Death*, p. 66.

26 *Chronica Monasterii de Melsa*, in Horrox, *The Black Death*, p. 67.

27 'Wills: 24 Edward III (1350–1)', in *Calendar of Wills Proved and Enrolled in the Court of Husting, London: Part 1, 1258–1358*, ed. R. R. Sharpe (London, 1889), British History Online, british-history.ac.uk/court-husting-wills/vol1.

28 ibid.

29 W. Mark Ormrod, *Edward III* (New Haven: Yale University Press, 2013), p. 358.

30 Wellcome Institute for the History of Medicine, London: Western MS 668 fos. 97v-98, in Horrox, *The Black Death*, p. 149.

31 Robert of Avesbury, quoted in Horrox, *The Black Death*, pp. 153–4.

32 British Library, Harleian MS 2398, fos. 93–4, in Horrox, *The Black Death*, p. 134.

33 British Library, Harleian MS 2398, in Horrox, *The Black Death*, pp. 93–4.

34 Horrox, *The Black Death*, pp. 126–33

35 Ormrod, *Edward III*, p. 358.

36 TNA, E 101/391/18

18. New Beginnings

1 Petrarch, *Epistolae de Rebus Familiaribus et variate*, ed. Joseph Fracassetti (Florence, 1859), vol. I, p. 13, in Rosemary Horrox (ed. and trans.), *The Black Death* (Manchester: Manchester University Press, 1994), p. 248.

2 William Newburgh, *The History of William of Newburgh, The Chronicles of Robert de Monte* (United Kingdom: Seeleys, 1856), p. 658.

3 British Library, Cotton Nero A. X, art.3, f.42.

4 *Pearl*, trans. Simon Armitage (London: Faber & Faber, 2017).

5 For more on the language of plague in *Pearl*, see David. K. Coley, *Death and the Pearl Maiden: Plague, Poetry, England* (Columbus: Ohio State University Press), pp. 56–77; on death and dying in *Pearl*, see D. Vance Smith, *Arts of Dying: Literature and Finitude in Medieval England* (Chicago: University of Chicago Press, 2020), pp. 152–71.

6 James Belich, *The World the Plague Made: The Black Death and the Rise of Europe* (Princeton: Princeton University Press, 2022), pp. 83–105.

7 *CCR*, Edward III, vol. 10, 1354–60, *British History Online*.

8 Gillian Adler and Paul Strohm, *Alle Thyng Hath Tyme: Time and Medieval Life* (London: Reaktion Books, 2023), p. 35.

9 For a detailed analysis of the changes that occurred globally following the Black Death, see Belich, *The World the Plague Made*.

10 On brewsters and ale wives in England, see Judith M. Bennett, *Ale, Beer, and Brewsters in England: Women's Work in a Changing World, 1300–1600* (Oxford: Oxford University Press, 1999).

11 Sarah Rees Jones, 'Women and Citizenship in Later Medieval York', in Deborah Simonton (ed.), *The Routledge History Handbook of Gender and the Urban Experience* (New York: Routledge, 2017), p. 176.

12 Bruce Campbell, *The Great Transition: Climate, Disease and Society in the Late Medieval World* (Cambridge: Cambridge University Press, 2016), p. 287.

13 Mark Bailey, *After the Black Death: Economy, Society and the Law in Fourteenth-Century England* (Oxford: Oxford University Press, 2021), pp. 10–11.

14 TNA, C 54/185, m. 8d.

15 There are two schools of thought in regard to the so-called 'Golden Age', the 'optimists' and the 'pessimists'. For an analysis of both arguments, see Belich, *The World the Plague Made*, pp. 83–105.

19. Winner and Waster

1 On the household, all is taken from C. M. Woolgar, *The Great Household in Late Medieval England* (New Haven: Yale University Press, 1999).

2 Royal or wealthy households were often separate, the lord having his household and the lady hers. However, it was common for them to still live together.

3 Marion Turner, *Chaucer: A European Life* (Princeton: Princeton University Press, 2019), p. 46.

4 Hilary M. Carey, *Courting Disaster: Astrology at the English Court and University in the Later Middle Ages* (New York: Palgrave Macmillan, 1992), p. 89.

5 Henry Knighton, *Knighton's Chronicle, 1337–1396*, ed. and trans. G. H. Martin (Oxford: Clarendon Press, 1995), pp. 145–9.

6 ibid.

7 ibid., p. 151.

8 ibid.; W. Mark Ormrod, *Edward III* (New Haven: Yale University Press, 2013), p. 387.

9 McCauley (ed.), Froissart, *Chronicles* (1895), (Macmillian: London, 1913), p. 134.

10 Quoted in Ormrod, *Edward III*, p. 387.

11 Knighton, *Knighton's Chronicle*, p. 155.

12 Turner, *Chaucer*, p. 58.

13 Stella Mary Newton, *Fashion in the Age of the Black Prince: A Study of the Years 1340–1365* (Woodbridge: Boydell Press, 1980), pp. 44–5.

14 ibid., p. 46.

15 ibid.

16 W. Mark Ormrod, 'The Foundation and Early Development of the Order of the Garter in England, 1348–1399' *Frühmittelalterliche Studien*, vol. 50, no. 1 (2016) p. 369.

17 ibid., p. 387.

18 For a detailed analysis and a translation of the Jousting Letters, see Philip E. Bennett, Sarah Carpenter, and Louise Gardiner, 'Chivalric Games at the Court of Edward III: The Jousting Letters of EUL MS 183', *Medium Ævum*, vol. 87, no. 2 (2018), 304–42.

19 W. Mark Ormrod, 'The Foundation and Early Development of the Order of the Garter', p. 376.

20 Quoted in W. Mark Ormrod, *Winner and Waster and Its Contexts: Chivalry, Law and Economics in Fourteenth-Century England* (Cambridge: D. S. Brewer, 2021), p. 18.

21 British Library, Additional MS 31042; Ormrod, *Winner and Waster and Its Contexts*, pp. 15–37; Turner, *Chaucer*, pp. 64–5.

20. Lions and Leopards

1 *Chronique de Jean le Bel*, ed. Jules Viard and Eugène Déprez (Paris: Libraire de la Société de l'histoire de France, 1906), p. 256.

2 Natasha O'Hear, 'The Angers Apocalypse Tapestry: A Fourteenth-Century Walking Tour of the Book of Revelation', in *Contrasting Images of the Book of Revelation in Late Medieval and Early Modern Art: A Case Study in Visual Exegesis* (Oxford: Oxford Theological Monographs, 2011), p. 47.

3 ibid., p. 66.

4 ibid., p. 67.

5 With thanks to Professor Michael Livingstone for discussing mounted archers with me.

6 *Anonimalle Chronicle, 1333–1381, from a MSS Written at St Mary's Abbey, York and now in the Possession of Lieut. Col. Sir William Ingleby, Bart.*, eds. V. H. Galbraith and William Ingleby (Manchester: Manchester University Press, 1927), p. 43.

7 'Scalacronica', in Clifford J. Rogers (ed.), *The Wars of Edward III* (Woodbridge: Boydell Press 1999), p. 176.

8 David Green, *The Hundred Years War: A People's History* (New Haven: Yale University Press, 2015), p. 51.

9 Jean de Venette, 'Chronicle', in Rogers, *The Wars of Edward III*, p. 169.

10 Jonathan Sumption, *The Hundred Years War*, vol. 2, *Trial by Fire* (London: Faber & Faber, 2001), p. 429.

11 ibid.

12 Deuteronomy 20:10–154.

13 Marion Turner, *Chaucer: A European Life* (Princeton: Princeton University Press, 2019), pp. 80–82; Anne Walters Robertson, *Guillaume de Machaut and Reims: Context and Meaning in His Musical Works* (Cambridge: Cambridge University Press, 2002), pp. 202–4.

14 Robertson, *Guillaume de Machaut and Reims*, p. 203.

15 Sumption, *Trial by Fire*, p. 431.

16 Henry Knighton, *Knighton's Chronicle, 1337–1396*, ed. and trans. G. H. Martin (Oxford: Clarendon Press, 1995), p. 177.

17 Sumption, *Trial by Fire*, p. 438.

18 ibid., p. 440.

19 ibid.

20 There was some change to the treaty when it was formalised at Calais, when Jean II's formal renunciation of his rights and sovereignty in place of Edward was put into another document, set to be confirmed a year later – it never was. It was this administrative change that gave reason to extend the war; see John Le Patourel, 'The Treaty of Brétigny, 1360', *Transactions of the Royal Historical Society*, vol. 10 (1960), 19–39.

21 £500,000: this comes to around £250 million by today's standards, see https://www.nationalarchives.gov.uk/currency-converter.

22 Stella Mary Newton, *Fashion in the Age of the Black Prince: A Study of the Years 1340–1365* (Woodbridge: Boydell Press, 1980), p. 44; the amount of squirrel bellies used to clothe the nobility in this period suggest extraordinary levels of squirrel culling across England. In a single year, 80,000 squirrels were killed for the royal household alone. Squirrels were also sometimes enjoyed as pets, walked on a leash and kept in hutches; see Kathleen Walter-Meikle, *Medieval Pets* (Woodbridge: Boydell Press, 2012), pp. 51–2.

23 T. Rymer (ed.), *Rymer's Foedera* (London, 1739–45), *British History Online*, british-history.ac.uk/rymer-foedera, vol. 1, p. 412.

24 King Jean's Letter on the Treaty of Brétigny, A. Bardonnnet, 'Procès-verbal de déliverance à Jean Chandos, commissaire du roi d'Angleterre, des places françaises abandonnées par le traité de Brétigny', in Rogers, *The Wars of Edward III*, p. 183.; Knighton, *Knighton's Chronicle*, pp. 181–3.

25 'Regesta 240: 1359–1360', in W. H. Bliss (ed.), *Calendar of Papal Registers Relating to Great Britain and Ireland: Volume 3, 1342–1362* (London, 1897), pp. 628–32, f.93–95d.

26 *Anonimalle Chronicle,* quoted in W. Mark Ormrod, *Edward III* (New Haven: Yale University Press, 2013), p. 412.

21. Prince of Aquitaine

1 TNA, SC 7/22/16.

2 W. Mark Ormrod, *Edward III* (New Haven: Yale University Press, 2013), p. 419.

3 Marion Turner, *The Wife of Bath: A Biography* (Princeton: Princeton University Press, 2023), p. 70.

4 Jean Froissart, quoted in Michael Jones, *The Black Prince* (London: Head of Zeus, 2017).

5 T. Rymer (ed.), *Rymer's Foedera* (London, 1739–45), *British History Online,* british-history.ac.uk/rymer-foedera, vol. I, p. 418.

6 Henry Knighton, *Knighton's Chronicle, 1337–1396,* ed. and trans. G. H. Martin (Oxford: Clarendon Press, 1995), p. 185.

7 Jones, *The Black Prince*, p. 259.

8 Knighton, *Knighton's Chronicle*, p. 185.

9 TNA, C 47/26/22. A series of petitions outlines the issues that people had with the change in regime and the requests they had for the new prince of Aquitaine.

10 Jean Froissart, *Chronicles of England and France*, trans. Thomas Johnes, vol. 1 (London: W. Smith, 1844), p. 339.

11 *The True Chronicles of Jean Le Bel, 1290–1360,* trans. Nigel Bryant (Woodbridge: Boydell Press, 2011), p. 260.

12 ibid., pp. 260–61.

13 Jonathan Sumption, *The Hundred Years War*, vol. 2, *Trial by Fire* (London: Faber & Faber, 2001), pp. 475–8.

14 Jones, *The Black Prince,* p. 267.

15 David Green, *Edward the Black Prince: Power in Medieval Europe* (Harlow: Pearson/Longman, 2007), p. 107

16 'Elle introduisit la mode des corsets fendus sur les côtés et bordés d'hermine. Ceintures de soie avec plaques d'orfévrerie émaillées ou dorées,

fourrures de vair, voiles de lin, voiles de soie venus de Lyon, d'Alep ou d'Alexandrie, hautes coiffures constellées de perles, tout servait à la princesse pour rehausser l'éclat de ses toilettes' : Joseph Moisant, *Le Prince Noir en Aquitaine 1355–1356, 1362–1370* (Paris: A. Picard et fils, 1894), p. 109.

17 Green, *Edward the Black Prince*, p. 119.

18 Richard Barber, *Prince of Wales and Aquitaine: A Biography of the Black Prince* (Woodbridge: Boydell Press, 1978), p. 183.

19 Jonathan Sumption, *Trial by Fire*, p. 544.

20 Jones, *The Black Prince*, p. 283.

21 L. J. Andrew Villalon, 'Spanish Involvement in the Hundred Years War and the Battle of Nájera', in L. J. Andrew Villalon and Donald J. Kagay (eds.), *The Hundred Years War: A Wider Focus* (Boston: Brill, 2005), p. 21; Richard Vernier, *The Flower of Chivalry: Bertrand Du Guesclin and the Hundred Years War* (Woodbridge: Boydell Press, 2007), p. 96.

22 Chandos Herald, *Life of the Black Prince*, ed. Mildred Katharine Pope and Eleanor Constance Lodge (Oxford: Clarendon Press, 1910), p. 150. Pedro also went via Portugal on his way to Bordeaux; see Jones, *The Black Prince*, p. 284.

23 Jean Froissart, quoted in Jones, *The Black Prince*, pp. 287–8; Chris Given-Wilson, 'Edward, the Black Prince, and Bertrand du Guesclin, Constable of France: Chivalry and Rivalry in Life and Death', in J. A. Lutkin and J. S. Hamilton (eds.), *Creativity, Contradictions and Commemoration in the Reign of Richard II: Essays in Honour of Nigel Saul* (Woodbridge: Boydell & Brewer, 2022), pp. 221–34.

24 Marion Turner, *Chaucer: A European Life* (Princeton: Princeton University Press, 2019), p. 112

25 L. P. Harvey, *Islamic Spain: 1250–1500* (Chicago: University of Chicago Press, 1990), p. 141.

26 Turner, *Chaucer*, pp. 106–7.

27 Sumption, *Trial by Fire*, p. 553; Herald, *Life of the Black Prince*, p. 162.

28 Herald, *Life of the Black Prince*, p. 162.

29 Froissart, *Chronicles of England and France*, p. 371.

30 ibid.

31 Pero López de Ayala, *Chronicle of King Pedro*, vols. 1–3, trans. Lord Berners, sel., ed. and intro. Gillian and William Anderson (London, 1963), p. 454.

32 ibid.

33 Sumption, *Trial by Fire*, p. 554.

34 Ayala, *Chronicle of King Pedro*, p. 457.

35 Sumption, *Trial by Fire*, p. 556.

36 Clara Estow, *Pedro the Cruel of Castile 1350–1369* (Leiden: E. J. Brill, 1995), pp. 242–3.

37 Froissart, *Chronicles of England and France*, p. 383.

38 ibid.

39 ibid.

40 Quoted in Jones, *The Black Prince*, p. 342.

41 Froissart, *Chronicles of England and France*, pp. 435–7.

42 ibid.

43 ibid., p. 459.

44 ibid.

22. A Parliament of Rats

1 In a will made weeks before his death, Lionel requested to be buried next to his first wife, Elizabeth de Burgh. His body was exhumed from Pavia and re-interred in Suffolk in the 1370s; see *The Cartulary of the Augustinian Friars of Clare*, ed. Christopher Harper-Bill, (Woodbridge: Published for the Suffolk Records Society by the Boydell Press, 1991), p. 76.

2 *Thomae Walsingham, quondam monachi S. Albani, historia Anglicana*, ed. H. T. Riley, 2 vols., pt 1 of *Chronica monasterii S. Albani*, Rolls Series, 28 (1863–4), vol. 2, p. 309.

3 London, Westminster Abbey Muniments, 'A Wigmore Chronicle, 1355–1377', ed. J. Taylor, in J. Taylor, *English Historical Literature in the Fourteenth Century* (Oxford, 1987), quoted in W. Mark Ormrod, *Edward III* (New Haven: Yale University Press, 2013), p. 471.

4 Ormrod, *Edward III*, p. 529.

5 There is no evidence to suggest that Edward had a stroke, but that was ultimately his cause of death. As W. Mark Ormrod points out, the king could well have had an accident while hunting: Ormrod, *Edward III*, p. 530.

6 ibid., p. 534.

7 Thomas Walsingham, *The Chronica Maiora of Thomas Walsingham, 1376–1422*, trans. David Preest, intro. and notes James G. Clark (Woodbridge: Boydell Press, 2005), p. 32.

8 Berwick Record Office, ZHG/I.A.

9 A ship called *La Alice* was sent to arrest sixty sailors in Kent on 28 January 1374: T. Rymer (ed.), *Rymer's Foedera* (London, 1739–45), *British History Online*, british-history.ac.uk/rymer-foedera, vol. 1, p. 467; 8 August 1373 p. 466.

10 They had one son named John Southray, who was appointed an esquire of the king's bedchamber in 1375: Ormrod, *Edward III*, p. 537.

11 E. M. Orsten, 'The Ambiguities in Langland's Rat Parliament, *Mediaeval Studies*, vol. 23 (1961), p. 221; G. Dodd, 'A Parliament Full of Rats? *Piers Plowman* and the Good Parliament of 1376', *Historical Research*, vol. 79, no. 203 (2006), 21–49.

12 W. R. Lethaby, 'English Primitives: The Painted Chamber and the Early Masters of the Westminster School', *Burlington Magazine for Connoisseurs*, vol. 7, no. 28 (1905), 257–69; Paul Binski, 'The Painted Chamber at Westminster and Its Documentation', *Walpole Society*, vol. 83 (2021), 1–68.

13 Binski, 'The Painted Chamber at Westminster', 29.

14 Lethaby, 'English Primitives', 11–14.

15 *PROME*, Edward III, April 1376; *Anonimalle Chronicle, 1333–1381, from a MSS Written at St Mary's Abbey, York and now in the Possession of Lieut. Col. Sir William Ingleby, Bart.*, eds. V. H. Galbraith and William Ingleby (Manchester: Manchester University Press, 1927), p. 81.

16 *Anonimalle Chronicle, 1333–1381*, p. 82.

17 *PROME*, Edward III, April 1376; *Anonimalle Chronicle, 1333–1381*, p. 87.

18 *PROME*, Edward III, April 1376.

19 ibid.

20 For Alice Perrers and the Good Parliament, see W. Mark Ormrod, 'The Trials of Alice Perrers', *Speculum*, vol. 83, no. 2 (2008), 366–96; Laura Tompkins, 'The Uncrowned Queen: Alice Perrers, Edward III and Political Crisis in Fourteenth-Century England, *1360–1377* (PhD thesis, University of St Andrews, 2013); *Anonimalle Chronicle, 1333–1381*, p. 87.

21 Ormrod, 'The Trials of Alice Perrers', 371.

22 John Gower, quoted in Ormrod, *Edward III*, p. 537.

23 Lambeth Palace Library, Reg. Sudbury, f. 90v, 91r, 91v. The will is printed in A. P. Stanley, *Historical Memorials of Canterbury: The Landing of Augustine, the Murder of Becket, Edward the Black Prince*, 10th edn (London: J. Murray, 1909), pp. 164–71; Donald F. Logan (ed.), *The Register of Simon*

Sudbury, *Archbishop of Canterbury, 1375–1381* (Woodbridge: Boydell Press, 2020), pp. 142–6.

24 Chandos Herald, *Life of the Black Prince*, ed. Mildred Katharine Pope and Eleanor Constance Lodge (Oxford: Clarendon Press, 1910), p. 240.

25 ibid.

26 Walsingham, *The Chronica Maiora of Thomas Walsingham*, p. 27.

27 Quoted in Michael Jones, *The Black Prince* (London: Head of Zeus, 2017), p. 395.

28 *PROME,* Edward III, April 1376.

29 Logan, *The Register of Simon Sudbury*, p. 143.

30 The chantries were established in observance of the Trinity, 'to honour the Holy Trinity, which we [the Black Prince and Joan of Kent] have always revered with a special devotion [ad honorem Sancte Trinitatis, quam peculiari devocione semper colimus]': 'Ordinance by Edward the Black Prince for the Two Chantries Founded by Him in the Undercroft of the South Transept, Canterbury Cathedral', in Stanley, *Historical Memorials of Canterbury*, p. 159.

31 The tombs of John of Gaunt, Philippa of Hainault, Edward II and Isabella of France were all carved from alabaster; see Jessica Barker, Graeme McArthur and Emily Pegues, '"Fully Armed in Plate of War": Making the Effigy of the Black Prince', *Burlington Magazine*, vol. 87, no. 2 (2021), 996–1007.

32 ibid., pp. 104–6.

33 ibid.; D. Tyson: 'The Epitaph of Edward the Black Prince', *Medium Ævum*, vol. 46, no. 1 (1977), 98–104.

34 Gaunt was not the only member of the royal family interested in Wycliffe's theology. Joan of Kent supported his views, and reform became fashionable in the 1370s–80s. Wycliffe's ideas around clerical wealth also supported Gaunt's patronage of the Carmelite Order, who lived without worldly possessions.

35 Margaret Aston, 'John Wycliffe's Reformation Reputation', *Past & Present*, no. 30 (1965), 24.

36 Walsingham, *The Chronica Maiora of Thomas Walsingham*, p. 30; Henry Knighton, *Knighton's Chronicle, 1337–1396*, ed. and trans. G. H. Martin (Oxford: Clarendon Press, 1995), pp. 298–301.

37 The most famous example of which was in the twelfth century and the argument between Thomas Becket and Henry II.

38 Anne Hudson (ed.), *Selections from English Wycliffe Writings* (Cambridge: Cambridge University Press, 1978), pp. 1–10.

39 Nicholas Orme, *Going to Church in Medieval England* (New Haven: Yale University Press, 2021), pp. 193–4.

40 Walsingham, *The Chronica Maiora of Thomas Walsingham*, p. 72.

41 Logan, *Register of Simon Sudbury*, p. 61.

42 ibid., pp. 61–2.

43 Anne Hudson and Anthony Kenny, 'John Wycliffe [called Doctor Evangelicus]', in *Oxford Dictionary of National Biography*, 2010.

44 Walsingham, *The Chronica Maiora of Thomas Walsingham*, p. 32.

45 Alice and William went on to continually petition for the return of Alice's properties that were removed in 1378: TNA, SC 8/146/7265; Laura Tompkins, 'Alice Perrers and the Goldsmiths' Mistery: New Evidence Concerning the Identity of the Mistress of Edward III', *The English Historical Review* 130, no. 547 (2015): 1361–91.

46 Jean Froissart, *Chronicles of England and France*, trans. Thomas Johnes, vol. I (London: W. Smith, 1844), p. 510.

47 ibid., p. 511.

48 Ormrod, *Edward III*, p. 578.

49 The death mask of Edward III and his wooden effigy still survive and are kept at Westminster Abbey.

50 Ormrod, *Edward III*, p. 578.

51 Knighton, *Knighton's Chronicle*, p. 197.

52 *An Inventory of the Historical Monuments in London*, vol. 1, *Westminster Abbey* (London, 1924), p. 30.

Part Five

23. Vox Clamantis

1 Nigel Saul, *Richard II* (New Haven: Yale University Press, 1999), p. 33.

2 TNA, SC 8/86/4257

3 *Anonimalle Chronicle*, pp. 107–9, in Alison K. McHardy (ed. and trans.), *The Reign of Richard II: From Minority to Tyranny, 1377–1397* (Manchester: Manchester University Press, 2012), pp. 28–9.

4 Thomas Walsingham, *The Chronica Maiora of Thomas Walsingham, 1376–1422*, trans. David Preest, intro. and notes James G. Clark (Woodbridge: Boydell Press, 2005), p. 40.

5 'Westminster Chronicle', in McHardy, *The Reign of Richard II*, p. 29.

6 Saul, *Richard II*, p. 57.

7 Walsingham, *The Chronica Maiora of Thomas Walsingham*, p. 109.

8 *PROME*, Richard II, November 1380.

9 Henry Knighton, *Knighton's Chronicle, 1337–1396*, ed. and trans. G. H. Martin (Oxford: Clarendon Press, 1995), p. 209.

10 ibid., pp. 207–9.

11 *Anonimalle Chronicle*, in *The Peasants' Revolt of 1381*, ed. and trans. R. B. Dobson (London and Basingstoke: Palgrave MacMillan, 1970), p. 125.

12 ibid., p. 125.

13 *Anonimalle Chronicle*, in *The Peasants' Revolt of 1381*, p. 127.

14 ibid., p. 155.

15 Vespers are evening prayers; ibid., p. 155.

16 Marion Turner, *Chaucer: A European Life* (Princeton: Princeton University Press, 2019), pp. 279–80.

17 Milan Pajic, *Flemish Textile Workers in England, 1331–1400: Immigration, Integration and Economic Development* (Cambridge: Cambridge University Press, 2023), p. 244.

18 *Anonimalle Chronicle*, in *The Peasants Revolt of 1381*, p. 163; Pajic, *Flemish Textile Workers in England*, p. 245.

19 Henry Thomas Riley (ed. and trans.), *Memorials of London and London Life in the Xiiith, XIVth, and IVth Centuries: Being a Series of Extracts, Local, Social, and Political, from the Early Archives of the City of London, A.D. 1276–1419* (London: Longmans, 1868), pp. 459, 448.

20 Geoffrey Chaucer, 'The Nun's Priest's Prologue and Tale', in *The Canterbury Tales: A Selection* (London: Penguin Classics, 1996), p. 201.

21 Frederick Devon (ed.), *Issues of the Exchequer: Being a Collection of Payments Made Out of His Majesty's Revenue, from King Henry III to King Henry VI Inclusive* (London: J. Murray, 1837), p. 217.

22 KB 27/482 rex m. 39d, in Sylvia Federico, 'The Imaginary Society: Women in 1381', *Journal of British Studies*, vol. 40, no. 2 (2001), 168.

23 Jean Froissart in *The Peasants' Revolt of 1381*, p. 193.

24 *Anonimalle Chronicle*, in *The Peasants' Revolt of 1381*, p. 164.

25 ibid., p. 165.

26 ibid.

27 ibid.

28 ibid., p. 166.

29 Thomas Walsingham, in *The Peasants' Revolt of 1381*, p. 164.

30 TNA, 2 KB 27/482 rex mm. 37, 37d, in Federico, 'The Imaginary Society', 167; TNA, 9 KB 9/166/1 m., in Federico, 'The Imaginary Society', 168.

31 TNA, KB 27/482 rex m. 39d., in Federico, 'The Imaginary Society', 168.; TNA, KB 27/484 rex m. 3, *The People of 1381 Online Database*, www.1381.online.

32 TNA, KB 9/166/1 m. 119, *The People of 1381 Online Database*.

33 Thomas Walsingham, in *The Peasants' Revolt of 1381*, p. 260.

34 Richard passed from 'pueritia' to 'adolescentia', see Saul, *Richard II*, p. 108.

24. Milky Way

1 Geoffrey Chaucer, *A Treatise on the Astrolabe*, ed. Walter W. Skeat (Amsterdam: Meridian, 1978).

2 Geoffrey Chaucer, quoted in Seb Falk, *The Light Ages: A Medieval Journey of Discovery* (London: Allen Lane, 2020), p. 133.

3 Marion Turner, *Chaucer: A European Life* (Princeton: Princeton University Press, 2019), pp. 233–4.

4 ibid., p. 219.

5 Jonathan Hughes, *The Rise of Fourteenth-Century Alchemy in England: Plantagenet Kings and the Search for the Philosopher's Stone* (London: Continuum, 2012), p. 130.

6 ibid., p. 198.

7 Thomas Walsingham, *The Chronica Maiora of Thomas Walsingham, 1376–1422*, trans. David Preest, intro. and notes James G. Clark (Woodbridge: Boydell Press, 2005), pp. 170–71.

8 'Westminster Chronicle', in Alison K. McHardy (ed. and trans.), *The Reign of Richard II: From Minority to Tyranny, 1377–1397* (Manchester: Manchester University Press, 2012), p. 93; Nigel Saul, *Richard II* (New Haven: Yale University Press, 1999), p. 443.

9 Walsingham, *The Chronica Maiora of Thomas Walsingham*, p. 251.

10 ibid., p. 216.

11 'Vita Ricardi Secundi', in McHardy, *The Reign of Richard II*, p. 116.

12 Walsingham, *The Chronica Maiora of Thomas Walsingham*, p. 217.

13 Hughes, *The Rise of Fourteenth-Century Alchemy in England*, p. 203.

14 Walsingham, *The Chronica Maiora of Thomas Walsingham*, p. 217.

15 'Westminster Chronicle', in McHardy, *The Reign of Richard II*, p. 81.

16 Henry Knighton, *Knighton's Chronicle, 1337–1396*, ed. and trans. G. H. Martin (Oxford: Clarendon Press, 1995), p. 335.

17 Walsingham, *The Chronica Maiora of Thomas Walsingham*, p. 224.

18 Saul, *Richard II*, p. 133.

19 'Vita Richardi Secundi', in McHardy, *The Reign of Richard II*, p. 124.

20 ibid., p. 127.

21 Saul, *Richard II*, p. 144.

22 Knighton, *Knighton's Chronicle*, pp. 336–8.

23 'Vita Ricardi Secundi', in McHardy, *The Reign of Richard II*, p. 128.

24 *PROME*, Richard II, October 1385.

25 Quoted in Helen Castor, *The Eagle and the Hart: The Tragedy of Richard II and Henry IV* (London: Allen Lane, 2024), p. 109.

26 Walsingham, *The Chronica Maiora of Thomas Walsingham*, p. 226.

25. *A Mirror for Kings*

1 Henry Knighton, *Knighton's Chronicle, 1337–1396*, ed. and trans. G. H. Martin (Oxford: Clarendon Press, 1995), p. 349.

2 Chris Given-Wilson, *Henry IV* (New Haven: Yale University Press, 2017), p. 41.

3 Thomas Walsingham, in Alison K. McHardy (ed. and trans), *The Reign of Richard II: From Minority to Tyranny, 1377–1397* (Manchester: Manchester University Press, 2012), p. 144.

4 *Calendar of Letter-Books of the City of London: Letter-Book H*, ed. Reginald R. Sharpe, (London, 1907), pp. 285–6, 288–9.

5 William Thorne, 'Chronica', in McHardy, *The Reign of Richard II*, p. 147.

6 Given-Wilson, *Henry IV*, p. 41.

7 *PROME*, Richard II, October 1386.

8 ibid.

9 ibid.

10 ibid.

11 Henry Knighton, in McHardy, *The Reign of Richard II*, p. 169.

12 Thomas Walsingham, in McHardy, *The Reign of Richard II*, p. 171.

13 'Westminster Chronicle', in McHardy, *The Reign of Richard II*, p. 171.

14 McHardy, *The Reign of Richard II*, pp. 181–2.

15 "Eulogium", in McHardy, *The Reign of Richard II*, p. 183.

16 'Westminster Chronicle', in McHardy, *The Reign of Richard II*, p. 191.

17 Knighton, *Knighton's Chronicle*, p. 419.

18 ibid.

19 ibid., pp. 421–425.

20 Thomas Walsingham, in McHardy, *The Reign of Richard II*, p. 197.

21 The original petition that was prepared for the 1388 parliament – probably before November 1387 – is at the National Archives; see C 65/47, m.8.

22 *PROME*, Richard II, February 1388.

23 Thomas Favent, quoted in *PROME*, 'Richard II: February 1388'.

24 *PROME*, Richard II, February 1388.

25 ibid.

26 ibid.

27 'Bishop Wakefield's Register', in McHardy, *The Reign of Richard II*, p. 220.

28 *PROME*, Richard II, February 1388.

29 ibid.

30 'Kirkstall Chronicle', in McHardy, *The Reign of Richard II*, p. 228.

31 ibid., p. 229.

32 Knighton, *Knighton's Chronicle*, p. 531.

33 Thomas Walsingham, in McHardy, *The Reign of Richard II*, p. 248.

26. Renaissance

1 For Richard's personality and an analysis over his lack of confidence, see an excellent argument by Alison K. McHardy, 'Richard II: A Personal Portrait', in *The Reign of Richard II*, ed. Gwilym Dodd (Stroud: Tempus, 2000), pp. 11–32.

2 Nigel Saul, *Richard II* (New Haven: Yale University Press, 1999), p. 238.

3 Sylvia Federico, 'The Chivalry of Richard II: 1381 and 1399', in Dodd, *The Reign of Richard II*, p. 52.

4 John Gower, *Confessio Amantis* (Cambridge University Library, MS Dd 8.19).

5 Marion Turner, *Chaucer: A European Life* (Princeton: Princeton University Press, 2019), pp. 384, 392.

6 Jean Froissart, in McHardy, *The Reign of Richard II*, p. 259.

7 Henry Knighton, *Knighton's Chronicle, 1337–1396*, ed. and trans. G. H. Martin (Oxford: Clarendon Press, 1995), p. 537.

8 I am grateful to Helen Castor's clear and detailed account of Richard's fallout and repair with the Londoners between 1390 and 1392; see Helen Castor, *The Eagle and the Hart: The Tragedy of Richard II and Henry IV* (London: Allen Lane, 2024), pp. 193–203.

9 *Calendar of Close Rolls, Richard II: Volume 4, 1389–1392*, ed. H. C. Maxwell Lyte (London, 1922), pp. 25–527. *British History Online.*

10 'Brut Chronicle', in McHardy, *The Reign of Richard II*, p. 269.

11 ibid., p. 271.

12 Anne of Bohemia died on 7 June 1394: 'Vita Ricardi Secundi', in McHardy, *The Reign of Richard II*, p. 255.

13 See Kristen L. Seaman, 'Anne of Bohemia and Her Struggle to Conceive', *Social History of Medicine*, vol. 29, no. 2 (2016), 224–44.

14 'Saint Alban's Chronicle', in McHardy, *The Reign of Richard II*, p. 286.

15 'Vita Ricardi Secundi', in McHardy, *The Reign of Richard II*, p. 255; TNA, E 364/36 rot.H.

16 'Vita Ricardi Secundi', in McHardy, *The Reign of Richard II*, p. 302.

17 'Issue of the Exchequer', in McHardy, *The Reign of Richard II*, p. 304.

18 Helen Carr, *The Red Prince: John of Gaunt, Duke of Lancaster* (London: Oneworld, 2021), pp. 204–15.

19 *PROME*, Richard II, September 1397.

20 Sylvia Huot, 'An Iconography of Trauma: The Fraught Identity of Charles VI in Its Literary and Cultural Context', *Digital Philology: A Journal of Medieval Cultures*, vol. 12, no. 1 (2023), 1–29; Robert Knecht, *The Valois: Kings of France 1328–1589* (London: Bloomsbury Academic, 2007), p. 57.

21 Anne Curry, 'Richard II and the War with France', in Dodd, *The Reign of Richard II*, p. 35.

22 *The Chronicle of Adam of Usk, 1377–1421*, ed. Chris Given-Wilson (Oxford: Oxford University Press, 1997), p. 103.

27. The Last Plantagenets

1 *Calendar of Close Rolls, Richard II: Volume 6, 1396–1399*, ed. A. E. Stamp (London, 1927), pp. 137–49, *British History Online*.

2 'Vita Ricardi Secundi', in *Chronicles of the Revolution*, ed. and trans. Chris Given-Wilson (Manchester: Manchester University Press, 1993), p. 54.

3 Walsingham, in *Chronicles of the Revolution*, p. 72.

4 *Close Rolls, Richard II*: July 1397, pp. 137–149.

5 'Vita Ricardi Secundi', in *Chronicles of the Revolution*, p. 55.

6 Nigel Saul, *Richard II* (New Haven: Yale University Press, 1999), p. 404.

7 *PROME*, Richard II, September 1397.

8 ibid.

9 Gloucester was probably killed on 8 September, nine days before the opening of parliament.

10 *PROME*, Richard II, September 1397.

11 ibid.; 'Eulogium', in *Chronicles of the Revolution*, p. 67.

12 Chris Given-Wilson, 'Richard II, Edward II, and the Lancastrian Inheritance', *English Historical Review*, vol. 109, no. 432 (1994), 553–71, 554.

13 *Chronique de la traïson et mort de Richart II, Roy d'Angleterre* (1846), ed. Benjamin Williams, p. 19; Chris Given-Wilson, *Henry IV* (New Haven: Yale University Press, 2017), p. 114.

14 Given-Wilson, *Henry IV*, p. 122.

15 Tim Thornton, 'Cheshire: The Inner Citadel of Richard's kingdom?', in Dodd, *The Reign of Richard II*, p. 94.

16 British Library, MS Harley 1319.

17 'Jean Creton', in Given-Wilson, *Chronicles of the Revolution*, p. 150.

18 'Adam of Usk', in Given-Wilson, *Chronicles of the Revolution*, p. 161.

19 *Chronique de la traïson et mort de Richart II, Roy d'Angleterre* (1846), ed Benjamin Williams, p. 62.

20 'Dieulacres Chronicle', Given-Wilson, *Chronicles of the Revolution*, p. 155.

21 The 'Record and Process', in Given-Wilson, *Chronicles of the Revolution*, pp. 168–89.

22 Given-Wilson, *Henry IV*, p. 143.

23 English had been used at court since 1362, when it became the compul-
    sory language of oral communication in royal and seigniorial courts – not
    ecclesiastical, which remained in Latin. But the first recorded reference
    of a monarch using English in a formal declaration was in 1399 with
    the accession of Henry IV; see W. Mark Ormrod, 'The Use of English
    Language, Law and Political Culture in Fourteenth-Century England',
    Speculum, vol. 78 (2003), 750; Given-Wilson, *Henry IV*, p. 144.

Note on Sources

Historians working today are blessed by the number of records that have now been digitised, mostly governmental records held at the National Archives in Kew. The most useful of these are the rolls of the royal chancery, which recorded copies of the various types of letters sent out from the king. They are known as the Chancery Rolls. Many of these have been translated and published in English and are widely available through, particularly, *British History Online*. Among them are the Parliament Rolls of Medieval England – the formal record of all parliaments held since the reign of Edward I.

The full list of sources I have used are outlined in my bibliography. In order to gain some insight into the lives and feelings of regular folk I have relied on the digitised collection of wills, the *Calendar of Wills Proved and Enrolled in the Court of Husting, London*, which is also available on *British History Online*.

The Gascon Rolls Project, which contains records from the government in Aquitaine, as well as *The People of 1381 Project*, have been incredibly useful databases that also include digitised records.

Other records have been printed. *Northern Petitions*, edited by Constance Fraser, containing the plights and pleas of people living in the north of England over the course of the Scottish Wars of Independence, has been particularly useful to me. Like wills, I find petitions a useful source for the experiences of the general populace – petitions are also an excellent way of accessing voice, as one of the few sources available to historians that *can* contain direct speech or oration from women. I have found other petitions in the National Archives as part of the *SC8 Ancient Petitions Series*. Most non-digitised or non-printed sources like these have come from the National Archives, including the wardrobe accounts of Edward II, Edward III and Richard II. References to manuscripts have mostly come from the fine collection of medieval manuscripts held by the British Library.

Much of the 'colour' of what we know of the fourteenth century comes thanks to the surviving chronicle accounts of the period. Chroniclers were contemporary historians, mostly non-secular (belonging to the Church), living as monks and working out of a scriptorium, such as Thomas Walsingham, author of *The Saint Alban's Chronicle: The Chronica Maiora of Thomas Walsingham* and *Historia Anglicana*. Occasionally this changes and we have chroniclers who are attached to members of the royal court, such as Jean Froissart, or are even soldiers, like Thomas Gray, the author of *Scalacronica*. These men recorded events of their time as well as their own views of the past. One example would be the *Brut* chronicle, which begins its chronology with the settling of Britain by Brutus and the latter tales of King Arthur. It is a collection of prose chronicles, used since the fifteenth century as the main account of English history. Although chronicles can shed light and detail on events of the fourteenth century that administrative records cannot, these accounts are often flawed. Based on hearsay and written to fit personal, political or religious agendas, chronicles offer a biased view of the period and as a result these chronicles should sometimes be taken with a pinch of salt. It is not uncommon for a chronicler to exaggerate their account or even make blind assertions for the sake of a good yarn. Yet various narratives are often corroborated by other chronicles, which offers valuable insight and makes these stories a crucial source in a medieval historian's arsenal and have been consulted liberally and joyfully over the course of this book.

Of the modern literature on the kings and other characters in this book, a foolproof starting point has been the *Oxford Dictionary of National Biography*, available online through most libraries. The *Yale English Monarchs* series has also been essential reading, providing biographies of the four kings who straddle the fourteenth century. Books that I have returned to time and time again, deserving special attention, are the collected primary sources on the Black Death edited by Rosemary Horrox, R. B. Dobson's edited volume of sources on the Peasants' Revolt, as well as Chris Given-Wilson's *Chronicles of the Revolution* and A. K. McHardy's volume of sources on the reign of Richard II. Other influential books are Marion Turner's splendid

Chaucer: A European Life, which has influenced my take on the four-teenth century. I have equally relied on Helen Castor's *Eagle and the Hart: The Tragedy of Richard II and Henry IV*, for her unpicking of complex politics and power structures in the second part of the four-teenth century. The *Fourteenth Century England* series are volumes of essays penned by some of the best medieval historians of our time. These collections have been immensely useful, offering valuable insight into the people and politics of the fourteenth century.

These sources are a handful of many that have informed my understanding of the fourteenth century. An exhaustive list, as well as the full details of those mentioned above, can be found in my bibliography.

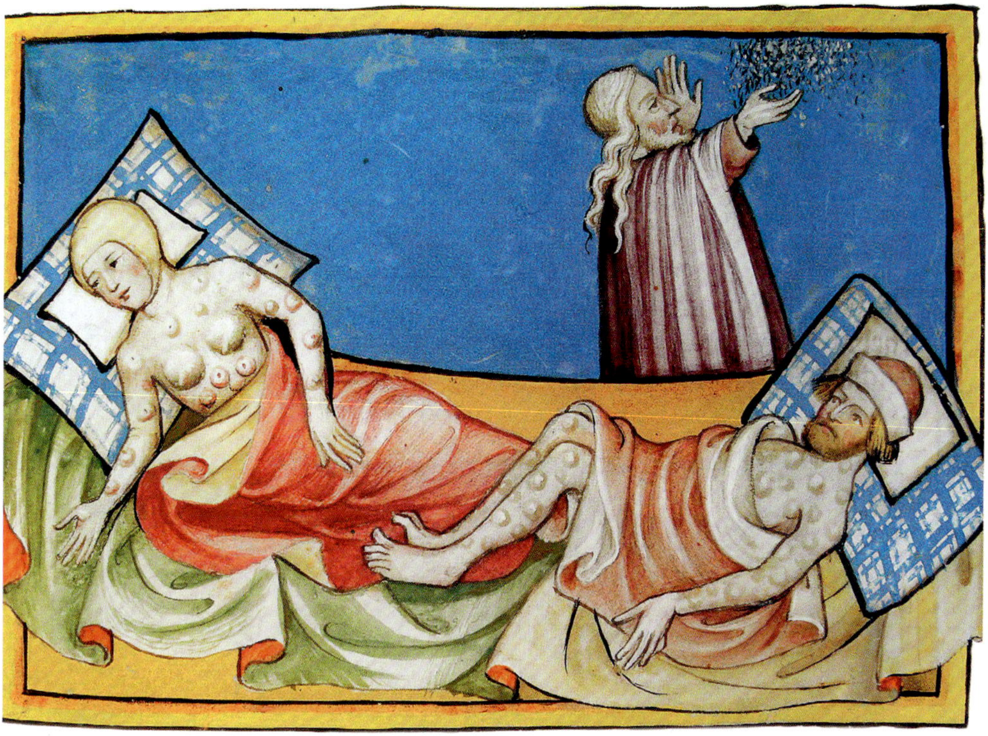

16. Victims of the bubonic plague, otherwise known as the Black Death, depicted in the *Toggenburg Bible*.

17. The execution of Hugh Despenser the Younger at Hereford in Jean Froissart's *Chronicles*.

18. The Battle of Crécy, as depicted in Jean Froissart's *Chronicles*.

13. The Wilton Diptych showing the child Richard II and his army of angels wearing his badge, the White Hart.

14. The coronation chair commissioned by Edward I *c.*1297 to house the Stone of Scone, Westminster Abbey.

15. The Wheel of Fortune from the *Holkham Bible*, *c.*1320-30, a common textual symbol in the fourteenth century.

7. The Angers Apocalypse Tapestry commissioned by Louis I of Anjou. The tapestries were so large they had to be displayed outdoors.

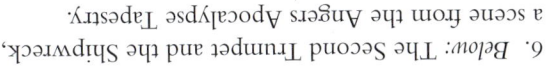
5. *Left:* Richard II at the zenith of his kingship enthroned in majesty, c.1390s.

6. *Below:* The Second Trumpet and the Shipwreck, a scene from the Angers Apocalypse Tapestry.

4. Edward III granting Edward the Black Prince the dukedom of Aquitaine and Gascony, wearing the quartered arms of England and France, inside a historiated initial E.

12. The tomb of Edward, the Black Prince, fully armed in plate of war, at Canterbury Cathedral.

10. The Stone of Scone, Scotland's coronation stone stolen by Edward I in 1296 and kept beneath the coronation chair at Westminster until 1996.

11. A fourteenth-century astrolabe, 'thou maist turnen [it] up and doun as thyself liketh' (you may turn it up and down however you like).

8. *Above:* Isabella of France meeting her brother Charles IV in 1325, depicted in Jean Froissart's *Chronicles*.

9. *Right:* The tomb effigy of Philippa of Hainault, queen of England and wife of Edward III.

1. A contemporary image of King Edward I (otherwise known as 'Edward Longshanks') from Westminster Abbey.

3. The official charter granting Piers Gaveston the earldom of Cornwall in 1307, as indicated by the black Cornish choughs decorating the margins and his arms being linked with the royal coat of arms above.

2. A contemporary image of King Edward II receiving his crown, possibly at his coronation. From this point onwards, Edward's reign was riddled with conflict between the king and his nobles.

Bibliography

Archives

The Bodleian Library, Oxford.
The British Library, London.
The National Archives, London.
The Parker Library, Corpus Christi College, Cambridge University.

Calendars, Online and Printed

Calendar of Close Rolls, vols. 4-6, *British History Online*.
Calendar of Documents Relating to Scotland Preserved in Her Majesty's Public Record Office, London, vols. 2–4, ed. Joseph Bain (Edinburgh: H. M. General Register House, 1881–8).
Calendar of the Fine Rolls Preserved in the Public Record Office, vol. 3, *Edward II A.D. 1319–1327* (London: Her Majesty's Stationery Office, 1911).
Calendar of Papal Registers Relating to Great Britain and Ireland, vols. 2–5, ed. W. H. Bliss, *British History Online*.
Calendar of Patent Rolls, vols. 1–6, *British History Online*.
Calendar of the Plea and Memoranda Rolls of the City of London, vol. 1, *1323–1364*, ed. A. H. Thomas (London, 1926), *British History Online*, british-history. ac.uk/plea-memoranda-rolls/vol1.
Calendar of Wills Proved and Enrolled in the Court of Husting, London: Part 1, 1258–1358, ed. R. R. Sharpe (London, 1889), *British History Online*, british-history.ac.uk/court-husting-wills/vol1.
Parliament Rolls of Medieval England, eds. Chris Given-Wilson, Paul Brand, Seymour Phillips, Mark Ormrod, Geoffrey Martin, Anne Curry, Rosemary Horrox (Woodbridge, 2005), *British History Online*, british-history. ac.uk/no-series/parliament-rolls-medieval.

Chronicles

The Anonimalle Chronicle 1307 to 1334: From Brotherton Collection MS 29, eds. Wendy R. Childs and John Taylor (Cambridge: Cambridge University Press, 2013).

The Anonimalle Chronicle, 1333 to 1381, from a MSS Written at St Mary's Abbey, York and now in the Possession of Lieut. Col. Sir William Ingleby, Bart., eds. V. H. Galbraith and William Ingleby (Manchester: Manchester University Press, 1927).

The Black Death, ed. and trans. Rosemary Horrox (Manchester: Manchester University Press, 1994).

'Bohemian Chronicle', *Die Königssaaler Geschichtsquellen*, ed. Johann Loserth, in *Fontes herum Austricarum, Scriptores VIII* (Vienna, 1875).

The Brut, or, The Chronicles of England, ed. Friedrich W. D. Brie (London: Kegan Paul, Trench, Trübner, for the Early English Text Society, 1906).

Chandos Herald, *Life of the Black Prince*, eds. Mildred Katharine Pope and Eleanor Constance Lodge (Oxford: Clarendon Press, 1910).

The Chronicle of Adam of Usk, 1377–1421, ed. Chris Given-Wilson (Oxford: Oxford University Press, 1997).

The Chronicle of Geoffrey le Baker, trans. David Preest, intro. and notes Richard Barber (Woodbridge: Boydell & Brewer, 2018).

The Chronicle of Lanercost, 1272–1346, ed. and trans. Henry Maxwell (Glasgow: J. Maclehose, 1913).

Chronicles of the Mayors and Sheriffs of London 1188–1274, ed. Henry T. Riley (London: Trübner, 1863).

The Chronicle of Pierre de Langtoft: In French Verse from the Earliest Period to the Death of King Edward I, 2 vols, ed. Thomas Wright (London: Longmans, Green, Reader and Dyer, 1866).

Chronicles of the Reigns of Edward I and Edward II, vol. 1, *Annales Londonienses and Annales Paulini*, ed. William Stubbs (London: Longman, 1882).

Chronicles of the Revolution, 1397–1400: The Reign of Richard II, ed. and trans. Chris Given-Wilson (Manchester: Manchester University Press, 1993).

The Chronicle of William de Rishanger of the Barons' War: The Miracles of Simon de Montfort, ed. James Halliwell-Phillips (London: Printed for the Camden Society by J. B. Nichols and Son, 1840).

Froissart, Jean, *Chronicles of England, France, Spain, and the Adjoining Countries, from the Latter Part of the Reign of Edward II to the Coronation of Henry IV*, trans. Thomas Johnes (London: W. Smith, 1844).

Gray, Thomas, *Scalacronica* (Cambridge, Corpus Christi College, MS 133).

Gray, Thomas, *Scalacronica (1272–1363)*, ed. and trans. Andy King, Publications of the Surtees Society, 209 (Woodbridge: Boydell & Brewer, 2005).

Holinshed, Raphael, *Holinshed's Chronicles of England, Scotland and Ireland*, vol. 6, ed. Henry Ellis (London: J. Johnson et al., 1807).

Knighton, Henry, *Knighton's Chronicle, 1337–1396*, ed. and trans. G. H. Martin (Oxford: Clarendon Press, 1996).

López de Ayala, Pero, *Chronicle of King Pedro*, vols. 1–3, trans. Lord Berners, sel., ed. and intro. Gillian and William Anderson (Liverpool University Press, 1963).

McHardy, Alison K. (ed. and trans.), *The Reign of Richard III: From Minority to Tyranny, 1377–97* (Manchester: Manchester University Press, 2012).

Murimuth, Adam, *Continuatio Chronicarum: Robertus de Avesbury de Gestis Mirabilibus Regis Edwardi Tertii*, ed. Edmund Maunde Thompson (Cambridge: Cambridge University Press, 2012).

Paris, Matthew, *Flores Historiarum*, vol. III (London: Eyre & Spottiswoode, 1890), p. 324.

The Peasants' Revolt of 1381, ed. and trans. R. B. Dobson (London and Basingstoke: Palgrave MacMillan, 1970).

Trokelowe, John de, and Henry Blaneforde, *Chronica et Annales*, ed. Henry T. Riley (London: Longmans, Green, Reader and Dyer, 1866).

The True Chronicles of Jean Le Bel, 1290–1360, trans. Nigel Bryant (Woodbridge: Boydell Press, 2011).

Vita Edwardi Secundi: The Life of Edward the Second, ed. and trans. Wendy R. Childs (Oxford: Clarendon Press, 2005).

Walsingham, Thomas, *The Chronica Maiora of Thomas Walsingham, 1376–1422*, trans. David Preest, intro. and notes James G. Clark (Woodbridge: Boydell Press, 2005).

Other Primary Sources

An Inventory of the Historical Monuments in London, vol. 1, Westminster Abbey (London, 1924).

Ayloffe, J., 'XLIII. An Account of the Body of King Edward the First, as It Appeared on Opening His Tomb in the Year 1774. By Sir Joseph Ayloffe, Bart. V.P.S.A. and F.R.S.', *Archaeologia*, vol. 3 (1775), 376–413.

Blackley, F. D., and G. Hermansen (eds.), *The Household Book of Queen Isabella of England, for the Fifth Regnal Year of Edward II, 8th July 1311 to 7th July 1312*, The University of Alberta, Classical and Historical Studies, vol. 1 (Edmonton: University of Alberta Press, 1971).

Boccaccio, Giovanni, *Decameron*, a new English version by Cormac Ó Cuilleanáin, based on John Payne's 1886 translation (Hertfordshire: Wordsworth Classics of World Literature, 2004).

Chaplais, Pierre (ed.), *The War of Saint-Sardos (1323–1325): Gascon Correspondence, and Diplomatic Documents* (London: Offices of the Royal Historical Society, 1954).

Chaucer, Geoffrey, 'The Nun's Priest's Prologue and Tale', in *The Canterbury Tales: A Selection* (London: Penguin Classics, 1996).

Chaucer, Geoffrey, *A Treatise on the Astrolabe*, ed. Walter W. Skeat (Amsterdam: Meridian, 1978).

Colvin, H. M. (ed.), *The History of the King's Works, Middle Ages*, vol. I (London: Her Majesty's Stationery Office, 1963).

Davies, James Conway, 'The First Journal of Edward II's Chamber', *English Historical Review*, vol. 30, no. 120 (1915), 662–80.

Devon, Frederick (ed.), *Issues of the Exchequer: Being a Collection of Payments Made out of His Majesty's Revenue, from King Henry III to King Henry VI Inclusive* (London: J. Murray, 1837).

Fraser, C. M. (ed.), *Northern Petitions Illustrative of Life in Berwick, Cumbria and Durham in the Fourteenth Century*, 194 (London: Surtees Society, 1981).

Gower, John, *Confessio Amantis* (Cambridge University Library, MS Dd 8.19).

Harper-Bill, Christopher (ed.), *The Cartulary of the Augustinian Friars of Clare* (Woodbridge: Published for the Suffolk Records Society by the Boydell Press, 1991).

Hippocrates, *The Genuine Works of Hippocrates*, vol. 1, trans. Francis Adams (London: Printed for the Sydenham Society, 1849).

Inventaire sommaire des archives départementales antérieures à 1790, Gironde, Archives ecclésiastiques, Série G (Nos 1 à 920): Inventaire des Fonds de l'Archevêché et du chapitre métropolitain de Bordeaux, vol. 1 (Bordeaux: G. Gounouilhou, 1892).

Liechtenstein, von, *Frauendienst*, trans. J. W. Thomas, intro. Kelly DeVries (Woodbridge: Boydell Press, 2004).

Logan, F. Donald (ed.), *The Register of Simon Sudbury, Archbishop of Canterbury, 1375–1381* (Woodbridge: Boydell Press, 2020).

William Newburgh, *The History of William of Newburgh, The Chronicles of Robert de Monte* (United Kingdom: Seeleys, 1856).

Nicolas, N. H., 'I. Observations on the Institution of the Most Noble Order of the Garter. By Sir Nicholas Harris Nicolas, G.C.M.G., addressed to Hudson Gurney, Esq., F.R.S., Vice-President; illustrated by the Accounts of the Great Wardrobe of King Edward the Third, from the 29th of September 1344 to the 1st of August 1345; and again from the 21st of December 1345 to the 31st of January 1349', *Archaeologia*, vol. 31 (1846), 1–163.

Raine, James (ed.), *Historical Papers and Letters from the Northern Registers* (London: Longman, 1873).

Riley, Henry Thomas (ed. and trans.), *Memorials of London and London Life in the XIIIth, XIVth, and IVth Centuries: Being a Series of Extracts, Local, Social,* and Political, from the Early Archives of the City of London, A.D. 1276–1419 (London: Longmans, 1868).

Rymer, T. (ed.), *Rymer's Foedera* (London, 1739–45), *British History Online*, www.british-history.ac.uk/rymer-foedera.

Stanley, A. P., *Historical Memorials of Canterbury: The Landing of Augustine, the Murder of Becket, Edward the Black Prince*, 10th edn (London: J. Murray, 1909).

Twysden, Roger (ed.), *Historiae Anglicanae Scriptores X* (London, 1652).

Secondary Sources

Aberth, John (ed.), *The Black Death: The Great Mortality of 1348–1350: A Brief History with Documents* (London: St Martin's Press, 2005).

Adler, Gillian, and Paul Strohm, *Alle Thyng Hath Tyme: Time and Medieval Life* (London: Reaktion Books, 2023).

Aston, Margaret, 'John Wycliffe's Reformation Reputation', *Past & Present*, no. 30 (1965), 23–51.

Bailey, Mark, *After the Black Death: Economy, Society and the Law in Fourteenth-Century England* (Oxford: Oxford University Press, 2021).

Barber, Richard, 'Edward III's Arthurianisms Re-visited: Perceforest in the Context of Philippa of Hainault and the Round Table Feast of 1344', in Elizabeth Archibald and David F. Johnson (eds.), *Arthurian Literature* (Woodbridge: Boydell & Brewer, 2013).

Barber, Richard, *Prince of Wales and Aquitaine: A Biography of the Black Prince* (Woodbridge: Boydell Press, 1978).

Barber, Richard, 'The Round Table Feast of 1344', in Julian Munby, Richard Barber and Richard Brown (eds.), *Edward III's Round Table at Windsor* (Woodbridge: Boydell Press, 2007).

Bartlett, Robert, *The Making of Europe: Conquest, Colonization and Cultural Change, 950–1350* (London: Allen Lane, 1993).

Barker, Jessica, Graeme McArthur and Emily Pegues, ' "Fully Armed in Plate of War": Making the Effigy of the Black Prince', *Burlington Magazine*, vol. 163, no. 1424 (2021), 996–1007.

Belich, James, *The World the Plague Made: The Black Death and the Rise of Europe* (Princeton: Princeton University Press, 2022).

Bengry, Justin, 'Can and Should We Queer the Past?', in *What Is History, Now?*, ed. Helen Carr and Suzannah Lipscomb (London: W&N, 2021).

Bennett, Judith M., *Ale, Beer, and Brewsters in England: Women's Work in a Changing World, 1300–1600* (Oxford: Oxford University Press, 1999).

Bennett, Judith M., *Women in the Medieval English Countryside: Gender and Household in Brigstock before the Plague* (Oxford: Oxford University Press, 1987).

Bennett, Michael, *Richard II and the Revolution of 1399* (Stroud: Sutton Publishing, 1999).

Bennett, Philip E., Sarah Carpenter and Louise Gardiner, 'Chivalric Games at the Court of Edward III: The Jousting Letters of EUL MS 183', *Medium Ævum*, vol. 87, no. 2 (2018), 304–42.

Binski, Paul, 'The Painted Chamber at Westminster and Its Documentation', *Walpole Society*, vol. 83 (2021), 1–68.

Binski, Paul, *Westminster Abbey and the Plantagenets: Kingship and the Representation of Power, 1200–1400* (New Haven: Yale University Press, 1995).

Booker, Sparky, 'Intermarriage in Fifteenth-Century Ireland: The English and Irish in the "Four Obedient Shires"', *Proceedings of the Royal Irish Academy. Section C: Archaeology, Celtic Studies, History, Linguistics, Literature*, vol. 113C (2013), 219–250.

Bothwell, James, 'An Emotional Pragmatism: Edward III and Death', in Gwilym Dodd and Craig Taylor (eds.), *Monarchy, State and Political Culture in Late Medieval England: Essays in Honour of W. Mark Ormrod* (York: York Medieval Press, 2020), 39–70.

Briggs, Chris, 'Empowered or Marginalized? Rural Women and Credit in Later Thirteenth- and Fourteenth-Century England', *Continuity and Change*, vol. 19, no. 1 (2004), 13–43.

Brown, Elizabeth A. R., and Nancy Freeman Regaldo, 'Universitas et communitas: The Parade of the Parisians at the Pentecost Feast of 1313', in Kathleen Ashley (ed.), *Moving Object: Processional Performance in the Middle Ages and the Renaissance* (Amsterdam: Rodopi, 2001), 117–54.

Brown, Michael, *Bannockburn: The Scottish War and the British Isles, 1307–1323* (Edinburgh: Edinburgh University Press, 2008).

Bruce, Mark P., and Katherine H. Terrell (eds.), *The Anglo-Scottish Border and the Shaping of Identity, 1300–1600* (London: Palgrave Macmillan, 2012).

Bullock-Davies, Constance, 'Lanval and Avalon', *Bulletin of the Board of Celtic Studies*, vol. 23, no. 2 (1969), 128–42.

Burt, Caroline, and Richard Partington, *Arise, England: Six Kings and the Making of the English State* (London: Faber & Faber, 2024).

Bury Palliser, Mrs, *Historic Devices, Badges, and War-cries* (London: Sampson Low, Son & Marston, 1870).

Campbell, Bruce, *The Great Transition: Climate, Disease and Society in the Late Medieval World* (Cambridge: Cambridge University Press, 2016).

Capwell, Tobias, *Arms and Armour of the Medieval Joust* (Leeds: Royal Armouries Museum, 2018).

Carey, Hilary M., *Courting Disaster: Astrology at the English Court and University in the Later Middle Ages* (London: Palgrave Macmillan, 1992).

Carr, Helen, *The Red Prince: John of Gaunt, Duke of Lancaster* (London: Oneworld, 2021).

Castor, Helen, *She-Wolves: The Women Who Ruled England Before Elizabeth* (London: Faber & Faber, 2011).

Castor, Helen, *The Eagle and the Hart: The Tragedy of Richard II and Henry IV* (London: Allen Lane, 2024).

Coley, David K., *Death and the Pearl Maiden: Plague, Poetry, England* (Columbus: Ohio State University Press, 2019).

Cornelius, Ian, 'Gower and the Peasants' Revolt', *Representations*, vol. 131, no. 1 (2015), 22–51.

Cox, R., 'Women on the Edge: The de Clare sisters and the Marches of Wales in the Early Fourteenth Century' (unpublished PhD thesis, University of Bristol, 2024).

Crooks, Peter, David Green and W. Mark Ormrod (eds.), *The Plantagenet Empire, 1259–1453: Proceedings of the 2014 Harlaxton Symposium* (Donington: Shaun Tyas, 2016).

Dixon, M. C., 'The Knightly Families of Northumberland: A Crisis in the Early Fourteenth Century' (Masters thesis, Durham University, 2000).

Dodd, Gwilym, 'A Parliament Full of Rats? *Piers Plowman* and the Good Parliament of 1376', *Historical Research*, vol. 79, no. 203 (2006), 21–49.

Dodd, Gwilym, *Justice and Grace: Private Petitioning and the English Parliament in the Late Middle Ages* (Oxford: Oxford University Press, 2007).

Dodd, Gwilym (ed.), *The Reign of Richard II* (Stroud: Tempus, 2000).

Dodd, Gwilym and Anthony Musson (eds.), *The Reign of Edward II: New Perspectives* (York: York University Press, 2006).

Doherty, Paul, *Isabella and the Strange Death of Edward II* (London: Constable and Robinson, 2003).

Dryburgh, Paul, 'The Career of Roger Mortimer, First Earl of March (c.1287– 1330)' (PhD thesis, University of Bristol, 2002).

Estow, Clara, *Pedro the Cruel of Castile 1350–1369* (Leiden: E. J. Brill, 1995).

Falk, Seb, *The Light Ages: A Medieval Journey of Discovery* (London: Allen Lane, 2020).

Febvre, Lucien, *A Geographical Introduction to History*, trans. E. G. Mountford and J. H. Paxton (London: Routledge, 1996).

Federico, Sylvia, 'The Imaginary Society: Women in 1381', *Journal of British Studies*, vol. 40, no. 2 (2001), 159–83.

Fourteenth Century England, vols. I–XII (Woodbridge: Boydell Press, 2000–2022).

Fryde, Natalie, *The Tyranny and Fall of Edward II: 1321–1326* (Cambridge: Cambridge University Press, 1979).

Given-Wilson, Chris, 'Edward, the Black Prince, and Bertrand du Guesclin, Constable of France: Chivalry and Rivalry in Life and Death', in J. A. Lutkin and J. S. Hamilton (eds.), *Creativity, Contradictions and Commemoration in the Reign of Richard II: Essays in Honour of Nigel Saul* (Woodbridge: Boydell & Brewer, 2022), 221–34.

Given-Wilson, Chris, *Henry IV* (New Haven: Yale University Press, 2016).

Given-Wilson, Chris, 'Richard II, Edward II, and the Lancastrian Inheritance', *English Historical Review*, vol. 109, no. 432 (1994), 553–71.

Green, David, *Edward the Black Prince: Power in Medieval Europe* (Harlow: Pearson/Longman, 2007).

Green, David, *The Hundred Years War: A People's History* (New Haven: Yale University Press, 2015).

Green, Mary Anne Everett, *Lives of the Princesses of England*, vol. 3 (London: Longman, 1857).

Green, Monica, 'The Four Black Deaths', *American Historical Review*, vol. 125, no. 5 (2020), 1601–31.

Haines, Roy Martin, 'Sumptuous Apparel for a Royal Prisoner: Archbishop Melton's Letter, 14 January 1330', *English Historical Review*, vol. 124, no. 509 (2009), 885–94.

Hanawalt, Barbara A., *Of Good and Ill Repute: Gender and Social Control in Medieval England* (Oxford: Oxford University Press, 1998).

Hanawalt, Barbara A., *The Wealth of Wives: Women, Law, and the Economy in Late Medieval London* (Oxford: Oxford University Press, 2007).

Hanley, Catherine, *Two Houses, Two Kingdoms: A History of France and England, 1100–1300* (New Haven: Yale University Press, 2023).

Harvey, L. P, *Islamic Spain: 1250–1500* (Chicago: University of Chicago Press, 1990).

Harwood, Sophie, *Medieval Women and War: Female Roles in the Old French Tradition* (London: Bloomsbury Academic, 2020).

Heffran, Matthew, 'Edward III's Household Knights and the Crécy Campaign of 1346', *Historical Research*, vol. 92, no. 255 (2019), 24–49.

Heffran, Matthew, *The Household Knights of Edward III: Warfare, Politics and Kingship in Fourteenth-Century England* (Woodbridge: Boydell Press, 2021).

Heyam, Kit, *The Reputation of Edward II, 1307–1697* (Amsterdam: Amsterdam University Press, 2020).

Higham, Nicholas J., *King Arthur: The Making of a Legend* (New Haven: Yale University Press, 2018).

Holmes, G. A., 'Judgement on the Younger Despenser, 1326', *English Historical Review*, vol. 70, no. 275 (1955), 261–7.

Holmes, G. A., 'A Protest against the Despensers, 1326', *Speculum*, vol. 30, no. 2 (1955), 207–12.

Horrox, Rosemary, and W. Mark Ormrod, *A Social History of England, 1200–1500* (Cambridge: Cambridge University Press, 2006).

Hudson, Anne (ed.), *Selections from English Wycliffe Writings* (Cambridge: Cambridge University Press, 1978).

Hughes, Jonathan, *The Rise of Fourteenth-Century Alchemy in England: Plantagenet Kings and the Search for the Philosopher's Stone* (London: Continuum, 2012).

Huot, Sylvia, 'An Iconography of Trauma: The Fraught Identity of Charles VI in Its Literary and Cultural Context', *Digital Philology: A Journal of Medieval Cultures*, vol. 12, no. 1 (2023), 1–29.

Jones, Dan, *The Plantagenets: The Kings Who Made England* (London: William Collins, 2012).

Jones, Michael, *The Black Prince* (London: Head of Zeus, 2017).

Jones, Sarah Rees, 'Women and Citizenship in Later Medieval York', in Deborah Simonton (ed.), *The Routledge History Handbook of Gender and the Urban Experience* (London: Routledge, 2017).

Jordan, William Chester, *The Great Famine: Northern Europe in the Early Fourteenth Century* (Princeton: Princeton University Press, 1998).

Kane, Bronach C., *Popular Memory and Gender in Medieval England: Men, Women, and Testimony in the Church Courts, c.1200–1500* (Woodbridge: Boydell Press, 2019).

Kane, Bronach, and Fiona Williamson (eds.), *Women, Agency and the Law, 1300–1700* (London: Pickering & Chatto, 2013).

Kershaw, Ian, 'The Great Famine and Agrarian Crisis in England 1315–22', *Past & Present*, no. 59 (1973), 3–50.

King, Andy, *Sir Thomas Gray: Scalacronica (1272–1363)*, Publications of the Surtees Society, 209 (Woodbridge: Boydell Press, 2005).

King, Andy, and Michael Penman (eds.), *England and Scotland in the Fourteenth Century: New Perspectives* (Woodbridge: Boydell Press, 2007).

Knecht, Robert, *The Valois: Kings of France 1328–1589* (London: Bloomsbury Academic, 2007).

Le Patourel, John, 'The Treaty of Brétigny, 1360', *Transactions of the Royal Historical Society*, vol. 10 (1960).

Lethaby, W. R., 'English Primitives: The Painted Chamber and the Early Masters of the Westminster School', *Burlington Magazine for Connoisseurs*, vol. 7, no. 28 (1905), 257–69.

Lieberman, Max, *The Medieval March of Wales: The Creation and Perception of a Frontier, 1066–1283* (Cambridge: Cambridge University Press, 2010).

Livingstone, Michael, and Kelly DeVries (eds.), *The Battle of Crécy: A Casebook* (Liverpool Liverpool University Press, 2015).

McDougall, Sarah, 'The Opposite of the Double Standard: Gender, Marriage, and Adultery Prosecution in Late Medieval France', *Journal of the History of Sexuality*, vol. 23, no. 2, (2014), 206–25.

MacInnes, Iain A., *Scotland's Second War of Independence 1332–1357* (Woodbridge: Boydell Press, 2016).

McHardy, Alison K. (ed. and trans), *The Reign of Richard II: From Minority to Tyranny, 1377–1397* (Manchester: Manchester University Press, 2012).

McKisack, May, *The Fourteenth Century 1307–1399* (Oxford: Clarendon Press, 1963).

McLaughlin, Megan, 'The Woman Warrior: Gender, Warfare and Society in Medieval Europe', *Women's Studies*, vol. 17, nos. 3–4 (1990), 193–209.

McLaughlin, Rhian Elizabeth, 'Gentry Perceptions of Violence in Fourteenth-Century England' (PhD thesis, University of York, 2014).

McNamee, Colm, *The Wars of the Bruces: Scotland, England and Ireland 1306–1328* (East Linton: Tuckwell Press, 1997).

Maddicott, J. R., *Thomas of Lancaster, 1307–1322: A Study in the Reign of Edward II* (Oxford: Oxford University Press, 1970).

Mitchell, Shelagh, 'Ladies of the Garter: Edward III; Richard II; Elizabeth II', *Court Historian*, vol. 22, no. 2 (2017), 151–67.

Moisant, Joseph, *Le Prince Noir en Aquitaine 1355–1356, 1362–1370* (Paris: A. Picard et fils, 1894).

Morris, Marc, *A Great and Terrible King: Edward I and the Forging of Britain* (London: Windmill Books, 2008).

Mortimer, Ian, *Medieval Horizons: Why the Middle Ages Matter* (London: The Bodley Head, 2023).

Mortimer, Ian, 'Sermons of Sodomy: A Reconsideration of Edward II's Sodomitical Reputation', in Gwilym Dodd and Anthony Musson (eds.), *The Reign of Edward II: New Perspectives* (York: York University Press, 2006), 48–60.

Munby, Julian, Richard Barber and Richard Brown, *Edward III's Round Table at Windsor* (Woodbridge: Boydell Press, 2007).

Neville, Cynthia J., *Violence, Custom and Law: The Anglo-Scottish Border Lands in the Later Middle Ages* (Edinburgh: Edinburgh University Press, 1998).

Newton, Stella Mary, *Fashion in the Age of the Black Prince: A Study of the Years 1340–1365* (Woodbridge: Boydell Press, 1980).

Nicholson, Ranald, 'The Siege of Berwick, 1333', *Scottish Historical Review*, vol. 40, no. 129 (1961), 19–42.

O'Hear, Natasha, 'The Angers Apocalypse Tapestry: A Fourteenth-Century Walking Tour of the Book of Revelation', in *Contrasting Images of the Book of Revelation in Late Medieval and Early Modern Art: A Case Study in Visual Exegesis* (Oxford: Oxford Theological Monographs, 2011), 43–68.

Orme, Nicholas, *Going to Church in Medieval England* (New Haven: Yale University Press, 2021).

Ormrod, W. Mark, *Edward III* (New Haven: Yale University Press, 2013).

Ormrod, W. Mark, 'The Foundation and Early Development of the Order of the Garter in England, 1348–1399', *Frühmittelalterliche Studien*, vol. 50, no. 1 (2016), 361–92.

Ormrod, W. Mark, 'The Trials of Alice Perrers', *Speculum,* vol. 83, no. 2 (2008), 366–96.

Ormrod, W. Mark, 'The Use of English Language, Law and Political Culture in Fourteenth-Century England', *Speculum,* vol. 78, no. 3 (2003), 750–87.

Ormrod, W. Mark, *Winner and Waster and Its Contexts: Chivalry, Law and Economics in Fourteenth-Century England* (Cambridge: D. S. Brewer, 2021).

Ormrod, W. Mark, Gwilym Dodd and Anthony Musson (eds.), *Medieval Petitions: Grace and Grievance* (Woodbridge: Boydell & Brewer, 2009).

Orsten, E. M., 'The Ambiguities in Langland's Rat Parliament', *Mediaeval Studies*, vol. 23 (1961), 216–39.

Pajic, Milan, *Flemish Textile Workers in England, 1331–1400: Immigration, Integration and Economic Development* (Cambridge: Cambridge University Press, 2023).

Pearl, trans. Simon Armitage (London: Faber & Faber, 2017).

Pegg, Mark Gregory, *Beatrice's Last Smile: A New History of the Middle Ages* (Oxford: Oxford University Press, 2023).

Penman, Michael, *Robert the Bruce: King of the Scots* (New Haven: Yale University Press, 2014).

Phillips, Seymour, *Edward II* (New Haven: Yale University Press, 2010).

Phipps, Teresa and Deborah Youngs (eds.), *Litigating Women: Gender and Justice in Europe, c.1300–1800* (London: Routledge, 2022).

Pine, S., ' " Comme Nostre Frere": Knightly Ritual Brotherhood Reconsidered', *Cultural and Social History*, vol. 19, no. 3 (2022), 227–45.

Podd, Rachel, 'Reconsidering Maternal Mortality in Medieval England: Aristocratic Englishwomen, c.1236–1503', *Continuity and Change*, vol. 35, no. 2 (2020), 115–37, doi.org/10.1017/S0268416020000156.

Prestwich, Michael, 'The Court of Edward II', in Gwilym Dodd and Anthony Musson (eds.), *The Reign of Edward II: New Perspectives* (York: York University Press, 2006), 61–75.

Prestwich, Michael, *Edward I* (London: Methuen, 1988).

Raven, Matt, 'The Earldom Endowments of 1337: Political Thought and the Practice of Kingship in Late Medieval England', *English Historical Review*, vol. 136, no. 580 (2021), 498–529.

Robertson, Anne Walters, *Guillaume de Machaut and Reims: Context and Meaning in His Musical Works* (Cambridge: Cambridge University Press, 2002).

Rodwell, Warwick, *The Coronation Chair and Stone of Scone: History, Archaeology and Conservation* (Oxford: Oxbow, 2013).

Rogers, Clifford J. (ed.), *The Wars of Edward III: Sources and Interpretations* (Woodbridge: Boydell Press, 1999).

St John, Lisa Benz, 'In the Queen's Best Interest: Isabella, Edward II and the Image of a Functional Relationship', in Jeffrey S. Hamilton (ed.), *Fourteenth Century England*, vol. VIII (Woodbridge: Boydell & Brewer, 2014).

Saul, Nigel, *Richard II* (New Haven: Yale University Press, 1999).

Scammel, Jean, 'Robert I and the North of England', *English Historical Review*, vol. 73, no. 288 (1958), 385–403.

Seabourne, Gwen, *Imprisoning Medieval Women: The Non-judicial Confinement and Abduction of Women in England, c. 1170–1509* (Farnham: Ashgate, 2011).

Seabourne, Gwen, *Women in the Medieval Common Law: c.1200–1500* (London: Routledge, 2021).

Seaman, Kristen L., 'Anne of Bohemia and Her Struggle to Conceive', *Social History of Medicine*, vol. 29, no. 2 (2016), 224–44.

Smith, D. Vance, *Arts of Dying: Literature and Finitude in Medieval England* (Chicago: University of Chicago Press, 2020).

Smith, Thomas W., and Helen Killick (eds.), *Petitions and Strategies of Persuasion in the Middle Ages: The English Crown and the Church, c.1200–1550* (York: York Medieval Press, 2018).

Sumption, Jonathan, *The Hundred Years War*, vol. 1, *Trial by Battle* (London: Faber & Faber, 1990).

Sumption, Jonathan, *The Hundred Years War*, vol. 2, *Trial by Fire* (London: Faber & Faber, 2001).

Tanner, Heather J. (ed.), *Medieval Elite Women and the Exercise of Power, 1100–1400. Moving Beyond the Exceptionalism Debate* (London: Palgrave Macmillan, 2019).

Taylor, Craig, *Chivalry and the Ideals of Knighthood in France During the Hundred Years War* (Cambridge: Cambridge University Press, 2013).

Tompkins, Laura, 'The Uncrowned Queen: Alice Perrers, Edward III and Political Crisis in Fourteenth-Century England, 1360–1377' (PhD thesis, University of St Andrews, 2013).

Turner, Marion, *Chaucer: A European Life* (Princeton: Princeton University Press, 2019).

Turner, Marion, *The Wife of Bath: A Biography* (Princeton: Princeton University Press, 2023).

Tyson, D., 'The Epitaph of Edward the Black Prince', *Medium Ævum*, vol. 46, no. 1 (1977), 98–104.

Vale, Juliet, *Edward III and Chivalry: Chivalric Society and Its Context 1270–1350* (Woodbridge: Boydell Press, 1982).

Valente, Claire, 'The "Lament of Edward II": Religious Lyric, Political Propaganda', *Speculum*, vol. 77, no. 2 (2002), 422–39.

Vernier, Richard, *The Flower of Chivalry: Bertrand Du Guesclin and the Hundred Years War* (Woodbridge: Boydell Press, 2007).

Villalon, L. J. Andrew, 'Spanish Involvement in the Hundred Years War and the Battle of Nájera', in *The Hundred Years War: A Wider Focus*, ed. L. J. Andrew Villalon and Donald J. Kagay (Boston: Brill, 2005), 3–74.

Walter-Meikle, Kathleen, *Medieval Pets* (Woodbridge: Boydell Press, 2012).

Ward, J. C., *The Estates of the de Clare Family, 1066–1317* (PhD thesis, Queen Mary University London, 1962).

Warner, Kathryn, *Edward II's Nieces: The Clare Sisters: Powerful Pawns of the Crown* (Yorkshire: Pen & Sword History, 2020).

Waugh, Scott L., *England in the Reign of Edward III* (Cambridge: Cambridge University Press, 1991).

Whalen, Logan. E. (ed.), *A Companion to Marie de France* (Leiden: Brill, 2011).

Woolgar, C. M., *The Great Household in Late Medieval England* (New Haven: Yale University Press, 1999).

Online Blogs and Databases

The Breaking of Britain: Cross Border Society and Scottish Independence 1216–1314, breakingofbritain.ac.uk.

England's Immigrants 1330–1550: Resident Aliens in the Late Middle Ages, englandsimmigrants.com.

The Gascon Rolls Project, 1317–1468, gascon rolls.org.

The Northern Way: The Archbishops of York & The North of England 1304–1405, archbishopsregisters.york.ac.uk/northernway.

People of Medieval Scotland 1093–1371, poms.ac.uk.

The People of 1381 Online Database, www.1381.online.

Kathryn Warner, *Edward II Blog*, edwardthesecond.blogspot.com.

Index